Twitter® Application Development FOR DUMMIES®

by Dusty Reagan

Wiley Publishing, Inc.

Twitter® Application Development For Dummies®
Published by
Wiley Publishing, Inc.
111 River Street
Hoboken, NJ 07030-5774

www.wiley.com

Published by Wiley Publishing, Inc., Indianapolis, Indiana

Published simultaneously in Canada

For general information on our other products and services, please contact our Customer Care Department within the U.S. at 877-762-2974, outside the U.S. at 317-572-3993, or fax 317-572-4002.

For technical support, please visit www.wiley.com/techsupport.

Wiley also publishes its books in a variety of electronic formats. Some content that appears in print may not be available in electronic books.

Library of Congress Control Number: 2010921232

ISBN: 978-0-470-56862-0

Manufactured in the United States of America

10 9 8 7 6 5 4 3 2 1

About the Author

Dusty Reagan launched a Web development company called Floating Head Studios in 2007. He developed the popular Twitter app Friend or Follow in 2008, and a few months later launched FeaturedUsers, a niche ad network for the Twitter ecosystem.

Follow Dusty on Twitter at @dustyreagan.

Dedication

This book is dedicated to my parents, Randy & Sandy Reagan.

Author's Acknowledgments

This book would not have been possible without the patience, love, and encouragement of my wonderful wife, Sharlee. She was beside me through the whole journey, proofreading every word, acting as my sounding board, and being my emotional rock during those tight deadlines. Thank you Shar. I love you!

To all of my friends and family who put up with my social absence during the writing of this book, thank you for your encouragement and for enthusiastically accepting me back into your lives when I crawled out of my writing cave, back into the daylight.

Thanks to Chris Treadaway for introducing me to Katie Feltman. Katie, you are a wonderful project editor and writer's therapist. Thank you for guiding me through this wonderful experience.

Pat O'Brien, thank you for your professionalism and editing expertise. Somehow you and Debbye Butler managed to make even my writing publishable.

Thank you Jaisen Mathai (@jmathai) and Abraham Williams (@abraham) for your technical help with OAuth. You are both masters of your trade and exceptionally generous with your knowledge. Follow them on Twitter and pay attention to what they have to say about Twitter API happenings.

Thank you for reading. I hope this book brings value to your endeavors.

Publisher's Acknowledgments

We're proud of this book; please send us your comments at http://dummies.custhelp.com. For other comments, please contact our Customer Care Department within the U.S. at 877-762-2974, outside the U.S. at 317-572-3993, or fax 317-572-4002.

Some of the people who helped bring this book to market include the following:

Acquisitions, Editorial, and Media Development

Project Editor: Pat O'Brien

Acquisitions Editor: Katie Feltman

Copy Editor: Melba Hopper

Technical Editor: Vince McCune

Editorial Manager: Kevin Kirschner

Media Development Project Manager: Laura Moss-Hollister

Media Development Assistant Project Manager: Jenny Swisher

Media Development Associate Producers: Josh Frank, Marilyn Hummel, Douglas Kuhn, and Shawn Patrick

Editorial Assistant: Amanda Graham

Sr. Editorial Assistant: Cherie Case

Cartoons: Rich Tennant (www.the5thwave.com)

Composition Services

Project Coordinator: Sheree Montgomery

Layout and Graphics: Ashley Chamberlain, Carl Byers, Joyce Haughey, Melissa K. Jester

Proofreader: Sossity R. Smith

Indexer: Becky Hornyak

Publishing and Editorial for Technology Dummies

Richard Swadley, Vice President and Executive Group Publisher

Andy Cummings, Vice President and Publisher

Mary Bednarek, Executive Acquisitions Director

Mary C. Corder, Editorial Director

Publishing for Consumer Dummies

Diane Graves Steele, Vice President and Publisher

Composition Services

Debbie Stailey, Director of Composition Services

Contents at a Glance

Introduction **1**

Part I: Catching Up to Twitter and App Development **5**

Chapter 1: Catching Twitter's Coat Tails 7
Chapter 2: Web Development Refresher Course 13
Chapter 3: Setting Up to Create Twitter Apps 39

Part II: Ideation — Coming Up with an Idea **45**

Chapter 4: Getting to Know the Twitter Application Ecosystem 47
Chapter 5: Introducing the Twitter API 63
Chapter 6 : Logging In and Managing Your Account 79
Chapter 7: Managing Users and Their Relationships 105
Chapter 8: Communication Through Tweets 179
Chapter 9: Selecting an Idea 241

Part III: Creation — Developing Your Application **249**

Chapter 10: Selecting Libraries, Design Patterns, and Frameworks 251
Chapter 11: Hosting In the Clouds 255
Chapter 12: Coding Your Application 269
Chapter 13: Making It Pretty Makes It Credible 309
Chapter 14: What You Need to Know to Grow 315

Part IV: Monetization — Making Money with Your Application **321**

Chapter 15: How Twitter Makes Money 323
Chapter 16: Advertising 327
Chapter 17: Monetizing with Other Models 335
Chapter 18: Promoting Your Application 345

Part V: The Part of Tens **355**

Chapter 19 : Ten Traits of a Respectable Twitter Developer 357
Chapter 20: Ten Twitter API Tips 361

Appendix A: Twitter API Reference............................ 365
Appendix B: Gallery of Twitter Applications............... 395
Index.. 413

Table of Contents

Introduction 1

About This Book 1
What You Don't Need to Read 2
Foolish Assumptions 2
How This Book Is Organized 2
  Part I: Catching Up to Twitter and App Development 2
  Part II: Ideation — Coming Up with an Idea 3
  Part III: Creation — Developing Your Application 3
  Part IV: Monetization — Making Money with Your Application 3
  Part V: The Part of Tens 3
Icons Used in This Book 3
Where to Go from Here 4

Part I: Catching Up to Twitter and App Development 5

Chapter 1: Catching Twitter's Coat Tails 7

Why Do People Tweet? 7
What Makes Twitter So Special? 8
  Asymmetrical relationships 9
  Follow and update using SMS 10
  Trends and search 10
  The open API 11
Why Should You Develop a Twitter App? 11
Turning Motivation into Action 12

Chapter 2: Web Development Refresher Course 13

Writing HTML & CSS 13
  HTML Elements 16
Styling Your HTML 18
Formatting in XML & JSON 24
The Basics of PHP 25
  Conditional Statements 26
  Loops 28
  Functions 29
  Arrays 30
  cURL 31
  PHP DOMDocument Class 33
  PHP json_decode Function 35
Understanding MySQL 35

Chapter 3: Setting Up to Create Twitter Apps.....39

Create Your Developer Account.....39
The Importance of Version Control.....40
Hello Twitter!.....41

Part II: Ideation — Coming Up with an Idea.....45

Chapter 4: Getting to Know the Twitter Application Ecosystem.....47

Desktop Client.....47
TweetDeck.....48
Seesmic Desktop.....48
Twitterrific.....49
Mobile Clients.....49
Tweetie.....49
TweetDeck.....50
Tiny Twitter.....50
Web Applications.....50
Customer relationship management (CRM).....51
Contact management.....52
Statistics.....53
Media Sharing.....54
Information aggregation.....55
Information publishing.....57
Advertising.....58
Twitter Bots.....59
Twittercal (@gcal).....59
Remember The Milk (@rtm).....60
Tweetname (@tweetname).....60
Hardware.....60
BakerTweet.....61
Botanicalls Kit.....61
Tweet-a-Watt.....61

Chapter 5: Introducing the Twitter API.....63

Play Nice and Follow the Terms of Service.....63
General Twitter Rules.....64
Developer Etiquette.....65
There Are Actually Two APIs.....65
Twitter API Versioning.....66
Rate Limits and How to Get White Listed.....67
REST API Rate Limit.....67
Search API Rate Limit.....68
Getting Blacklisted.....69

HTTP Response Status Codes and Errors 69
Defining the Payload 71
The User Object 71
The Status Object 72
Authentication 73

Chapter 6: Logging In and Managing Your Account 79

Account Methods 79
Verify a user's credentials 80
Check your rate limit 81
End a user's session 83
Updating a user's notification device 85
Update a user's profile 86
Update a user's profile colors 89
Update a user's profile picture 91
Update a user's background image 93
OAuth Methods 95
Log a user in with OAuth 95
Get an OAuth request token 96
Get an OAuth access token 99

Chapter 7: Managing Users and Their Relationships 105

User Methods 105
Get the details of a user 106
Get user details of your friends and followers 109
Social Graph Methods 112
Get the user IDs of your friends and followers 112
List Methods 115
Create a new list 116
Update an existing list 118
Get a user's lists 120
Get details on a specific list 122
Delete a list 124
Get a list's timeline 126
Get the lists a user belongs to 129
Get the lists a user follows 132
List Members Methods 134
Get a list's members 134
Add a member to a list 136
Remove a list member 138
Test if user is a list member 140
List Subscribers Methods 142
Get a list's subscribers 143
Follow a list 145
Stop following a list 147
Test if user follows a list 149

Friendship Methods 151
Follow a user 152
Stop following a user 154
Check if one user follows another user 156
Get information about the relationship between two users 158
Notification Methods 161
Follow a user to your phone 161
Stop receiving notifications 163
Block Methods 165
Block a user 166
Unblock a user 168
Check if a user is blocked 170
Get a user details list of blocked users 172
Retrieve a list of blocked users IDs 174
Spam Reporting Method 176
How to report a Twitter account as spam 176

Chapter 8: Communication Through Tweets 179

Status Methods 179
Get the details of a specific tweet 180
Create a new tweet 182
Delete a tweet 184
Retweet a tweet 186
Retrieve retweets of a particular tweet 188
Direct Messages Methods 190
Retrieve direct messages 191
Send a direct message 194
Delete a received direct message 196
Timeline Methods 198
Get tweets from the public timeline 199
Get your aggregated friends timeline 201
Get a user's tweets 203
Get tweets that mention your screen name 207
Get status updates retweeted by you 210
Get your friend's retweets 212
Get the retweets of a specific tweet 215
Favorite Methods 217
Retrieve a user's favorite tweets 217
Add a tweet to your favorites 220
Remove a tweet from your favorites 222
Saved Searches Methods 224
Retrieve all your saved searches 225
Get the details of a saved search 227
Create a saved search 229
Remove a saved search 231
Search API Methods 233
How to search for tweets with the API 233
Get the current trending topics 235

Get the days trending topics 237
Get the weeks trending topics 239

Chapter 9: Selecting an Idea 241

Imagining a Successful Twitter App 241
What Is Your Motivation? 242
Enjoyment 242
Make money 242
Filling a need 243
Make it better 243
Build your brand's reputation 244
Support a cause 244
Why Do People Use a Twitter App? 244
Solves a problem 245
It's entertaining 245
It's easy to use 245
They trust it 246
Do You Have the Skill and Resources to Build Your App? 246
Enough Jibber Jabber! Start Building! 247

Part III: Developing Your Application 249

Chapter 10: Selecting Libraries, Design Patterns, and Frameworks 251

Twitter API Libraries Can Speed Up Development 251
Web Application Frameworks 252
Model View Control 253

Chapter 11: Hosting in the Clouds 255

Types of Web Hosting Solutions 255
Shared web hosting 255
Dedicated web hosting 256
Cloud computing 256
Choosing a Hosting Provider 257
Setting Up Your Servers 258
Setting up Apache and PHP 258
Setting up your MySQL server 263
Uploading Files to Your Web Server 266
Setting Up Your Domain Name 267

Chapter 12: Coding Your Application 269

Setting Up the Zend Framework 269
Create your project's initial directories 270
Install the Zend Framework 271

Bootstrapping your application 272
Create your .htaccess file 273
Create your index.php file 273
Create your bootstrap file 275
Create your config file 276
Create your layout template 277
Create your first view and controller 278
Setting Up Your Data Structure 280
Build the User table 280
Build the Tweet table 282
Create Your Data Models 283
Define your tables 283
Create the Tweet model 284
Create the User model 286
The Cron Jobs 295
1. Creating your auto-follow script 295
2. Creating your Tweet monitor script 301
Schedule your Cron jobs 303
Creating the Scoreboard 303
Update your IndexController 303
Add your pagination template 305
Update your Index view 306
Release Early and Often 307

Chapter 13: Making It Pretty Makes It Credible 309

Hire a Designer 309
PSD to XHTML 310
Integrating Your Design 311

Chapter 14: What You Need to Know to Grow 315

Automating Acceptance Testing 315
Unit Testing 317
Continuous Integration 317
Performance Concerns 318

Part IV: Monetization — Making Money with Your Application 321

Chapter 15: How Twitter Makes Money 323

Understanding Venture Capital 323
How to Fund Your Application 325
Self-funding 325
Outside investors 326

Chapter 16: Advertising 327

Selecting a Traditional Ad Network 327
Pay Per Click (PPC) 328
Cost Per Thousand (CPM) 329
Pay Per Action (PPA) 330
Cost Per Time (CPT) 331
Going Vertical 332
The Magpie Network 332
The Featured Users Network 332
Do It Yourself 333

Chapter 17: Monetizing with Other Models 335

Requesting Payment for Service 335
Ask for donations 336
Sell your software 337
Sell subscriptions 338
Selling Goods 339
Physical goods 340
Virtual goods 341
Building Your Business 342
Brand awareness 342
Be acquired 343

Chapter 18: Promoting Your Application 345

Social Networking 346
Twitter strategy 346
Facebook strategy 347
Web site blog 348
Opt-in e-mail list 349
Go Viral 349
Public Relations Strategies 351
Network in your industry 351
Toot your own horn 351
Be authentic 352
Advertise 352
SEO 353

Part V: The Part of Tens 355

Chapter 19: Ten Traits of a Respectable Twitter Developer 357

Ask Permission 357
Read the Documentation First 358

Stay Within Your Rate Limit 358
Don't Promote Mass Following 358
Be Cautious of Trademarks 359
Give Back 359
Cache Your Data 359
Use OAuth 359
Don't Be Evil 360
Communicate with Your Users 360

Chapter 20: Ten Twitter API Tips 361

Develop Defensively 361
Degrade Gracefully 361
Don't Rely on screen_name 362
Use 64-Bit Integers 362
Subscribe to the Google Group 362
Access the API in the Background 362
Use JSON 363
Optimize Caching 363
Support International Characters 363
Do It Client Side 363

Appendix A: Twitter API Reference 365

Account Methods 365
- account/verify_credentials 365
- account/rate_limit_status 366
- account/end_session 366
- account/update_delivery_device 366
- account/update_profile_colors 366
- account/update_profile_image 367
- account/update_profile_background_image 367
- account/update_profile 368

Block Methods 368
- blocks/blocking 369
- blocks/blocking/ids 369
- blocks/create 369
- blocks/destroy 370
- blocks/exists 370

Direct Message Methods 371
- direct_messages 371
- direct_messages/sent 372
- direct_messages/new 372
- direct_messages/destroy 373

Favorite Methods....373
favorites....373
favorites/create....374
favorites/destroy....374
Social Graph Methods....375
followers/ids....375
friends/ids....375
Friendship Methods....376
friendships/create....376
friendships/destroy....376
friendships/exists....377
friendships/show....377
Help Methods....378
help/test....378
Notification Methods....378
notifications/follow....379
notifications/leave....379
OAuth Methods....379
oauth/access_token....380
oath/authenticate....380
oauth/authorize....380
oauth/request_token....380
Saved Searches Methods....380
saved_searches....381
saved_searches/create....381
saved_searches/destroy....381
saved_searches/show....382
Search Methods....382
search....382
trends....383
trends/daily....383
trends/current....384
trends/weekly....384
Spam Reporting Methods....384
report_spam....385
Status Methods....385
statuses/destroy....386
statuses/followers....386
statuses/friends....387
statuses/friends_timeline....388
statuses/home_timeline....389
statuses/mentions....389
statuses/public_timeline....390
statuses/retweet....390
statuses/retweeted_by_me....390

statuses/retweeted_of_me 390
statuses/retweeted_to_me 391
statuses/retweets 392
statuses/show 392
statuses/update 392
statuses/user_timeline 393
User Methods 394
users/show 394

Appendix B: Gallery of Twitter Applications 395

Index 413

Introduction

Welcome to the first edition of *Twitter Application Development For Dummies,* the book written especially for people who want to create Twitter applications but haven't a clue about how to start.

About This Book

There are a couple of ways to use this book, depending on your preferences and experience.

If you're a Twitter newbie, you can start reading and working with Chapter 1 and keep going until you reach the index at the end. Everything falls in sequence as you build experience and knowledge.

This book also works like a reference. Start with the topic you want to find out about. Look for it in the table of contents or in the index to get going. The table of contents is detailed enough that you should be able to find most of the topics you're looking for. If not, turn to the index, where you can find even more detail.

After you find your topic in the table of contents or the index, turn to the area of interest and read as much as you need or want. Then close the book and get on with it.

Of course, this book is loaded with information, so if you want to take a brief excursion into your topic, you're more than welcome. If you want to know the ins and outs of building an online store, read the whole chapter on storefronts. If you just want to know how to post a product on your site, read just the section on adding products. You get the idea.

This book rarely directs you elsewhere for information — just about everything that you need to know about is right here. If you find the need for additional information on related topics, plenty of other *For Dummies* books can help.

What You Don't Need to Read

Aside from the topics you can use right away, some of this book is skippable. I carefully placed extra-technical information in self-contained sidebars and clearly marked them so that you can steer clear of them. Don't read this stuff unless you're really into technical explanations and want to know a little of what's going on behind the scenes. Don't worry; my feelings won't be hurt if you don't read every word.

Foolish Assumptions

I'm making only one assumption about who you are: You're a computer user.

How This Book Is Organized

Inside this book, you find chapters arranged in five parts. Each chapter breaks down into sections that cover various aspects of the chapter's main subject. The chapters are in a logical sequence, so reading them in order (if you want to read the whole thing) makes sense. But the book is modular enough that you can pick it up and start reading at any point.

Here's the lowdown on what's in each of the five parts.

Part I: Catching Up to Twitter and App Development

The chapters in this part present a layperson's introduction to what Twitter development is all about.

The best thing about this part is that it starts at the very beginning and doesn't assume you know how to download and upload and extract and install software. It also suggests simple solutions on how to get started. In other words, this part is aimed at ordinary people who know almost nothing.

Part II: Ideation — Coming Up with an Idea

The goal of the chapters in this section is to get you started working on a great Twitter application. There are technical details, and blue-sky tips.

Part III: Creation — Developing Your Application

The chapters in this part show you how to take control of your application and detail it.

Part IV: Monetization — Making Money with Your Application

Hey, there's more to life than money. That's why we keep the money stuff safely tucked away here.

Part V: The Part of Tens

This wouldn't be a *For Dummies* book without a collection of lists of interesting snippets.

Icons Used in This Book

Those nifty little pictures in the margin aren't there just to pretty up the place. They have practical functions:

Hold it — technical details lurk just around the corner. Read on only if you have a pocket protector.

Pay special attention to this icon; it lets you know that some particularly useful tidbit is at hand — perhaps a shortcut or a little-used command that pays off big.

Did I tell you about the memory course I took?

Danger, Will Robinson! This icon highlights information that may help you avert disaster.

Where to Go from Here

Yes, you can get there from here. With this book in hand, you're ready to build your own robust and useful Twitter application. Browse through the table of contents and decide where you want to start. Be bold! Be courageous! Be adventurous! Above all, have fun!

Part I

Catching Up to Twitter and App Development

"I'd respond to this person's comment on Twitter, but I'm a former Marine, Bernard, and a Marine never retweets."

In this part . . .

The chapters in this part present a layperson's introduction to what Twitter development is all about.

Chapter 1

Catching Twitter's Coat Tails

In This Chapter

- Why Twitter is a compelling platform
- The rationale behind building a Twitter app

A few years ago a small Web site called Twitter appeared on the Internet. Twitter is kind of like a blog, but your posts must be less than 140 characters. Twitter users call their posts *tweets.* Of course, your tweets have to be that small to be sent as a text message to your followers. That's Twitter lingo for subscribers to your Twitter updates, usually your friends, family, and fans. As it turns out, my dad is one of my biggest fans. All of my small daily updates about my life go straight to his cell phone. Likewise, all of his updates go to my phone. This way we get to share little things we wouldn't otherwise take the time to call and talk about. This helps bring us closer together, even though we live miles apart.

The idea of keeping in touch with friends and family is comforting and increases Twitter's appeal, but Twitter has even larger implications.

Why Do People Tweet?

You already know one reason I tweet, to stay close to friends and family. But there are several other reasons why people might be compelled to get involved with Twitter. Here are a few examples:

- Stay in touch with friends and family.
- Get instant advice from friends.
- Meet new people.
- Keep informed of stock market trends.
- Build cool stuff with their open API.
- Build a business around Twitter.

- Promote a business with Twitter and interact with customers.
- Get involved in politics.
- Stay informed of breaking current events as they happen.
- Talk to influential people and celebrities.

These are just a few common reasons why someone might be on Twitter. There are even more creative uses of Twitter. In Chapter 4, you learn about a plant that tweets when it needs to be watered. You can also use Twitter to update your Google Calendar by sending a direct message to @gcal. If you want to know the time in London, you can follow @big_ben_clock that bongs every hour on the hour.

Perhaps a more practical example of creative Twitter use is @AusTraffic, run by the *Austin American Statesmen* newspaper. The account includes only tweets on traffic conditions in Austin, Texas. People can even direct message (DM) the account to send traffic reports, which are then shared with all the account's followers. If you follow this account to your phone, you have an instant, real-time feed of traffic conditions in Austin.

One of Twitter's strengths is that it doesn't limit what people can do with it. Nor do they presume to know exactly how everyone should interact with it. The founders of Twitter have left it up to the users to discover what Twitter is to be used for and how.

Some now common features of Twitter were originally derived out of how the Twitter community decided to use the application. @ replies for instance were invented and adopted by the Twitter community first. @ replies are used when one Twitter user references another Twitter user's screen name. For example, if someone wanted to mention me in a tweet, they would type @DustyReagan. Twitter noticed how people were using the @ sign when they referred to another Twitter account, and to make the @ sign more helpful, Twitter linked it to the referred users account. Then they made it so you could search for all mentions of your screen name. Some other conventions that came out of the Twitter community include *hashtags* and *retweets*.

What Makes Twitter So Special?

Twitter's premise is simple, but its effects are wide-reaching. Here are four features of Twitter that make it more than a blog with 140 character posts:

- Asymmetrical relationships
- Follow and update using SMS
- Trends and Search
- Open API

A brief glossary of terms

If you haven't been around the Twitter block, you need to learn a few Twitter-specific terms to communicate with your new Twitter friends and colleagues.

- direct message — Sometimes referred to as a DM, a direct message is a private message sent to you, or by you, over Twitter.
- FailWhale — In the early days of Twitter, the small company suffered from growing pains as its application became popular. Unfortunately, this caused Twitter to crash frequently. When Twitter was down, an illustration of several birds lifting a whale out of the sea via ropes held from their beaks was displayed. This image became known as the *FailWhale.*
- hashtag — A word proceeded with a # sign. Hashtags are used to signify that a status update is about a particular topic to allow for easy searching. For example, conference goers may tag all of their updates with a hashtag unique to the conference so other attendees can read all the updates pertaining to the event.
- @ replies — Pronounced "at replies." @ replies are how you reference another Twitter user. For example, I am @DustyReagan. You use @ replies to direct a tweet to a user or to mention a user in passing. @ replies are sometimes referred to as "mentions" or a "mention."
- retweet — Abbreviated RT. A retweet is a status update from someone you follow that you share with your followers, by using Twitter's built-in retweet feature or by copying the update attributing the original author and posting it from your Twitter account.
- tweet — A tweet is another word for a status update. It can be used as a noun or a verb. For example, you can tweet a tweet.
- twoosh — A tweet that is exactly 140 characters.

Asymmetrical relationships

Twitter's relationships structure is simple, but revolutionary. Before Twitter, most social networking sites, such as Facebook (`http://facebook.com`) and MySpace (`http://myspace.com`), required mutual friendships. You couldn't see a user's information if he or she didn't specify you as a friend. Twitter threw this model out the window.

On Twitter, you can follow the updates of anyone who has a public account, and they don't have to follow you back. This means celebrities and politicians can communicate with their fans and constituents without becoming friends with half of the Internet's population. This asymmetrical relationship model parallels relationships in real life. There are people whom I admire, who have simply never met me. Now I have a way to stalk those people! I can even send their updates to my phone. I write this with tongue in cheek — well, the stalking part anyway. Unless your account is private, tweets are intended to be public broadcasts of information.

Follow and update using SMS

I usually attend one or two technical conferences per year. These conferences usually last a few days, and I may know a few people at the event. Attending the panels is straightforward enough, but there is valuable time in-between panels and after the conference when people meet up, have a good time, exchange ideas, and so on. At these times, you have two options: find out where everyone is hanging out and join them, or go back to the hotel.

Twitter is my lifeline during these times. At conferences, I follow the people I know using SMS updates that are sent to my phone. This way, I know where the good parties are, where the free beer is, and where the conference presenters are hanging out.

Still not convinced about the usefulness of SMS updates? Here's another example.

Many news organizations have seen the potential of broadcasting news to Twitter. If you want to stay up-to-date on current events, you can't get much more current than having headlines sent to your phone in near real-time.

Along with receiving updates to your mobile phone, you can post updates to Twitter using SMS. This feature allows users to update their Twitter status while they're on the go, in real-time. The next time you go downtown for drinks or head to the coffee shop for a mid-afternoon cup of espresso, you can alert your friends. This may cause an impromptu gathering of good friends.

Trends and search

Following the Twitter accounts of news organizations to stay on top of current events is one option, but using Twitter, you can get information on newsworthy events even before the news organizations do.

One way to do this is by monitoring trending words and phrases on Twitter. Twitter has this functionality built in and provides the current trending topics to all users. When real-time events occur, they often spread organically by word of mouth, bubbling up in popularity until they become a trending topic.

A frequently referenced Twitter news-breaking event happened on December 20, 2008, when Mike Wilson (@2drinksbehind) tweeted that he was just in a plane crash. Thirty-eight people in the crash were injured. Everyone survived. News of the event spread quickly on Twitter before any major media outlet could cover the event.

Trends are helpful in finding recent interesting topics, but if you're looking for news on a particular subject, you can use Twitter's search functionality. Using Twitter Search, you can monitor Twitter for words and phrases in near real-time. You can even limit your results to tweets from particular geographical locations.

Search is also useful for monitoring mentions of your company's brand name or product. You can then interact with users who are talking about your brand from your company's Twitter account. Never before has it been this easy for a brand to contact customers about their concerns before their customers contact them.

The open API

The real reason Twitter is so appealing to developers, inventors, hackers, and entrepreneurs is the open API. Twitter provides all its data and functionality for free as an open API. This means you can invent and build new applications around Twitter's functionality. You can even create a whole new Twitter interface from the ground up.

Twitter encourages development with its API and has even acquired companies that build spectacular applications on top of Twitter. Twitter's current search engine was once an independent company called Summize.

The open API is probably the reason you picked up this book.

Why Should You Develop a Twitter App?

Opportunities to build interesting and compelling things in and around Twitter abound. Some third-party applications have started to show themselves as the leader in a particular facet of the Twitter ecosystem. But these leaders could use some competition, and there are still opportunities to use Twitter in ways no one has even thought of before. Developers are constantly pushing the envelope on how Twitter can be useful and entertaining.

I built my first Twitter app, Friend Or Follow (`http://friendorfollow.com`), because I wanted to know who wasn't following me back on Twitter. Plus it was something fun to do on the weekend. As it turned out, other people found Friend Or Follow useful as well. As my app's popularity began to grow, I realized I could make money with it through advertising. Suddenly I had a small business built on top of Twitter.

If you're looking for a reason to build a Twitter app, money could be one of them. However, it can also be fun and rewarding to learn something new, and if you're fortunate enough to gain an audience with your app, it can be really gratifying to build something people appreciate.

Here are few reasons why you might want to develop a Twitter app:

- **Make money:** Twitter is trendy right now, and its user base is growing every day. There are numerous ways to make money developing Twitter applications. I cover this in detail in Part IV.
- **Build your reputation:** Twitter is a social platform. If you build something people find useful or entertaining, you will gain a reputation with the users of your app.
- **Support a cause:** Leveraging the social nature of Twitter, you could build an app that raises awareness and money for a charitable cause or a philosophical idea. See TwitCause (`http://twitcause.com`) for an example of this.
- **Fill a need:** If there is something you don't like about Twitter, you can fix it using the API. It's quite likely several other people share your sentiments and will enjoy your fix.
- **Promote a brand:** In much the same way in which you can support a cause building a Twitter app, you can promote a brand with a Twitter app. For example, @twelpforce is a Twitter account used by Best Buy. They built an internal application that allows their employees to respond easily to technical inquiries directed to the account.
- **Scratch an itch:** Sometimes you just want to build something cool. You can't help it, and that's awesome! Build something cool because it's fun.

Turning Motivation into Action

I hope you're now motivated to start building a Twitter app. Now it's time to turn that motivation into action.

The next chapter is a refresher course on Web application development using a LAMP (Linux, Apache, MySQL, and PHP) stack.

If your Web development skills are strong, feel free to head straight to Chapter 3 where you post your first message to Twitter using the API.

Chapter 2

Web Development Refresher Course

In This Chapter

- The basics of Web development
- A look at the LAMP stack
- Reference material for the Web developer

An interesting thing about Twitter application development is you can interact with the API in any language and on any platform. Windows clients, iPhone applications, and Android apps use different programming languages and still interact with the Twitter API in similar ways.

In this book, I use a typical LAMP (Linux, Apache, MySQL, and PHP) stack to demonstrate the Twitter API. I use the Web platform as a teaching tool because it has become prevalent, multiplatform, and Twitter itself is a Web app. I use a LAMP stack because it is a widely adopted development platform and all the components are open source and free.

If you're already an expert LAMP user, you can skip to Chapter 3.

If Web programming isn't your native language, read this chapter. However, this isn't a definitive LAMP resource. The topics in this chapter could easily fill several books on their own. My aim here is to show you enough to get you through the rest of the book.

Writing HTML & CSS

If you've done Web development work before, you're probably familiar with HTML and CSS. HTML (Hypertext Markup Language) is the language of the Web. Web browsers interpret the semantics of the HTML elements, called tags, and render a human readable page for the visitor. CSS (Cascading Style

Sheets) is the markup language that tells the browser how the HTML elements are to be styled and displayed. In the early days of the Web, HTML often contained both the content of the Web page and information on how the page was to be styled. Developers would often inappropriately use HTML tables to structure page elements, and the HTML specification included tags that defined display style such as "font" and "bold." These tags have since been deprecated. The modern practice is to separate content from style.

There are several reasons to separate content from style.

- Style changes are simple. For example, using external CSS you can change style elements site wide, like font size and background color.
- HTML code is easier to read with the style elements removed. This makes maintenance easier.
- File sizes are decreased, which increases the speed of your Web site.
- Coding to Web standards increases the likelihood your site will render correctly in a wide variety of Web browsers.
- The order of your content can be structured logically like a document because you can rearrange elements aesthetically using CSS. This means in cases where aesthetics are irrelevant, such as screen readers for the blind, and search engine spiders, your Web page will still be readable.

The organization that writes the standards on HTML, CSS, XML, and numerous other Internet protocols is the W3C (World Wide Web Consortium). This organization is made up of organizations that have a stake in Web standards. Some obvious examples are companies that build Web browsers, such as Microsoft, Mozilla, and Apple. Without the W3C there would be numerous proprietary versions of HTML and developers would be forced to develop to the most popular browsers.

The W3C writes specification documents on how each version of HTML is to function. With each new version of HTML comes a new specification document. Web browsers are supposed to render your HTML based on the specification document, called a *doctype,* which you choose and declare in your HTML. So if you declare your page HTML 4.01, the browser should render your page based on HTML 4.01 rules. Current doctypes include

- HTML 2.0
- HTML 3.2
- HTML 4.01
    - Frameset
    - Transitional
    - Strict

- XHTML 1.0
  - Frameset
  - Transitional
  - Strict
- XHTML 1.1

Unless your target audience is known to run legacy browsers, use either HTML 4.01 Strict or XHTML 1.0 Strict.

The "strict" doctype of HTML 4.01 and XHTML 1.0 removes many deprecated tags and creates a more future proof document than transitional or frameset doctypes. These later two doctypes include some deprecated tags to make the transition for older Web sites easier.

XHTML (Extensible Hypertext Markup Language) is an HTML specification that is designed to make HTML more like a semantic collection of data, similar to XML. It relies on CSS to define the page's design. The key difference between HTML and XHTML is that XHTML must be valid XML. The rules for HTML are much more lenient in this regard.

Here are some rules to make your HTML valid XHTML:

- The root element must be html and must contain an xmlns attribute that defines the XHTML namespace.
- You must always close XHTML tags including empty elements like the break and image tag. A closed break tag looks like this: `<br />`
- All XHTML tags must be lowercase.
- All XHTML tag attributes must have a value. You cannot shorten an attribute such as `readonly`. That attribute must appear as: `readonly="readonly"`.
- All XHTML tag attributes must be surrounded by quotes.

Here is an example of a short valid XHTML document:

```
<!DOCTYPE html
     PUBLIC "-//W3C//DTD XHTML 1.0 Strict//EN"
     "http://www.w3.org/TR/xhtml1/DTD/xhtml1-strict.dtd">
<html xmlns="http://www.w3.org/1999/xhtml" xml:lang="en" >
   <head>
      <title>Example XHTML Document</title>
   </head>
   <body>
      <p>Tags must be lowercase and closed,<br />
         including singleton tags like the break tag.</p>
   </body>
</html>
```

HTML Elements

HTML documents contain two main sections: the head and the body.

The head occurs at the top of the file and is denoted by the `<head>` tag. It contains non-visual information about the page, and usually contains these tags:

- title: Denotes the name of the Web page. This usually appears at the top of the browser window, and is used in bookmark labels and search engine results.
- link: The link tag is used to link other resources to this Web page. Examples include external CSS files and favicons (the tiny 16 x 16 icon that is displayed in your bookmarks and browser address bar).
- meta: The meta tag is used to define ancillary information about a Webpage, such as keywords, a short description, or copyright information.
- style: Used to embed document wide CSS code directly in the head section.
- script: Both embedded and external JavaScript code make use of the script tag.

The body of the HTML document, denoted by the `<body>` tag, is where the content of the page resides. All content tags can be categorized into two groups: block-level elements and inline elements.

By default, block-level elements occur on a new line. Block-level elements may contain nested block-level tags and inline tags. Examples include

- Headings: Heading tags are used to separate a document by topics and sub-topics. Example:

  ```
  <h1>Animals</h1>
     <h2>Domestic</h2>
        <h3>Dogs</h3>
        <h3>Cats</h3>
  ```

- Paragraphs: Paragraph tags are naturally used to define a paragraph.

  ```
  <p>This is a paragraph.</p>
  ```

- Unordered lists: Used for bulleted lists.

  ```
  <ul>
     <li>eggs</li>
     <li>bacon</li>
     <li>milk</li>
  </ul>
  ```

- Tables: Used for tabular data, tables contain other block-level elements to define the header row <th>, a row <tr>, and a column <td>.

```
<table>
   <th>
      <td>Name</td>
      <td>Number</td>
   </th>
   <tr>
      <td>Dusty</td>
      <td>555-2368</td>
   </tr>
   <tr>
      <td>Jenny</td>
      <td>867-5309</td>
   </tr>
</table>
```

- Forms: Forms are used to send user input data back to the hosting server. Forms are vital part of HTML and are necessary for nearly all ecommerce and Web applications, including Twitter. While the form tag is a block-level element, the field tags are inline elements.

```
<form name="input" action="login.php" method="post">
   Username: <input type="text" name="username" />
   Password: <input type="password" name="password">
   <input type="submit" value="Submit" />
</form>
```

- DIVs: The div tag is a generic block-level element. It is used primarily to wrap sections of your document in logical blocks, so they can be easily manipulated and styled with CSS.

```
<div id="footer">
   <p>Copyright 2011</p>
</div>
```

In contrast to block-level elements, inline elements may only contain other inline tags. Examples include

- Anchor links: Anchor tags make the World Wide Web a Web. Links to external sites and internal pages weave a Web of information and connects the Web. The anchor tag contains an important element called “target” that tells the browser to open the link in a new or the current window. By default the link will open in the current window. You can specify target=”_blank” to have a link open in a new window.

```
<a href="http://twitter.com" target="_blank">Twitter</
      a>
```

- Images: Image tags display images. They contain several important attributes including alt, title, height, and width. The alt attribute is short for alternative text; it's used to provide text description of the image. The title attribute is the text that will appear in a browser tooltip when your cursor is hovering over the image. Naturally. the height and width attributes define the images height and width. By defining an image's height and width, the browser doesn't have to wait for the image to finish download to correct render the elements around the image. You can also use height and width to force an image's size. However, this doesn't alter its file size.

```
<img src="http://twitter.com/logo.gif" alt="Twitter
        Logo" title="Twitter" height="100" width="80"
        />
```

- Strong: The strong tag is used to denote a word or phrase as important. Its default behavior is to bold the word or phrase. However, using CSS you may style the important text however you wish.

```
Please do <strong>not</strong> delete these files.
```

- Line break: Browsers ignore line breaks in HTML markup. To tell the browser you want a new line, you must use a `<br />` tag.

```
<p>The White House<br />
1600 Pennsylvania Avenue NW<br />
Washington, DC 20500</p>
```

Styling Your HTML

You can style HTML with CSS in three different ways:

- Inline: You can use the style attribute on any HTML tag to add style to an element. It looks like this:

```
<p style="margin:10px">Hello Twitter!</p>
```

  This is a poor method for styling your page, because your style only applies to the element it's on. So if you want all your paragraphs to have a margin of 10px, you have to add this style to every paragraph tag. This also means that if you want to change the design, you have to update every tag.

- Embedded: You can embed your style in the head section of your HTML page by placing your CSS in between the style tags, like this:

```
<!DOCTYPE html
      PUBLIC "-//W3C//DTD XHTML 1.0 Strict//EN"
      "http://www.w3.org/TR/xhtml1/DTD/xhtml1-strict.
         dtd">
<html xmlns="http://www.w3.org/1999/xhtml"
         xml:lang="en" >
   <head>
      <title>Example XHTML Document</title>
      <style type="text/css">
         p { margin: 20px; }
      </style>
   </head>
   <body>
      <p>Hello Twitter!</p>
   </body>
</html>
```

Embedding your CSS centralizes your style elements. If you want to make a style change, you only have to change it once at the top of the page.

- External File: The best option is to create an external CSS file with all your styles in it and link to it from your HTML file, like this:

```
<!DOCTYPE html
      PUBLIC "-//W3C//DTD XHTML 1.0 Strict//EN"
      "http://www.w3.org/TR/xhtml1/DTD/xhtml1-strict.
         dtd">
<html xmlns="http://www.w3.org/1999/xhtml"
         xml:lang="en" >
   <head>
      <title>Example XHTML Document</title>
      <link rel="stylesheet" type="text/css"
         href="test.css" />
   </head>
   <body>
      <p>Hello Twitter!</p>
   </body>
</html>
```

Using an external CSS file is the best way to style your Web site. The external file can be applied to multiple Web pages, centralizing the design for your entire site. This also decreases your Web site's download size, because the user doesn't have to download redundant style data.

If these three methods are applied to the same element at the same time, the inline CSS takes precedence over the embedded CSS, which takes precedence over the external CSS file.

When styling your CSS, you use selectors to specify what HTML attributes you want to style. There are four main CSS selectors you should know for this book:

- Type selectors: Type selectors use the HTML tag name to identify what tags you want to style. For example, to give all the paragraphs on your Web site a margin of 10px, you would do this:

  ```
  p { margin:10px;}
  ```

- Class selectors: You can add a class attribute to any HTML tag and select elements with a particular class name using a dot followed by the class name. For example, you might want to add a class called e-mail to all link tags that link to an e-mail address. To select and style all those e-mail links, you would do this:

  ```
  .email { color:red; }
  ```

- ID selectors: You can give any HTML element an ID attribute. However, the ID you give the element must be unique to the page. You can't have duplicate IDs on the same page. To select an element based on its ID you use a pound sign like this:

  ```
  #navigation { margin-top:20px; }
  ```

- Descendant selectors: You can select elements nested inside of other elements by using a descendant selector. For example, if you wanted to select all the links inside of a div tag with and ID called "footer" you would do this:

  ```
  #footer a { color:red; }
  ```

These are the primary CSS selectors you need to have a firm grasp on.

When dealing with CSS selectors, you need to consider the nature of cascading style sheets. Cascading styles work by applying the styles of the most general selector first, then overwriting those styles with more specific selectors. The order of which the rules are encountered by the browser is irrelevant. To give you an example, a general selector could be a style applied to all paragraphs like this:

```
p { margin:10px; color: red;}
```

A more specific selector might pick a specific paragraph with an ID of "intro" like this:

```
p #intro { color:blue; }
```

In this example, the 1st CSS rule will give all your paragraphs a 10px margin and red text. The specific "intro" paragraph will have a 10px margin like all the other paragraphs. However, because we have a second rule that styles the "intro" paragraph specifically, that style will make the "intro" paragraph text blue instead of red.

Here are the most basic CSS styles you will encounter regularly in the wild.

The Box Model

The box model is an HTML element's margin, border, padding, height, and width. Look at Figure 2-1 for an illustration of each one of these spaces. The most common units of measurement to adjust spacing are px for pixels and em for em-length. Em-length is defined as the width of the letter "m" in your currently selected font.

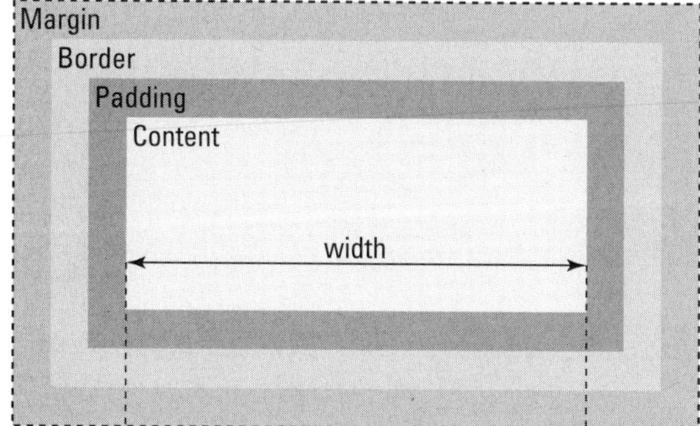

Figure 2-1: Use the box model to adjust spacing on your page.

Margin & Padding

You can specify the side of the box you want to apply your margin, or padding, by using the indicators top, right, bottom, or left, seen in Listing 2-1.

Listing 2-1: Margin and Padding

```
#contentBox {
   margin-top: 10px;
   padding-bottom: 10px;
}
```

If you just apply one measurement, it's applied to all sides of the box. You can also use shorthand by putting the measurements in the order of top, right, bottom, left, as seen in Listing 2-2.

Listing 2-2: Margin and Padding Shorthand

```
#contentBox {
   margin: 10px;
   padding: 10px 5px 10px 5px;
}
```

Border

You can set the border's width, style, and color. Like the margin and padding, it can be applied to specific sides using the indicators top, right, bottom, left, or it can be applied to all sides at once.

Listing 2-3 shows an example of how to set the border CSS.

Listing 2-3: Border Styles

```
#contentBox {
   border: 2px solid #000;
   border-bottom: 5px dashed red;
}
```

Height & Width

Setting the height and width of an element is straightforward. See Listing 2-4.

Listing 2-4: Height and Width

```
#contentBox {
   height: 100px;
   width: 200px;
}
```

Font Styles

You can alter fonts by changing their size, font-family, weight, style, and color. You can change the alignment of your text by using the text-align style. Possible alignments include left, right, center, and justify. Listing 2-5 shows an example of how to decorate your fonts.

Listing 2-5: Font Decorations

```
p {
    font-family: "Times New Roman", Georgia, Serif;
    font-style: italic;
    font-weight: bold;
    font-size: 16px;
    color: #333;
    text-align: center;
}
```

Floating

The floating style is used to position an element to the left or right on the surrounding elements. It's commonly used to position images in text, but can also be used to layout other page elements. See the example in Listing 2-6.

Listing 2-6: Font Decorations

```
img {
    float: left;
}
```

Display

The display style can be used to change a block level HTML element into an inline element, and vice versa, but the main reason you need to know about the display style is because it can hide elements if you set the property to none. This is useful for dynamic JavaScript elements and can make a Web page feel truly interactive. See Listing 2-7.

Listing 2-7: Hide an Element with display:none

```
img {
    display:none;
}
```

Background Styles

You can alter the background image or color on any element using background styles. The example in Listing 2-8 sets the background color to white, and positions a non-repeating background image in the top left-corner.

Listing 2-8: Background Styles

```
body {
 background:#fff url('example.png') no-repeat top left;
}
```

Formatting in XML & JSON

XML (Extensible Markup Language) and JSON (JavaScript Object Notation) are types of textual data formatting. By formatting textual data in a standard format, the data can be easily exchanged and parsed. This is particularly useful for Web site data exchange through Web services and APIs, such as Twitter's API. When you make a request to Twitter, they respond by returning XML or JSON data, depending on which data format you requested. You can then parse that data and go merrily on your programming way.

If you're writing a JavaScript application, JSON is the data format for you. Using JSON, you can take the response from the Twitter API and access natively like an object. You can see an example JSON response from Twitter in Listing 2-9.

Listing 2-9: Example JSON Object


```
{"trends":[{"name":"#amazonfail","url":"http:\/\/search.twitter.com\/
        search?q=%23amazonfail"},... truncated ...],"as_of":"Mon, 13 Apr
        2009 20:48:29 +0000"}
```


XML is a popular data formatting choice because it has been around for a while. XHTML is a type of XML. It is made up of tags, elements, and attributes. Due to the establishment of XML, most program languages either have native parsers or open source libraries with XML parsers that you can use to easily extract data out of an XML file. You can see an example XML response in Listing 2-10.

Listing 2-10: Example XML Object


```
<?xml version="1.0" encoding="UTF-8"?>
<status>
   <created_at>Tue Apr 07 22:52:51 +0000 2009</created_at>
   <id>1472669360</id>
   <text>At least I can get your humor through tweets. RT @abdur: I don't mean
        this in a bad way, but genetically speaking you're a cul-de-sac.</
        text>
   <source><a href="http://www.tweetdeck.com/">TweetDeck</a></source>
   <truncated>false</truncated>
   <in_reply_to_status_id></in_reply_to_status_id>
   <in_reply_to_user_id></in_reply_to_user_id>
   <favorited>false</favorited>
   <in_reply_to_screen_name></in_reply_to_screen_name>
   <geo/>
</status>
```

The Basics of PHP

PHP is an open-source server side programming language. It is used to dynamically create Web pages on the fly. With a language like PHP, you can create a custom experience for every viewer.

The examples in this book are written for PHP version 5 and newer. PHP is so prevalent on the Web that most Web hosting companies come with PHP preinstalled. If you don't already have a favorite Web hosting company to try the PHP examples in this book on, I recommend Nearly Free Speech (`http://nearlyfreespeech.net`).

PHP is a rich language with a huge library of built-in functionality. In this chapter, I cover the essentials you need to understand the Twitter API examples in this book, including

- Conditional Statements
- Loops
- Functions
- Arrays
- cURL
- PHP DOMDocument Class
- PHP JSON Functions

The first thing you need to know about PHP is the echo command. Echo simply prints a string to the screen, as seen in Listing 2-11.

Listing 2-11: Print a String to the Screen

```
<?php

echo "Hello world!";

?>
```

The next thing you need to know about PHP is its comments syntax. I use comments in example code throughout this book to help you understand what is going on in the code. Example of PHP comments syntax can be seen in Listing 2-12.

Listing 2-12: PHP Comments Syntax

```
<?php

echo "This will be printed";

// This will not

# Nor will this

/*
This also won't print,
and is useful for commenting out multiple lines.
*/

?>
```

Conditional Statements

Conditional statements are programming statements that perform different actions depending on whether a specified condition is true or false. Conditional statements are a common structure across most programming languages.

The conditional statement used most often in this book is the if-then-else statement. It works just like the name implies: if a condition is true, then perform a task. Else perform a different task. The code for an if-then-else statement in PHP looks like Listing 2-13.

Listing 2-13: If-Then-Else

```
<?php

if($x == 1)
{
   echo "x equals 1";
}
else
{
   echo "x does not equal 1";
}

?>
```

To determine whether a condition is true or false, a comparison operator is used. PHP comparison operators you need to know for this book include

- == equal to

  Example: (1 == 2) returns false
- != not equal to

  Example: (1 != 2) returns true
- < less than

  Example: (1 < 2) returns true
- > greater than

  Example: (1 > 2) returns false
- <= less than or equal to

  Example: (1 <= 2) returns true
- >= greater than or equal to

  Example: (1 >= 2) returns false

You can test for multiple conditions using logical operators. Logical operators you need to know for this book include

- && and

  Example: ($x && $y) return TRUE if $x and $Y are both TRUE.
- || or

  Example: ($x || $y) return TRUE if either $x or $Y are TRUE.
- ! not

  Example: (!$x) return TRUE if $x is not TRUE.

Another conditional statement that is used in this book is the elseif part. You can use one or more elseif parts in an if-then-else to combine multiple statements. The first statement that is found to be true is executed. The other statements are ignored, including the final else statement. Listing 2-14 shows an example if-then-else statement with an elseif part.

Listing 2-14: ElseIf Part

```
<?php

if($x == $y)
{
   echo "x equals y";
}
elseif($x > $y)
{
   echo "x is greater than y";
}
else
{
   echo "x is less than y";
}

?>
```

Loops

There are occasions in any programming language when you need to repeat a task until a certain condition is met. For these scenarios, it is appropriate to use a loop. For the examples in this book I use two types of PHP loops:

- foreach
- do while

foreach

Foreach loops iterate over every element inside of an array, starting with the first element. Foreach only works on arrays, and will produce an error if you try using it on anything other than an array.

You can use a foreach loop one of two ways. The first way, shown in Listing 2-15, iterates over the given array and assigns the value of the current element to a variable I named $value.

Listing 2-15: foreach

```
<?php

foreach($arrayElements as $value)
{
   echo "Value: $value";
}

?>
```

The second way to use a foreach is to assign the current elements value to a variable, and also assign that element's key value to a variable. This is helpful for arrays with key value pairs. Listing 2-16 shows an example of how to assign the key value as well as the elements value.

Listing 2-16: foreach

```
<?php

foreach($arrayElements as $key => $value)
{
    echo "Key: $key";
    echo "Value: $value";
}

?>
```

do-while

Do-while loops work by "doing" something over and over "while" a condition remains true. As soon as that condition is no longer true, the do-while loop stops. A do-while loop will always run at least once. Listing 2-17 shows an example of a do-while loop counting to 10.

Listing 2-17 uses the shorthand $x++. Placing two pluses behind a variable is the functional equivalent of writing $x = $x + 1.

Listing 2-17: do-while Loop that Counts to 10

```
<?php

$x = 0;
do
{
    $x++;
    echo "$x<br />";
}
while($x < 10)

?>
```

Functions

Another common programming structure in PHP and the examples in this book, is a function. Functions are chunks of code that can be referenced and reused. The purpose of functions is to reduce code duplication and make code more readable. Functions can also take input in the form of parameters and return a value as output. An example of a function with parameters and a return value is show in Listing 2-18.

Listing 2-18: An Example of a Function

```
<?php

function addTwoNumbers($x, $y)
{
   $z = $x + $y;
   return $z;
}

echo addTwoNumbers(1, 2);

?>
```

Arrays

An array is a collection of data stored in memory. Each element in an array contains a key identifier and a value.

- The value can be any type, including an integer, string, object, or even another array.
- The key must be either an integer or a string.

  If no key is specified, PHP will assign the key:

  - If no integer key currently exists, PHP assigns a key of 0.
  - If there are already integer keys, PHP assigns the next higher integer key.

Listing 2-19 shows an example of how to create an array with keys and values.

Listing 2-19: Creating an Array

```
<?php

$exampleArray = array("publisher" => "Wiley", true);
echo $exampleArray [0]; // 1
echo $exampleArray ["publisher"]; // Wiley

?>
```

To create an empty array, you would write: $myArray = array();

To add a value to the end of the array, write: $myArray[] = $x;

PHP includes numerous functions that allow you to work with and manipulate arrays and their contents. The online PHP manual includes a list of all the array functions (`http://php.net/manual/en/function.array.php`). For the purpose of the examples in this book, you need to be familiar with the following array functions:

- array_intersect: Takes two arrays, compares the contents of each array, and returns a new array of the duplicate content.

  Example: $mutualFollows = array_intersect($friendsIds, $followersIds);
- array_diff: Compares the contents of two array and returns a new array with the elements that exist in the first array, but don't exist in the second array.

  Example: $notFollowingYouBack = array_diff($following, $followers);
- array_merge: Combines two arrays into one new array:
  - If string keys are duplicated, the later key value is assigned.
  - If numeric keys are duplicated, the keys are reassigned in numerical order.

  Example: $newArray = array_merge($array1, $array2);
- array_values: Discards an array's keys and returns a new array with the original array's values but with numerical keys.

  This is useful if you want to merge arrays with duplicate keys.

  Example: $newArray = array_values($array1);
- count: Returns the amount of elements in the array.

  Example: $length = count($myArray);
- ksort: Sorts the array by the name of the key.

  Example: ksort($myArray);

cURL

cURL stands for client for URLs. It is an open source software project that consists of two products:

- libcurl
- curl

Libcurl is a multi-platform C-based URL transfer library. It supports numerous protocols, and runs on every platform from Linux to Windows. PHP has functions built in to support libcurl, making it super easy to interact with the Twitter API over HTTP.

Curl is a client-side command line tool used to interact with the libcurl library. With the curl client, you can play with the Twitter API via a basic command line. To get started, you need to know a few basic case-sensitive command line options, including

- -u: The username and password to use.
- -d: The data to send in a post request.
- -k: Turn off SSH certificate verification.

Listings 2-20 and 2-21 are some examples of how to interact with the Twitter API using the curl command line client.

Listing 2-20: Pull Up the Public Timeline

```
curl http://twitter.com/statuses/public_timeline.xml
```

Listing 2-21: Post a Tweet

```
curl -u username:password -k -d "status=Testing curl." https://twitter.com/
            statuses/update.xml
```

To interact with libcurl using PHP, you need the help of a few built-in functions. The functions you need to know for this book include

- curl_init: Create the object to interact with libcurl.
- curl_setopt: Sets the options for the connection, such as post data, URL, and authentication.
- curl_exec: Executes the connection and returns to remote servers response.
- curl_getinfo: Use to get information on the last request, such as transfer speed, and header data.
- curl_close: Closes the connection to the remote server and frees system resources.

To set the curl_setopt function, there are a few predefined constants you need to know.

- CURLOPT_URL: The URL you are requesting.
- CURLOPT_USERAGENT: A string that will identify your requests to hosting server.
- CURLOPT_RETURNTRANSFER: A Boolean that, when set to TRUE or 1, returns the response of the request as a string return value of the curl_exec function.
- CURLOPT_POST: A Boolean that indicates the request is a HTTP POST.
- CURLOPT_POSTFIELDS: The fields you want to include in a HTTP POST request.
- CURLOPT_SSL_VERIFYPEER: A Boolean on whether you want to verify a SSH certificate.
- CURLOPT_USERPWD: The username and password for an authenticated request.

Put all these pieces together, and you see the example in Listing 2-22 that posts to your Twitter stream.

Listing 2-22: Post a Tweet

```
$url = "https://api.twitter.com/1/statuses/update.xml";

$curlHandle = curl_init();

curl_setopt($curlHandle, CURLOPT_URL, "$url");
curl_setopt($curlHandle, CURLOPT_USERAGENT, "Twitter App Development For
                Dummies: Example");
curl_setopt($curlHandle, CURLOPT_POST, 1);
curl_setopt($curlHandle, CURLOPT_RETURNTRANSFER, 1);
curl_setopt($curlHandle, CURLOPT_SSL_VERIFYPEER, false);
curl_setopt($curlHandle, CURLOPT_POSTFIELDS, "status=test");
curl_setopt($curlHandle, CURLOPT_USERPWD, "$username:$password");

$apiResponse = curl_exec($curlHandle);
$info = curl_getinfo($curlHandle);

curl_close($curlHandle);
```

PHP DOMDocument Class

PHP provides a class to parse any standard DOM (Document Object Model) markup. XML fits this category, so you can use PHP's DOMDocument class to parse the XML results from the Twitter API.

To get started, create a new DOMDocument object and then call its loadXML class, as seen in Listing 2-23. The loadXML class loads an XML document from a string.

cURL's curl_exec method returns the response from Twitter in a string. When requesting XML from Twitter, you simply load that response string into the DOMDocument object using the loadXML method.

Listing 2-23: Creating a DOMDocument Object

```
$xml = new DOMDocument();
$xml->loadXML($apiResponse);
```

Now that your DOMDocument is loaded with your XML data, you can parse the data using the getElementsByTagName method. This method returns a class called DOMNodeList. It's essentially a list of all the nodes the method found. See Listing 2-24.

Listing 2-24: getElementsByTagName

```
$nodesFound = $xml->getElementsByTagName('nameOfSomeTag');
```

You can evaluate a collection of tags by using the nodeValue property and a foreach loop. Listing 2-25 shows an example of how to do this.

Listing 2-25: Loop through a DOMNodeList Object

```
$screenNameNodes = $xml->getElementsByTagName("screen_name");

foreach($screenNameNodes as $screenNameNode)
{
   $screenName = $screenNameNode->nodeValue;
   echo $screenName;
}
```

If you know that your DOMNodeList only contains one node, you can go straight to that node using the item method, and print its value. See Listing 2-26.

Listing 2-26: Go Straight to the First Node in a DOMNodeList Object

```
$errorMessage = $errors->item(0)->nodeValue;
```

You can check the amount of nodes found by reading the public property `length` on the DOMNodeList object. If the length is greater than 1, you have found the tag (or tags) you're looking for.

I often use the length attribute in the API example to check when any error tags were found in the returned XML. If so, I print them; else, I continue on.

Listing 2-27 shows an example of this.

Listing 2-27: Check the Length of DOMNodeList

```
$errors = $xml->getElementsByTagName("error");

if($errors->length > 0)
{
   $errorMessage = $errors->item(0)->nodeValue;
   echo "<h1>$errorMessage</h1>";
}
else
{
   // continue with process
}
```

PHP json_decode Function

The json_decode function, included in PHP version 5 and greater, takes a string of JSON formatted data and returns an object of that data.

In this book, I use the json_decode function to parse Twitter API search results.

An example of how this function works can be seen in Listing 2-28.

Listing 2-28: getElementsByTagName

```
<?php

$json = '{"screenname": DustyReagan}';

$obj = json_decode($json);

echo $obj->screenname; // displays: DustyReagan

?>
```

Understanding MySQL

MySQL is an open source relational database server and structured query language (SQL). It is a common fixture in Web development and is found as an optional add-on on most Web hosting companies.

Relational databases are collections of related tables that store data in fields. To interact with the databases you use the MySQL query language. You will need to know a few basic MySQL commands for this book, including

- select: Use to query the database.
- create: Create a new table.
- insert: Insert a new row into a table.
- update: Update the values in a database.
- delete: Delete a row.

The select query is probably the most common MySQL command. It is used to query data in the database. It also uses some common MySQL clauses that you will recognize in other MySQL commands. These common clauses are

- from: Specifies the table you want to query.
- join: Allows you to include the data from another table with your query, by joining the two tables on a common row identifier, such as an id field.
- where: Limit the results of the query to data that meets the conditions specified in the where clause.
- group by: Group data by common fields.
- having: Use to limit data after it has grouped by the conditions specified in the having clause.
- order by: Sort the data by a column or multiple columns.
- limit: Use to limit the row count to a specific number. Useful for getting a sample of an extremely large result set.

To use the select query, you must specify the fields you want to return, and the database and table you want to query. You can return all the fields in the table by using an asterisk *. To start, select the database you want to work with the command:

```
use databaseName;
```

Once you select your database, you can run a simple select query, as seen in Listing 2-29, to return all the rows in a table.

Listing 2-29: A Basic SQL Select Query

```
select *
from tableName;
```

If you have data stored in two different tables, it might be necessary to join those tables based on a common id field. An example of this is seen in Listing 2-30.

Listing 2-30: A SQL Select Query Using a Join

```
select *
from tableName t1
join tableName2 t2 on t1.id = t2.id;
```

In Listing 2-31, I show you the proper syntax for a where, order by, and limit clause. In this query, I get the ten products that are lowest in stock.

Listing 2-31: A Select Query Using a Where, Order By, and Limit Clause

```
select productName, quantityInStock
from tableName
where quantityInStock < 100
order by quantityInStock
limit 0, 10;
```

Listing 2-32 is an example of a group by and having clause. The count(*) statement returns the amount of rows.

Listing 2-32: Group By and Having

```
select year, count(*)
from tableName
group by year
having count(*) > 5;
```

To create a new table in MySQL, use the create statement. When you create a new table, you must specify the field names, their data type, whether they are allowed to contain a NULL value, whether they should be indexed for quick searching, and whether they should be indexed as the primary key. The primary key exists for unique row identifiers, and is perfectly suitable for ids that join tables together. Create keys for fields that you want indexed for quick searching, but are not unique row identifiers. Listing 2-33 shows an example of a create statement.

Listing 2-33: A Create Statement

```
create table 'exampleTable' (
   exampleTableId int(6) not null,
   firstName varchar(60) not null,
   lastName varchar(60) not null,
   dateOfBirth timestamp not null,
   cellPhoneNumber default null
) engine=innodb default charset=utf-8;
```

Inserting a new row into a table requires the use of the insert statement, as seen in Listing 2-34.

Listing 2-34: An Insert Statement

```
insert into exampleTable (column1, column2)
values (value1, value2);
```

To update the data in a table, use the update statement as seen in Listing 2-35. Use the where clause you can limit the field updates to one particular row or a set of rows.

Listing 2-35: An Update Statement

```
update exampleTable
set column1 = bacon, column2 = eggs
where meal == 'breakfast';
```

The delete statement can be used to delete rows, tables, and even databases. In Listing 2-36, I delete a few rows from a table whose ids are less than 10.

Listing 2-36: A Delete Statement

```
delete from exampleTable
where id > 10;
```

Chapter 3

Setting Up to Create Twitter Apps

In This Chapter

- Signing up for Twitter
- Establishing version control
- Creating your first Twitter app

In this chapter, you create your first Twitter application. Don't get too excited. The example Twitter app in this chapter is not the next "killer app." But it does illustrate how to work with the Twitter API. I also cover the importance of version control software, which helps you manage your code files

Create Your Developer Account

Before you can start writing Twitter applications, you need a Twitter account. I assume that since you are interested in developing Twitter apps, you must have some experience with Twitter using a personal account. If not, no worries; now is an excellent time to create your personal account. However, you will also need an account dedicated to your application.

Your application needs a Twitter account to authenticate with Twitter's API. You can use your personal account to do this, but if any problems arise with your application, your personal account may be penalized. There's no reason to take that risk.

Creating a Twitter account for development is easy:

1. **Go to `https://twitter.com/signup` and fill out the provided fields.**
2. **Twitter asks if you want to look up any of your e-mail contacts on Twitter.**

   I don't recommend this option.

Twitter recommends a list of popular Twitter accounts for you to follow. Since this account is dedicated to your application and is not used for light reading, I recommend not following any of the suggested users.

3. **Click the Finish button, and you're done creating your account.**

The Importance of Version Control

Use a *hosted version control repository* instead of installing and managing your own server. You can easily get up and running in minutes with version control by going to a site like Beanstalk (`http://beanstalkapp.com`), Unfuddle (`http://unfuddle.com`), or GitHub (`http://github.com`), signing up for a free account, and using their online repository URL and Web-based administration tools.

Version control software makes programming more manageable in a few different ways:

- Track file changes over time.

  This is useful to development teams because they can resolve conflicts that arise when two or more developers simultaneously update the same line of code. When this happens, version control software is used to inspect the differences and correctly merge the files.

- Compare the differences between the current version of a file and an older version of the same file.
- Roll a file back to a previous version.

  This is a lifesaver if you accidentally introduce a debilitating bug into your program because you can simply roll your code back to the last known working version while you chase down the new bug. Even if you're coding by yourself and you're not on a team, version control can give you the security to try new things with your code because you can always roll any changes back if you break something.

If you're new to version control, I recommend signing up for a free Subversion account with Beanstalk.. Subversion is a widely adopted version control system and it's easy to learn. By using Beanstalk, you don't have to set up or manage your own Subversion servers. They do that for you. To create your free Beanstalk Subversion account, sign up at `https://signup.beanstalkapp.com/accounts/new?plan=free`.

Hello Twitter!

It's time to write your first Twitter app! Writing the app is actually a lot easier than you might think. Follow these steps:

1. **Create a new file titled `HelloTwitter.html` and save it anywhere on your local hard drive.**

   This is a great chance to try a version control program, like Subversion.

2. **In the new file, add the HTML from Listing 3-1.**

Listing 3-1: HelloTwitter.html

```
<html>
   <head>
      <title>Hello Twitter!</title>
   </head>
   <body>

      <form name="input"
            action="http://username:password@twitter.com/statuses/update.xml"
            method="post">
         Tweet: <textarea cols="40" rows="3" name="status">Hello Twitter!</
               textarea><br />
         <input type="submit" value="Submit" />
      </form>

   </body>
</html>
```

   Listing 3-1 is an HTML form that posts the status message "Hello Twitter!" to your Twitter account:

   a. The form's action performs an HTTP POST to the address `twitter.com/statuses/update.xml`.

   b. The post address passes your Twitter login credentials to the API method.

   c. The field named "status" allows you to input the text of your status update.

3. **Replace `username` and `password` in the form action (seen bolded in Listing 3-1) with your application's Twitter account credentials (as created previously in this chapter).**

   Do not upload this file to the Internet or use this example for production code. Your username and password are clearly viewable in this file, and that is a major security hole. You do not want the general public to have access to your Twitter account credentials.

4. **Open this file locally on your computer with your Web browser (I recommend using Firefox or Internet Explorer to properly view the results); then click the Submit button.**

Some browsers don't display XML in a human readable format. I use either Firefox or Internet Explorer to view XML files. If you are using Safari or Google Chrome, you need to view the source code of the response page to see code that looks similar to Listing 3-2. You can view the source code by right clicking on the results page, then selecting "View Source" in the popup menu.

After you click the Submit button, Twitter responds with the details of the status message you just submitted. The status message details include the details of the user account. The response is an XML file that should look similar to Listing 3-2.

Listing 3-2: Twitter Status Update XML Response

```
<?xml version="1.0" encoding="UTF-8"?>
<status>
  <created_at>Sat Sep 19 04:19:17 +0000 2009</created_at>
  <id>4096090186</id>
  <text>Hello World!</text>

  <source>
    <a href="http://apiwiki.twitter.com/" rel="nofollow">API</a>
  </source>
  <truncated>false</truncated>
  <in_reply_to_status_id/>
  <in_reply_to_user_id/>
  <favorited>false</favorited>
  <in_reply_to_screen_name/>

  <user>
    <id>75155000</id>
    <name>testfordummies</name>
    <screen_name>testfordummies</screen_name>
    <location/>
    <description/>
    <profile_image_url>
    http://s.twimg.com/a/1253301564/images/default_profile_4_normal.png
    </profile_image_url>
    <url/>
    <protected>false</protected>
    <followers_count>0</followers_count>
    <profile_background_color>9ae4e8</profile_background_color>
    <profile_text_color>000000</profile_text_color>
    <profile_link_color>0000ff</profile_link_color>
    <profile_sidebar_fill_color>e0ff92</profile_sidebar_fill_color>
    <profile_sidebar_border_color>87bc44</profile_sidebar_border_color>
```

(continued)

Listing 3-2 *(continued)*

```
        <friends_count>0</friends_count>
        <created_at>Fri Sep 18 00:19:49 +0000 2009</created_at>
        <favourites_count>0</favourites_count>
        <utc_offset/>
        <time_zone/>

        <profile_background_image_url>
        http://s.twimg.com/a/1253301564/images/themes/theme1/bg.png
        </profile_background_image_url>
        <profile_background_tile>false</profile_background_tile>
        <statuses_count>3</statuses_count>
        <notifications>false</notifications>
        <verified>false</verified>
        <following>false</following>
    </user>
</status>
```

5. **Open the Twitter account and verify that the form updated your status.**

Congratulations! You've written your first Twitter application!

Chapter 4 covers several areas of the Twitter application ecosystem and will provide you with inspiration and a general idea of what you can do with the API.

Part II

Ideation — Coming Up with an Idea

"These are the parts of our life that aren't on Twitter."

In this part . . .

The goal of the chapters in this section is to get you started working on a great Twitter application.

Chapter 4

Getting to Know the Twitter Application Ecosystem

In This Chapter

- Types of Twitter applications
- Examples of Twitter applications
- Sources for inspiration

Twitter has strategically taken on a role as a communication platform and is seemingly not out to solve every user requested feature demand. With their open API, this allows developers to find a niche in the Twitter application ecosystem by identifying a feature that Twitter users want but that Twitter itself does not address.

Before you jump in and start creating your Twitter application, you need to investigate the various applications that have already been developed. This is your opportunity to learn from those applications and gain inspiration, identify opportunities, and find your niche.

The Twitter application ecosystem can be broken into five different categories: desktop clients, mobile clients, Web applications, Twitter bots, and hardware. There are over 10,000 Twitter applications. In this chapter, I profile 34 example applications across all five categories just identified. You will get a sense of what each application is about, who made it, and how it is monetized, if it is monetized at all. Popular applications that don't have a direct revenue stream may still benefit the creators indirectly by increasing their name recognition, providing them with job leads, or simply satisfying their need to create. However, in the applications profiled in this chapter, I focus on how they create cash directly. Many of these applications are illustrated in Appendix B.

Desktop Client

Desktop clients are applications that run directly on your operating system whether that is Linux, Windows, or OS X. One of the key strengths of Twitter desktop applications is that they allow you to keep a constant eye on your Twitter stream due to the dedicated application window and process. Here are a few popular Twitter desktop clients.

TweetDeck

Web site: `http://tweetdeck.com`

Creator: TweetDeck, Inc. Founded by Iain Dodsworth (@iaindodsworth)

Description: TweetDeck's claim to fame is its multiple column layout. This allows users to segment their Twitter streams into groups. For example, you can add your close friends to one column and your professional contacts to another column. You can also create a column for search terms, @ replies, and direct messages. Additionally, TweetDeck integrates with Facebook. TweetDeck is an Adobe Air application so it can run on any operating system that Adobe Air can run on. There is also a complimentary iPhone application and Web version of this popular Twitter client. TweetDeck will even backup and sync your column settings across environments.

Monetization: TweetDeck is a funded company that has not settled on a revenue stream. However, TweetDeck is experimenting with allowing other Twitter services to bid on having their service integrated into TweetDeck. It is unclear whether any deals of this nature have been made.

Seesmic Desktop

Web site: `http://seesmic.com`

Creator: Seesmic, Inc. Founded by Loic Le Meur (@loic)

Description: Seesmic Desktop is TweetDeck's primary competitor. They purchased Twhirl, another popular Twitter desktop client, in 2009 and added column-based grouping similar to TweetDeck's. Since that time, TweetDeck and Seesmic Desktop have been in an arms race to add features and improve usability. Both clients have very similar features, and choosing between the two seemingly boils down to personal preference regarding the user interface.

Monetization: Similar to TweetDeck, Seesmic is a funded company that has not yet settled on a revenue stream. However, Seesmic founder, Loic Le Meur, has mentioned a paid pro version.

Twitterrific

Web site: `http://twitterrific.com`

Creator: The Iconfactory

Description: Twitterrific is a Twitter client for OS X and iPhone. It has a long history with Twitter users and has been around since early 2007. It is strictly a Twitter client and does not interface with other social networking sites such as Facebook. It also cannot manage multiple Twitter accounts, but its small desktop footprint and simple interface make it a popular choice among Twitter users.

Monetization: Twitterrific is shareware. The free shareware version is fully functional and ad-supported. The full version can be purchased for just under $15 and removes the ads.

Mobile Clients

Twitter is all about broadcasting to the world what is going on in your life at this very moment. However, not everyone sits near their computer all day waiting to tweet something interesting about their lives. As it turns out, interesting tweet-worthy events frequently happen to people when they are away from their computers. Twitter has addressed this problem by including text messaging with its service. If you have a cell phone, you can update your status anytime, anywhere. With smartphones becoming more prevalent, a market has opened up for mobile Twitter clients that provide a more enriching experience than text messaging.

Tweetie

Web site: `http://atebits.com/tweetie-iphone`

Creator: Loren Britcher (@atebits)

Description: Due to its simple interface and its ability to manage multiple Twitter accounts on the go, Tweetie has become one of the most popular Twitter clients for the iPhone. Nearly anything you can do on Twitter's Web site, you can do easily using Tweetie, including viewing popular trends, and saving searches. Tweetie also provides features absent from Twitter's Web site such as posting pictures directly to TwitPic, creating a Google Maps link based on your GPS location, and retweeting a post with one button click.

Monetization: Tweetie is sold in the Apple iPhone store for $2.99. Tweetie also has a free OS X desktop client that generates revenue through ads.

TweetDeck

Web site: `http://tweetdeck.com/iphone`

Creator: TweetDeck, Inc. Founder Iain Dodsworth (@iaindodsworth)

Description: TweetDeck for iPhone provides much of the same functionality as TweetDeck for the desktop. Its signature draw is the ability to group the tweets of the people you're following into multiple columns. The other interesting aspect of TweetDeck is that it can back up and sync your groups and settings to your TweetDeck desktop client, and vice versa.

Monetization: Like the desktop version, TweetDeck for the iPhone is currently free.

Tiny Twitter

Web site: `http://tinytwitter.com`

Creator: Kevin Cawley (@kcbigring)

Description: Tiny Twitter is a Java-based Twitter client that works on any Java enabled phone including Blackberry, Windows Mobile, and Pocket PC. It has many of the same features found on Twitter's Web site and most notably, allows you to save money on text messaging costs.

Monetization: Tiny Twitter is free and has no monetization scheme that I am aware of.

Web Applications

Web applications are applications that you can access on the Internet through your Web browser. Twitter.com itself is an example of a Web application. Web applications have a lower barrier to entry for end users than desktop applications because the user does not need to install software. Web applications also don't typically require a specific operating system to run. This increases the potential market for Web applications.

There are probably more Twitter Web applications than any other type of Twitter application. To help in reviewing the Twitter Web application ecosystem,

I've identified seven popular types of Twitter Web applications including customer relationship management (CRM), contact management, statistics, media sharing, information aggregation, information publishing, and advertising.

Customer relationship management (CRM)

CRM applications help businesses communicate effectively with customers by helping the organization keep track of who communicated with the customer, what they talked about, and when. As businesses begin to rely on Twitter as a customer communication channel, the demand for a Twitter CRM system grows. And it's not just businesses that benefit from using a Twitter CRM system. Any Twitter account with multiple editors can use a CRM system to keep from stepping on each other's toes and improve communication with their readers.

HootSuite

Web site: `http://hootsuite.com`

Creator: Invoke Media Inc.

Description: HootSuite may have been first to address the growing need of a Twitter CRM system. Its interface allows you to manage multiple Twitter accounts and to assign multiple editors to a Twitter profile. Each editor receives a unique login, so you don't have to share the organization's primary Twitter login credentials.

Monetization: HootSuite currently accepts donations. However, I suspect it will eventually implement a paid pro version of its Web application.

CoTweet

Web site: `http://cotweet.com`

Creator: CoTweet Inc.

Description: CoTweet has similar features to HootSuite, but you can also assign tweets to specific editors and leave notes about previous conversations with the customer. Assigning tweets to a specific editor keeps members of the organization from addressing a customer more than once on a single issue.

Monetization: CoTweet is currently in free beta. It has plans to create a paid pro version of its application.

Contact management

Twitter has two basic types of contacts: those you follow and those who follow you. This raises the question of whom should I follow and whom should I allow to follow me. Twitter's interface for managing contacts is a relatively simple paged list. The simplicity of Twitter's own contact management solution has created an opportunity in the Twitter API developer world to improve contact management. Here are a few examples of contact management applications.

Friend Or Follow

Web site: `http://friendorfollow.com`

Creator: Dusty Reagan (@dustyreagan; and author of this book)

Description: Friend Or Follow shows users whom they're following who aren't following them back, and vice versa, using a visual grid of profile pictures. It also shows users their reciprocated followers. The users can sort their contact list by a variety of options such as name, last tweet, and location.

Friend Or Follow is probably the most useful, well written, and sexiest application on the Internet, according to your author, the creator of Friend Or Follow. Please send money.

Monetization: Friend Or Follow makes its revenue through the Featured Users ad network and by giving its creator enough exposure to land a book deal on Twitter application development.

Mr. Tweet

Web site: `http://mrtweet.com`

Creator: Yu-Shan Fung (@ambivalence) and Ming Yeow Ng (@mingyeow)

Description: Mr. Tweet recommends users for you to follow by comparing your social graph to other users, weighing recommendations from other Twitter users, and other user commonalities.

Monetization: Mr.Tweet currently does not have a revenue stream.

WeFollow

Web site: `http://wefollow.com`

Creator: Kevin Rose (@kevinrose)

Description: WeFollow.com is a tag-based Twitter user directory where you select up to three tags that you believe best describe your Twitter account.

To be allowed in the directory, you must tweet your selected tags, adding to the viral nature of the directory.

Monetization: We Follow monetizes with Google Ad Sense.

Statistics

Statistical Twitter analysis became a hot topic when businesses started marketing on Twitter. This is because businesses are interested in determining their marketing reach and the return on their marketing efforts. Twitter statistics can also be fun and interesting to non-business users who are curious about how they interact on Twitter. Twitter statistics are also useful for academic research.

TwitterCounter

Web site: `http://twittercounter.com`

Creator: Boris Veldhuijzen van Zanten (@boris) and Arjen Schat (@arjenschat)

Description: TwitterCounter tracks Twitter users' follower count over time. Users can proudly display their follower count on their Web site or blog using the TwitterCounter badge. TwitterCounter also keeps an updated list of the most followed profiles on Twitter.

Monetization: TwitterCounter sells a featured user position on its Web site that Twitter users use to promote their profile and gain new followers.

TweetReach

Web site: `http://tweetreach.com`

Creator: Hayes Davis (@hayesdavis)

Description: TweetReach calculates how many people have seen a word or phrase you've shared on Twitter. It does this by counting the amount of tweets that contain your word or phrase and then counts how many Twitter profiles may have seen those tweets. The tweets are broken into retweets, @ replies, and regular tweets.

Monetization: TweetReach searches at a fixed depth, but the user can pay a fee to get a deeper and more accurate report. TweetReach also uses the Featured Users advertising network to make money.

TweetStats

Web site: `http://tweetstats.com`

Creator: Damon Cortesi (@dacort)

Description: TweetStats graphs your personal Twitter stats including your tweets per hour, your tweets per month, your tweet timeline, and your reply statistics. It also generates a tag cloud of your most tweeted words.

Monetization: TweetStats users can order custom-built reports from Damon. TweetStats also makes money using the Featured Users advertising network.

Follow Cost

Web site: `http://followcost.com`

Creator: Luke Francl (@lof) and Barry Hess (@bjhess)

Description: You can use Follow Cost to see how frequently a user tweets per day. Creators Luke Francl and Barry Hess also humorously provide the average tweets per day in milliscobles, a unit of measurement they created that was inspired by the prolific Twitterer Robert Scoble (@scobleizer). Aside from visiting the Web site to get a user's average tweets per day, you can use the site's bookmarklet or Fluid/Greasemonkey script.

Monetization: Follow Cost makes its revenue through the Featured Users ad network.

Media Sharing

Twitter limits status updates to 140 characters or less. However, users aren't always content with this limitation. There are times when you might like to share pictures, movies, or long URLs with your followers. This need has generated several apps like the ones below.

TwitPic

Web site: `http://twitpic.com`

Creator: Noah Everett (@noaheverett)

Description: TwitPic is the most popular photo-sharing site on Twitter. It owes most of its popularity to its ease of adoption and API. Anyone with a Twitter account automatically has a TwitPic account, and the API has allowed third-party Twitter clients to integrate with TwitPic. For example, the iPhone app, Tweetie, allows users to take a picture using their iPhone and post the picture directly to their Twitter stream using TwitPic's API.

Monetization: TwitPic generates ad revenue using a combination of the video ad network VideoEgg and Google AdSense.

SnapTweet

Web site: `http://snaptweet.com`

Creator: Damon Clinkscales (@damon)

Description: Using SnapTweet, you can easily post a link to your Flickr photos to Twitter. SnapTweet does this by monitoring your Flickr stream looking for new pictures or pictures with a specific tag that marks that the photo should be posted to Twitter. You can also direct-message a request to have a photo tweeted.

Monetization: SnapTweet currently does not have a revenue model.

Blip.fm

Web site: `http://blip.fm`

Creator: Blip.fm. Founded by Brian Venneman & Jeff Yasuda (@jeffyasuda)

Description: You can use Blip.fm to share and discover music with your friends. You start by creating a profile and typing in a song you want to share. Blip.fm searches for the song on various public sites such as youtube.com. It then allows you to post that song along with a comment to your Blip.fm music stream, where all your friends can listen to it. Blip.fm can also cross-post your song selections to Twitter and Facebook.

Monetization: Blip.fm monetizes through advertising, selling merchandise, and by making referral sales on iTunes and Amazon.

Information aggregation

Your Twitter stream is a flow of information. However, that stream is unfiltered, and it is difficult to key in on any one particular topic. You may be reading your graduate professor's tweet on quantum physics, while right above it is your grandmother's tweet about her cat Fluffo. Here is an opportunity to create an application that aggregates topical information in a central location.

CheapTweet

Web site: `http://cheaptweet.com`

Creator: Hayes Davis (@hayesdavis) and Jenn Deering Davis (@jdeeringdavis) of Appozite, LLC

Description: CheapTweet is a social search engine for deals on Twitter. It automatically aggregates and categorizes tweets about coupons, discounts, and promotions into an easily searchable index. The CheapTweet user community votes on the deals, and the most popular ones filter into the "Cheapest Tweets" list.

Monetization: CheapTweet monetizes its Web site using paid sponsorships. Businesses and individuals can pay to have their Twitter profiles featured on the Web site. CheapTweet also has sponsored Tweets where a business can pay to have its tweeted deal placed on the top of the deal list. Retailers can also pay for the privilege of having a page totally dedicated to the deals of that particular store.

ExecTweets

Web site: `http://exectweets.com`

Creator: Federated Media, in partnership with Microsoft

Description: ExecTweets is a Web site that aggregates the tweets from numerous business executives from large companies. Users vote on the tweets they find most compelling, and ExecTweets then posts the most popular tweets to its @ExecTweets Twitter stream. There is also a list of the current most popular links that the executives are tweeting about.

Monetization: Federated Media makes money through Microsoft's sponsorship.

Tweeting Too Hard

Web site: `http://tweetingtoohard.com`

Creator: Trey Philips (@treyp), Michael Cummings (@michaelcummings), Jacob Morse (@jacobmorse), and Keith Hanson (@big_love)

Description: Tweeting Too Hard was created to give attention to Tweets that are braggadocios or arrogant. Users submit tweets they feel fit in this vein, and then the community votes the tweets up or down. The most self-important tweets get featured on the front page.

Monetization: Tweeting Too Hard makes its revenue through the Featured Users ad network.

Twistori

Web site: `http://twistori.com`

Creator: Amy Hoy (@amyhoy) and Thomas Fuchs (@thomasfuchs) of slash7

Description: Twistori has a unique twist on information aggregation. Instead of aggregating tweets by topics such as celebrities or deals, Twistori.com aggregates tweets by emotions. It includes a scrolling list of tweets that contain phrases such as "I love," "I hate," and "I think."

Monetization: Twistori sells a desktop version that allows users to visualize their own search terms.

Hashtags.org

Web site: `http://hashtags.org`

Creator: Cody Marx Bailey (@superphly), Aaron Farnham (@afarnham), Brian Smith (@brianthecoder), & Ben Burkert (@benburkert)

Description: Hashtags.org is a Web site that tracks the frequency that a hashtag is used on Twitter. You can search for a hashtag, and it will show you a graph of the hashtags use over time. You can also drill down and get details on a hashtag, such as the tweets that contained the hashtags, the people who tweeted about the hashtag, and related hashtags. Hashtags.org also shows you the current most popular hashtags, and it provides a directory of hashtags.

Monetization: Hashtags.org is monetized through the use of the ad network Featured Users and user donations. It is also exploring other revenue models.

Information publishing

I'll admit "information publishing" is a pretty broad category for Twitter. After all, tons of Twitter applications post information to Twitter. But what I'm focusing on here are applications that specialize in posting tweets to Twitter in unique ways. Read on; you'll see what I mean.

SecretTweet

Web site: `http://secrettweet.com`

Creator: Kevin Smith (@mozunk)

Description: SecretTweet user's can anonymously post their secrets to the Web site, allowing the curious to read all about them on SecretTweet's Twitter account, @SecretTweetor, on the Web site.

Monetization: SecretTweet generates its revenue through banner advertising using BuySellAds, Google AdSense, and Featured Users.

Twitterfeed

Web site: `http://twitterfeed.com`

Creator: Twitterfeed, Inc. Founded by Mario Menti (@mario)

Description: Twitterfeed allows users to push RSS feed updates to Twitter, Laconcia, Ping.fm, or HelloText automatically. It was originally created as a side project by Mario Menti and has since become its own company, receiving investments from Betaworks and TAG.

Monetization: Twitterfeed currently has no publicly disclosed revenue source.

Advertising

Twitter has opened a new channel for business owners, brands, and personalities to communicate with their customers, fans, and critics. Along with the ability to communicate, an advertising opportunity has emerged. Brands want to gain exposure to the millions of people twittering, but Twitter itself does not have a means for these brands to advertise on Twitter. However, a few third-party solutions have arisen to cater to advertisers' needs. Here are a few examples.

Featured Users

Web site: `http://featuredusers.com`

Creator: Dusty Reagan (@dustyreagan; and author of this book)

Description: Featured Users is an ad network where Twitter users promote their Twitter profile across a network of third-party Twitter applications by purchasing banner impressions. It provides a means for Twitter application developers to monetize their site with relevant ads, and it provides advertisers with the ability to promote their brand to Twitter users.

Monetization: Featured Users makes money by taking a percentage of each ad sale.

Magpie

Web site: `http://be-a-magpie.com`

Creator: Magpie and Friends Ltd. (@beamagpie)

Description: Magpie is a Twitter ad network where advertisers pay Twitter users to tweet a marketing message to their followers. Magpie brokers the transaction and facilitates the whole process, including matching advertisers to Twitter users, reporting click stats, and giving the Twitter users the ability to manage the type and frequency of ads that are posted to their Twitter stream.

Monetization: Magpie takes a percentage of each transaction.

Twittad

Web site: `http://twittad.com`

Creator: James Eliason (@jameseliason)

Description: Twittad allows advertisers to purchase and advertise on the background image of a Twitter user's profile for a limited amount of time. Twitter users pay a small fee to have their listing posted on Twittad; then they set the price and duration they're willing to sell their background. Advertisers then select from the list of Twitter users who have put their Twitter backgrounds up for sale. When advertisers select a Twitter account, they pay Twittad the money, which then releases the money to the Twitter user after each day of advertising.

Monetization: Twittad makes its revenue by taking a percentage of each transaction, and it makes a small fee for each Twitter publisher listing.

Twitter Bots

Twitter bots are Twitter accounts that are automated to accomplish a certain task. They may alert you of events on Twitter, such as when someone stopped following you, or they may perform a task if you tweet them a command. One compelling aspect to Twitter bots is Twitter's built-in support for text messaging. Twitter bots can leverage Twitter's text message support to allow users to accomplish tasks from their cell phones. You could consider Twitter accounts that are simply an automated import of blog's RSS feed a Twitter bot. However, I review some more complex and compelling Twitter bots next.

Twittercal (@gcal)

Web site: `http://twittercal.com`

Creator: Fred Brunel (@fbrunel)

Description: Twittercal is a Twitter bot that updates your Google calendar. Simply start following @gcal and grant access to your Google Calendar account at its Web site, twittercal.com. Then you can direct-message @gcal events.

Monetization: Twittercal has no monetization strategy.

Remember The Milk (@rtm)

Web site: `http://rememberthemilk.com/services/twitter`

Creator: Remember The Milk Pty Ltd.

Description: Remember The Milk is a Web-based to-do list. They have a Twitter bot you can follow and send direct messages to in order to update your to-do list. This is helpful because by using this Twitter bot, you can update your Remember The Milk to-do list via text message.

Monetization: The Remember The Milk Twitter bot is free. However, the bot adds value to the Remember The Milk Web service and encourages the user to purchase the pro account.

Tweetname (@tweetname)

Web site: `http://tweetname.com`

Creator: Philip Kaplan (@pud)

Description: With Tweetname, you can check domain name availability and purchase domain names impulsively by direct messaging the Tweetname bot. To do this, you must first register your payment information at Tweetname. com. Tweetname stores your payment information and associates it with your Twitter account. Then when you want to check on the availability of or purchase a domain name, you simply direct-message @tweetname the command.

Monetization: Tweetname makes a commission on every domain name it sells.

Hardware

Probably one of the least pioneered applications of the Twitter API is in the area of hardware integration. There are a few good reasons this area is relatively underdeveloped. For one, the Twitter API is constantly changing, and there is a risk that a Twitter hardware device will become obsolete if Twitter makes a change to its API. You have the same risk with software, but it's much easier to roll out a change to a Web site, and users are used to upgrading software. There is also a high cost barrier to manufacture and distribute Twitter hardware devices to a mass market. Therefore, most Twitter hardware devices are left to the do-it-yourself crowd. Still, the potential is there, and you may eventually see mass-market devices with Twitter integration built in.

BakerTweet

Web site: `http://bakertweet.com`

Creator: Poke

Description: BakerTweet is a wireless device for bakeries that alerts their customers on Twitter when something fresh has come out of the oven. The plain white box contains a simple text display, a dial, and one button. The baker uses the dial on BakerTweet to select the baked goods that just came out of the oven and then presses the button to tweet the news. The baker can customize BakerTweets preprogrammed tweets and items via a Web interface.

Monetization: Poke sells BakerTweet on a custom order basis.

Botanicalls Kit

Web site: `http://botanicalls.com`

Creator: Botanicalls

Description: Botanicalls is a company that aims to bridge the communication gap between humans and plants. It sells a do-it-yourself plant monitoring kit. The kit consists of a leaf-shaped circuit board, soil probes, Ethernet port, power adapter, and various transistors, resistors, and other circuitry-related bits. Once assembled, the Bontanicalls Kit will alert you via your plant's Twitter account when your plant needs water or if it has been over-watered.

Monetization: The Botanicalls Kit can be purchased on several popular technology and DIY-related Web sites.

Tweet-a-Watt

Web site: `http://adafruit.com`

Creator: Phil Torrone (@ptorrone) of Adafruit Industries

Description: Tweet-a-Watt is a do-it-yourself kit used to hack a P3 Kill-a-Watt power meter. Tweet-a-Watt plugs into any standard 140-volt US electrical outlet and tracks the power consumption of the device you plug into Tweet-a-Watt. As the name suggests, Tweet-a-Watt tweets your device's power consumption. It also allows you to log and graph the power consumption over time on your computer.

Monetization: Adafruit Industries sells the kit on its Web site.

Chapter 5

Introducing the Twitter API

In This Chapter

- Defining an API
- Interacting with Twitter's API

API stands for Application Programming Interface. It's kind of like a user interface, except instead of delivering content that humans can read and use, an API delivers content that software can read and use. For example, a Web site can deliver beautiful graphics that are thoughtfully laid out, with large readable fonts, so that the user can easily find and read the information he or she is looking for. This type of human-oriented design is difficult for a program to read because it relies on context. A program can access the same Web site using an API. The API returns an XML or JSON data file that can then be parsed and processed easily.

An API does more than allow your program to easily read data. It also allows you to perform actions on the remote system. With the Twitter API, by simply requesting a URL with a few HTTP POST parameters, you can post a tweet or send a direct message.

Twitter's API is designed to be RESTful. REST (Representational State Transfer) is a software design pattern for creating APIs. In a nutshell, it means the API is designed to leverage HTTP requests, such as GET, POST, DELETE, and PUT. And it means that requesting data from the API is as straightforward as requesting a Web page.

Play Nice and Follow the Terms of Service

When developing your Twitter application, keep in mind that you're eating at Twitter's dinner table and you're their guest. Be respectful, gracious, follow the rules of the house, and don't take more than your share. If you're not a good guest, your dinner host may throw you out and not invite you back to dinner.

You need to be aware of and follow two sets of rules. The first set consists of the general rules that apply to all Twitter users. The second set consists of those that apply to developers of the API.

Both sets of rules apply to you as a Twitter application developer.

General Twitter Rules

A regular Twitter user could be banned from Twitter for breaking any of the following rules. As a developer you may not only have your account banned, but your application as well. So pay special attention to the following rules:

- Do not impersonate someone else.
- Do not infringe on anyone else's trademarks or copyrights.
- Do not publish anyone's private or confidential information without his or her permission.
- Do not threaten violence against other users.
- Do not copy and use the Verified Account badge anywhere on your Twitter profile, unless Twitter provides it to you.
- You may not use pornographic images in your background or profile picture.
- Do not mass create serial accounts for disruptive purposes.
- Do not *name squat*. Name squatting means signing up for an account name and not using it, for the sole purpose of preventing other people from using it.
- Do not sell usernames you have control of.
- Do not publish links to malware, phishing sites, or viruses.
- Do not engage in *follower churn*.

  Follower churn is the act of egregiously following thousands of users, dropping the ones who don't follow back, and then repeating the act over and over to grow your follower base.
- Do not post the same link or tweet over and over again.
- Do not @ reply everyone in your follow list with the same tweet.

Stay Informed with Online Resources

For updates on the latest Twitter API developments, consult these online resources:

- @twitterapi — The Official Twitter API Twitter account
- @twitter — The Official Twitter account
- Twitter Development Talk Google Group — `http://groups.google.com/group/twitter-development-talk`
- Twitter API Announcements Only Google Group — `http://groups.google.com/group/twitter-api-announce`
- Twitter API wiki and documentation — `http://apiwiki.twitter.com`
- Chat via #twitterapi on irc.freenode.net.

Developer Etiquette

The following rules are not applicable to regular Twitter users, but as a developer you need to be conscious of them:

- Do not tweet or perform any other behavior on users' behalf without first asking them to do so.
- Call the API as little as possible to achieve your goal. Keeping a local cache of results can aid greatly in this effort.
- Be conscientious of your API rate limit. Avoid making requests after your limit is reached.
- Do not create applications that perform follower churn.
- Stay informed about API developments and updates using the Developer Google Group.

There Are Actually Two APIs

The Twitter API is actually made up of two different RESTful APIs.

- `http://api.twitter.com`
- `http://search.twitter.com`

The Streaming API Is Around the Corner

Twitter currently has a Streaming API in alpha testing. The Streaming API is a near–real-time feed of Twitter status updates that developers can tap into. To work with the Streaming API, you open a connection to the feed and parse the data as it constantly flows.

The Streaming API contains the legendary `statuses/firehose` method, often referred to as the Firehose. The Firehose returns all real-time public statuses as fast as possible. This method has only been made available to exclusive parties that have partnered with Twitter. However, Twitter has announced that this method will eventually be made available to all developers.

The Streaming API is currently under heavy development and isn't ready for production applications, but you can learn more about what is going on with the Streaming API on the Twitter wiki at `http://apiwiki.twitter.com/Streaming-API-Documentation`.

The `http://api.twitter.com` API contains the majority of Twitter's API methods. It is commonly referred to as the REST API. `http://search.twitter.com` contains only five search-specific methods, including:

- `search`
- `trends`
- `trends/current`
- `trends/daily`
- `trends/weekly`

The Search API is currently separate from the rest of the Twitter API because a company named Summize built it independently of Twitter. Twitter acquired Summize in 2008 and integrated Search into its front end, but hasn't yet integrated the Search API with the rest of its system. However, the Search API is planned to be integrated into the rest of the Twitter API soon.

Twitter API Versioning

Twitter has a version for every API method, starting with version 1, except for methods in the Search API.

This is done so Twitter can release new updates as new version numbers without breaking developer code that uses an older version number.

The methods in this book refer to the latest version as of the time of this writing, version 1 of the API. The version number of the method is specified in the URL between the domain name and the method specification. In the following code, you can see the number `1` between the domain and the `users/show` method. That signifies I'm requesting version 1 of the `users/show` method.

```
http://api.twitter.com/1/users/show
```

Consult Twitter's online documentation at `http://apiwiki.twitter.com` for the latest version of each method.

Rate Limits and How to Get White Listed

Twitter places limits on how frequently developers and users can interact with the system. The current limits are

- 1,000 status updates per day
- 250 direct messages per day
- 150 REST API requests per hour

There is also a limit on the number of people you can follow. This limit starts at 2,000 people. Once you have followed 2,000 people, the limit may increase based on an undocumented algorithm that considers the ratio of friends to followers you have.

These limits are in place to prevent edge case users from straining the Twitter servers. Fortunately, these limits are reasonable for most normal Twitter interactions.

These limits have a history of changing as Twitter grows. For the most recent update limits, see `http://help.twitter.com/forums/10711/entries/15364`.

REST API Rate Limit

The REST API rate limit is based on IP address and Twitter account. If you authenticate a Twitter account with your API requests, that Twitter account will be subject to the rate limit. If you don't authenticate a Twitter account, the IP address the request is made from is subject to the rate limit.

Only GET requests are subject to the REST API rate limit. REST API methods that use HTTP POST do not affect your rate limit.

With every GET request you make, Twitter includes three HTTP response headers in the results that show details on your rate limit status. These headers are

- `X-RateLimit-Limit` - your maximum rate limit
- `X-RateLimit-Remaining` - your remaining API hits
- `X-RateLimit-Reset` - the time your rate limit resets in epoch time

You can also use the `account/rate_limit_status` method, profiled in Chapter 6, to retrieve your current rate limit status. Calling this method does not count against your rate limit.

As a Twitter application developer, you may be able to increase your API rate limit to 20,000 requests per hour by submitting your application for *white listing*. You can have a Twitter account or IP address white listed. The application for white listing can be found here: `http://twitter.com/help/request_whitelisting`. It may take up to a week before you receive an email response to your white listing request.

IP addresses that are white listed have their rate limit reduced before authenticated accounts from that address. That means if your application has numerous authenticating users, you can save those users' rate limit by having your IP address white listed.

Search API Rate Limit

The Search API has a rate limit independent of the REST API based entirely on the requesting IP address. Twitter does not document the maximum rate limit for the Search API and there is no white listing available for this API. However, if you include a unique User Agent string in your HTTP Request Header, Twitter increases the amount of Search API calls you can make. Listing 5-1 shows an example of how to specify the User Agent string using PHP and cURL.

Listing 5-1: Specify The User Agent to Increase Your Rate Limit

```
// The Twitter search method
$url = "http://search.twitter.com/search.json?lang=en&q=twitter";

// Get Twitter API results with cURL
$curlHandle = curl_init();
curl_setopt($curlHandle, CURLOPT_URL, "$url");
curl_setopt($curlHandle, CURLOPT_USERAGENT, "Twitter App Development For
            Dummies: Example User Agent");
curl_setopt($curlHandle, CURLOPT_RETURNTRANSFER, 1);
$apiResponse = curl_exec($curlHandle);
curl_close($curlHandle);
```

If you hit the Search API rate limit, you receive an HTTP response code of 420 and an included response header called `Retry-After`. `Retry-After` specifies the amount of seconds until you can access the Search API again.

Getting Blacklisted

If your application consistently ignores the API rate limits, your account or IP address may be blacklisted. Blacklisted accounts and IP address receive no response from the Twitter API.

If you believe you've been erroneously blacklisted, you can contact api@twitter.com to discuss your situation.

HTTP Response Status Codes and Errors

Anytime you make a request to the Twitter API, Twitter attempts to return an appropriate HTTP status code.

An HTTP status code is a number sent in the header information of a Web request. The Web browser doesn't display this number, but you can retrieve the status code programmatically when you work with the API.

In Listing 5-2, there is an example of how to read an HTTP status code using PHP and cURL.

Listing 5-2: Reading an HTTP Status Code With PHP and cURL

```
<?php

// The Twitter users/show method
$url = 'http://api.twitter.com/1/users/show/dustyreagan.xml ';

// Get API results using curl
$curlHandle = curl_init();
curl_setopt($curlHandle, CURLOPT_URL, "$url");
curl_setopt($curlHandle, CURLOPT_RETURNTRANSFER, 1);
$apiResponse = curl_exec($curlHandle);

// Get HTTP Status Code
$info = curl_getinfo($curlHandle);
$http_code = $info['http_code'];
echo "<h1>HTTP Status Code: $http_code</h1>";

// Close cURL connection
curl_close($curlHandle);

?>
```

Every status code has a meaning that informs you what happened when you made your last request. For example, a status code of 404 means that the file or resource you requested was not found on the server. Here is a complete list of possible status codes you could receive from Twitter, and their meanings:

- 200 OK: Everything was successful.
- 304 Not Modified: Nothing has changed since your last request. Used to save bandwidth and processing power, this request does not include message content. You have to rely on data gathered from your previous request.
- 400 Bad Request: There is an error in your request. This is common if you fail to provide a method with valid or required parameters. A 400 code can also mean you've exceeded your rate limit allowance. Twitter also returns an error message to help explain why your request is invalid.
- 401 Not Authorized: Your account credentials are incorrect or missing.
- 403 Forbidden: This error is returned if you hit an update limit. Update limits differ from rate limits; they refer to such actions as posting the maximum amount of tweets per day or following too many people
- 404 Not Found: The resource you requested can't be found on the server. This is common if a Twitter username can't be found or if you provide an incorrect API method path.
- 406 Not Acceptable: The Search API returns this status code if you request a format that is invalid or that it does not support.
- 420 Rate Limited: This code is returned if you hit your rate limit.
- 500 Internal Server Error: This usually indicates something is broken on Twitter's end. You can alert them by posting to the Twitter Developer's Google Group (`http://groups.google.com/group/twitter-development-talk`).
- 502 Bad Gateway: Twitter is down for maintenance.
- 503 Service Unavailable: Twitter is overloaded with traffic so your request temporarily failed. Try again.

When possible, Twitter provides an explanation for the error in the response body. Listing 5-3 shows the error message after trying to delete a direct message that has already been deleted. The accompanying HTTP status code with this error is 404.

Listing 5-3: Example Error Message in XML

```
<?xml version="1.0" encoding="UTF-8"?>
<hash>
  <request>/1/direct_messages/destroy/486489555.xml</request>
  <error>No direct message with that ID found.</error>
</hash>
```

Defining the Payload

The payload is what Twitter calls the results it sends back to you after an API call. That could mean XML, JSON, RSS or any data type.

You might also call this the *output,* or the *result set.*

These payloads are usually made of common sets of data called objects, which represent concepts in the Twitter universe like a "user," a "status," and so on. It is not guaranteed that all payloads will contain common objects, but Twitter does strive for consistency. Many methods return an array or list of common objects. For example, requesting the public timeline returns an array of `status` objects. Some methods return only a list of IDs or a simple true or false value.

Here are the two most common objects returned by the Twitter API: the `user` object and the `status` object. You will see these objects included in most Twitter API responses.

The `User` Object

The `user` object contains all the details about a Twitter user and includes their last tweet in an embedded `status` object. If the user account is protected, the last tweet is omitted from the `user` details.

Listing 5-4 shows my `user` object.

Listing 5-4: An Example `User` Object in XML

```
<user>
  <id>973261</id>
  <name>Dusty Reagan</name>
  <screen_name>DustyReagan</screen_name>
  <location>Austin, TX</location>
  <description>Started Jelly in Austin. Co-Founded Conjunctured. Made
              FriendOrFollow.com and FeaturedUsers.com. Writing Twitter App
              Development For Dummies.</description>
 <profile_image_url>http://a3.twimg.com/profile_images/500150827/2209569192_816b
              28049d_bigger_normal.jpg</profile_image_url>
  <url>http://dustyreagan.com</url>
  <protected>false</protected>
  <followers_count>2742</followers_count>
  <profile_background_color>8B542B</profile_background_color>
  <profile_text_color>333</profile_text_color>
  <profile_link_color>9D582E</profile_link_color>
  <profile_sidebar_fill_color>EADEAA</profile_sidebar_fill_color>
```

(continued)

Listing 5-4 *(continued)*

```
  <profile_sidebar_border_color>D9B17E</profile_sidebar_border_color>
  <friends_count>496</friends_count>
  <created_at>Mon Mar 12 01:39:06 +0000 2007</created_at>
  <favourites_count>31</favourites_count>
  <utc_offset>-21600</utc_offset>
  <time_zone>Central Time (US &amp; Canada)</time_zone>
  <profile_background_image_url>http://a1.twimg.com/profile_background_
            images/976552/bar.jpg</profile_background_image_url>
  <profile_background_tile>false</profile_background_tile>
  <statuses_count>3192</statuses_count>
  <notifications></notifications>
  <geo_enabled>false</geo_enabled>
  <verified>false</verified>
  <following></following>
  <status>
    <created_at>Tue Nov 10 00:38:21 +0000 2009</created_at>
    <id>5574474617</id>
    <text>@btruax Agreed. I like the freemium model. Free base, paid tiers. I
            think some startups are getting carried away &amp; shrinking their
            market.</text>
    <source>web</source>
    <truncated>false</truncated>
    <in_reply_to_status_id>5574372577</in_reply_to_status_id>
    <in_reply_to_user_id>21057898</in_reply_to_user_id>
    <favorited>false</favorited>
    <in_reply_to_screen_name>btruax</in_reply_to_screen_name>
    <geo/>
  </status>
</user>
```

The Status Object

The `status` object includes all the details about a particular tweet and has the complete `user` object of the author embedded in it.

Listing 5-5 shows the `status` object of the first tweet.

Listing 5-5: An Example `status` Object in XML

```
<?xml version="1.0" encoding="UTF-8"?>
<status>
  <created_at>Tue Mar 21 20:50:14 +0000 2006</created_at>
  <id>20</id>
  <text>just setting up my twttr</text>
  <source>web</source>
  <truncated>false</truncated>
  <in_reply_to_status_id>0</in_reply_to_status_id>
  <in_reply_to_user_id></in_reply_to_user_id>
```

```
  <favorited>false</favorited>
  <in_reply_to_screen_name></in_reply_to_screen_name>
  <user>
    <id>12</id>
    <name>Jack Dorsey</name>
    <screen_name>jack</screen_name>
    <location>NYC &amp; San Francisco</location>
    <description>Creator, Co-founder and Chairman of Twitter</description>
 <profile_image_url>http://a1.twimg.com/profile_images/54668082/Picture_2_
             normal.png</profile_image_url>
    <url></url>
    <protected>false</protected>
    <followers_count>1428625</followers_count>
    <profile_background_color>8B542B</profile_background_color>
    <profile_text_color>333333</profile_text_color>
    <profile_link_color>9D582E</profile_link_color>
    <profile_sidebar_fill_color>EADEAA</profile_sidebar_fill_color>
    <profile_sidebar_border_color>D9B17E</profile_sidebar_border_color>

    <friends_count>689</friends_count>
    <created_at>Tue Mar 21 20:50:14 +0000 2006</created_at>
    <favourites_count>682</favourites_count>
    <utc_offset>-28800</utc_offset>
    <time_zone>Pacific Time (US &amp; Canada)</time_zone>
 <profile_background_image_url>http://s.twimg.com/a/1257465343/images/themes/
             theme8/bg.gif</profile_background_image_url>
    <profile_background_tile>false</profile_background_tile>
    <statuses_count>5458</statuses_count>
    <notifications></notifications>
    <geo_enabled>false</geo_enabled>
    <verified>false</verified>
    <following></following>
  </user>
  <geo/>
</status>
```


Authentication

In order to see and do some things on Twitter's Web site, you need to be logged in, whereas you can see and do other things without logging in. For example, when you're not logged in, you can still view the public timeline, search, and view public profile pages. However, you can't follow people, view a timeline of the people you follow, or tweet.

The API works in exactly the same way. For this reason, some API methods require you to log in (authenticate), while other methods are publicly available without a login. There are two ways to authenticate with the Twitter API:

- Basic HTTP authentication
- OAuth

Basic HTTP authentication is the login method that Twitter was founded on. It is very simple for developers to grasp and easy to start working with. For this reason, I use basic HTTP authentication for the examples in this book. However, it has one major disadvantage. If you are doing a task using the API for another user, which happens quite frequently, you need to authenticate your application as that user. To do that using basic authentication, you have to ask the user for his or her Twitter username and password. This is a bad thing.

As a developer, handling users' passwords carries a great deal of liability and responsibility. You need to take care that you store the passwords in an encrypted format and that you use SSH to secure the HTTP connection when users submit their login credentials. Asking for users' passwords also creates a barrier to entry on your application. Before users can use your app, they must consider whether they trust your application enough to give you their usernames and passwords. This could be a deal breaker for some users, and it may cause you to lose traffic.

Fortunately, there is a solution to basic authentication: OAuth (`http://oauth.net`). OAuth is an open protocol that Twitter implemented in March 2009, with the promise to solve the downfalls of basic authentication. The wonderful thing about OAuth is that it doesn't require users to give Twitter application developers their passwords. Using OAuth, users give your application permission to interact with their Twitter account, Twitter gives you a token to authenticate with, and you never have to ask for or handle the users' passwords.

The typical user sign-in workflow for OAuth looks like Figure 5-1.

An application can request read or read and write access to your Twitter account. When you grant an application permission to your Twitter account, the application is then listed in your Twitter settings under "Connections" here: `http://twitter.com/account/connections`. From that page, you have the option to revoke access to applications you authorized in the past.

Once an application has a user's authorization to interface with his or her Twitter account, the app doesn't have to ask for it again.

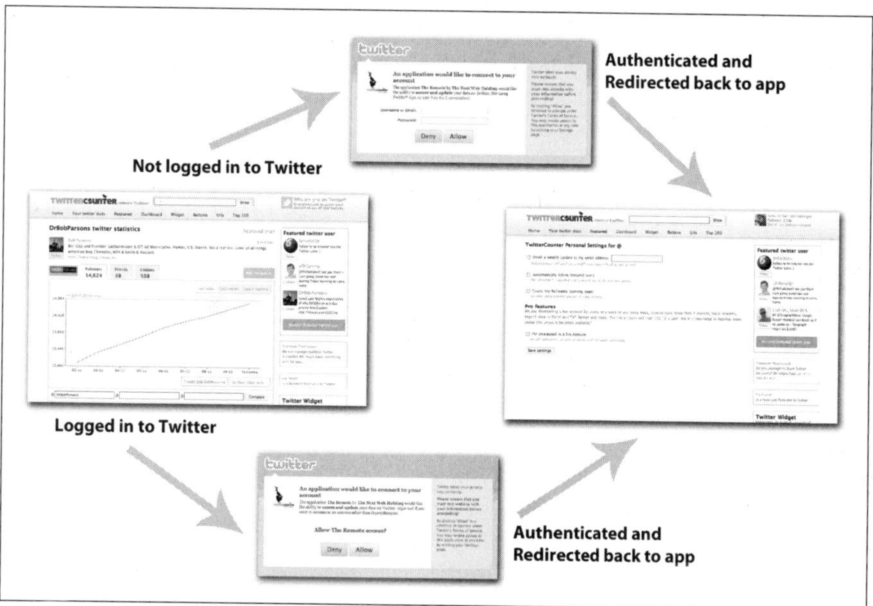

Figure 5-1: OAuth login workflow.

Twitter provides four methods for working with OAuth.

- oauth/authenticate
- oauth/authorize
- oauth/request_token
- oauth/access_token

Two of these methods are used as links for your users to login. Here are the two methods used as links:

- oauth/authenticate
- oauth/authorize

With the oauth/authenticate URL, if users are logged in to Twitter and have already approved your application, they will immediately be redirected back to your Web site. The oauth/authorize URL will always ask the user to reconfirm your application's permissions. If you're building a desktop application, you must use oauth/authorize.

From the developer's point of view, OAuth takes six steps.

1. Register your application with Twitter, if you have not already, to get a consumer token and secret for your application. (You only need to do this once.)
2. Pass your application's assigned consumer token and secret to the `oauth/request_token` method to get a request token from Twitter.
3. Present the user with a link to either `oauth/authenticate` or `oauth/authorize` and include the request token as a query string value named `oauth_token`.
4. When the user clicks on the `oauth/authenticate` or `oauth/authorize` URL, he or she is taken to Twitter.com to log in and approve your application. Once completed, the user is redirected back to your application with the original request token included in the URL query string labeled `oauth_token`.
5. Once the user is back on your application, pass the request token to the `oauth/access_token` method. That method returns the access token in the body of the response.
6. Use the access token to make your API calls to Twitter on behalf of the user. You can store this access token and use it to make future calls.

To implement this process, the first thing you must do is register your application with Twitter.

There is a link to the application registration page in your Twitter settings under the Connection tab. Alternatively, you can visit this URL: `http://twitter.com/apps`.

1. **Click the Register a new application link.**

   The registration page is shown in Figure 5-2.

   At the bottom of the registration form is a check box labeled Use Twitter for login.

2. **Check the box if you intend to log your users into your application by checking if they are logged in to Twitter.**

   If you're not sure, check the box.

3. **Complete the rest of the fields and click save.**

When you submit the registration form, Twitter assigns you

- A consumer key
- A consumer secret

These keys are unique to your application and are used as parameters in the `oauth/request_token` and `oauth/access_token` methods.

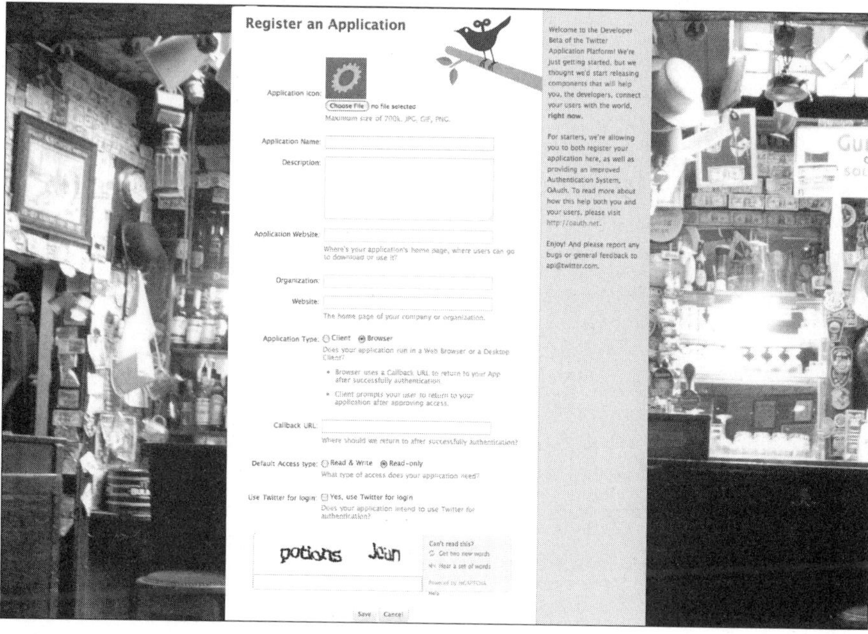

Figure 5-2: Twitter application OAuth registration form.

Another nice thing about registering your application with Twitter is that when you use OAuth to tweet from an authorized account, the tweet contains your application's name and a link to your application's Web site. Figure 5-3 shows a tweet from @Starbucks sent from the Twitter application CoTweet. You can see the link in small print below the tweet text.

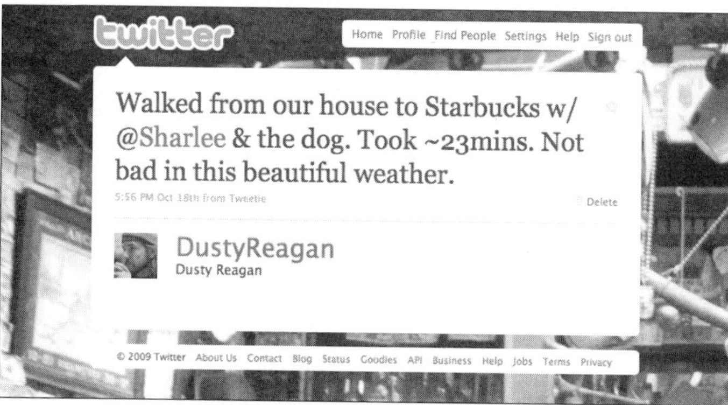

Figure 5-3: Tweeting using OAuth includes your application as the source of the tweet.

The tricky part in dealing with OAuth authentication is passing the required parameters to the OAuth methods correctly. OAuth specifications require very particular parameter encoding, and it's easy to make small mistakes in the encoding process that are very hard to identify and fix. If you get any part of the encoding incorrect, you receive a 401 "Failed to validate oauth signature and token" HTTP status error, which doesn't help identify the encoding problem.

OAuth parameter-encoding requirements are highly convoluted and will drive even the most patient developers batty. Due to this, I highly recommend that you not roll your own OAuth authentication methods and instead use an open source Twitter API and OAuth library. There are libraries in numerous languages available, and because they're open source, you have the ability to manipulate them and see their inner workings. Using a library will hide the technical implementation of OAuth from you, and all you have to worry about is the high-level workflow. There is a fairly comprehensive Twitter API library list maintained by Twitter employees on the Twitter wiki at `http://apiwiki.twitter.com/Libraries`.

An excellent PHP library with OAuth functionality is Twitter-async (`http://github.com/jmathai/twitter-async`), created by Jaisen Mathai (@jmathai). You can download an example Twitter-async OAuth implementation at `http://jaisenmathai.com/blog/2009/04/30/letting-your-users-sign-in-with-twitter-with-oauth`.

If you are persistent in rolling your own OAuth implementation, Chapter 6 profiles each of the Twitter OAuth methods and includes some PHP code examples to get you started.

Chapter 6

Logging In and Managing Your Account

In This Chapter

- Manage a user's account from the API
- Logging in with OAuth methods
- Working examples of the API in PHP

This chapter profiles methods for logging in and managing your account. This includes

- Account methods
- OAuth methods

You can use account management methods to do things like change your profile picture, update personal information, view your API rate limit, and so on. The details on the OAuth methods can help you roll your own OAuth login system.

Account Methods

Account methods are used to modify or view data pertaining to a particular Twitter profile. Profile data includes things such as your name, location, bio, Web page link, profile background, and profile colors. It also includes methods that verify the provided account credentials, check the profiles remaining rate limit, and end the users Twitter session.

Here are the Twitter account methods:

- `account/verify_credentials`
- `account/rate_limit_status`

- account/end_session
- account/update_delivery_device
- account/update_profile
- account/update_profile_colors
- account/update_profile_image
- account/update_profile_background_image

Verify a user's credentials

To verify a user's supplied Twitter credentials, authenticate and call the account/verify_credentials method.

This method presumes you are asking users for their Twitter credentials to carry out API calls on their behalf. This type of authentication is not necessary anymore, and Twitter recommends that you use OAuth to authenticate users. However, this method is provided for applications still using basic authentication.

This method requires a GET request and is not rate limited.

Output

This method has two output formats:

- XML
- JSON

A successful request and authentication returns an HTTP status code of 200 and the authenticating user's user details object. A failed attempt to authenticate returns a 401 not authorized HTTP status code and an error message.

Input

This method has no input parameters.

Example

Listing 6-1 shows you an example of how to test a user's Twitter login credentials.

Listing 6-1: Check a User's Twitter Username and Password

```
<?php

// Set username and password to test
$username = 'username';
$password = 'password';

// The Twitter account/verify_credentials method
$url = "https://api.twitter.com/1/account/verify_credentials.xml";

// GET Twitter API using cURL
$curlHandle = curl_init();
curl_setopt($curlHandle, CURLOPT_URL, "$url");
curl_setopt($curlHandle, CURLOPT_USERAGENT, "Twitter App Development For
            Dummies: Example");
curl_setopt($curlHandle, CURLOPT_RETURNTRANSFER, 1);
curl_setopt($curlHandle, CURLOPT_SSL_VERIFYPEER, false);
curl_setopt($curlHandle, CURLOPT_USERPWD, "$username:$password");
$apiResponse = curl_exec($curlHandle);

// Get HTTP Status Code
$info = curl_getinfo($curlHandle);
$http_code = $info['http_code'];
echo "<h1>HTTP Status Code: $http_code</h1>";

// Close cURL connection
curl_close($curlHandle);

if($http_code == 200)
   echo "<h1>Login Credentials Are Valid</h1>";
else if($http_code == 401)
   echo "<h1>Login Credentials Are NOT Valid</h1>";

?>
```

Check your rate limit

You should always be conscious about how much you are accessing the Twitter API. It's good Twitter developer etiquette to request the API as little as possible; going over your rate limit frequently is grounds to have your access to the API taken away. To check your rate limit, Twitter provides the `account/rate_limit_status` method.

If you provide the `account/rate_limit_status` method authentication credentials, it will return the authenticating user's rate limit status. If you do not provide authentication credentials, it will check the rate limit for the requesting IP address.

This method requires a GET request and is not rate limited.

Output

This method has two output formats:

- XML
- JSON

A successful request returns the remaining API requests allowed, the hourly limit, the time the limit will be reset, and the seconds remaining until a reset.

Input

This method has no input parameters.

Example

Listing 6-2 shows you an example of how to look up your rate limit.

Listing 6-2: Look Up Your Rate Limit Status

```
<?php

// Set username and password to test
$username = 'username';
$password = 'password';

// The Twitter account/verify_credentials method
$url = "https://api.twitter.com/1/account/rate_limit_status.xml";

// GET Twitter API results using cURL
$curlHandle = curl_init();
curl_setopt($curlHandle, CURLOPT_URL, "$url");
curl_setopt($curlHandle, CURLOPT_USERAGENT, "Twitter App Development For
              Dummies: Example");
curl_setopt($curlHandle, CURLOPT_RETURNTRANSFER, 1);
curl_setopt($curlHandle, CURLOPT_SSL_VERIFYPEER, false);
curl_setopt($curlHandle, CURLOPT_USERPWD, "$username:$password");
$apiResponse = curl_exec($curlHandle);

// Get HTTP Status Code
$info = curl_getinfo($curlHandle);
```

```
$http_code = $info['http_code'];
echo "<h1>HTTP Status Code: $http_code</h1>";

// Close cURL connection
curl_close($curlHandle);

$xml = new DOMDocument();
$xml->loadXML($apiResponse);

// Check for an error tag
$errors = $xml->getElementsByTagName("error");

// If found, print the error. Else, success!
if($errors->length > 0)
{
   $errorMessage = $errors->item(0)->nodeValue;
   echo "<h1>$errorMessage</h1>";
}
else
{
   $remainingHitsNode = $xml->getElementsByTagName("remaining-hits");
   $remainingHits = $remainingHitsNode->item(0)->nodeValue;
   echo $remainingHits;
}

?>
```

End a user's session

You can end an established persistent Basic HTTP Authentication user session by calling `account/end_session`.

This method requires a POST request and is not rate limited.

Output

This method has two output formats:

- XML
- JSON

Input

This method has no input parameters.

Example

Listing 6-3 shows you an example of how to log a user out.

Listing 6-3: End a Persistent Basic HTTP Auth Session

```
<?php

// Set username and password to test
$username = 'username';
$password = 'password';

// The Twitter account/verify_credentials method
$url = "https://api.twitter.com/1/account/end_session.xml";

// GET Twitter API results using cURL
$curlHandle = curl_init();
curl_setopt($curlHandle, CURLOPT_URL, "$url");
curl_setopt($curlHandle, CURLOPT_USERAGENT, "Twitter App Development For
              Dummies: Example");
curl_setopt($curlHandle, CURLOPT_POST, 1);
curl_setopt($curlHandle, CURLOPT_RETURNTRANSFER, 1);
curl_setopt($curlHandle, CURLOPT_SSL_VERIFYPEER, false);
curl_setopt($curlHandle, CURLOPT_USERPWD, "$username:$password");
$apiResponse = curl_exec($curlHandle);

// Get HTTP Status Code
$info = curl_getinfo($curlHandle);
$http_code = $info['http_code'];
echo "<h1>HTTP Status Code: $http_code</h1>";

// Close cURL connection
curl_close($curlHandle);

$xml = new DOMDocument();
$xml->loadXML($apiResponse);

// Check for an error tag
$errors = $xml->getElementsByTagName("error");

// If found, print the error. Else, success!
if($errors->length > 0)
{
   $errorMessage = $errors->item(0)->nodeValue;
   echo "<h1>$errorMessage</h1>";
}
else
{
   print_r($apiResponse);
}

?>
```

Updating a user's notification device

The `account/update_delivery_device` method is designed to allow you to update a user's notification device. This method was originally designed to allow you to switch between SMS, IM, and none as your delivery device. However, IM is currently unavailable, and there is no talk of it being re-enabled. Furthermore, trying to switch the device to SMS via this method currently does nothing. So really the only thing you can do with this method is turn off SMS notifications. There is no way to turn SMS back on with this method.

This method requires a POST request and is not rate limited.

Output

This method has two output formats:

- XML
- JSON

On a successful post, this method will return the updated user details object. A failed post receives an error message.

Input

This method requires one of the following parameters:

- `device` — Values include: sms or none.

  Example: `device=none`

Example

Listing 6-4 is an example of how to programmatically update your Twitter profile's device settings using PHP and cURL to post to the `account/update_delivery_device` method.

Listing 6-4: How to Programmatically Update Your Device Settings

```
<?php

// Set username and password
$username = 'username';
$password = 'password';

// The Twitter account/update_profile method
```

(continued)

Listing 6-4 *(continued)*

```
$apiUrl = "https://api.twitter.com/1/account/update_delivery_device.xml";

// POST to Twitter API using cURL
$curlHandle = curl_init();
curl_setopt($curlHandle, CURLOPT_URL, "$apiUrl");
curl_setopt($curlHandle, CURLOPT_USERAGENT, "Twitter App Development For
               Dummies: Example");
curl_setopt($curlHandle, CURLOPT_POST, 1);
curl_setopt($curlHandle, CURLOPT_RETURNTRANSFER, 1);
curl_setopt($curlHandle, CURLOPT_POSTFIELDS, "device=none");
curl_setopt($curlHandle, CURLOPT_SSL_VERIFYPEER, false);
curl_setopt($curlHandle, CURLOPT_USERPWD, "$username:$password");
$apiResponse = curl_exec($curlHandle);

// Print HTTP Status Code
$info = curl_getinfo($curlHandle);
$http_code = $info['http_code'];
echo "<h1>HTTP Status Code: $http_code</h1>";

// Close cURL connection
curl_close($curlHandle);

$xml = new DOMDocument();
$xml->loadXML($apiResponse);

// Check for an error tag
$errors = $xml->getElementsByTagName("error");

// If found, print the error. Else, success!
if($errors->length > 0)
{
   $errorMessage = $errors->item(0)->nodeValue;
   echo "<h1>$errorMessage</h1>";
}
else
{
   $nameNode = $xml->getElementsByTagName("name");
   $name = $nameNode->item(0)->nodeValue;
   echo "<p>Turned off notification for: $name</p>";
}

?>
```

Update a user's profile

To update a user's profile fields, including name, URL, location, and description, use the `account/update_profile` method.

This method requires a POST request and is not rate limited.

Output

This method has two output formats:

- XML
- JSON

On a successful post, this method will return the updated user details object. A failed post receives an error message.

Input

This method requires one of the following parameters:

- `name` — A string under 20 characters intended for the full name of the user.

  Example: `name=Dusty+Reagan`
- `url` — A string under 100 characters intended for the personal URL of the user. "http://" is added if not already included.

  Example: `url=http%3A%2F%2Fdustyreagan.com`
- `location` — A string under 30 characters intended for the geographical location of the user.

  Example: `location=Austin+Texas`
- `description` — A string under 160 characters intended to describe the user.

  Example: `description=They+think+he's+a+righteous+dude`

Example

Listing 6-5 is an example of how to programmatically update your Twitter profile using PHP and cURL to post to the `account/update_profile` method.

Listing 6-5: How to Programmatically Update Your Twitter Profile

```
<?php

// Set username and password
$username = 'username';
$password = 'password';

$name = urlencode("Dusty Reagan");
$url = "http://dustyreagan.com";
$location = urlencode("Austin, TX");
$description = urlencode("Writing Twitter App Development For Dummies.");

// The Twitter account/update_profile method
```

(continued)

Listing 6-5 *(continued)*

```
$apiUrl = "https://api.twitter.com/1/account/update_profile.xml";

// POST to Twitter API using cURL
$curlHandle = curl_init();
curl_setopt($curlHandle, CURLOPT_URL, "$apiUrl");
curl_setopt($curlHandle, CURLOPT_USERAGENT, "Twitter App Development For
              Dummies: Example");
curl_setopt($curlHandle, CURLOPT_POST, 1);
curl_setopt($curlHandle, CURLOPT_RETURNTRANSFER, 1);
curl_setopt($curlHandle, CURLOPT_POSTFIELDS,
   "name=$name&url=$url&location=$location&description=$description");
curl_setopt($curlHandle, CURLOPT_SSL_VERIFYPEER, false);
curl_setopt($curlHandle, CURLOPT_USERPWD, "$username:$password");
$apiResponse = curl_exec($curlHandle);

// Print HTTP Status Code
$info = curl_getinfo($curlHandle);
$http_code = $info['http_code'];
echo "<h1>HTTP Status Code: $http_code</h1>";

// Close cURL connection
curl_close($curlHandle);

$xml = new DOMDocument();
$xml->loadXML($apiResponse);

// Check for an error tag
$errors = $xml->getElementsByTagName("error");

// If found, print the error. Else, success!
if($errors->length > 0)
{
   $errorMessage = $errors->item(0)->nodeValue;
   echo "<h1>$errorMessage</h1>";
}
else
{
   $nameNode = $xml->getElementsByTagName("name");
   $name = $nameNode->item(0)->nodeValue;
   echo "<p>name: $name</p>";

   $urlNode = $xml->getElementsByTagName("url");
   $url = $urlNode->item(0)->nodeValue;
   echo "<p>url: $url</p>";

   $locationNode = $xml->getElementsByTagName("location");
   $location = $locationNode->item(0)->nodeValue;
   echo "<p>location: $location</p>";

   $descriptionNode = $xml->getElementsByTagName("description");
```

```
    $description = $descriptionNode->item(0)->nodeValue;

    echo "<p>description: $description</p>";
}

?>
```

Update a user's profile colors

To update a user's profile colors, including background color, text, links, and sidebar, use the `account/update_profile_colors` method.

This method requires a POST request and is not rate limited.

Output

This method has two output formats:

- XML
- JSON

On a successful post, this method will return the updated user details object. A failed post receives an error message.

Input

This method requires one of the following parameters:

- `profile_background_color` — Hexadecimal color code for the background, if no background image is present.

  Example: `profile_background_color=333`
- `profile_text_color` — Hexadecimal color code for text.

  Example: `profile_text_color=000000`
- `profile_link_color` — Hexadecimal color code for links.

  Example: `profile_link_color=00C2FC`
- `profile_sidebar_fill_color` — Hexadecimal color code for the background of the sidebar.

  Example: `profile_sidebar_fill_color=fff`
- `profile_sidebar_border_color` — Hexadecimal color code for the border around the sidebar.

  Example: `profile_sidebar_border_color=000`

Listing 6-6 is an example of how to programmatically update your Twitter profile colors using PHP and cURL to post to the `account/update_profile_colors` method.

Listing 6-6: How to Update Your Twitter Profile Colors

```
<?php

// Set username and password
$username = 'username';
$password = 'password';

$profile_background_color = "fff";
$profile_text_color = "333333";
$profile_link_color = "990000";
$profile_sidebar_fill_color = "003";
$profile_sidebar_border_color = "090";

// The Twitter account/update_profile_colors method
$apiUrl = "https://api.twitter.com/1/account/update_profile_colors.xml";

// POST to Twitter API using cURL
$curlHandle = curl_init();
curl_setopt($curlHandle, CURLOPT_URL, "$apiUrl");
curl_setopt($curlHandle, CURLOPT_USERAGENT, "Twitter App Development For
              Dummies: Example");
curl_setopt($curlHandle, CURLOPT_POST, 1);
curl_setopt($curlHandle, CURLOPT_RETURNTRANSFER, 1);
curl_setopt($curlHandle, CURLOPT_POSTFIELDS,
   "profile_background_color=$profile_background_color&" .
   "profile_text_color=$profile_text_color&" .
   "profile_link_color=$profile_link_color&" .
   "profile_sidebar_fill_color=$profile_sidebar_fill_color&" .
   "profile_sidebar_border_color=$profile_sidebar_border_color");
curl_setopt($curlHandle, CURLOPT_SSL_VERIFYPEER, false);
curl_setopt($curlHandle, CURLOPT_USERPWD, "$username:$password");
$apiResponse = curl_exec($curlHandle);

// Print HTTP Status Code
$info = curl_getinfo($curlHandle);
$http_code = $info['http_code'];
echo "<h1>HTTP Status Code: $http_code</h1>";

// Close cURL connection
curl_close($curlHandle);

$xml = new DOMDocument();
$xml->loadXML($apiResponse);

// Check for an error tag
```

```
$errors = $xml->getElementsByTagName("error");

// If found, print the error. Else, success!
if($errors->length > 0)
{
   $errorMessage = $errors->item(0)->nodeValue;
   echo "<h1>$errorMessage</h1>";
}
else
{
   echo "<h1>Updated your profile colors.</h1>";
}

?>
```

Update a user's profile picture

To update a user's profile picture use the `account/update_profile_image` method.

This method requires a POST request and is not rate limited.

Output

This method has two output formats:

- XML
- JSON

On a successful post, this method will return the updated user details object. A failed post receives an error message.

Input

This method requires one of the following parameters:

- `image` — A GIF, JPG, or PNG image less than 700 kilobytes. Widths greater than 500 pixels are scaled down.

  Example: `image=@mypic.gif;type=image/gif`

Listing 6-7 is an example of how to programmatically update your Twitter profile picture using PHP and cURL to post to the `account/update_profile` method.

Listing 6-7: How to Programmatically Update Your Twitter Picture

```
<?php

// Set username and password
$username = 'username';
$password = 'password';

$imageFilename = "mypic.jpg";

// The Twitter account/update_profile_image method
$apiUrl = "https://twitter.com/account/update_profile_image.xml";

// POST to Twitter API using cURL
$curlHandle = curl_init();
curl_setopt($curlHandle, CURLOPT_URL, "$apiUrl");
curl_setopt($curlHandle, CURLOPT_USERAGENT, "Twitter App Development For
                Dummies: Example");
curl_setopt($curlHandle, CURLOPT_POST, 1);
curl_setopt($curlHandle, CURLOPT_HTTPHEADER, array('Expect:'));
curl_setopt($curlHandle, CURLOPT_RETURNTRANSFER, 1);
curl_setopt($curlHandle, CURLOPT_SSL_VERIFYPEER, false);
curl_setopt($curlHandle, CURLOPT_USERPWD, "$username:$password");
curl_setopt($curlHandle, CURLOPT_POSTFIELDS,array('image' =>
                "@$imageFilename;type=image/jpg"));

$apiResponse = curl_exec($curlHandle);

// Print HTTP Status Code
$info = curl_getinfo($curlHandle);
$http_code = $info['http_code'];
echo "<h1>HTTP Status Code: $http_code</h1>";

// Close cURL connection
curl_close($curlHandle);

$xml = new DOMDocument();
$xml->loadXML($apiResponse);

// Check for an error tag
$errors = $xml->getElementsByTagName("error");

// If found, print the error. Else, success!
if($errors->length > 0)
{
   $errorMessage = $errors->item(0)->nodeValue;
   echo "<h1>$errorMessage</h1>";
}
else
{
   $picNode = $xml->getElementsByTagName("profile_image_url");
   $profile_image_url = $picNode->item(0)->nodeValue;
```

```
    echo "<h1>Updated your picture to:</h1>";
    echo "<img src=\"$profile_image_url\" />";
}

?>
```

Update a user's background image

To update a user's profile background image, use the `account/update_profile_background_image` method.

This method requires a POST request and is not rate limited.

Output

This method has two output formats:

- XML
- JSON

On a successful post, this method will return the updated user details object. A failed post receives an error message.

Input

This method requires one of the following parameters:

- `image` — A GIF, JPG, or PNG image less than 800 kilobytes. Widths greater than 2048 pixels are scaled down.

  Example: `image=@mypic.gif;type=image/gif`
- `tile` — Tile the background image by setting a value of true.

  Example: `tile=true`

Listing 6-8 is an example of how to programmatically update your Twitter profile background image using PHP and cURL to post to the `account/update_profile_background_image` method.

Listing 6-8: How to Programmatically Update Your Twitter Background

```
<?php

// Set username and password
$username = 'username';
```

(continued)

Listing 6-8 *(continued)*

```
$password = 'password';

$imageFilename = "TwitterBackground.gif";

// The Twitter account/update_profile_background_image method
$apiUrl = "https://twitter.com/account/update_profile_background_image.xml";

// POST to Twitter API using cURL
$curlHandle = curl_init();
curl_setopt($curlHandle, CURLOPT_URL, "$apiUrl");
curl_setopt($curlHandle, CURLOPT_USERAGENT, "Twitter App Development For
              Dummies: Example");
curl_setopt($curlHandle, CURLOPT_POST, 1);
curl_setopt($curlHandle, CURLOPT_HTTPHEADER, array('Expect:'));
curl_setopt($curlHandle, CURLOPT_RETURNTRANSFER, 1);
curl_setopt($curlHandle, CURLOPT_SSL_VERIFYPEER, false);
curl_setopt($curlHandle, CURLOPT_USERPWD, "$username:$password");
curl_setopt($curlHandle, CURLOPT_CONNECTTIMEOUT, 4);
curl_setopt($curlHandle, CURLOPT_POSTFIELDS,array('image' =>
              "@$imageFilename;type=image/gif"));

$apiResponse = curl_exec($curlHandle);

// Print HTTP Status Code
$info = curl_getinfo($curlHandle);
$http_code = $info['http_code'];
echo "<h1>HTTP Status Code: $http_code</h1>";

// Close cURL connection
curl_close($curlHandle);

$xml = new DOMDocument();
$xml->loadXML($apiResponse);

// Check for an error tag
$errors = $xml->getElementsByTagName("error");

// If found, print the error. Else, success!
if($errors->length > 0)
{
   $errorMessage = $errors->item(0)->nodeValue;
   echo "<h1>$errorMessage</h1>";
}
else
{
   $backgroundNode = $xml->getElementsByTagName("profile_background_image_url");
   $profile_background_image_url = $backgroundNode->item(0)->nodeValue;

   $backgroundTileNode = $xml->getElementsByTagName("profile_background_tile");
   $profile_background_tile = $backgroundTileNode->item(0)->nodeValue;

   $tileBackgroundCSS = "repeat";
```

```
    if($profile_background_tile == "false")
       $tileBackgroundCSS = "no-repeat";

    echo "<body style=\"
       background-image:url('$profile_background_image_url');
       background-repeat:$tileBackgroundCSS;
    \">";
    echo "<h1>Updated your background!</h1>";
    echo "</body>";
}

?>
```

OAuth Methods

Twitter's API OAuth methods are used to authenticate a user using the open OAuth protocol (`http://oauth.net`). In Chapter 5, I cover the OAuth workflow. Here, I cover each of the methods used in that workflow, and include examples of how these methods are used in PHP. There are four OAuth methods:

- `oauth/authenticate`
- `oauth/authorize`
- `oauth/request_token`
- `oauth/access_token`

You can use an open source Twitter API and OAuth library to save yourself a lot of time. You can find a list of Twitter API libraries at `http://apiwiki.twitter.com/Libraries`.

Log a user in with OAuth

To log a user in with OAuth, you must use either one of the following:

- `oauth/authenticate`
- `oauth/authorize`

However, these are not API methods like the rest of the Twitter API. These are actual links that direct users back to Twitter.com so they can log in and approve or disapprove your application.

With the authenticate URL, if users are logged in to Twitter and have already approved your application, they will immediately be redirected. The authorize URL will always ask users to reconfirm your application's permissions. If you're building a desktop application, you must use `oauth/authorize`.

Both links require that you pass a request token in the URL query string as a parameter named `oauth_token`. You can get a request token using the `oauth/request_token` method.

After users log in and authenticate your application from Twitter.com, Twitter redirects them back to your application. At this point, you can trade your request token in for an access token using the `oauth/access_token` method.

Get an OAuth request token

The `oauth/request_token` method is used to create the `oauth_token` parameter that you pass to the OAuth authenticate URL: `http://twitter.com/oauth/authenticate`.

This method requires a GET request and is not rate limited.

Output

The `request_token` method returns an `oauth_token` parameter and an `oauth_token_secret` parameter in the response body. Listing 6-9 shows an example of the results.

Listing 6-9: An Example oauth/request_token Response Body

```
oauth_token=Y2e1altZ2krvwtgksGbzy4BnZhjrVhqGOPsqSfTVkk&oauth_token_secret=Tv0Uwv
                H7UPTy2fLM4P8zSLsqd6i3RaYFuCr6aVzpng
```

You must parse the string to get the `oauth_token` parameter. You use that parameter to create the authentication login URL seen in Listing 6-10.

Listing 6-10: An Example Authentication Login URL

```
http://twitter.com/oauth/authenticate?oauth_token=
                Y2e1altZ2krvwtgksGbzy4BnZhjrVhqGOPsqSfTVkk
```

A failed request is usually due to malformed input parameters, and it will return a 401 "Failed to validate oauth signature and token" error.

Input

These input parameters are all required and must be passed in the authorization header. Note that this is not the usual GET and POST HTTP parameter passing. See the code example in Listing 6-12 on how to pass parameters in the authorization header using cURL.

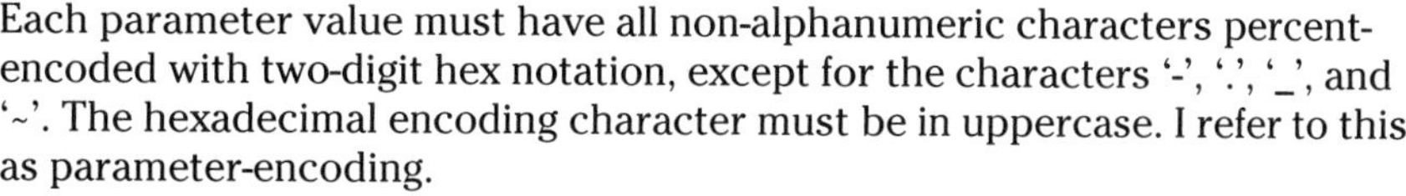

Each parameter value must have all non-alphanumeric characters percent-encoded with two-digit hex notation, except for the characters '-', '.', '_', and '~'. The hexadecimal encoding character must be in uppercase. I refer to this as parameter-encoding.

In practical terms, this means you must use PHP's `rawurlencode` function on the parameter value, except for the '~' character and spaces.

- `oauth_nonce` — A random number used to prevent replay attacks.

  Example: `oauth_nonce="d9a1704f6dd2bfe2dc2e201dfe3274dd"`
- `oauth_consumer_key` — The consumer key assigned to your application by Twitter. (It can be found here: `http://twitter.com/oauth`.)

  Example: `oauth_consumer_key="W2uDOozuH1286mV7k10qPg"`
- `oauth_version` — The version of OAuth you're using.

  Example: `oauth_version="1.0a"`
- `oauth_token` — This parameter is left empty for this method request.

  Example: `oauth_token=""`
- `oauth_timestamp` — The current Unix timestamp.

  Example: `oauth_timestamp="1256877296"`
- `oauth_signature_method` — The cryptography method used on the parameters. Twitter only accepts HMAC-SHA1.

  Example: `oauth_signature_method ="HMAC-SHA1"`
- `oauth_signature` — You must create this string value by:

  1. Concatenating the HTTP request method (GET), the full URL of the method you're requesting (`http://twitter.com/oauth/request_token`), and all the other parameters in alphabetical order, and all these parameters must be separated by the '&' character and be parameter-encoded. Listing 6-11 shows an example of this string.
  2. Next, you must encrypt the string using HMAC-SHA1 encryption.
  3. Finally, you must parameter-encode the encrypted string.

  Example: `oauth_signature="bQleSDqD4GQkJkuBIm%2B099oDyys%3D"`

Listing 6-11: An Example of the Concatenated oauth_signature String Before It's Encrypted and Finally Parameter Encoded

```
GET&http%3A%2F%2Ftwitter.com%2Foauth%2Frequest_token&oauth_consumer_key%3
            DF6uCOoyuH1414mV7k00qtg%26oauth_nonce%3Dc4a56f5c142e4ff3024
            0084923c36446%26oauth_signature_method%3DHMAC-SHA1%26oauth_
            timestamp%3D1257853543%26oauth_token%3D%26oauth_version%3D1.0
```

Example

In Listing 6-12 is an example of how you can generate a request token to create a Twitter authorization link. The parameter-encoding can get pretty confusing. Use the code comments to help you understand what's going on.

Listing 6-12: Generating a Request Token

```
<?php
// This is how to encode OAuth parameters
function encode_rfc3986($string)
{
   return str_replace('+', ' ', str_replace('%7E', '~',
             rawurlencode(($string))));
}

// These values are given to you by Twitter
// http://twitter.com/oauth
$consumerSecret = "YOUR_CONSUMER_SECRET";
$oauth_consumer_key = "YOUR_CONSUMER_KEY";

// The Twitter oauth/request_token method
$url = "http://twitter.com/oauth/request_token";

// OAuth paramaters
$oauth_nonce = md5(uniqid(rand(), true));
$oauth_version = "1.0a";
$oauth_token = "";
$oauth_timestamp = time();
$oauth_signature_method = "HMAC-SHA1";

// Create $oauth_signature
// First concatenate all parameters except oauth_signature
$parametersSoFar = "oauth_consumer_key=$oauth_consumer_key&" .
"oauth_nonce=$oauth_nonce&" .
"oauth_signature_method=$oauth_signature_method&" .
"oauth_timestamp=$oauth_timestamp&" .
"oauth_token=$oauth_token&" .
"oauth_version=$oauth_version";

// Next encode them to OAuth spec
$encodedParams = encode_rfc3986($parametersSoFar);

// Next create your signature base string
$signatureBaseString = "GET&" . encode_rfc3986($url) . "&" .
             $encodedParams;

// Next create your key, hash your signature base string, and encode
             the new parameter
$key = "$consumerSecret&$oauth_token";
```

```
$oauth_signature = encode_rfc3986(base64_encode(hash_hmac('sha1',
            $signatureBaseString, $key, true)));

// Now create your Authorization Header with all of your parameters
$authorizationHeader = "Authorization: OAuth
            oauth_consumer_key=\"$oauth_consumer_key\",oauth_
            token=\"$oauth_token\",oauth_nonce=\"$oauth_nonce\",oauth_
            timestamp=\"$oauth_timestamp\",oauth_signature_
            method=\"$oauth_signature_method\",oauth_version=\"$oauth_
            version\",oauth_signature=\"$oauth_signature\"";

$_header[] = 'Expect:';
$_header[] = $authorizationHeader;

// GET Twitter API results using cURL
$curlHandle = curl_init();
curl_setopt($curlHandle, CURLOPT_URL, "$url");
curl_setopt($curlHandle, CURLOPT_RETURNTRANSFER, 1);
curl_setopt($curlHandle, CURLOPT_HTTPHEADER, $_header);
$apiResponse = curl_exec($curlHandle);

// Get HTTP Code
$info = curl_getinfo($curlHandle);
$http_code = $info['http_code'];

// Close cURL connection
curl_close($curlHandle);

// The tokens are returned in the body of the cURL response
// Dig them out here
list($oauth_token, $oauth_token_secret) = explode("&",
            $apiResponse);
$oauth_token = str_replace("oauth_token=", '', $oauth_token);
$oauth_token_secret = str_replace("oauth_token_secret=", '', $oauth_
            token_secret);

echo "<h1>HTTP Status Code: $http_code</h1>";

echo "<p>$apiResponse</p>";

// Deliver the authorization link
echo "<a href=\"http://twitter.com/oauth/authenticate?oauth_
            token=$oauth_token\">Authorize with Twitter</a>";
?>
```

Get an OAuth access token

The `oauth/access_token` method is used to create the `oauth_token` used to make API calls on behalf of the user. Note this method is very similar to the `oauth/request_token` method.

This method requires a GET request and is not rate limited.

Output

The access_token method returns an oauth_token, an oauth_token_secret parameter, the authorized user's Twitter ID and screen name. Listing 6-13 shows an example of the results.

Listing 6-13: An Example oauth/access_token Response Body

```
oauth_token=973261-wpmln1iUOElP982jwBAylJlkCIamagZiSmRRmRLTQ0&oauth_token_secret=
        mA6WrrvP92e27QXGmCUkPbD32SwAIhpMz1QiodZpEu8&user_id=973261&screen_
        name=DustyReagan
```

You must parse the string to get the oauth_token and oauth_token_secret.

A failed request is usually due to malformed input parameters and will return a 401 "Failed to validate oauth signature and token" error.

Input

These input parameters are all required and must be passed in the authorization header. Note that this is not the usual GET and POST HTTP parameter passing. See the code example in Listing 6-15 on how to pass parameters in the authorization header using cURL.

Each parameter value must have all non-alphanumeric characters percent-encoded with two-digit hex notation, except for the characters '-', '.', '_', and '~'. The hexadecimal encoding character must be in uppercase. I refer to this as parameter-encoding.

In practical terms, this means you must use PHP's rawurlencode function on the parameter value, except for the '~' character and spaces.

- oauth_nonce — A random number used to prevent replay attacks.

  Example: oauth_nonce="d9a1704f6dd2bfe2dc2e201dfe3274dd"

- oauth_consumer_key — The consumer key assigned to your application by Twitter. (It can be found here: http://twitter.com/oauth.)

  Example: oauth_consumer_key="W2uDOozuH1286mV7k10qPg"

- oauth_version — The version of OAuth you're using.

  Example: oauth_version="1.0a"

- oauth_token — This is the request token.

  Example: auth_token="mn2NKdCfnHAOShW2eDGt1m9rPOXJXR3E7zp3ZfddSk"

- oauth_timestamp — The current Unix timestamp.

  Example: oauth_timestamp="1256877296"

- oauth_signature_method — The cryptography method used on the parameters. Twitter only accepts HMAC-SHA1.

  Example: oauth_signature_method ="HMAC-SHA1"

- oauth_signature — You must create this string value by:

  1. Concatenating the HTTP request method (GET), the full URL of the method you're requesting (http://twitter.com/oauth/access_token), and all the other parameters in alphabetical order, and all these parameters must be separated by the '&' character and be parameter-encoded. Listing 6-14 shows an example of this string.
  2. Next, you must encrypt the string using HMAC-SHA1 encryption.
  3. Finally, you must parameter-encode the encrypted string.

  Example: oauth_signature="bQleSDqD4GQkJkuBIm%2B099oDyys%3D"

Listing 6-14: An Example of the Concatenated oauth_signature String Before It's Encrypted and Finally Parameter-Encoded

```
GET&http%3A%2F%2Ftwitter.com%2Foauth%2Faccess_token&oauth_consumer_key%3D
                F6uCOoyuH1414mV7k00qtg%26oauth_nonce%3D941862b6d24bfbc2e4f9
                181869dc5386%26oauth_signature_method%3DHMAC-SHA1%26oauth_
                timestamp%3D1257855285%26oauth_token%3DKWVYLK3xg8YW2PAAdOksTCMdK3K
                J187qnnIRhOu90%26oauth_version%3D1.0
```

Example

In Listing 6-15 is an example of how you can generate an access token to access the Twitter API. The parameter-encoding can get pretty confusing. Use the code comments to help you understand what's going on.

Listing 6-15: Generating an Access Token

```
<?php
// This is how to encode OAuth parameters
function encode_rfc3986($string)
{
   return str_replace('+', ' ', str_replace('%7E', '~',
            rawurlencode(($string))));
}

// These values are given to you by Twitter
// http://twitter.com/oauth
$consumerSecret = "YOUR_CONSUMER_SECRET";
```

(continued)

Listing 6-15 ***(continued)***

```
$oauth_consumer_key = "YOUR_CONSUMER_KEY";

// The Twitter oauth/access_token method
$url = "http://twitter.com/oauth/access_token";

// OAuth paramaters
$oauth_nonce = md5(uniqid(rand(), true));
$oauth_version = "1.0a";
$oauth_token = $_GET['oauth_token'];
$oauth_timestamp = time();
$oauth_signature_method = "HMAC-SHA1";

// Create $oauth_signature
// First concatenate all parameters except oauth_signature
$parametersSoFar = "oauth_consumer_key=$oauth_consumer_key&" .
"oauth_nonce=$oauth_nonce&" .
"oauth_signature_method=$oauth_signature_method&" .
"oauth_timestamp=$oauth_timestamp&" .
"oauth_token=$oauth_token&" .
"oauth_version=$oauth_version";

// Next encode them to OAuth spec
$encodedParams = encode_rfc3986($parametersSoFar);

// Next create your signature base string
$signatureBaseString = "GET&" . encode_rfc3986($url) . "&" .
            $encodedParams;

// Next create your key, hash your signature base string, and encode
            the new parameter
$key = "$consumerSecret&$oauth_token";
$oauth_signature = encode_rfc3986(base64_encode(hash_hmac('sha1',
            $signatureBaseString, $key, true)));

// Now create your Authorization Header with all of your parameters
$authorizationHeader = "Authorization: OAuth
            oauth_consumer_key=\"$oauth_consumer_key\",oauth_
            token=\"$oauth_token\",oauth_nonce=\"$oauth_
            nonce\",oauth_timestamp=\"$oauth_timestamp\",oauth_
            signature_method=\"$oauth_signature_method\",oauth_
            version=\"$oauth_version\",oauth_signature=\"$oauth_
            signature\"";

$_header[] = 'Expect:';
$_header[] = $authorizationHeader;

// GET Twitter API results using cURL
$curlHandle = curl_init();
curl_setopt($curlHandle, CURLOPT_URL, "$url");
```

```
curl_setopt($curlHandle, CURLOPT_RETURNTRANSFER, 1);
curl_setopt($curlHandle, CURLOPT_HTTPHEADER, $_header);
$apiResponse = curl_exec($curlHandle);

// Get HTTP Code
$info = curl_getinfo($curlHandle);
$http_code = $info['http_code'];

// Close cURL connection
curl_close($curlHandle);

// The tokens are returned in the body of the cURL response
// Dig them out here
list($oauth_token, $oauth_token_secret) = explode("&",
            $apiResponse);
$oauth_token = str_replace("oauth_token=", '', $oauth_token);
$oauth_token_secret = str_replace("oauth_token_secret=", '', $oauth_
             token_secret);

echo "<h1>HTTP Status Code: $http_code</h1>";
echo "<p>$apiResponse</p>";

// Token parameters
echo "<p>OAuth Token: parameter: $oauth_token</p>";
echo "<p>OAuth Token Secret: parameter: $oauth_token_secret</p>";
```

Chapter 7

Managing Users and Their Relationships

In This Chapter

- Working examples of the API in PHP
- Getting data on users and their friends
- Managing Twitter lists
- Following, unfollowing, blocking, and reporting spam

This chapter covers Twitter API methods that deal with users and their relationships with other Twitter users. It covers 17 methods that you can use to do things like:

- Follow a new user
- Get a list of users friends
- Create and manage a list of users
- Block a user
- Report a user as a spammer

User Methods

Every Twitter user has site usage data, such as their profile information, how many followers they have, their last status update, the date they created their account, their total amount of tweets, and et cetera. To get at that data you need to pull the user object for that Twitter user. You can get that data with API most effectively, using these three methods:

- `users/show`
- `statuses/friends`
- `statuses/followers`

Get the details of a user

You can get the complete details of any public user on Twitter by using the `users/show` method.

This method doesn't require authentication, but to get the details of a protected Twitter account, you must

- Authenticate your API call
- Have permission to view the protected account.

This method requires a GET request and is rate limited. The sidebar "Hard Knocks" explains the concern with rate limits.

Output

This method has two output formats:

- XML
- JSON

On a successful method call it returns the complete user object, which contains the last status update.

If an account doesn't exist or is disabled by Twitter, you will receive an error message and a HTTP status code of 404.

Input

This method requires only one of three parameters:

- `id`: The user's screen name or numerical user ID.
  Example: `/users/show/bob.xml`
- `user_id`: The numerical IDof the user.
  Example: `/users/show.xml?user_id=12345`
- `screen_name`: The screen name of the user.
  Example: `/users/show.xml?screen_name=101010`

Avoid using the `id` parameter and use `user_id`, over `screen_name` if possible. The sidebar "Hard Knocks" explains why.

Hard Knocks

I make mistakes so you don't have to! In this section are tips to avoid some common API pitfalls. I refer to these tips throughout this chapter.

- I don't use the `id` parameter in cases where it can take either a screen name or numeric user ID, because I can't be sure who it finds. It's possible for one user's screen name to be the same numbers as another user's numeric userID. For example, a user's screen name might be 101010. There might also be a numeric user ID 101010.
- Whenever possible, I use the `user_id` parameter over `screen_name`. A user can change their screen name at any time, but their account's `user_id` never changes.
- I store API results locally and try to call the Twitter API as little as possible, because I don't want to use up my hourly rate limit. Twitter limits access to their API with hourly "rate limits." Every IP address and Twitter account has a rate limit allowance. If you call a method that is rate limited, your rate limit is reduced by 1. To increase your rate limit allowance, request white listing at: `http://twitter.com/help/request_whitelisting`.

Example

You can try the `users/show` method easily by typing `http://api.twitter.com/1/users/show.xml?screen_name=dustyreagan` into your browser's URL address bar.

One example of how you can use the `users/show` method is by customizing your applications appearance to match the user's profile settings. For example, if you wanted to get the background color of a Twitter user for use on your application results page, you could call this method and parse the background color out of the XML results. In Listing 7-1, I use PHP to get a user's background color and their profile image and print it to a HTML page.

Listing 7-1: Get User Data with the Users/Show Method

```
<?php
// Set username and password
$username = 'username';
$password = 'password';

// The Twitter users/show method
$url = 'https://api.twitter.com/1/users/show/dustyreagan.xml ';

// GET API results using curl
$curlHandle = curl_init();
```

(continued)

Listing 7-1 *(continued)*

```
curl_setopt($curlHandle, CURLOPT_URL, "$url");
curl_setopt($curlHandle, CURLOPT_USERAGENT, "Twitter App Development For
             Dummies: Example");
curl_setopt($curlHandle, CURLOPT_RETURNTRANSFER, 1);
curl_setopt($curlHandle, CURLOPT_SSL_VERIFYPEER, false);
curl_setopt($curlHandle, CURLOPT_USERPWD, "$username:$password");
$apiResponse = curl_exec($curlHandle);

// Get HTTP Status Code
$info = curl_getinfo($curlHandle);
$http_code = $info['http_code'];
echo "<h1>HTTP Status Code: $http_code</h1>";

// Close cURL connection
curl_close($curlHandle);

// Get XML
$xml = new DOMDocument();
$xml->loadXML($apiResponse);

// Check for an error tag.
$errors = $xml->getElementsByTagName("error");

// If found, print the error. Else, success!
if($errors->length > 0)
{
   $errorMessage = $errors->item(0)->nodeValue;
   echo "<h1>$errorMessage</h1>";
}
else
{
   $elements = $xml->getElementsByTagName("profile_background_color");
   $profile_background_color = $elements->item(0)->nodeValue;

   // Parse XML for profile image
   $elements = $xml->getElementsByTagName("profile_image_url");
   $profile_image_url = $elements->item(0)->nodeValue;

   // Use profile data in HTML
   echo "
      <body style=\"background-color:#$profile_background_color\">
         <img src=\"$profile_image_url\" />
      </body>";
}
?>
```

Get user details of your friends and followers

You can get an array of user details objects for each of the user's followers and for the people a user is following by using:

- `statuses/friends`: Retrieves user details for members a user is following.
- `statuses/followers`: Retrieves user details for members following a user.

These methods don't require authentication, but to get the details of a protected Twitter account, you must

- Authenticate your API call
- Have permission to view the protected account.

Both of these methods require a GET request and are rate limited. The sidebar "Hard Knocks" explains the concern with rate limits.

Output

These methods have two output formats:

- XML
- JSON

On a successful method call they return:

- An array of user objects 100 users at time.
- If the optional cursor parameter is provided, `next_cursor` and `previous_cursor` nodes are also returned.

If the requested user account doesn't exist or is disabled by Twitter, you will receive an error message and a HTTP status code of 404.

Input

Both methods require only one of three parameters:

- `id`: The user's screen name or numerical user ID.
  Example: `/statuses/friends/bob.xml`
- `user_id`: The numerical id of the user.
  Example: `/statuses/friends.xml?user_id=12345`
- `screen_name`: The screen name of the user.
  Example: `/statuses/friends.xml?screen_name=101010`

Avoid using the id parameter and use user_id, over screen_name if possible. The sidebar "Hard Knocks" explains why.

There is one optional parameter:

- cursor: Use to retrieve additional sets of user data.
  Example: /statuses/friends/bob.xml?cursor=-1

Example

You can try the users/show method easily by typing http://api.twitter.com/1/ statuses/friends.xml?screen_name=dustyreagan into your browser's URL address bar.

To retrieve more than 100 user accounts, you must call the method multiple times. To advance through the user list, pass the parameter cursor=-1 to the method. It will then return two more values in addition to the user objects:

- next_cursor
- previous_cursor.

On your next method call, pass the cursor parameter with the value contained in next_cursor. The results from this call will give you 100 new users and a new next_cursor and previous_cursor that you can use on your next call. For an example of how to page through the list of a user's friends using the cursor parameter and print each user's profile picture, see Listing 7-2. You can page through a user's followers by changing the method call in Listing 7-2 from statuses/friends to statuses/followers.

Listing 7-2: Use the Cursor to Print the Profile Picture of People You Follow

```
<?php

function getFriendsPage($screen_name, $cursor)
{
   // Set username and password
   $username = 'username';
   $password = 'password';

   // The Twitter statuses/friends method
   $url =
"https://api.twitter.com/1/statuses/friends.xml?screen_name=$screen_
              name&cursor=$cursor";

   // GET API results using curl
   $curlHandle = curl_init();
   curl_setopt($curlHandle, CURLOPT_URL, "$url");
   curl_setopt($curlHandle, CURLOPT_USERAGENT, "Twitter App Development For
              Dummies: Example");
```

```
    curl_setopt($curlHandle, CURLOPT_RETURNTRANSFER, 1);
    curl_setopt($curlHandle, CURLOPT_SSL_VERIFYPEER, false);
    curl_setopt($curlHandle, CURLOPT_USERPWD, "$username:$password");
    $apiResponse = curl_exec($curlHandle);

    // Get HTTP Status Code
    $info = curl_getinfo($curlHandle);
    $http_code = $info['http_code'];
    echo "<h1>HTTP Status Code: $http_code</h1>";

    // Close cURL connection
    curl_close($curlHandle);

    return $apiResponse;
}

$cursor = -1;
do {
    // Get response from Twitter statuses/friends method
    $apiResponse = getFriendsPage('dustyreagan', $cursor);

    // Get XML
    $xml = new DOMDocument();
    $xml->loadXML($apiResponse);

    // Parse XML for profile image
    $elements = $xml->getElementsByTagName("profile_image_url");

    // Print user's profile picture
    foreach($elements as $node)
    {
        $profile_image_url = $node->nodeValue;
        echo "<img src=\"$profile_image_url\" width=\"48\" height=\"48\" />";
    }

    // Look for next_cursor
    $elements = $xml->getElementsByTagName("next_cursor");

    // Get next_cursor. Break if you can't find it.
    if(!empty($elements))
    {
        $cursor = $elements->item(0)->nodeValue;
        echo "<h1>cursor: $cursor</h1>";
    }
    else
    {
        echo "<h1>No cursor found</h1>";
        break;
    }
} while($cursor != 0);

?>
```

Social Graph Methods

Every Twitter user has a collection of followers and people whom they are following. You can get a detailed list of all of these accounts using these two methods from the previous section on user methods:

- `statuses/friends`
- `statuses/followers`

However, these methods can return only 100 users per page, and they return a lot of data, possibly more than you need. This may be too much overhead for processing a large social graph.

The most straightforward way to find who a user is following and is being followed by is to use the two social graph methods:

- `friends/ids`
- `followers/ids`

These methods only return the user IDs, and in batches of 5000 or more.

Get the user IDs of your friends and followers

To get a list of people a user is following, use the `friends/ids method`. To get a list of a user's followers, use the `followers/ids` method. Beyond this difference, these methods function exactly the same. These methods don't require authentication, but to get the details of a protected Twitter account, you must

- Authenticate your API call
- Have permission to view the protected account.

Both of these methods require a GET request and are rate limited. The sidebar "Hard Knocks" explains the concern with rate limits.

Output

These methods have two output formats:

- XML
- JSON

On a successful method call they return:

- A complete list of all the requested userIDs.
- If the optional cursor parameter is provided, `next_cursor` and `previous_cursor` nodes are also returned.

If the requested user account doesn't exist or is disabled by Twitter, you will receive an error message and a HTTP status code of 404.

Input

Both methods require only one of three parameters:

- `id`: The user's screen name or numerical user ID.
  Example: `/friends/ids/bob.xml`
- `user_id`: The numerical ID of the user.
  Example: `/friends/ids.xml?user_id=12345`
- `screen_name`: The screen name of the user.
  Example: `/friends/ids.xml?screen_name=101010`

Avoid using the `id` parameter and use `user_id`, over `screen_name` if possible. The sidebar "Hard Knocks" explains why.

There is one optional parameter:

- `cursor`: Use to page through results 5000 IDs per call.
  Example: `/friends/ids/bob.xml?cursor=-1`

These methods return the entire following or follower list of user IDs. If the list is greater than a couple thousand users, your request may timeout. Use the cursor parameter to page through the ids at 5000 IDs per call to avoid timeouts.

To advance through the ID list, pass the parameter `cursor=-1` to the method. It will then return two more values in addition to the user objects:

- `next_cursor`
- `previous_cursor`

On your next method call, pass the cursor parameter with the value contained in `next_cursor`. The results from this call will give you 100 new users and a new `next_cursor` and `previous_cursor` that you can use on your next call. For an example of how to use the cursor parameter on the similar method `statuses/friends`, see Listing 7-2.

Example

You can try the users/show method by typing `http://api.twitter.com/1/friends/ids.xml?screen_name=dustyreagan` into your browser's URL address bar.

Both the `friends/ids` and `followers/ids` methods are to be used in conjunction with a local cache of detailed user data. For example, if you keep a database of user details, you can use the `friends/ids` or `followers/ids` methods to get an update of a user's social graph, and then look up the details for those users in your database based on the user ID.

In Listing 7-3, I show you how to use the `friends/ids` and `followers/ids` methods to create a list of people you follow who also follow you back.

Listing 7-3: Get the User IDs of Mutual Followers

```
<?php

function getApiResponse($method, $screen_name)
{
   // Set username and password
   $username = 'username';
   $password = 'password';

   // The Twitter statuses/friends method
   $url = "https://api.twitter.com/1/$method/ids.xml?screen_name=$screen_name";

   // Get API results using curl
   $curlHandle = curl_init();
   curl_setopt($curlHandle, CURLOPT_URL, "$url");
   curl_setopt($curlHandle, CURLOPT_USERAGENT, "Twitter App Development For
              Dummies: Example");
   curl_setopt($curlHandle, CURLOPT_RETURNTRANSFER, 1);
   curl_setopt($curlHandle, CURLOPT_SSL_VERIFYPEER, false);
   curl_setopt($curlHandle, CURLOPT_USERPWD, "$username:$password");
   $apiResponse = curl_exec($curlHandle);

   // Get HTTP Status Code
   $info = curl_getinfo($curlHandle);
   $http_code = $info['http_code'];
   echo "<h1>HTTP Status Code: $http_code</h1>";

   // Close cURL connection
   curl_close($curlHandle);

   return $apiResponse;
}
```

```
// Get array of IDs from API response
function getIdArray($apiResponse)
{
   // Get XML
   $xml = new DOMDocument();
   $xml->loadXML($apiResponse);

   $domelements = $xml->getElementsByTagName("id");

   $ids = array();
   foreach($domelements as $node)
      array_push($ids, $node->nodeValue);

   return $ids;
}

$screen_name = 'dustyreagan';

$apiResponseFriends = getApiResponse('friends', $screen_name);
$apiResponseFollowers = getApiResponse('followers', $screen_name);

$friendsIds = getIdArray($apiResponseFriends);
$followersIds = getIdArray($apiResponseFollowers);

// Get the IDs that are in both your following and followers list.
$mutualFollows = array_intersect($friendsIds, $followersIds);

echo "<h1>You have: " . count($mutualFollows) . " mutual followers.</h1>";

?>
```

List Methods

Lists in Twitter allow you to group individuals however you wish to create a custom Twitter stream with the people in the list. You could create a list of close friends, family, entrepreneurs, or Twitter developers.

The list methods behave differently than the other REST API methods. For instance, a list method may do one thing when you issue an HTTP POST request, and something else when you give the same method a GET request.

When you see a colon in a method path, that signifies a required variable. For example, if I call `:user/lists` for my Twitter account @dustyreagan, the method would be written as `dustyreagan/lists`.

- POST `:user/lists`
- POST `:user/lists/:id`
- GET `:user/lists`
- GET `:user/lists/:id`
- DELETE `:user/lists/:id`
- GET `:user/lists/:list_id/statuses`
- GET `:user/lists/memberships`
- GET `:user/lists/subscriptions`

Create a new list

To create a new list for the authenticated user, you can POST to the `:user/lists` method.

This method is not rate limited, but each user may only have up to 20 lists.

Output

This method has two output formats:

- XML
- JSON

A successful POST returns a `list` object that includes the detailed `user` object for the authenticated user. A failed POST returns an error message explaining why the list creation failed.

Input

The `:user/lists` method requires two parameters:

- `user`: The screen name of the user you're creating a list for. This variable is passed in the method path.
  Example: `dustyreagan/lists`
- `name`: The desired name of the list, passed as a POST field.
  Example: `name=austin`

These parameters are optional and passed as a POST field:

- mode: Pass the values private or public to set the mode of the list. If no mode parameter is passed, the list is set to public as default.
  Example: mode=private
- description: A description of your list.
  Example: description=Twitter+developers+in+Austin

Example

Listing 7-4 illustrates how to create a list with the :users/list method.

Listing 7-4: Creating a List

```
<?php

// Set username and password
$username = 'username';
$password = 'password';

// The Twitter create list method
$url = "http://api.twitter.com/1/$username/lists.xml";

$name = urlencode("Twitter Developers");
$description = urlencode("My favorite Twitter developers");

// Get API results using curl
$curlHandle = curl_init();
curl_setopt($curlHandle, CURLOPT_URL, "$url");
curl_setopt($curlHandle, CURLOPT_USERAGENT, "Twitter App Development For
              Dummies: Example");
curl_setopt($curlHandle, CURLOPT_POST, 1);
curl_setopt($curlHandle, CURLOPT_RETURNTRANSFER, 1);
curl_setopt($curlHandle, CURLOPT_SSL_VERIFYPEER, false);
curl_setopt($curlHandle, CURLOPT_POSTFIELDS, "name=$name&description=$descript
              ion");
curl_setopt($curlHandle, CURLOPT_USERPWD, "$username:$password");
$apiResponse = curl_exec($curlHandle);

// Get HTTP Status Code
$info = curl_getinfo($curlHandle);
$http_code = $info['http_code'];
echo "<h1>HTTP Status Code: $http_code</h1>";

// Close cURL connection
curl_close($curlHandle);

// Get XML
$xml = new DOMDocument();
```

(continued)

Listing 7-4 ***(continued)***

```
$xml->loadXML($apiResponse);

// Check for an error tag.
$errors = $xml->getElementsByTagName("error");

// If found, print the error and break. Else, keep going!
if($errors->length > 0)
{
   $errorMessage = $errors->item(0)->nodeValue;
   echo "<h1>$errorMessage</h1>";
   break;
}
else
{
   // Get new list URL
   $uriNode = $xml->getElementsByTagName("uri");
   $uri = $uriNode->item(0)->nodeValue;

   echo "<a href=\"http://twitter.com/$uri\">$uri</a>";
}

?>
```

Update an existing list

To update the authenticated user's existing list, use the `:user/lists/:id` method.

This method is not rate limited, and you can perform an HTTP POST or PUT request.

Output

This method has two output formats:

- XML
- JSON

A successful POST or PUT returns a `list` object that includes the detailed `user` object for the list's owner. A failed POST or PUT returns an error message explaining why the list creation failed.

Input

The :user/lists/:id POST method requires two parameters:

- user: The screen name of the user whose list you're updating. This variable is passed in the method path.
  Example: dustyreagan/lists
- id: The list's numeric ID or the list's slug, passed in the method path.
  Example: dustyreagan/lists/5065754.xml
  Example: dustyreagan/lists/twitter-developers.xml

To update the list, you can provide the following optional parameters in the POST or PUT fields.

- name: The desired name of the list.
  Example: name=austin
- mode: Pass the values private or public to set the access value of the list. If no mode parameter is passed, the list is set to public as default.
  Example: mode=private
- description: A description of your list.
  Example: description=Twitter+developers+in+Austin

Example

Listing 7-5 illustrates how to update a list with the :users/list/:id method.

Listing 7-5: Updating a List

```
<?php

// Set username and password
$username = 'username';
$password = 'password';

$listId = 5065754;

// The Twitter lists update method
$url = "http://api.twitter.com/1/$username/lists/$listId.xml";

$name = urlencode("Updated: Twitter Developers");
$description = urlencode("Updated: My favorite Twitter developers");

// Get API results using curl
$curlHandle = curl_init();
curl_setopt($curlHandle, CURLOPT_URL, "$url");
```

(continued)

Listing 7-5 *(continued)*

```
curl_setopt($curlHandle, CURLOPT_USERAGENT, "Twitter App Development For
               Dummies: Example");
curl_setopt($curlHandle, CURLOPT_POST, 1);
curl_setopt($curlHandle, CURLOPT_RETURNTRANSFER, 1);
curl_setopt($curlHandle, CURLOPT_SSL_VERIFYPEER, false);
curl_setopt($curlHandle, CURLOPT_POSTFIELDS, "name=$name&description=$descript
               ion");
curl_setopt($curlHandle, CURLOPT_USERPWD, "$username:$password");
$apiResponse = curl_exec($curlHandle);

// Get HTTP Status Code
$info = curl_getinfo($curlHandle);
$http_code = $info['http_code'];
echo "<h1>HTTP Status Code: $http_code</h1>";

// Close cURL connection
curl_close($curlHandle);

// Get XML
$xml = new DOMDocument();
$xml->loadXML($apiResponse);

// Check for an error tag.
$errors = $xml->getElementsByTagName("error");

// If found, print the error and break. Else, keep going!
if($errors->length > 0)
{
   $errorMessage = $errors->item(0)->nodeValue;
   echo "<h1>$errorMessage</h1>";
   break;
}
else
{
   // Get new list URL
   $uriNode = $xml->getElementsByTagName("uri");
   $uri = $uriNode->item(0)->nodeValue;

   echo "<a href=\"http://twitter.com/$uri\">$uri</a>";
}

?>
```

Get a user's lists

You can get a list of a user's Twitter lists by issuing a GET request to the `:user/lists` method.

This method is rate limited and you must be authenticated.

Output

This method has two output formats:

- XML
- JSON

A successful GET request returns an array of `list` objects that includes the detailed `user` object for the list's creator. If the user you are requesting is the authenticated user, the method results include their private lists. Otherwise, only that user's public lists are returned.

A failed GET request returns an error message explaining why the request failed.

Input

The `:user/lists` method requires one parameter:

- `user`: The screen name of the user you're pulling list data for. This variable is passed in the method path.
  Example: `dustyreagan/lists.xml`

Listing 7-6 illustrates how to get a list of a user's lists using the :user/lists method.

Listing 7-6: Get a User's List of Lists

```
<?php

// Set username and password
$username = 'username';
$password = 'password';

$requstedUser = 'dustyreagan';

// The Twitter GET lists method
$url = "http://api.twitter.com/1/$requstedUser/lists.xml";

// Get API results using curl
$curlHandle = curl_init();
curl_setopt($curlHandle, CURLOPT_URL, "$url");
curl_setopt($curlHandle, CURLOPT_USERAGENT, "Twitter App Development For
            Dummies: Example");
curl_setopt($curlHandle, CURLOPT_RETURNTRANSFER, 1);
curl_setopt($curlHandle, CURLOPT_SSL_VERIFYPEER, false);
curl_setopt($curlHandle, CURLOPT_USERPWD, "$username:$password");
$apiResponse = curl_exec($curlHandle);

// Get HTTP Status Code
```

(continued)

Listing 7-6 *(continued)*

```
$info = curl_getinfo($curlHandle);
$http_code = $info['http_code'];
echo "<h1>HTTP Status Code: $http_code</h1>";

// Close cURL connection
curl_close($curlHandle);

// Get XML
$xml = new DOMDocument();
$xml->loadXML($apiResponse);

// Check for an error tag.
$errors = $xml->getElementsByTagName("error");

// If found, print the error and break. Else, keep going!
if($errors->length > 0)
{
   $errorMessage = $errors->item(0)->nodeValue;
   echo "<h1>$errorMessage</h1>";
   break;
}
else
{
   $lists = $xml->getElementsByTagName("list");

   foreach($lists as $list)
   {
      $nameNode = $list->getElementsByTagName("name");
      $name = $nameNode->item(0)->nodeValue;

      $uriNode = $list->getElementsByTagName("uri");
      $uri = $uriNode->item(0)->nodeValue;

      echo "<a href=\"http://twitter.com/$uri\">$name</a><br />";
   }
}

?>
```

Get details on a specific list

To get the details on a specific user list, issue a GET request on the `:user/lists/:id` method.

This method is rate limited and you must be authenticated.

Output

This method has two output formats:

- XML
- JSON

A successful GET request returns the detailed `list` object that includes the detailed `user` object for the lists creator. To view the details of a private list, you must be authenticated as that list's owner.

A failed request returns an error message explaining why the request failed.

Input

The `:user/lists/:id` GET method requires two parameters:

- `user`: The screen name of the user whose list you're retrieving details for. This variable is passed in the method path.
  Example: `dustyreagan/lists`
- `id`: The list's numeric ID or the list's slug, passed in the method path.
  Example: `dustyreagan/lists/5065754.xml`
  Example: `dustyreagan/lists/twitter-developers.xml`

Listing 7-7 illustrates how to get a list's details by issuing a GET request to the `:user/lists/:id` method.

Listing 7-7: Get List Details

```
<?php

// Set username and password
$username = 'username';
$password = 'password';

$listId = 'twitter-developers';

// The Twitter lists update method
$url = "http://api.twitter.com/1/$username/lists/$listId.xml";

// Get API results using curl
$curlHandle = curl_init();
curl_setopt($curlHandle, CURLOPT_URL, "$url");
curl_setopt($curlHandle, CURLOPT_USERAGENT, "Twitter App Development For
            Dummies: Example");
curl_setopt($curlHandle, CURLOPT_RETURNTRANSFER, 1);
curl_setopt($curlHandle, CURLOPT_SSL_VERIFYPEER, false);
```

(continued)

Listing 7-7 ***(continued)***

```
curl_setopt($curlHandle, CURLOPT_USERPWD, "$username:$password");
$apiResponse = curl_exec($curlHandle);

// Get HTTP Status Code
$info = curl_getinfo($curlHandle);
$http_code = $info['http_code'];
echo "<h1>HTTP Status Code: $http_code</h1>";

// Close cURL connection
curl_close($curlHandle);

// Get XML
$xml = new DOMDocument();
$xml->loadXML($apiResponse);

// Check for an error tag.
$errors = $xml->getElementsByTagName("error");

// If found, print the error and break. Else, keep going!
if($errors->length > 0)
{
   $errorMessage = $errors->item(0)->nodeValue;
   echo "<h1>$errorMessage</h1>";
   break;
}
else
{
   // Get new list URL
   $uriNode = $xml->getElementsByTagName("uri");
   $uri = $uriNode->item(0)->nodeValue;

   echo "<a href=\"http://twitter.com/$uri\">$uri</a>";
}

?>
```

Delete a list

To delete an authenticated users list, issue an HTTP DELETE command to the `:user/lists/:id` method. If you can't issue a DELETE command, you can POST with the added parameter `_method=DELETE`.

This method is not rate limited.

Output

This method has two output formats:

- XML
- JSON

A successful DELETE returns the deleted list's `list` object, which includes the detailed `user` object for list's owner. A failed DELETE returns an error message explaining why the list deletion failed.

Input

The `:user/lists/:id` method requires two parameters:

- `user`: The screen name of the user you're deleting a list for. This variable is passed in the method path.
  Example: `dustyreagan/lists`
- `id`: The list's numeric ID or the list's slug, passed in the method path.
  Example: `dustyreagan/lists/5065754.xml`
  Example: `dustyreagan/lists/twitter-developers.xml`

Example

Listing 7-8 illustrates how to delete a list with the `:users/lists/:id` method.

Listing 7-8: Delete a List

```
<?php

// Set username and password
$username = 'dustytest2';
$password = 'password77';

$listId = 'twitter-developers';

// The Twitter delete list method
$url = "http://api.twitter.com/1/$username/lists/$listId.xml";

$name = urlencode("Twitter Developers");
$description = urlencode("My favorite Twitter developers");

// Get API results using curl
$curlHandle = curl_init();
curl_setopt($curlHandle, CURLOPT_URL, "$url");
curl_setopt($curlHandle, CURLOPT_USERAGENT, "Twitter App Development For
            Dummies: Example");
```

(continued)

Listing 7-8 *(continued)*

```
curl_setopt($curlHandle, CURLOPT_CUSTOMREQUEST, "DELETE");
curl_setopt($curlHandle, CURLOPT_RETURNTRANSFER, 1);
curl_setopt($curlHandle, CURLOPT_SSL_VERIFYPEER, false);
curl_setopt($curlHandle, CURLOPT_USERPWD, "$username:$password");
$apiResponse = curl_exec($curlHandle);

// Get HTTP Status Code
$info = curl_getinfo($curlHandle);
$http_code = $info['http_code'];
echo "<h1>HTTP Status Code: $http_code</h1>";

// Close cURL connection
curl_close($curlHandle);

// Get XML
$xml = new DOMDocument();
$xml->loadXML($apiResponse);

// Check for an error tag.
$errors = $xml->getElementsByTagName("error");

// If found, print the error and break. Else, keep going!
if($errors->length > 0)
{
   $errorMessage = $errors->item(0)->nodeValue;
   echo "<h1>$errorMessage</h1>";
}
else
{
   // Get new list URL
   $uriNode = $xml->getElementsByTagName("uri");
   $uri = $uriNode->item(0)->nodeValue;

   echo "<a href=\"http://twitter.com/$uri\">$uri</a>";
}

?>
```

Get a list's timeline

To get the tweets for all the members of a specific list, use a GET request on the `:user/lists/:list_id/statuses` method.

This method is rate limited and does not require authentication.

Output

This method has three output formats:

- XML
- JSON
- ATOM

A successful method request returns the complete `status` object for the 20 most recent tweets. A failed request returns an error message explaining why the list's tweets could not be returned.

Input

The `:user/lists/:list_id/statuses` method requires two parameters:

- `user`: The screen name of the user you're deleting a list for. This variable is passed in the method path.
  Example: `dustyreagan/lists`
- `list_id`: The list's numeric ID or the list's slug, passed in the method path.
  Example: `dustyreagan/lists/5065754/statuses.xml`
  Example: `dustyreagan/lists/twitter-developers/statuses.xml`

The following parameters are optional:

- `since_id`: The numerical ID of a tweet. Use to return list tweets that are more recent than the id specified.
  Example: `/dustyreagan/lists/twitter/statuses.xml?since_id=12345`
- `max_id`: The numerical ID of a tweet. Use to return list tweets that are older than the ID specified.
  Example: `/dustyreagan/lists/twitter/statuses.xml?max_id=54321`
- `per_page`: Limits the results per page to an amount specified that is less than 200.
  Example: `/dustyreagan/lists/twitter/statuses.xml?count=100`
- `page`: Page backwards to retrieve older list tweets.
  Example: `/dustyreagan/lists/twitter/statuses.xml?page=5`

Example

In Listing 7-9 I use the `page` and `per_page` parameter loop through the `:user/lists/:list_id/statuses` method to display the maximum amount of tweets in a list that the API will allow.

Listing 7-9: Getting a List's Tweets

```
<?php
function getStatusesPage($page)
{
   // Set username and password
   $username = 'username';
   $password = 'password';

   // The Twitter list timeline method
   $url = "https://api.twitter.com/1/dustyreagan/lists/twitter-developers/
              statuses.xml?per_page=200&page=$page";

   // Get API results using curl
   $curlHandle = curl_init();
   curl_setopt($curlHandle, CURLOPT_URL, "$url");
   curl_setopt($curlHandle, CURLOPT_USERAGENT, "Twitter App Development For
              Dummies: Example");
   curl_setopt($curlHandle, CURLOPT_RETURNTRANSFER, 1);
   curl_setopt($curlHandle, CURLOPT_SSL_VERIFYPEER, false);
   curl_setopt($curlHandle, CURLOPT_USERPWD, "$username:$password");
   $apiResponse = curl_exec($curlHandle);

   // Get HTTP Code
   $info = curl_getinfo($curlHandle);
   $http_code = $info['http_code'];
   echo "<h1>HTTP Status Code: $http_code</h1>";

   // Close cURL connection
   curl_close($curlHandle);

   return $apiResponse;
}

$page = 1;
do
{
   echo "<h1>Page: $page</h1>";
   // Get a page of statuses
   $apiResponse = getStatusesPage($page);

   // Get XML
   $xml = new DOMDocument();
   $xml->loadXML($apiResponse);

   // Check for an error tag.
   $errors = $xml->getElementsByTagName("error");

   // If found, print the error and break. Else, keep going!
   if($errors->length > 0)
   {
      $errorMessage = $errors->item(0)->nodeValue;
      echo "<h1>$errorMessage</h1>";
```

```
            break;
        }
        else
        {
            // Get tweets
            $statusNodes = $xml->getElementsByTagName("status");

            foreach($statusNodes as $statusNode)
            {
                // Get the tweet text
                $textNode = $statusNode->getElementsByTagName("text");
                $text = $textNode->item(0)->nodeValue;

                // Get the author's picture
                $senderNode = $statusNode->getElementsByTagName("user");
                $profilePicNode = $senderNode->item(0)->getElementsByTagName("profile_
                      image_url");
                $profile_image_url = $profilePicNode->item(0)->nodeValue;

                echo "<img style=\"float:left\" src=\"$profile_image_url\" width=\"48\"
                      height=\"48\" />";
                echo "<p>$text</p>";
                echo "<hr style=\"clear:both\" />";
            }
        }

        // increment page count and loop
        $page++;
    }
    while($statusNodes->length > 0)

?>
```

Get the lists a user belongs to

You can get all of the lists a user is listed in by using a GET request on the `:user/lists/memberships` method.

This method is rate limited and requires authentication.

Output

This method has two output formats:

- XML
- JSON

A successful method request returns an array of `list` objects of the most recent 20 lists the user was added to. Each list object includes the detailed `user` object of the creator of the list. A failed request returns an error message explaining why the lists could not be returned.

Input

The `:user/lists/memberships` method requires the `user` parameter:

- `user`: The screen name of the user you're deleting a list for. This variable is passed in the method path.
  Example: `dustyreagan/lists`

The `cursor` parameter is optional:

- `cursor`: Use to retrieve additional sets of user data.
  Example: `/:user/lists/memberships.xml?cursor=-1`

Example

Listing 7-10 illustrates how to pull a list of lists a user belongs to using the `:user/lists/memberships` method.

Listing 7-10: Getting the Lists a User Belongs To

```
<?php

function getListsPage($screen_name, $cursor)
{
   // Set username and password
   $username = 'username';
   $password = 'password';

   // The Twitter method
   $url =
"http://api.twitter.com/1/$screen_name/lists/memberships.xml?cursor=$cursor";

   // GET API results using curl
   $curlHandle = curl_init();
   curl_setopt($curlHandle, CURLOPT_URL, "$url");
   curl_setopt($curlHandle, CURLOPT_USERAGENT, "Twitter App Development For
            Dummies: Example");
   curl_setopt($curlHandle, CURLOPT_RETURNTRANSFER, 1);
   curl_setopt($curlHandle, CURLOPT_SSL_VERIFYPEER, false);
   curl_setopt($curlHandle, CURLOPT_USERPWD, "$username:$password");
   $apiResponse = curl_exec($curlHandle);

   // Get HTTP Status Code
   $info = curl_getinfo($curlHandle);
```

```
    $http_code = $info['http_code'];
    echo "<h1>HTTP Status Code: $http_code</h1>";

    // Close cURL connection
    curl_close($curlHandle);

    return $apiResponse;
}

$cursor = -1;
do {
    // Get lists for user
    $apiResponse = getListsPage('dustyreagan', $cursor);

    // Get XML
    $xml = new DOMDocument();
    $xml->loadXML($apiResponse);

    $lists = $xml->getElementsByTagName("list");

    foreach($lists as $list)
    {
        $nameNode = $list->getElementsByTagName("name");
        $name = $nameNode->item(0)->nodeValue;

        $uriNode = $list->getElementsByTagName("uri");
        $uri = $uriNode->item(0)->nodeValue;

        echo "<a href=\"http://twitter.com$uri\">$name</a><br />";
    }

    // Look for next_cursor
    $elements = $xml->getElementsByTagName("next_cursor");

    // Get next_cursor. Break if you can't find it.
    if(!empty($elements))
    {
        $cursor = $elements->item(0)->nodeValue;
        echo "<h1>cursor: $cursor</h1>";
    }
    else
    {
        echo "<h1>No cursor found</h1>";
        break;
    }
} while($cursor != 0);

?>
```

Get the lists a user follows

To get the lists a user subscribes to, you can issue a GET request to the `:user/lists/subscriptions` method.

This method requires authentication and is rate limited.

Output

This method has two output formats:

- XML
- JSON

A successful method request returns an array of `list` objects of the lists the user subscribes to. Each `list` object includes the detailed `user` object of the creator of the list. A failed request returns an error message explaining why the lists could not be returned.

Input

The `:user/lists/subscriptions` method requires the `user` parameter:

- `user`: The screen name of the user whose list subscriptions you want. This variable is passed in the method path.
  Example: `dustyreagan/lists/subscriptions.xml`

The `cursor` parameter is optional:

- `cursor`: Use to retrieve additional sets of user data.
  Example: `/dustyreagan/lists/subscriptions.xml?cursor=-1`

Example

Listing 7-11 illustrates how to pull a list of lists a user subscribes to using the `:user/lists/subscriptions` method.

Listing 7-11: Getting the Lists a User Subscribes To

```
<?php

function getListsPage($screen_name, $cursor)
{
   // Set username and password
   $username = 'username';
   $password = 'password';

   // The Twitter method
```

```
    $url =
"http://api.twitter.com/1/$screen_name/lists/subscriptions.xml?cursor=$cursor";

    // GET API results using curl
    $curlHandle = curl_init();
    curl_setopt($curlHandle, CURLOPT_URL, "$url");
    curl_setopt($curlHandle, CURLOPT_USERAGENT, "Twitter App Development For
                Dummies: Example");
    curl_setopt($curlHandle, CURLOPT_RETURNTRANSFER, 1);
    curl_setopt($curlHandle, CURLOPT_SSL_VERIFYPEER, false);
    curl_setopt($curlHandle, CURLOPT_USERPWD, "$username:$password");
    $apiResponse = curl_exec($curlHandle);

    // Get HTTP Status Code
    $info = curl_getinfo($curlHandle);
    $http_code = $info['http_code'];
    echo "<h1>HTTP Status Code: $http_code</h1>";

    // Close cURL connection
    curl_close($curlHandle);

    return $apiResponse;
}

$cursor = -1;
do {
    // Get lists for user
    $apiResponse = getListsPage('Scobleizer', $cursor);

    // Get XML
    $xml = new DOMDocument();
    $xml->loadXML($apiResponse);

    $lists = $xml->getElementsByTagName("list");

    foreach($lists as $list)
    {
        $nameNode = $list->getElementsByTagName("name");
        $name = $nameNode->item(0)->nodeValue;

        $uriNode = $list->getElementsByTagName("uri");
        $uri = $uriNode->item(0)->nodeValue;

        echo "<a href=\"http://twitter.com$uri\">$name</a><br />";
    }

    // Look for next_cursor
    $elements = $xml->getElementsByTagName("next_cursor");
```

(continued)

Listing 7-11 *(continued)*

```
    // Get next_cursor. Break if you can't find it.
    if(!empty($elements))
    {
       $cursor = $elements->item(0)->nodeValue;
       echo "<h1>cursor: $cursor</h1>";
    }
    else
    {
       echo "<h1>No cursor found</h1>";
       break;
    }
} while($cursor != 0);

?>
```

List Members Methods

List members are the Twitter user's a list follows. You can view, add, and remove members, as well as check for membership using the four list members methods:

- GET `:user/:list_id/members`
- POST `:user/:list_id/members`
- DELETE `:user/:list_id/members`
- GET `:user/:list_id/members/:id`

Get a list's members

To get the users a list includes, issue a GET request to the `:user/:list_id/members` method.

This method requires authentication and is rate limited.

Output

This method has two output formats:

- XML
- JSON

A successful method request returns an array of `user` objects. A failed request returns an error message explaining why the lists could not be returned.

Input

The :user/:list_id/members method requires two parameters:

- user: The screen name of the user whose list you're querying. This variable is passed in the method path.
  Example: /dustyreagan/twitter-developers/members.xml
- list_id: The list's numeric ID or the list's slug, passed in the method path.
  Example: /dustyreagan/5065754/members.xml
  Example: /dustyreagan/twitter-developers/members.xml

The cursor parameter is optional:

- cursor: Use to retrieve additional sets of user data.
  Example: /dustyreagan/twitter-developers/members.xml?cursor=-1

Example

Listing 7-12 illustrates how to get a list of users a list follows using the :user/:list_id/members method.

Listing 7-12: Getting the Users a List Follows

```
<?php

function getMembersPage($cursor)
{
    // Set username and password
    $username = 'dustytest2';
    $password = 'password77';

    // The Twitter method
    $url =
"https://api.twitter.com/1/dustyreagan/twitter-developers/members.
            xml?cursor=$cursor";

    // GET API results using curl
    $curlHandle = curl_init();
    curl_setopt($curlHandle, CURLOPT_URL, "$url");
    curl_setopt($curlHandle, CURLOPT_USERAGENT, "Twitter App Development For
            Dummies: Example");
    curl_setopt($curlHandle, CURLOPT_RETURNTRANSFER, 1);
    curl_setopt($curlHandle, CURLOPT_SSL_VERIFYPEER, false);
    curl_setopt($curlHandle, CURLOPT_USERPWD, "$username:$password");
    $apiResponse = curl_exec($curlHandle);

    // Get HTTP Status Code
    $info = curl_getinfo($curlHandle);
```

(continued)

Listing 7-12 *(continued)*

```
    $http_code = $info['http_code'];
    echo "<h1>HTTP Status Code: $http_code</h1>";

    // Close cURL connection
    curl_close($curlHandle);

    return $apiResponse;
}

$cursor = -1;
do {
    // Get lists for user
    $apiResponse = getMembersPage($cursor);

    // Get XML
    $xml = new DOMDocument();
    $xml->loadXML($apiResponse);

    $users = $xml->getElementsByTagName("user");

    foreach($users as $user)
    {
        $nameNode = $user->getElementsByTagName("screen_name");
        $name = $nameNode->item(0)->nodeValue;

        echo "<a href=\"http://twitter.com/$name\">$name</a><br />";
    }

    // Look for next_cursor
    $elements = $xml->getElementsByTagName("next_cursor");

    // Get next_cursor. Break if you can't find it.
    if(!empty($elements))
    {
        $cursor = $elements->item(0)->nodeValue;
        echo "<h1>cursor: $cursor</h1>";
    }
    else
    {
        echo "<h1>No cursor found</h1>";
        break;
    }
} while($cursor != 0);

?>
```

Add a member to a list

To add a user to a list, issue a POST request to the `:user/:list_id/members` method. You must be authenticated as the owner of the list to add a new member to the list.

This method is not rate limited, however lists are limited to 500 members. This method requires authentication.

Output

This method has two output formats:

- XML
- JSON

A successful POST returns a list object of the list you added a new user to. The list object includes a detailed user object for the lists owner. A failed POST returns an error message explaining why the user couldn't be added.

Input

The :user/:list_id/members POST method requires three parameters:

- user: The screen name of the user whose list you're updating. This variable is passed in the method path.
  Example: /dustyreagan/twitter-developers/members.xml
- list_id: The list's numeric ID or the list's slug, passed in the method path.
  Example: /dustyreagan/5065754/members.xml
  Example: /dustyreagan/twitter-developers/members.xml
- id: The numeric ID of the user you want to add passed as a POST field.
  Example: id=1234

Example

Listing 7-13 illustrates how to add a new member to a list with the :user/:list_id/members method.

Listing 7-13: Add a New List Member

```
<?php

// Set username and password
$username = 'username';
$password = 'password';

$listId = 'twitter-developers';

// The Twitter add list member method
$url = "https://api.twitter.com/1/$username/$listId/members.xml";

$userId = 973261;

// Get API results using curl
```

(continued)

Listing 7-13 *(continued)*

```
$curlHandle = curl_init();
curl_setopt($curlHandle, CURLOPT_URL, "$url");
curl_setopt($curlHandle, CURLOPT_USERAGENT, "Twitter App Development For
              Dummies: Example");
curl_setopt($curlHandle, CURLOPT_POST, 1);
curl_setopt($curlHandle, CURLOPT_RETURNTRANSFER, 1);
curl_setopt($curlHandle, CURLOPT_SSL_VERIFYPEER, false);
curl_setopt($curlHandle, CURLOPT_POSTFIELDS, "id=$userId");
curl_setopt($curlHandle, CURLOPT_USERPWD, "$username:$password");
$apiResponse = curl_exec($curlHandle);

// Get HTTP Status Code
$info = curl_getinfo($curlHandle);
$http_code = $info['http_code'];
echo "<h1>HTTP Status Code: $http_code</h1>";

// Close cURL connection
curl_close($curlHandle);

// Get XML
$xml = new DOMDocument();
$xml->loadXML($apiResponse);

// Check for an error tag.
$errors = $xml->getElementsByTagName("error");

// If found, print the error and break. Else, keep going!
if($errors->length > 0)
{
   $errorMessage = $errors->item(0)->nodeValue;
   echo "<h1>$errorMessage</h1>";
}
else
{
   // Get list URL
   $uriNode = $xml->getElementsByTagName("uri");
   $uri = $uriNode->item(0)->nodeValue;

   echo "<a href=\"http://twitter.com$uri\">$uri</a>";
}

?>
```

Remove a list member

To remove a user that a list is following, authenticate as the list's owner and issue a HTTP DELETE command to the `:user/:list_id/members` method. If you can't issue a DELETE command, you can POST with the added parameter `_method=DELETE`.

This method is not rate limited.

Output

This method has two output formats:

- XML
- JSON

A successful DELETE returns the modified list's `list` object details, which includes the detailed `user` object for the list's owner. A failed DELETE returns an error message explaining why the user couldn't be removed.

Input

The `:user/:list_id/members` DELETE method requires three parameters:

- `user`: The screen name of the user whose list you're updating. This variable is passed in the method path.
  Example: `/dustyreagan/twitter-developers/members.xml`
- `list_id`: The list's numeric ID or the list's slug, passed in the method path.
  Example: `/dustyreagan/5065754/members.xml`
  Example: `/dustyreagan/twitter-developers/members.xml`
- `id`: The numeric ID of the user you want to remove passed as a POST field.
  Example: `id=1234`

Example

Listing 7-14 shows how to remove a user from a list by issuing an HTTP DELETE command to the `:user/:list_id/members` method.

Listing 7-14: Remove a List Member

```
<?php

// Set username and password
$username = 'username';
$password = 'password';

$listId = 'twitter-developers';

// The Twitter list method
$url = "http://api.twitter.com/1/$username/$listId/members.xml";

$userId = 973261;

// Get API results using curl
```

(continued)

Listing 7-14 *(continued)*

```
$curlHandle = curl_init();
curl_setopt($curlHandle, CURLOPT_URL, "$url");
curl_setopt($curlHandle, CURLOPT_USERAGENT, "Twitter App Development For
              Dummies: Example");
curl_setopt($curlHandle, CURLOPT_CUSTOMREQUEST, "DELETE");
curl_setopt($curlHandle, CURLOPT_RETURNTRANSFER, 1);
curl_setopt($curlHandle, CURLOPT_SSL_VERIFYPEER, false);
curl_setopt($curlHandle, CURLOPT_POSTFIELDS, "id=$userId");
curl_setopt($curlHandle, CURLOPT_USERPWD, "$username:$password");
$apiResponse = curl_exec($curlHandle);

// Get HTTP Status Code
$info = curl_getinfo($curlHandle);
$http_code = $info['http_code'];
echo "<h1>HTTP Status Code: $http_code</h1>";

// Close cURL connection
curl_close($curlHandle);

// Get XML
$xml = new DOMDocument();
$xml->loadXML($apiResponse);

// Check for an error tag.
$errors = $xml->getElementsByTagName("error");

// If found, print the error and break. Else, keep going!
if($errors->length > 0)
{
   $errorMessage = $errors->item(0)->nodeValue;
   echo "<h1>$errorMessage</h1>";
}
else
{
   // Get list URL
   $uriNode = $xml->getElementsByTagName("uri");
   $uri = $uriNode->item(0)->nodeValue;

   echo "<a href=\"http://twitter.com/$uri\">$uri</a>";
}

?>
```

Test if user is a list member

You can check if a user is being followed by a specific list by issuing a GET request to the `:user/:list_id/members/:id` method.

This method is rate limited, and requires authentication.

Output

This method has two output formats:

- XML
- JSON

If the user is a member of the specified list, the method returns the checked user's `user` object and an HTTP status code of 200. If the user is not a member, an error message containing the explanation: "The specified user is not a member of this list" is returned, along with an HTTP status code of 404.

Input

The `:user/:list_id/members/:id` GET method requires three parameters:

- `user`: The screen name of the user whose list you're checking. This variable is passed in the method path.
  Example: `/dustyreagan/5065754/members/1234.xml`
- `list_id`: The list's numeric ID or the list's slug, passed in the method path.
  Example: `/dustyreagan/5065754/members/1234.xml`
  Example: `/dustyreagan/twitter-developers/members/1234.xml`
- `id`: The numeric ID of the user you want to check passed in the method path.
  Example: `/dustyreagan/twitter-developers/members/1234.xml`

Example

Listing 7-15 shows how to check if a user is a member of a list using a GET request on the `:user/:list_id/members/:id` method.

Listing 7-15: Check if a User Is a Member of a List

```
<?php

// Set username and password
$username = 'username';
$password = 'password';

$listId = 'twitter-developers';
$userId = 973261;
// The Twitter check list method
$url = "http://api.twitter.com/1/$username/$listId/members/$userId.xml";
```

(continued)

Listing 7-15 *(continued)*

```
// Get API results using curl
$curlHandle = curl_init();
curl_setopt($curlHandle, CURLOPT_URL, "$url");
curl_setopt($curlHandle, CURLOPT_USERAGENT, "Twitter App Development For
              Dummies: Example");
curl_setopt($curlHandle, CURLOPT_RETURNTRANSFER, 1);
curl_setopt($curlHandle, CURLOPT_SSL_VERIFYPEER, false);
curl_setopt($curlHandle, CURLOPT_USERPWD, "$username:$password");
$apiResponse = curl_exec($curlHandle);

// Get HTTP Status Code
$info = curl_getinfo($curlHandle);
$http_code = $info['http_code'];
echo "<h1>HTTP Status Code: $http_code</h1>";

// Close cURL connection
curl_close($curlHandle);

// Get XML
$xml = new DOMDocument();
$xml->loadXML($apiResponse);

// Check for an error tag.
$errors = $xml->getElementsByTagName("error");

// If found, print the error. Else, print the user's picture.
if($errors->length > 0)
{
   $errorMessage = $errors->item(0)->nodeValue;
   echo "<h1>$errorMessage</h1>";
}
else
{
   $profileImageNode = $xml->getElementsByTagName("profile_image_url");
   $profile_image_url = $profileImageNode->item(0)->nodeValue;

   echo "<img src=\"$profile_image_url\" width=\"48\" height=\"48\" />";
}

?>
```

List Subscribers Methods

List subscribers are the people who follow a Twitter list. You can view a list's subscribers, follow a list, unfollow a list, and test if a user is following a list using the four list subscribers methods:

- GET `:user/:list_id/subscribers`
- POST `:user/:id/subscribers`

- DELETE `:user/:list_id/subscribers`
- GET `:user/:list_id/subscribers/:id`

Get a list's subscribers

To get the users that follow a list, issue a GET request to the `:user/:list_id/subscribers` method.

This method requires authentication and is rate limited.

Output

This method has two output formats:

- XML
- JSON

A successful method request returns an array of `user` objects. A failed request returns an error message explaining why the list's subscribers could not be returned.

Input

The `:user/:list_id/subscribers` method requires two parameters:

- `user`: The screen name of the user whose list you're querying. This variable is passed in the method path.
  Example: `/dustyreagan/twitter-developers/subscribers.xml`
- `list_id`: The list's numeric ID or the list's slug, passed in the method path.
  Example: `/dustyreagan/5065754/subscribers.xml`
  Example: `/dustyreagan/twitter-developers/subscribers.xml`

The `cursor` parameter is optional:

- `cursor`: Use to retrieve additional sets of user data.
  Example: `/dustyreagan/twitter-developers/subscribers.xml?cursor=-1`

Example

Listing 7-16 illustrates how to use the cursor method to loop through the `:user/:list_id/subscribers` method and print all of a list's subscribers.

Listing 7-16: Getting a List's Followers

```
<?php

function getSubscribersPage($cursor)
{
   // Set username and password
   $username = 'dustytest2';
   $password = 'password77';

   // The Twitter method
   $url =
"https://api.twitter.com/1/dustyreagan/twitter-developers/subscribers.
               xml?cursor=$cursor";

   // GET API results using curl
   $curlHandle = curl_init();
   curl_setopt($curlHandle, CURLOPT_URL, "$url");
   curl_setopt($curlHandle, CURLOPT_USERAGENT, "Twitter App Development For
               Dummies: Example");
   curl_setopt($curlHandle, CURLOPT_RETURNTRANSFER, 1);
   curl_setopt($curlHandle, CURLOPT_SSL_VERIFYPEER, false);
   curl_setopt($curlHandle, CURLOPT_USERPWD, "$username:$password");
   $apiResponse = curl_exec($curlHandle);

   // Get HTTP Status Code
   $info = curl_getinfo($curlHandle);
   $http_code = $info['http_code'];
   echo "<h1>HTTP Status Code: $http_code</h1>";

   // Close cURL connection
   curl_close($curlHandle);

   return $apiResponse;
}

$cursor = -1;
do {
   // Get lists for user
   $apiResponse = getSubscribersPage($cursor);

   // Get XML
   $xml = new DOMDocument();
   $xml->loadXML($apiResponse);

   $users = $xml->getElementsByTagName("user");

   foreach($users as $user)
   {
      $nameNode = $user->getElementsByTagName("screen_name");
      $name = $nameNode->item(0)->nodeValue;
```

```
        echo "<a href=\"http://twitter.com/$name\">$name</a><br />";
    }

    // Look for next_cursor
    $elements = $xml->getElementsByTagName("next_cursor");

    // Get next_cursor. Break if you can't find it.
    if(!empty($elements))
    {
        $cursor = $elements->item(0)->nodeValue;
        echo "<h1>cursor: $cursor</h1>";
    }
    else
    {
        echo "<h1>No cursor found</h1>";
        break;
    }
} while($cursor != 0);

?>
```

Follow a list

The authenticated user can follow a list by issuing a POST request to the `:user/:list_id/subscribers` method.

This method is not rate limited, however you can only follow a maximum of 40 lists.

Output

This method has two output formats:

- XML
- JSON

A successful POST returns a `list` object of the list you followed. The `list` object includes a detailed `user` object for the list's owner. A failed POST returns an error message explaining why you can't follow the list.

Input

The `:user/:list_id/subscribers` POST method requires two parameters:

- `user`: The screen name of the user whose list you're updating. This variable is passed in the method path.
  Example: `dustyreagan/twitter-developers/subscribers.xml`
- `list_id`: The list's numeric ID or the list's slug, passed in the method path.
  Example: `dustyreagan/5065754/subscribers.xml`
  Example: `dustyreagan/twitter-developers/subscribers.xml`

Example

Listing 7-17 illustrates how to follow a list programmatically with the `:user/:list_id/subscribers` method.

Listing 7-17: Add a List Subscriber

```
<?php

// Set username and password
$username = 'username';
$password = 'password';

$listId = 'twitter-developers';

// The Twitter add list subscriber method
$url = "https://api.twitter.com/1/$username/$listId/members.xml";

$userId = 973261;

// Get API results using curl
$curlHandle = curl_init();
curl_setopt($curlHandle, CURLOPT_URL, "$url");
curl_setopt($curlHandle, CURLOPT_USERAGENT, "Twitter App Development For
          Dummies: Example");
curl_setopt($curlHandle, CURLOPT_POST, 1);
curl_setopt($curlHandle, CURLOPT_RETURNTRANSFER, 1);
curl_setopt($curlHandle, CURLOPT_SSL_VERIFYPEER, false);
curl_setopt($curlHandle, CURLOPT_POSTFIELDS, "id=$userId");
curl_setopt($curlHandle, CURLOPT_USERPWD, "$username:$password");
$apiResponse = curl_exec($curlHandle);

// Get HTTP Status Code
$info = curl_getinfo($curlHandle);
$http_code = $info['http_code'];
echo "<h1>HTTP Status Code: $http_code</h1>";
```

```
// Close cURL connection
curl_close($curlHandle);

// Get XML
$xml = new DOMDocument();
$xml->loadXML($apiResponse);

// Check for an error tag.
$errors = $xml->getElementsByTagName("error");

// If found, print the error and break. Else, keep going!
if($errors->length > 0)
{
   $errorMessage = $errors->item(0)->nodeValue;
   echo "<h1>$errorMessage</h1>";
}
else
{
   // Get list URL
   $uriNode = $xml->getElementsByTagName("uri");
   $uri = $uriNode->item(0)->nodeValue;

   echo "<a href=\"http://twitter.com$uri\">$uri</a>";
}

?>
```

Stop following a list

The authenticated user can stop following a list by issuing an HTTP DELETE command using the `:user/:list_id/subscribers` method. If you can't issue a DELETE command you can POST with the added field parameter `_method=DELETE`.

This method is not rate limited.

Output

This method has two output formats:

- XML
- JSON

A successful DELETE returns the `list` object of the unfollowed list, which includes the detailed `user` object for the list's owner. A failed DELETE returns an error message explaining why the list couldn't be unfollowed.

Input

The `:user/:list_id/members` DELETE method requires three parameters:

- `user`: The screen name of the user whose list you're updating. This variable is passed in the method path.
  Example: `dustyreagan/lists`
- `list_id`: The list's numeric ID or the list's slug, passed in the method path.
  Example: `dustyreagan/lists/5065754.xml`
  Example: `dustyreagan/lists/twitter-developers.xml`

Example

Listing 7-18 illustrates how to unfollow a list by issuing an HTTP DELETE command to the `:user/:list_id/subscribers` method.

Listing 7-18: Unfollow a List

```
<?php

// Set username and password
$username = 'username';
$password = 'password';

$listId = 'twitter-developers';

// The Twitter list method
$url = "http://api.twitter.com/1/$username/$listId/subscribers.xml";

$userId = 973261;

// Get API results using curl
$curlHandle = curl_init();
curl_setopt($curlHandle, CURLOPT_URL, "$url");
curl_setopt($curlHandle, CURLOPT_USERAGENT, "Twitter App Development For
               Dummies: Example");
curl_setopt($curlHandle, CURLOPT_CUSTOMREQUEST, "DELETE");
curl_setopt($curlHandle, CURLOPT_RETURNTRANSFER, 1);
curl_setopt($curlHandle, CURLOPT_SSL_VERIFYPEER, false);
curl_setopt($curlHandle, CURLOPT_POSTFIELDS, "id=$userId");
curl_setopt($curlHandle, CURLOPT_USERPWD, "$username:$password");
$apiResponse = curl_exec($curlHandle);

// Get HTTP Status Code
$info = curl_getinfo($curlHandle);
$http_code = $info['http_code'];
echo "<h1>HTTP Status Code: $http_code</h1>";
```

```
// Close cURL connection
curl_close($curlHandle);

// Get XML
$xml = new DOMDocument();
$xml->loadXML($apiResponse);

// Check for an error tag.
$errors = $xml->getElementsByTagName("error");

// If found, print the error and break. Else, keep going!
if($errors->length > 0)
{
   $errorMessage = $errors->item(0)->nodeValue;
   echo "<h1>$errorMessage</h1>";
}
else
{
   // Get list URL
   $uriNode = $xml->getElementsByTagName("uri");
   $uri = $uriNode->item(0)->nodeValue;

   echo "<a href=\"http://twitter.com/$uri\">$uri</a>";
}

?>
```

Test if user follows a list

You can check if a user is following a specific list by issuing a GET request on the `:user/:list_id/subscribers/:id` method.

This method is rate limited, and requires authentication.

Output

This method has two output formats:

- XML
- JSON

If the specified user follows the list, their user object is returned. A failed POST returns an error message explaining why the test could not be performed.

Input

The `:user/:list_id/subscribers/:id` GET method requires three parameters:

- `user`: The screen name of the user whose list you're checking. This variable is passed in the method path. Example: `dustyreagan/twitter-developers/subscribers/1234.xml`
- `list_id`: The list's numeric ID or the list's slug, passed in the method path. Example: `dustyreagan/5065754/subscribers/1234.xml` Example: `dustyreagan/twitter-developers/subscribers/1234.xml`
- `id`: The numeric ID of the user you want to check passed in the method path. Example: `dustyreagan/twitter-developers/subscribers/1234.xml`

Example

Listing 7-19 shows how to check if a user is following a list using a GET request on the `:user/:list_id/subscribers/:id` method.

Listing 7-19: Check if a User Is Following a List

```
<?php

// Set username and password
$username = 'username';
$password = 'password';

$listId = 'twitter-developers';
$userId = 'dustyreagan';

// The Twitter check list method
$url = "https://api.twitter.com/1/$username/$listId/subscribers/$userId.xml";

echo $url;

// Get API results using curl
$curlHandle = curl_init();
curl_setopt($curlHandle, CURLOPT_URL, "$url");
curl_setopt($curlHandle, CURLOPT_USERAGENT, "Twitter App Development For
            Dummies: Example");
curl_setopt($curlHandle, CURLOPT_RETURNTRANSFER, 1);
curl_setopt($curlHandle, CURLOPT_SSL_VERIFYPEER, false);
curl_setopt($curlHandle, CURLOPT_USERPWD, "$username:$password");

$apiResponse = curl_exec($curlHandle);
```

```
// Get HTTP Status Code
$info = curl_getinfo($curlHandle);
$http_code = $info['http_code'];
echo "<h1>HTTP Status Code: $http_code</h1>";

// Close cURL connection
curl_close($curlHandle);

// Get XML
$xml = new DOMDocument();
$xml->loadXML($apiResponse);

// Check for an error tag.
$errors = $xml->getElementsByTagName("error");

// If found, print the error. Else, print the user's picture.
if($errors->length > 0)
{
   $errorMessage = $errors->item(0)->nodeValue;
   echo "<h1>$errorMessage</h1>";
}
else
{
   $profileImageNode = $xml->getElementsByTagName("profile_image_url");
   $profile_image_url = $profileImageNode->item(0)->nodeValue;

   echo "<img src=\"$profile_image_url\" width=\"48\" height=\"48\" />";
}

?>
```

Friendship Methods

The term friendship in Twitter is used loosely. More appropriately, it means to follow someone's Twitter account. Using the friendship methods you can follow and unfollow a Twitter account, as well as check if one user follows another user. This is all done with these four methods:

- `friendships/create`
- `friendships/destroy`
- `friendship/exists`
- `friendships/show`

Follow a user

To programmatically follow a user on Twitter, you must authenticate as the follower and post the ID of the person you want to follow to the `friendship/create` method. Following a protected Twitter account will send a follower request to the account holder. They must approve your request before you begin following them.

This method requires a POST request and isn't rate limited. However, you may only follow an unspecified number of users per day. Twitter doesn't disclose how many.

Output

This method has two output formats:

- XML
- JSON

On a successful post, this method will return the user object of the person you followed. On a failed post, you will receive an error message explaining why the follow failed.

Input

The friendship/create method requires only one of three parameters:

- `id`: The user's screen name or numerical user id.
  Example: `/friendships/create/bob.xml`
  Example: `/friendships/create/12345.xml`
- `user_id`: The numerical id of the user.
  Example: `/friendships/create.xml?user_id=12345`
- `screen_name`: The screen name of the user.
  Example: `/friendships/create.xml?screen_name=101010`

Avoid using the `id` parameter and use `user_id`, over `screen_name` if possible. The sidebar "Hard Knocks" explains why.

In addition to following a user, the `friendships/create` method allows you to turn on SMS notifications at the same time with this optional parameter:

- `follow`: Use to turn on SMS notifications for the user.
  Example: `/friendships/create/bob.xml?follow=true`

Example

Listing 7-20 shows you an example of how to programmatically follow a new user by using curl to post to the `friendships/create` method.

Listing 7-20: How to Programmatically Follow a New User

```
<?php
// Set username and password
$username = 'username';
$password = 'password';

$follow = 'dustyreagan';

// The Twitter friendships/create method
$url = "https://api.twitter.com/1/friendships/create.xml";

// POST to Twitter API using curl
$curlHandle = curl_init();
curl_setopt($curlHandle, CURLOPT_URL, "$url");
curl_setopt($curlHandle, CURLOPT_USERAGENT, "Twitter App Development For
              Dummies: Example");
curl_setopt($curlHandle, CURLOPT_POST, 1);
curl_setopt($curlHandle, CURLOPT_RETURNTRANSFER, 1);
curl_setopt($curlHandle, CURLOPT_SSL_VERIFYPEER, false);
curl_setopt($curlHandle, CURLOPT_POSTFIELDS, "screen_name=$follow");
curl_setopt($curlHandle, CURLOPT_USERPWD, "$username:$password");
$apiResponse = curl_exec($curlHandle);

// Get HTTP Status Code
$info = curl_getinfo($curlHandle);
$http_code = $info['http_code'];
echo "<h1>HTTP Status Code: $http_code</h1>";

// Close cURL connection
curl_close($curlHandle);

// Get XML
$xml = new DOMDocument();
$xml->loadXML($apiResponse);

// Check for an error tag.
$errors = $xml->getElementsByTagName("error");

// If found, print the error. Else, success!
if($errors->length > 0)
{
   $errorMessage = $errors->item(0)->nodeValue;
   echo "<h1>$errorMessage</h1>";
}
else
{
   $profileImageNode = $xml->getElementsByTagName("profile_image_url");
   $profile_image_url = $profileImageNode->item(0)->nodeValue;
   echo "<h1>Now following: <img src=\"$profile_image_url\" width=\"48\"
              height=\"48\" alt=\"$follow\" /></h1>";
}
?>
```

Stop following a user

To stop following a user, authenticate as the user who's doing the unfollowing and post the ID of the person you want to unfollow to the `friendship/destroy` method.

This method requires a POST or DELETE request and isn't rate limited. However, you may only unfollow an unspecified number of users per day. Twitter doesn't disclose how many.

Output

This method has two output formats:

- XML
- JSON

On a successful post, this method will return the user object of the person you unfollowed. On a failed post, you will receive an error message explaining why you were unable to unfollow the user.

Input

The `friendships/destroy` method requires only one of three parameters:

- `id`: The user's screen name or numerical user ID.
  Example: `/friendships/destroy/bob.xml`
  Example: `/friendships/destroy/12345.xml`
- `user_id`: The numerical ID of the user.
  Example: `/friendships/destroy.xml?user_id=12345`
- `screen_name`: The screen name of the user.
  Example: `/friendships/destroy.xml?screen_name=101010`

Avoid using the `id` parameter and use `user_id`, over `screen_name` if possible. The sidebar "Hard Knocks" explains why.

Example

Listing 7-21 shows you an example of how to programmatically unfollow a new user by using curl to post to the `friendships/destroy` method.

Listing 7-21: How to Programmatically Unfollow a User

```
<?php

// Set username and password
$username = 'username';
```

```
$password = 'password';

$unfollow = 'dustyreagan';

// The Twitter friendships/destroy method
$url = "https://api.twitter.com/1/friendships/destroy.xml";

// POST to Twitter API using curl
$curlHandle = curl_init();
curl_setopt($curlHandle, CURLOPT_URL, "$url");
curl_setopt($curlHandle, CURLOPT_USERAGENT, "Twitter App Development For
              Dummies: Example");
curl_setopt($curlHandle, CURLOPT_POST, 1);
curl_setopt($curlHandle, CURLOPT_RETURNTRANSFER, 1);
curl_setopt($curlHandle, CURLOPT_SSL_VERIFYPEER, false);
curl_setopt($curlHandle, CURLOPT_POSTFIELDS, "screen_name=$unfollow");
curl_setopt($curlHandle, CURLOPT_USERPWD, "$username:$password");
$apiResponse = curl_exec($curlHandle);

// Get HTTP Status Code
$info = curl_getinfo($curlHandle);
$http_code = $info['http_code'];
echo "<h1>HTTP Status Code: $http_code</h1>";

// Close cURL connection
curl_close($curlHandle);

// Get XML
$xml = new DOMDocument();
$xml->loadXML($apiResponse);

// Check for an error tag.
$errors = $xml->getElementsByTagName("error");

// If found, print the error. Else, success!
if($errors->length > 0)
{
   $errorMessage = $errors->item(0)->nodeValue;
   echo "<h1>$errorMessage</h1>";
}
else
{
   $profileImageNode = $xml->getElementsByTagName("profile_image_url");
   $profile_image_url = $profileImageNode->item(0)->nodeValue;
   echo "<h1>Un-Followed: <img src=\"$profile_image_url\" width=\"48\"
              height=\"48\" alt=\"$unfollow\" /></h1>";
}

?>
```

Check if one user follows another user

If you want to check if one user is following another, you can run the `friendships/exists` method. It returns a simple true or false answer.

This method doesn't require authentication, but if either of the two user accounts you are checking is protected you must

- Authenticate your API call
- Have permission to view the protected accounts.

This method requires a GET request and is rate limited. The sidebar "Hard Knocks" explains the concern with rate limits.

Output

This method has two output formats:

- XML
- JSON

On a successful method call you will receive a value of true or false. If the either user accounts doesn't exist or is disabled by Twitter you will receive an error message and a HTTP status code of 404.

Input

This method requires two parameters:

- `user_a`: The user ID or screen name of a user
- `user_id`: The user ID or screen name of the user you want to know if user_a is following.

This method asks, "is user_a following user_b?"

Avoid using the `id` parameter and use `user_id` over `screen_name` if possible. The sidebar "Hard Knocks" explains why.

Example

You can try the friendships/exists method easily by typing `http://api.twitter.com/1/friendships/exists.xml?user_a=dustyreagan&user_b=ev` into your browser's URL address bar.

In Listing 7-22 you can see an example of how to test for friendships using PHP and cURL.

Listing 7-22: Testing if One User Follows Another

```
<?php
// Set username and password
$username = 'username';
$password = 'password';

$user_a = 'dustyreagan';
$user_b = 'z_bill';

// The Twitter friendships/exists method
$url = "https://api.twitter.com/1/friendships/exists.xml?user_a=$user_a&user_
               b=$user_b";

// POST to Twitter API using curl
$curlHandle = curl_init();
curl_setopt($curlHandle, CURLOPT_URL, "$url");
curl_setopt($curlHandle, CURLOPT_USERAGENT, "Twitter App Development For
               Dummies: Example");
curl_setopt($curlHandle, CURLOPT_RETURNTRANSFER, 1);
curl_setopt($curlHandle, CURLOPT_SSL_VERIFYPEER, false);
curl_setopt($curlHandle, CURLOPT_USERPWD, "$username:$password");
$apiResponse = curl_exec($curlHandle);

// Get HTTP Status Code
$info = curl_getinfo($curlHandle);
$http_code = $info['http_code'];
echo "<h1>HTTP Status Code: $http_code</h1>";

// Close cURL connection
curl_close($curlHandle);

// Get XML
$xml = new DOMDocument();
$xml->loadXML($apiResponse);

// Check for an error tag.
$errors = $xml->getElementsByTagName("error");

// If found, print the error. Else, success!
if($errors->length > 0)
{
   $errorMessage = $errors->item(0)->nodeValue;
   echo "<h1>$errorMessage</h1>";
}
else
{
   $friendsNode = $xml->getElementsByTagName("friends");
   $friends = $friendsNode->item(0)->nodeValue;
```

(continued)

Listing 7-22 *(continued)*

```
    if($friends == "true")
       echo "<h1>@$user_a follows @$user_b</h1>";
    else
       echo "<h1>@$user_a does NOT follow @$user_b</h1>";
}

?>
```

Get information about the relationship between two users

While the `friendships/exists` method will tell you if one user follows another, the `friendships/show` method will give you the bidirectional relationship between both users, as well as the user ID and screen name of both users.

So, if you want to know if user A follows user B, and you want to know if user B follows user A, you can do that in one call with the `friendships/show` method.

This method doesn't require authentication, but if either of the two user accounts you are checking is protected you must

- Authenticate your API call
- Have permission to view the protected accounts.

This method requires a GET request and is rate limited. The sidebar "Hard Knocks" explains the concern with rate limits.

Output

This method has two output formats:

- XML
- JSON

On a successful method call you will receive a response similar to Listing 7-23.

Listing 7-23: Example XML Response from the Friendships/Show Method

```
<?xml version="1.0" encoding="UTF-8"?>
<relationship>
  <source>
    <blocking type="boolean">false</blocking>
```

```
    <following type="boolean">true</following>
    <screen_name>DustyReagan</screen_name>
    <followed_by type="boolean">true</followed_by>
    <id type="integer">973261</id>
    <notifications_enabled type="boolean">true</notifications_enabled>
  </source>
  <target>
    <following type="boolean">true</following>
    <screen_name>z_bill</screen_name>
    <followed_by type="boolean">true</followed_by>
    <id type="integer">17643038</id>
  </target>
</relationship>
```

Notification data is private, so the notification_enabled element is only returned if the source user is the authenticated user.

If the either user accounts doesn't exist or is disabled by Twitter you will receive an error message and a HTTP status code of 404.

Input

This method has four parameters.

- source_id: The numerical ID of the source user. Example: /friendships/show.xml?source_id=123&target_id=456
- source_screen_name: The screen name of the source user. Example: /friendships/show.xml?source_screen_name=bob&target_id=456
- target_id: The numerical ID of the target user. Example: /friendships/show.xml?target_id=456
- target_screen_name: The screen name of the target user. Example: /friendships/show.xml?target_screen_name=bob

You are required to provide a source user and a target user to compare. You can do that using either their user ID or screen name. If you are authenticated, you can omit specifying the source user and the method will assume you are using the authenticated user as the source.

Example

You can try the friendships/show method easily by typing http://api.twitter.com/1/friendships/show.xml?source_screen_name=dustyreagan&target_screen_name=z_bill into your browser's URL address bar.

Listing 7-24 includes an example of how you can use the `friendships/show` method to show if two users follow each other.

Listing 7-24: Check if Two Users Follow Each Other

```
<?php

// Set username and password
$username = 'username';
$password = 'password';

$source_user = 'dustyreagan';
$target_user = 'z_bill';

// The Twitter friendships/exists method
$url =
"https://api.twitter.com/1/friendships/show.xml?source_screen_name=$source_
              user&target_screen_name=$target_user";

// POST to Twitter API using curl
$curlHandle = curl_init();
curl_setopt($curlHandle, CURLOPT_URL, "$url");
curl_setopt($curlHandle, CURLOPT_USERAGENT, "Twitter App Development For
              Dummies: Example");
curl_setopt($curlHandle, CURLOPT_RETURNTRANSFER, 1);
curl_setopt($curlHandle, CURLOPT_SSL_VERIFYPEER, false);
curl_setopt($curlHandle, CURLOPT_USERPWD, "$username:$password");
$apiResponse = curl_exec($curlHandle);

// Get HTTP Status Code
$info = curl_getinfo($curlHandle);
$http_code = $info['http_code'];
echo "<h1>HTTP Status Code: $http_code</h1>";

// Close cURL connection
curl_close($curlHandle);

// Get XML
$xml = new DOMDocument();
$xml->loadXML($apiResponse);

// Check for an error tag.
$errors = $xml->getElementsByTagName("error");

// If found, print the error. Else, success!
if($errors->length > 0)
{
   $errorMessage = $errors->item(0)->nodeValue;
   echo "<h1>$errorMessage</h1>";
}
else
```

```
{
   $sourceNode = $xml->getElementsByTagName("source");
   $followingNode = $sourceNode->item(0)->getElementsByTagName("following");
   $sourceFollowsTarget = $followingNode->item(0)->nodeValue;

   // does the source user follow the target user?
   if($sourceFollowsTarget == "true")
      echo "<h1>@$source_user follows @$target_user</h1>";
   else
      echo "<h1>@$source_user does NOT follow @$target_user</h1>";

   $targetNode = $xml->getElementsByTagName("target");
   $followingNode = $targetNode->item(0)->getElementsByTagName("following");
   $targetFollowSource = $followingNode->item(0)->nodeValue;

   // does the target user follow the source user?
   if($targetFollowSource == "true")
      echo "<h1>@$target_user follows @$source_user</h1>";
   else
      echo "<h1>@$target_user does NOT follow @$source_user</h1>";
}

?>
```

Notification Methods

The term notification in the Twitter API means to receive a specific user's tweets to your phone via SMS. You can manage who you receive notifications for using these two methods:

- `notifications/follow`
- `notifications/leave`

Follow a user to your phone

You can follow a user to your phone via SMS by calling the `notifications/follow` method. To follow a user to your phone you must

- Authenticate
- Be following the user

If the user you want to receive notifications on has a protected account, you must have permissions to view their tweets.

This method requires a POST request and isn't rate limited.

Output

This method has two output formats:

- XML
- JSON

On a successful post, this method will return the user object of the person you followed. On a failed post, you will receive an error message explaining why the follow failed.

Input

The notifications/follow method requires only one of three parameters:

- `id`: The user's screen name or numerical user ID.
  Example: `/notifications/follow/bob.xml`
  Example: `/notifications/follow/12345.xml`
- `user_id`: The numerical ID of the user.
  Example: `/notifications/follow.xml?user_id=12345`
- `screen_name`: The screen name of the user.
  Example: `/notifications/follow.xml?screen_name=101010`

Avoid using the `id` parameter and use `user_id`, over `screen_name` if possible. The sidebar "Hard Knocks" explains why.

Example

Listing 7-25 shows you an example of how to receive notifications from a user by using curl to post to the `notifications/follow` method.

Listing 7-25: How to Programmatically Receive Notifications from a User

```
<?php

// Set username and password
$username = 'username';
$password = 'password';

$follow = 'dustyreagan';

// The Twitter notifications/follow method
$url = "https://api.twitter.com/1/notifications/follow.xml";

// POST to Twitter API using curl
$curlHandle = curl_init();
curl_setopt($curlHandle, CURLOPT_URL, "$url");
```

```
curl_setopt($curlHandle, CURLOPT_USERAGENT, "Twitter App Development For
               Dummies: Example");
curl_setopt($curlHandle, CURLOPT_POST, 1);
curl_setopt($curlHandle, CURLOPT_RETURNTRANSFER, 1);
curl_setopt($curlHandle, CURLOPT_SSL_VERIFYPEER, false);
curl_setopt($curlHandle, CURLOPT_POSTFIELDS, "screen_name=$follow");
curl_setopt($curlHandle, CURLOPT_USERPWD, "$username:$password");
$apiResponse = curl_exec($curlHandle);

// Get HTTP Status Code
$info = curl_getinfo($curlHandle);
$http_code = $info['http_code'];
echo "<h1>HTTP Status Code: $http_code</h1>";

// Close cURL connection
curl_close($curlHandle);

// Get XML
$xml = new DOMDocument();
$xml->loadXML($apiResponse);

// Check for an error tag.
$errors = $xml->getElementsByTagName("error");

// If found, print the error. Else, success!
if($errors->length > 0)
{
   $errorMessage = $errors->item(0)->nodeValue;
   echo "<h1>$errorMessage</h1>";
}
else
{
   $profileImageNode = $xml->getElementsByTagName("profile_image_url");
   $profile_image_url = $profileImageNode->item(0)->nodeValue;
   echo "<h1>Now receiving notifications for: <img src=\"$profile_image_url\"
               width=\"48\" height=\"48\" alt=\"$follow\" /></h1>";
}

?>
```

Stop receiving notifications

To stop receiving SMS notifications for a user, authenticate and call the `notifications/leave` method.

This method requires a POST request and isn't rate limited.

Output

This method has two output formats:

- XML
- JSON

On a successful POST, this method will return the user object of the person you turned off notification for. On a failed POST, you will receive an error message explaining why you were unable to turn off notifications for the user.

Input

The `notifications/leave` method requires only one of three parameters:

- `id`: The user's screen name or numerical user ID.
  Example: `/notifications/leave/bob.xml`
  Example: `/notifications/leave/12345.xml`
- `user_id`: The numerical ID of the user.
  Example: `/notifications/leave.xml?user_id=12345`
- `screen_name`: The screen name of the user.
  Example: `/notifications/leave.xml?screen_name=101010`

Avoid using the `id` parameter and use `user_id` over `screen_name` if possible. The sidebar "Hard Knocks" explains why.

Example

Listing 7-26 shows you an example of how to programmatically turn off notifications for a user using curl to post to the `notifications/leave` method.

Listing 7-26: How to Programmatically Turn Off SMS Notifications

```
<?php

// Set username and password
$username = 'username';
$password = 'password';

$leave = 'dustyreagan';

// The Twitter notifications/leave method
$url = "https://api.twitter.com/1/notifications/leave.xml";

// POST to Twitter API using curl
$curlHandle = curl_init();
curl_setopt($curlHandle, CURLOPT_URL, "$url");
curl_setopt($curlHandle, CURLOPT_USERAGENT, "Twitter App Development For
              Dummies: Example");
```

```
curl_setopt($curlHandle, CURLOPT_POST, 1);
curl_setopt($curlHandle, CURLOPT_RETURNTRANSFER, 1);
curl_setopt($curlHandle, CURLOPT_SSL_VERIFYPEER, false);
curl_setopt($curlHandle, CURLOPT_POSTFIELDS, "screen_name=$leave");
curl_setopt($curlHandle, CURLOPT_USERPWD, "$username:$password");
$apiResponse = curl_exec($curlHandle);

// Get HTTP Status Code
$info = curl_getinfo($curlHandle);
$http_code = $info['http_code'];
echo "<h1>HTTP Status Code: $http_code</h1>";

// Close cURL connection
curl_close($curlHandle);

// Get XML
$xml = new DOMDocument();
$xml->loadXML($apiResponse);

// Check for an error tag.
$errors = $xml->getElementsByTagName("error");

// If found, print the error. Else, success!
if($errors->length > 0)
{
   $errorMessage = $errors->item(0)->nodeValue;
   echo "<h1>$errorMessage</h1>";
}
else
{
   $profileImageNode = $xml->getElementsByTagName("profile_image_url");
   $profile_image_url = $profileImageNode->item(0)->nodeValue;
   echo "<h1>Turned off notifications for: <img src=\"$profile_image_url\"
            width=\"48\" height=\"48\" alt=\"$leave\" /></h1>";
}

?>
```

Block Methods

Blocking a user in Twitter prevents them from following you and vice versa. You can block, unblock, and view existing user blocks using the API's block methods. These methods include:

- `blocks/create`
- `blocks/destroy`

- blocks/exists
- blocks/blocking
- blocks/blocking/ids

Block a user

Blocking a user removes them from the people you follow (if you're following them), and prevents the user from following you. To block a user with the API use the `blocks/create` method. To block a user you must be authenticated as the blocker.

This method requires a POST request and isn't rate limited. However, you may only block an unspecified number of users per day. Twitter doesn't disclose how many.

Output

This method has two output formats:

- XML
- JSON

On a successful POST, this method will return the user object of the person you blocked. On a failed POST, you will receive an error message explaining why you were unable to block the user.

Input

The `blocks/create` method requires only one of three parameters:

- `id`: The user's screen name or numerical user ID.
  Example: `/blocks/create/bob.xml`
  Example: `/blocks/create/12345.xml`
- `user_id`: The numerical ID of the user.
  Example: `/blocks/create.xml?user_id=12345`
- `screen_name`: The screen name of the user.
  Example: `/blocks/create.xml?screen_name=101010`

Avoid using the `id` parameter and use `user_id` over `screen_name` if possible. The sidebar "Hard Knocks" explains why.

Example

Listing 7-27 shows you an example of how to programmatically block a new user by using curl to post to the `blocks/create` method.

Listing 7-27: How to Programmatically Block a User

```
<?php
// Set username and password
$username = 'username';
$password = 'password';

$block = 'examplespammer';

// The Twitter blocks/create method
$url = "https://api.twitter.com/1/blocks/create.xml";

// POST to Twitter API using curl
$curlHandle = curl_init();
curl_setopt($curlHandle, CURLOPT_URL, "$url");
curl_setopt($curlHandle, CURLOPT_USERAGENT, "Twitter App Development For
               Dummies: Example");
curl_setopt($curlHandle, CURLOPT_POST, 1);
curl_setopt($curlHandle, CURLOPT_RETURNTRANSFER, 1);
curl_setopt($curlHandle, CURLOPT_SSL_VERIFYPEER, false);
curl_setopt($curlHandle, CURLOPT_POSTFIELDS, "screen_name=$block");
curl_setopt($curlHandle, CURLOPT_USERPWD, "$username:$password");
$apiResponse = curl_exec($curlHandle);

// Get HTTP Status Code
$info = curl_getinfo($curlHandle);
$http_code = $info['http_code'];
echo "<h1>HTTP Status Code: $http_code</h1>";

// Close cURL connection
curl_close($curlHandle);

// Get XML
$xml = new DOMDocument();
$xml->loadXML($apiResponse);

// Check for an error tag.
$errors = $xml->getElementsByTagName("error");

// If found, print the error. Else, success!
if($errors->length > 0)
{
   $errorMessage = $errors->item(0)->nodeValue;
   echo "<h1>$errorMessage</h1>";
}
else
{
   $profileImageNode = $xml->getElementsByTagName("profile_image_url");
   $profile_image_url = $profileImageNode->item(0)->nodeValue;
   echo "<h1>Blocked: <img src=\"$profile_image_url\" width=\"48\" height=\"48\"
               alt=\"$block\" /></h1>";
}

?>
```

Unblock a user

To unblock a user you previously blocked, use the `blocks/destroy` method. This method requires you authenticate as the user who's doing the unblocking and post the ID of the person you want to unblock to the `blocks/destroy` method.

This method requires a POST or DELETE request and isn't rate limited. However, you may only unblock an unspecified number of users per day. Twitter doesn't disclose how many.

Output

This method has two output formats:

- XML
- JSON

On a successful post, this method will return the user object of the person you unblocked. On a failed post, you will receive an error message explaining why you were unable to unblock the user.

Input

The `blocks/destroy` method requires only one of three parameters:

- `id`: The user's screen name or numerical user ID.
  Example: `/blocks/destroy/bob.xml`
  Example: `/blocks/destroy/12345.xml`
- `user_id`: The numerical ID of the user.
  Example: `/blocks/destroy.xml?user_id=12345`
- `screen_name`: The screen name of the user.
  Example: `/blocks/destroy.xml?screen_name=101010`

Avoid using the `id` parameter and use `user_id` over `screen_name` if possible. The sidebar "Hard Knocks" explains why.

Example

Listing 7-28 shows you an example of how to programmatically unfollow a new user by using curl to post to the `blocks/destroy` method.

Listing 7-28: How to Programmatically Unblock a User

```
<?php

// Set username and password
$username = 'username';
```

```
$password = 'password';

$block = 'examplespammer';

// The Twitter blocks/create method
$url = "https://api.twitter.com/1/blocks/destroy.xml";

// POST to Twitter API using curl
$curlHandle = curl_init();
curl_setopt($curlHandle, CURLOPT_URL, "$url");
curl_setopt($curlHandle, CURLOPT_USERAGENT, "Twitter App Development For
              Dummies: Example");
curl_setopt($curlHandle, CURLOPT_POST, 1);
curl_setopt($curlHandle, CURLOPT_RETURNTRANSFER, 1);
curl_setopt($curlHandle, CURLOPT_SSL_VERIFYPEER, false);
curl_setopt($curlHandle, CURLOPT_POSTFIELDS, "screen_name=$block");
curl_setopt($curlHandle, CURLOPT_USERPWD, "$username:$password");
$apiResponse = curl_exec($curlHandle);

// Get HTTP Status Code
$info = curl_getinfo($curlHandle);
$http_code = $info['http_code'];
echo "<h1>HTTP Status Code: $http_code</h1>";

// Close cURL connection
curl_close($curlHandle);

// Get XML
$xml = new DOMDocument();
$xml->loadXML($apiResponse);

// Check for an error tag.
$errors = $xml->getElementsByTagName("error");

// If found, print the error. Else, success!
if($errors->length > 0)
{
   $errorMessage = $errors->item(0)->nodeValue;
   echo "<h1>$errorMessage</h1>";
}
else
{
   $profileImageNode = $xml->getElementsByTagName("profile_image_url");
   $profile_image_url = $profileImageNode->item(0)->nodeValue;
   echo "<h1>Unblocked: <img src=\"$profile_image_url\" width=\"48\"
              height=\"48\" alt=\"$block\" /></h1>";
}

?>
```

Check if a user is blocked

You can test to see if the authenticating user is blocking another user by using the `blocks/exists` method.

This method requires a GET request and is rate limited. The sidebar "Hard Knocks" explains the concern with rate limits.

Output

This method has two output formats:

- XML
- JSON

If a user is blocked, you will receive the complete user object for the blocked user. If the user isn't blocked, or doesn't exist, you will receive an error message similar to Listing 7-29 and an HTTP status code of 404.

Listing 7-29: User Is Not Blocked Message

```
<?xml version="1.0" encoding="UTF-8"?>
<hash>
   <request>/blocks/exists.xml?user_id=z_bill</request>
   <error>You are not blocking this user.</error>
</hash>
```

Input

This method requires only one of three parameters:

- `id`: The user's screen name or numerical user ID.
  Example: `/blocks/exists /bob.xml`
- `user_id`: The numerical ID of the user.
  Example: `/blocks/exists.xml?user_id=12345`
- `screen_name`: The screen name of the user.
  Example: `/blocks/exists.xml?screen_name=101010`

Avoid using the `id` parameter and use `user_id`, over `screen_name` if possible. The sidebar "Hard Knocks" explains why.

Example

You can try the `blocks/exists` method easily by typing `http://api.twitter.com/1/blocks/exists.xml?screen_name=dustyreagan` into your browser's URL address bar.

You can see an example of how to use the `blocks/exists` method to programmatically test if a user is blocked in Listing 7-30.

Listing 7-30: Check if a User Is Blocked

```
<?php

// Set username and password
$username = 'username';
$password = 'password';

$testForBlock = 'examplespammer';

// The Twitter blocks/exists method
$url = "https://api.twitter.com/1/blocks/exists.xml?screen_name=$testForBlock";

// POST to Twitter API using curl
$curlHandle = curl_init();
curl_setopt($curlHandle, CURLOPT_URL, "$url");
curl_setopt($curlHandle, CURLOPT_USERAGENT, "Twitter App Development For
               Dummies: Example");
curl_setopt($curlHandle, CURLOPT_RETURNTRANSFER, 1);
curl_setopt($curlHandle, CURLOPT_SSL_VERIFYPEER, false);
curl_setopt($curlHandle, CURLOPT_USERPWD, "$username:$password");
$apiResponse = curl_exec($curlHandle);

// Get HTTP Status Code
$info = curl_getinfo($curlHandle);
$http_code = $info['http_code'];
echo "<h1>HTTP Status Code: $http_code</h1>";

// Close cURL connection
curl_close($curlHandle);

// Get XML
$xml = new DOMDocument();
$xml->loadXML($apiResponse);

// Check for an error tag.
$errors = $xml->getElementsByTagName("error");

// If found, print the error. Else, success!
if($errors->length > 0)
{
   $errorMessage = $errors->item(0)->nodeValue;
   if($errorMessage == "You are not blocking this user.")
      echo "<h1>$testForBlock is NOT blocked</h1>";
   else
      echo "<h1>$errorMessage</h1>";
}
```

(continued)

Listing 7-30 *(continued)*

```
else
{
   $profileImageNode = $xml->getElementsByTagName("profile_image_url");
   $profile_image_url = $profileImageNode->item(0)->nodeValue;
   echo "<h1>User is blocked: <img src=\"$profile_image_url\" width=\"48\"
            height=\"48\" alt=\"$testForBlock\" /></h1>";
}

?>
```

Get a user details list of blocked users

You can retrieve a list of user detail objects for all the users the authenticated user has blocked with the `details/blocking` method.

This method requires a GET request and is rate limited. The sidebar "Hard Knocks" explains the concern with rate limits.

Output

This method has two output formats:

- XML
- JSON

On a successful call this method returns a list of user objects with a documented maximum of 20 users returned per call. However, at the time of this writing all blocked user objects are returned at once.

If the method call fails it returns an error message and a HTTP status code of 404.

Input

This method has no required parameters, but has an optional page parameter to retrieve more than the maximum number of user objects per page.

- `page`: Page to retrieve older blocked user details. Example: `/blocks/blocking.xml?page=5`

The page parameter may eventually be replaced with the cursor parameter as seen in the statuses/friends, statuses/followers, followers/ids, and friends/ids methods. However, at the time of this writing, the page parameter is still the appropriate way to retrieve additional results for the `blocks/blocking` method.

Example

You can try the `blocks/blocking` method easily by typing `http://api.twitter.com/1/blocks/blocking.xml` into your browser's URL address bar.

The code example in Listing 7-31 displays the profile pictures of users blocked by the authenticated account.

Listing 7-31: Displays Blocked Users

```
<?php

// Set username and password
$username = 'username';
$password = 'password';

// The Twitter blocks/blocking/ids method
$url = "https://api.twitter.com/1/blocks/blocking.xml";

// POST to Twitter API using curl
$curlHandle = curl_init();
curl_setopt($curlHandle, CURLOPT_URL, "$url");
curl_setopt($curlHandle, CURLOPT_USERAGENT, "Twitter App Development For
            Dummies: Example");
curl_setopt($curlHandle, CURLOPT_RETURNTRANSFER, 1);
curl_setopt($curlHandle, CURLOPT_SSL_VERIFYPEER, false);
curl_setopt($curlHandle, CURLOPT_USERPWD, "$username:$password");
$apiResponse = curl_exec($curlHandle);

// Get HTTP Status Code
$info = curl_getinfo($curlHandle);
$http_code = $info['http_code'];
echo "<h1>HTTP Status Code: $http_code</h1>";

// Close cURL connection
curl_close($curlHandle);

// Get XML
$xml = new DOMDocument();
$xml->loadXML($apiResponse);

// Check for an error tag.
$errors = $xml->getElementsByTagName("error");

// If found, print the error. Else, success!
if($errors->length > 0)
{
   $errorMessage = $errors->item(0)->nodeValue;
   echo "<h1>$errorMessage</h1>";
}
```

(continued)

Listing 7-31 *(continued)*

```
else
{
   $screenNameNodes = $xml->getElementsByTagName("screen_name");

   echo "<p>You have blocked " . $screenNameNodes->length . " users.</p>";
   foreach($screenNameNodes as $screenNameNode)
   {
      $screenName = $screenNameNode->nodeValue;
      echo "<a href=\"http://api.twitter.com/1/users/show.xml?screen_
               name=$screenName\">$screenName</a><br />";
   }
}

?>
```

Retrieve a list of blocked users IDs

The `blocks/blocking` method is great for retrieving detailed blocked user records, but if you don't need that detailed user data, you can retrieve a list of only the user IDs of your blocked users with the `blocks/blocking/ids` method.

This method requires authentication, a GET request, and is rate limited. The sidebar "Hard Knocks" explains the concern with rate limits.

Output

This method has two output formats:

- XML
- JSON

A successful method call returns a list of all the blocked user IDs. A failed call returns an error message and a HTTP status code of 404.

Input

This method has no input parameters. It uses the authenticated user as the source.

Example

You can try the `blocks/blocking/id` method easily by typing `http://api.twitter.com/1/ /blocks/blocking/ids.xml` into your browser's URL address bar. When requested by your browser, enter your Twitter user name and password. Then you receive the IDs of your blocked users in XML format.

The `blocks/blocking/id` method is to be used in conjunction with a local cache of detailed user data. For example, if you keep a database of user details, you can use the `blocks/blocking/id` method to get a list of blocked users, then lookup the details for those users in your database based on the user ID.

In Listing 7-32 is an example of how to count the amount of users you have blocked, and return a list a blocked user IDs that link to the user details XML.

Listing 7-32: Get a Count and List of Blocked User IDs

```
<?php

// Set username and password
$username = 'username';
$password = 'password';

// The Twitter blocks/blocking/ids method
$url = "https://api.twitter.com/1/blocks/blocking/ids.xml";

// POST to Twitter API using curl
$curlHandle = curl_init();
curl_setopt($curlHandle, CURLOPT_URL, "$url");
curl_setopt($curlHandle, CURLOPT_USERAGENT, "Twitter App Development For
              Dummies: Example");
curl_setopt($curlHandle, CURLOPT_RETURNTRANSFER, 1);
curl_setopt($curlHandle, CURLOPT_SSL_VERIFYPEER, false);
curl_setopt($curlHandle, CURLOPT_USERPWD, "$username:$password");
$apiResponse = curl_exec($curlHandle);

// Get HTTP Status Code
$info = curl_getinfo($curlHandle);
$http_code = $info['http_code'];
echo "<h1>HTTP Status Code: $http_code</h1>";

// Close cURL connection
curl_close($curlHandle);

// Get XML
$xml = new DOMDocument();
$xml->loadXML($apiResponse);

// Check for an error tag.
$errors = $xml->getElementsByTagName("error");

// If found, print the error. Else, success!
if($errors->length > 0)
{
   $errorMessage = $errors->item(0)->nodeValue;
   echo "<h1>$errorMessage</h1>";
```

(continued)

Listing 7-32 *(continued)*

```
}
else
{
   $idNodes = $xml->getElementsByTagName("id");

   echo "<p>You have blocked " . $idNodes->length . " users.</p>";
   foreach($idNodes as $idNode)
   {
      $id = $idNode->nodeValue;
      echo "<a href=\"http://api.twitter.com/1/users/show.xml?user_id=$id\">$id</
              a><br />";
   }
}

?>
```

Spam Reporting Method

Reporting a user as spam blocks them from your account and sends a message to Twitter alerting them to investigate the account for spam activities. To mark a user as spam with the API you need one method:

- `report_spam`

How to report a Twitter account as spam

This method requires a POST request and isn't rate limited. However, you may only mark an unspecified number of users as spam per hour. Twitter doesn't disclose how many.

Output

This method has two output formats:

- XML
- JSON

On a successful POST, this method will return the user object of the person you marked as spam. On a failed POST, you will receive an error message explaining why you were unable to mark the user as spam.

Input

The report_spam method requires only one of three parameters:

- id: The user's screen name or numerical user ID.
  Example: /report_spam/bob.xml
  Example: /report_spam/12345.xml
- user_id: The numerical ID of the user.
  Example: /report_spam.xml?user_id=12345
- screen_name: The screen name of the user.
  Example: /report_spam.xml?screen_name=101010

Avoid using the id parameter and use user_id, over screen_name if possible. The sidebar "Hard Knocks" explains why.

Example

Listing 7-33 shows you an example of how to programmatically block a new user by using curl to post to the report_spam method.

Listing 7-33: How to Programmatically Mark a User as Spam

```
<?php

// Set username and password
$username = 'username';
$password = 'password';

$spammer = 'examplespammer';

// The Twitter report_spam method
$url = "https://api.twitter.com/1/report_spam.xml";

// POST to Twitter API using curl
$curlHandle = curl_init();
curl_setopt($curlHandle, CURLOPT_URL, "$url");
curl_setopt($curlHandle, CURLOPT_USERAGENT, "Twitter App Development For
            Dummies: Example");
curl_setopt($curlHandle, CURLOPT_POST, 1);
curl_setopt($curlHandle, CURLOPT_RETURNTRANSFER, 1);
curl_setopt($curlHandle, CURLOPT_SSL_VERIFYPEER, false);
curl_setopt($curlHandle, CURLOPT_POSTFIELDS, "screen_name=$spammer");
curl_setopt($curlHandle, CURLOPT_USERPWD, "$username:$password");
$apiResponse = curl_exec($curlHandle);

// Get HTTP Status Code
$info = curl_getinfo($curlHandle);
$http_code = $info['http_code'];
echo "<h1>HTTP Status Code: $http_code</h1>";
```

(continued)

Listing 7-33 *(continued)*

```
// Close cURL connection
curl_close($curlHandle);

// Get XML
$xml = new DOMDocument();
$xml->loadXML($apiResponse);

// Check for an error tag.
$errors = $xml->getElementsByTagName("error");

// If found, print the error. Else, success!
if($errors->length > 0)
{
   $errorMessage = $errors->item(0)->nodeValue;
   echo "<h1>$errorMessage</h1>";
}
else
{
   $profileImageNode = $xml->getElementsByTagName("profile_image_url");
   $profile_image_url = $profileImageNode->item(0)->nodeValue;
   echo "<h1>Marked as spam: <img src=\"$profile_image_url\" width=\"48\"
            height=\"48\" alt=\"$spammer\" /></h1>";
}

?>
```

Chapter 8

Communication Through Tweets

In This Chapter

- Working with API communication methods
- Update your Twitter status
- Manage a user's timeline
- More working examples of the API in PHP

This chapter covers API methods that allow users to communicate over Twitter. Communicating over Twitter involves consuming and creating tweets. Some ways you can work with tweets are by:

- Updating your status
- Sending a direct message
- Favoriting a tweet
- Searching for tweets

Status Methods

Status methods are methods that deal directly with tweets. They are used to create, delete, get details on, and retweet a tweet. There are six status methods, including:

- `statuses/show`
- `statuses/update`
- `statuses/destroy`
- `statuses/retweet`
- `statuses/retweets`

Get the details of a specific tweet

You can get the complete details of a tweet and the user who wrote it with the `statuses/show` method.

This method doesn't require authentication, but to get the details of a protected Twitter account, you must

- Authenticate your API call.
- Have permission to view the protected account.

This method requires a GET request and is rate limited. Chapter 7 explains the concern with rate limits.

Output

This method has two output formats:

- XML
- JSON

On a successful method call, it returns the complete status object, which contains the complete user object of the author.

If the tweet doesn't exist you will receive an error message and a HTTP status code of 404.

Input

This method requires one parameter, the id of the tweet.

- `id`: The numerical id of the status update.
  Example: `/statuses/show/1234.xml`

Example

You can try the `statuses/show` method easily by typing `http://api.twitter.com/1/statuses/show/20.xml` into your browser's URL address bar.

In Listing 8-1, I use the statuses/show method to pull the details of Twitter's first tweet and I display the author's picture with provided data.

Listing 8-1: Example of How to Get a Tweet's Details

```
<?php

// Set username and password
```

```
$username = 'username';
$password = 'password';

// The Twitter statuses/show method
$url = "https://api.twitter.com/1/statuses/show/20.xml";

// POST to Twitter API using curl
$curlHandle = curl_init();
curl_setopt($curlHandle, CURLOPT_URL, "$url");
curl_setopt($curlHandle, CURLOPT_USERAGENT, "Twitter App Development For
             Dummies: Example");
curl_setopt($curlHandle, CURLOPT_RETURNTRANSFER, 1);
curl_setopt($curlHandle, CURLOPT_SSL_VERIFYPEER, false);
curl_setopt($curlHandle, CURLOPT_USERPWD, "$username:$password");
$apiResponse = curl_exec($curlHandle);

// Get HTTP Status Code
$info = curl_getinfo($curlHandle);
$http_code = $info['http_code'];
echo "<h1>HTTP Status Code: $http_code</h1>";

// Close cURL connection
curl_close($curlHandle);

// Get XML
$xml = new DOMDocument();
$xml->loadXML($apiResponse);

// Check for an error tag.
$errors = $xml->getElementsByTagName("error");

// If found, print the error. Else, success!
if($errors->length > 0)
{
   $errorMessage = $errors->item(0)->nodeValue;
   echo "<h1>$errorMessage</h1>";
}
else
{
   // Get tweet text
   $textNode = $xml->getElementsByTagName("text");
   $text = $textNode->item(0)->nodeValue;

   // Get author's profile picture
   $profilePicNode = $xml->getElementsByTagName("profile_image_url");
   $profile_image_url = $profilePicNode->item(0)->nodeValue;

   // Print tweet and user's picture
   echo "<img src=\"$profile_image_url\" width=\"48\" height=\"48\" />";
   echo "<p>$text</p>";
}

?>
```

Create a new tweet

To post a new status update, authenticate as the author and post the tweet to the `statuses/update` method.

This method requires a GET request and isn't rate limited. However, there is an unspecified limit to the amount of status updates a user may tweet per day. If this limit is reached a 403 HTTP status error is returned.

Output

This method has two output formats:

- XML
- JSON

On a successful method call, it returns the complete status object, which contains the complete user object of the author. On a failed post attempt, this method returns an error message.

Input

This method requires one parameter, the id of the tweet.

- `status`: The contents of the tweet. Anything over 140 characters is truncated.
  Example: `status=Hello`
- `in_reply_to_status_id`: The id of a tweet that is being replied to. The new tweet reply must contain the username of the author of the original tweet, or this parameter is ignored.
  Example: `in_reply_to_status_id=1234`

At the time of this writing, Twitter was working on adding geolocation to individual status updates. They included two parameters on the `statuses/update` method to facilitate geolocation, but they weren't yet functional. These two parameters are

- `lat`: The geographical latitude of the tweet. Must be a valid latitude value between -90.0 and +90.0, the long parameter must be valid, and the user mustn't have `geo_enabled` disabled, otherwise this parameter is ignored.
  Example: lat=30.4
- `long`: The geographical longitude of the tweet. Must be a valid longitude value between -180.0 and +180.0, the lat parameter must be valid, and the user mustn't have `geo_enabled` disabled, otherwise this parameter is ignored.
  Example: long=-90.1

Example

In Listing 8-2, I programmatically send a status update to the authenticated user's Twitter account.

Listing 8-2: Use the API to Post a Tweet

```
<?php

// Set username and password
$username = 'username';
$password = 'password';

$status = urlencode("Testing Twitter's API. #TADD");

// The Twitter statuses/update method
$url = "https://api.twitter.com/1/statuses/update.xml";

// POST to Twitter API using curl
$curlHandle = curl_init();
curl_setopt($curlHandle, CURLOPT_URL, "$url");
curl_setopt($curlHandle, CURLOPT_USERAGENT, "Twitter App Development For
              Dummies: Example");
curl_setopt($curlHandle, CURLOPT_POST, 1);
curl_setopt($curlHandle, CURLOPT_RETURNTRANSFER, 1);
curl_setopt($curlHandle, CURLOPT_SSL_VERIFYPEER, false);
curl_setopt($curlHandle, CURLOPT_POSTFIELDS, "status=$status");
curl_setopt($curlHandle, CURLOPT_USERPWD, "$username:$password");
$apiResponse = curl_exec($curlHandle);

// Get HTTP Status Code
$info = curl_getinfo($curlHandle);
$http_code = $info['http_code'];
echo "<h1>HTTP Status Code: $http_code</h1>";

// Close cURL connection
curl_close($curlHandle);

// Get XML
$xml = new DOMDocument();
$xml->loadXML($apiResponse);

// Check for an error tag.
$errors = $xml->getElementsByTagName("error");

// If found, print the error. Else, success!
if($errors->length > 0)
{
   $errorMessage = $errors->item(0)->nodeValue;
   echo "<h1>$errorMessage</h1>";
}
else
```

(continued)

Listing 8-2 *(continued)*

```
{
    // Get the text from the new tweet
    $textNode = $xml->getElementsByTagName("text");
    $text = $textNode->item(0)->nodeValue;

    // Get author's profile picture
    $userNode = $xml->getElementsByTagName("user");
    $profilePicNode = $userNode->item(0)->getElementsByTagName("profile_image_
            url");
    $profile_image_url = $profilePicNode->item(0)->nodeValue;

    // Print tweet's text and user's picture
    echo "<h1>Successfully posted the following tweet:</h1>";
    echo "<img src=\"$profile_image_url\" width=\"48\" height=\"48\" />";
    echo "<p>$text</p>";
}

?>
```

Delete a tweet

To delete a status update, authenticate as the author of the tweet and pass the tweet's id to the `statuses/destroy` method.

This method requires a POST or DELETE request and isn't rate limited.

Output

This method has two output formats:

- XML
- JSON

On a successful post, this method will return the details of the tweet you just delete, including the complete user details object of the author.

On a failed post, you will receive an error message explaining why you were unable to delete the tweet.

Input

This method requires one parameter, the id of the tweet you want to delete.

- `id`: The numerical id of the status update.
  Example: `/statuses/destroy/1234.xml`

Example

Listing 8-3 is an example of how to programmatically delete a tweet by using curl to post to the `statuses/destroy` method. If a tweet is successfully deleted, it displays the text of the recently deleted tweet and the profile picture of the author.

Listing 8-3: How to Programmatically Delete a Tweet

```
<?php

// Set username and password
$username = 'username';
$password = 'password';

$tweetIdToDelete = 5348310879;

// The Twitter statuses/destroy method
$url = "http://api.twitter.com/1/statuses/destroy/$tweetIdToDelete.xml";

// POST to Twitter API using curl
$curlHandle = curl_init();
curl_setopt($curlHandle, CURLOPT_URL, "$url");
curl_setopt($curlHandle, CURLOPT_USERAGENT, "Twitter App Development For
                Dummies: Example");
curl_setopt($curlHandle, CURLOPT_POST, 1);
curl_setopt($curlHandle, CURLOPT_RETURNTRANSFER, 1);
curl_setopt($curlHandle, CURLOPT_SSL_VERIFYPEER, false);
curl_setopt($curlHandle, CURLOPT_POSTFIELDS, "");
curl_setopt($curlHandle, CURLOPT_USERPWD, "$username:$password");
$apiResponse = curl_exec($curlHandle);

// Get HTTP Status Code
$info = curl_getinfo($curlHandle);
$http_code = $info['http_code'];
echo "<h1>HTTP Status Code: $http_code</h1>";

// Close cURL connection
curl_close($curlHandle);

// Get XML
$xml = new DOMDocument();
$xml->loadXML($apiResponse);

// Check for an error tag.
$errors = $xml->getElementsByTagName("error");

// If found, print the error. Else, success!
if($errors->length > 0)
{
```

(continued)

Listing 8-3 *(continued)*

```
    $errorMessage = $errors->item(0)->nodeValue;
    echo "<h1>$errorMessage</h1>";
}
else
{
    // Get delete tweet text
    $textNode = $xml->getElementsByTagName("text");
    $text = $textNode->item(0)->nodeValue;

    // Get author's profile picture
    $profilePicNode = $xml->getElementsByTagName("profile_image_url");
    $profile_image_url = $profilePicNode->item(0)->nodeValue;

    // Print tweet and user's picture
    echo "<h1>Successfully deleted the following tweet:</h1>";
    echo "<img src=\"$profile_image_url\" width=\"48\" height=\"48\" />";
    echo "<p>$text</p>";
}
?>
```

Retweet a tweet

To retweet a tweet, authenticate and use the `statuses/retweet` method.

This method requires a POST or PUT request and isn't rate limited.

Output

This method has two output formats:

- XML
- JSON

On a successful post, this method will return the original tweet and retweet details, including the complete user details object of the author and the authenticated user.

On a failed post, you receive an error message explaining why you were unable to retweet. An HTTP 403 is returned if you hit an update limit.

Twitter ignores duplicate retweets and attempts to retweet your own tweets.

Input

This method requires one parameter, the id of the tweet you want to delete.

- `id`: The numerical id of the status update.
  Example: `/statuses/retweet/1234.xml`

Example

Listing 8-4 is an example of how to retweet a tweet by using curl to post to the `statuses/retweet` method. If a tweet is successfully retweeted, it displays the text tweet and the profile picture of the author.

Listing 8-4 How to Retweet a Tweet with the API

```
<?php

// Set username and password
$username = 'dustytest2';
$password = 'password77';

// The Twitter status id
$tweetId = 5608180464;

// The Twitter statuses/retweet method
$url = "https://api.twitter.com/1/statuses/retweet/$tweetId.xml";

// POST to Twitter API using curl
$curlHandle = curl_init();
curl_setopt($curlHandle, CURLOPT_URL, "$url");
curl_setopt($curlHandle, CURLOPT_USERAGENT, "Twitter App Development For
            Dummies: Example");
curl_setopt($curlHandle, CURLOPT_POST, 1);
curl_setopt($curlHandle, CURLOPT_RETURNTRANSFER, 1);
curl_setopt($curlHandle, CURLOPT_SSL_VERIFYPEER, false);
curl_setopt($curlHandle, CURLOPT_USERPWD, "$username:$password");
$apiResponse = curl_exec($curlHandle);

// Get HTTP Status Code
$info = curl_getinfo($curlHandle);
$http_code = $info['http_code'];
echo "<h1>HTTP Status Code: $http_code</h1>";

// Close cURL connection
curl_close($curlHandle);

// Get XML
$xml = new DOMDocument();
$xml->loadXML($apiResponse);

// Check for an error tag.
$errors = $xml->getElementsByTagName("error");

// If found, print the error. Else, success!
if($errors->length > 0)
{
   $errorMessage = $errors->item(0)->nodeValue;
   echo "<h1>$errorMessage</h1>";
}
```

(continued)

Listing 8-4 *(continued)*

```
else
{
   // Get the text from the new tweet
   $textNode = $xml->getElementsByTagName("text");
   $text = $textNode->item(0)->nodeValue;

   // Get author's profile picture
   $userNode = $xml->getElementsByTagName("user");
   $profilePicNode = $userNode->item(0)->getElementsByTagName("profile_image_
            url");
   $profile_image_url = $profilePicNode->item(0)->nodeValue;

   // Print tweet's text and user's picture
   echo "<h1>Successfully retweeted the following tweet:</h1>";
   echo "<img src=\"$profile_image_url\" width=\"48\" height=\"48\" />";
   echo "<p>$text</p>";
}

?>
```

Retrieve retweets of a particular tweet

You can retrieve a list of retweets of a specific tweet by using the `statuses/retweets` method.

This method requires authentication, a GET request, and is rate limited.

Output

This method has two output formats:

- XML
- JSON

On a successful call, this method returns a list of the 20 most recent retweets of a tweet. This list includes the complete status object for the original tweet and the retweet, which contains the complete user object of the original author and the retweeter. A failed call returns an error message.

Input

This method has two parameters:

- `id`: The numerical id of the original tweet.
  Example: `/statuses/retweet/1234.xml`
- `count`: Limits the results per page to an amount specified that is less than 100.
  Example: `/statuses/retweet/1234.xml?count=100`

You can try the `statuses/retweets` method easily by typing `http://api.twitter.com/1/statuses/retweets/5608180464.xml` into your browser's URL address bar. When requested by your browser, enter your Twitter user name and password. Then you receive the requested tweets last 20 retweets.

In Listing 8-5, I use the `statuses/retweets` method to retrieve the profile pictures and retweet text of the users who retweeted a specific tweet.

Example

Listing 8-5: Page Through All of Your Favorites and Print Them

```
<?php

// Set username and password
$username = 'dustytest2';
$password = 'password77';

// The Twitter statuses/friends method
$url = "http://api.twitter.com/1/statuses/retweets/5466220198.xml";

// Get API results using curl
$curlHandle = curl_init();
curl_setopt($curlHandle, CURLOPT_URL, "$url");
curl_setopt($curlHandle, CURLOPT_USERAGENT, "Twitter App Development For
            Dummies: Example");
curl_setopt($curlHandle, CURLOPT_RETURNTRANSFER, 1);
curl_setopt($curlHandle, CURLOPT_SSL_VERIFYPEER, false);
curl_setopt($curlHandle, CURLOPT_USERPWD, "$username:$password");
$apiResponse = curl_exec($curlHandle);
curl_close($curlHandle);

// Get XML
$xml = new DOMDocument();
$xml->loadXML($apiResponse);

// Check for an error tag.
$errors = $xml->getElementsByTagName("error");
```

(continued)

Listing 8-5 *(continued)*

```
// If found, print the error and break. Else, keep going!
if($errors->length > 0)
{
   $errorMessage = $errors->item(0)->nodeValue;
   echo "<h1>$errorMessage</h1>";
   break;
}
else
{
   // Get favorited tweets
   $statusNodes = $xml->getElementsByTagName("status");

   foreach($statusNodes as $statusNode)
   {
      // Get the tweet text
      $textNode = $statusNode->getElementsByTagName("text");
      $text = $textNode->item(0)->nodeValue;

      // Get the author's picture
      $profilePicNodes = $statusNode->getElementsByTagName("profile_image_url");
      $profile_image_url = $profilePicNodes->item(1)->nodeValue;

      echo "<img style=\"float:left\" src=\"$profile_image_url\" width=\"48\"
               height=\"48\" />";
      echo "<p>$text</p>";
      echo "<hr style=\"clear:both\" />";
   }
}

?>
```

Direct Messages Methods

Direct Messages (DMs) are private tweets that users can send to other Twitter users that are following them. Using the API Direct Messages methods you can view these DMs, send them, and delete them. There are four Direct Messages methods including:

- direct_messages
- direct_messages/sent
- direct_messages/new
- direct_messages/destroy

Retrieve direct messages

You can get a list of your most recently sent and received direct messages by authenticating and calling either:

- `direct_messages`: Received direct messages.
- `direct_messages/sent`: Sent direct messages.

Both of these methods require a GET request and are rate limited.

Output

These methods have four output formats:

- XML
- JSON
- RSS
- Atom

On a successful method call these methods return an array of detailed direct message objects that include the user details object for the sender and receiver of the message. By default these methods return the 20 most recent direct messages.

If the authenticated user has no direct messages, this method returns an empty array and a HTTP status of 200.

Input

These methods have four optional input parameters:

- `since_id`: The numerical id of direct message. Use to return direct messages that are more recent than the id specified.
  Example: `/direct_messages.xml?since_id=12345`
- `max_id`: The numerical id of a direct message. Use to return direct messages that are older than the id specified.
  Example: `/direct_messages.xml?max_id=54321`
- `count`: Limits the results per page to an amount specified that is less than 200.
  Example: `/direct_messages.xml?count=100`
- `page`: Page backwards to retrieve older direct messages.
  Example: `/direct_messages.xml?page=5`

Example

You can try the direct_messages method easily by typing http://api.twitter.com/1/direct_messages.xml into your browser's URL address bar. When requested by your browser, enter your Twitter user name and password. Then you receive your last 20 received direct messages in XML format. To try the direct_messages/sent method, type this URL in your browser's address bar: http://api.twitter.com/1/direct_messages/sent.xml.

In Listing 8-5, I retrieve more than the default 20 most recently received direct messages by setting the count parameter to the maximum 200 results per page, then I incrementally increase the page parameter until the direct_messages method returns no more results.

You can use this same example code found in Listing 8-6 to test the direct_messages/sent method. Simply update the $url variable in the example code to point to the direct_messages/sent method, like this:

```
$url = "http://api.twitter.com/1/direct_messages/sent.xml?count=200&page=$page";
```

Twitter will only let you go back about 4 pages with a count parameter of 200 until it stops returning data. To get older direct messages, you can use the max_id parameter. However, even the max_id parameter has an undocumented limit to how far in time it will go back.

If you have all the user's previously received direct messages, the next time you collect direct messages for the user, use the since_id parameter to save API calls.

Listing 8-6: Get Old Received Direct Messages Using Paging

```
<?php
function getDirectMessagesPage($page)
{
   // Set username and password
   $username = 'username';
   $password = 'password';

   // The Twitter direct_messages method
   $url = "https://api.twitter.com/1/direct_messages.xml?count=200&page=$page";

   // Get API results using curl
   $curlHandle = curl_init();
   curl_setopt($curlHandle, CURLOPT_URL, "$url");
   curl_setopt($curlHandle, CURLOPT_USERAGENT, "Twitter App Development For
            Dummies: Example");
   curl_setopt($curlHandle, CURLOPT_RETURNTRANSFER, 1);
   curl_setopt($curlHandle, CURLOPT_SSL_VERIFYPEER, false);
   curl_setopt($curlHandle, CURLOPT_USERPWD, "$username:$password");
   $apiResponse = curl_exec($curlHandle);
```

```
    // Get HTTP Code
    $info = curl_getinfo($curlHandle);
    $http_code = $info['http_code'];
    echo "<h1>HTTP Status Code: $http_code</h1>";

    // Close cURL connection
    curl_close($curlHandle);

    return $apiResponse;
}

$page = 1;
do
{
    echo "<h1>Page: $page</h1>";
    // Get a page of direct messages
    $apiResponse = getDirectMessagesPage($page);

    // Get XML
    $xml = new DOMDocument();
    $xml->loadXML($apiResponse);

    // Check for an error tag.
    $errors = $xml->getElementsByTagName("error");

    // If found, print the error and break. Else, keep going!
    if($errors->length > 0)
    {
        $errorMessage = $errors->item(0)->nodeValue;
        echo "<h1>$errorMessage</h1>";
        break;
    }
    else
    {
        // Get direct messages
        $dmNodes = $xml->getElementsByTagName("direct_message");

        foreach($dmNodes as $dm)
        {
            // Get the tweet text
            $textNode = $dm->getElementsByTagName("text");
            $text = $textNode->item(0)->nodeValue;

            // Get the author's picture
            $senderNode = $dm->getElementsByTagName("sender");
            $profilePicNode = $senderNode->item(0)->getElementsByTagName("profile_
                image_url");
            $profile_image_url = $profilePicNode->item(0)->nodeValue;

            echo "<img style=\"float:left\" src=\"$profile_image_url\" width=\"48\"
                height=\"48\" />";
```

(continued)

Listing 8-6 *(continued)*

```
            echo "<p>$text</p>";
            echo "<hr style=\"clear:both\" />";
        }
    }

    // increment page count and loop
    $page++;
}
while($dmNodes->length > 0)
?>
```

Send a direct message

You can send a direct message by authenticating as the sender using the `direct_messages/new` method. However, to send a direct message the receiver must be following you.

This method requires a POST request and isn't rate limited.

Output

This method has two output formats:

- XML
- JSON

On a successful post, this method will return the details of the direct message you just sent, including the complete user detail of the sender and receiver of the message.

On a failed post, you will receive an error message explaining why you were unable to send the message.

Input

This method requires two parameters, the numeric user id or screen name of the recipient, and the text content of the direct message.

- `user_id`: The numerical id of the user.
  Example: `user_id=12345`
- `screen_name`: The screen name of the user.
  Example: `screen_name=101010`
- `text`: The content of the direct message URL encoded. Must be fewer than 140 characters.
  Example: `text=test`

Be sure to URL encode the `text` parameter. Your message mayn't be sent properly otherwise. In PHP you can use the urlencode function, like I have in Listing 8-7.

Example

Listing 8-7 is an example of how to programmatically send a direct message by using cURL and PHP to post to the `direct_messages/new` method. If a message is successfully sent, it displays the text of the recently sent message and the profile picture of the sender.

Listing 8-7: How to Programmatically Send a Direct Message

```
<?php

// Set username and password
$username = 'username';
$password = 'password';

$sendToUser = 'dustyreagan';
$dmText = urlencode("Hey! This is a test DM sent from the API");

// The Twitter direct_messages/new method
$url = "https://api.twitter.com/1/direct_messages/new.xml";

// POST to Twitter API using curl
$curlHandle = curl_init();
curl_setopt($curlHandle, CURLOPT_URL, "$url");
curl_setopt($curlHandle, CURLOPT_USERAGENT, "Twitter App Development For
            Dummies: Example");
curl_setopt($curlHandle, CURLOPT_POST, 1);
curl_setopt($curlHandle, CURLOPT_RETURNTRANSFER, 1);
curl_setopt($curlHandle, CURLOPT_SSL_VERIFYPEER, false);
curl_setopt($curlHandle, CURLOPT_POSTFIELDS, "screen_name=$sendToUser&text=$dmT
            ext");
curl_setopt($curlHandle, CURLOPT_USERPWD, "$username:$password");
$apiResponse = curl_exec($curlHandle);

// Get HTTP Status Code
$info = curl_getinfo($curlHandle);
$http_code = $info['http_code'];
echo "<h1>HTTP Status Code: $http_code</h1>";

// Close cURL connection
curl_close($curlHandle);

// Get XML
$xml = new DOMDocument();
$xml->loadXML($apiResponse);

// Check for an error tag.
```

(continued)

Listing 8-7 *(continued)*

```
$errors = $xml->getElementsByTagName("error");

// If found, print the error. Else, success!
if($errors->length > 0)
{
    $errorMessage = $errors->item(0)->nodeValue;
    echo "<h1>$errorMessage</h1>";
}
else
{
    // Get new DM text
    $textNode = $xml->getElementsByTagName("text");
    $text = $textNode->item(0)->nodeValue;

    // Get author's profile picture
    $senderNode = $xml->getElementsByTagName("sender");
    $profilePicNode = $senderNode->item(0)->getElementsByTagName("profile_image_
               url");
    $profile_image_url = $profilePicNode->item(0)->nodeValue;

    // Print DM and user's picture
    echo "<h1>Successfully sent the following DM:</h1>";
    echo "<img src=\"$profile_image_url\" width=\"48\" height=\"48\" />";
    echo "<p>$text</p>";
}

?>
```

Delete a received direct message

You can delete a direct message you received by authenticating and passing the id of the direct message to the `direct_messages/destroy` method.

This method requires a POST or DELETE request and isn't rate limited.

Output

This method has two output formats:

- XML
- JSON

On a successful post, this method will return the details of the direct message you just delete, including the complete user detail of the sender and receiver of the message.

On a failed post, you will receive an error message explaining why you were unable to delete the message.

Input

This method requires one parameter, the id of the direct message you want to delete.

- `id`: The numerical id of the direct message.
  Example: `/direct_messages/destroy/1234.xml`

Example

Listing 8-8 is an example of how to programmatically delete a direct message by using curl to post to the `direct_messages/destroy` method. If a message is successfully deleted, it displays the text of the recently deleted tweet and the profile picture of the sender.

Listing 8-8: How to Programmatically Delete a Direct Message

```
<?php

// Set username and password
$username = 'username';
$password = 'password';

$messageIdToDelete = 486489555;

// The Twitter direct_messages/destroy method
$url = "https://api.twitter.com/1/direct_messages/destroy/$messageIdToDelete.
            xml";

// POST to Twitter API using curl
$curlHandle = curl_init();
curl_setopt($curlHandle, CURLOPT_URL, "$url");
curl_setopt($curlHandle, CURLOPT_USERAGENT, "Twitter App Development For
            Dummies: Example");
curl_setopt($curlHandle, CURLOPT_POST, 1);
curl_setopt($curlHandle, CURLOPT_RETURNTRANSFER, 1);
curl_setopt($curlHandle, CURLOPT_SSL_VERIFYPEER, false);
curl_setopt($curlHandle, CURLOPT_POSTFIELDS, "");
curl_setopt($curlHandle, CURLOPT_USERPWD, "$username:$password");
$apiResponse = curl_exec($curlHandle);

// Get HTTP Status Code
$info = curl_getinfo($curlHandle);
$http_code = $info['http_code'];
echo "<h1>HTTP Status Code: $http_code</h1>";
```

(continued)

Listing 8-8 *(continued)*

```
// Close cURL connection
curl_close($curlHandle);

// Get XML
$xml = new DOMDocument();
$xml->loadXML($apiResponse);

// Check for an error tag.
$errors = $xml->getElementsByTagName("error");

// If found, print the error. Else, success!
if($errors->length > 0)
{
    $errorMessage = $errors->item(0)->nodeValue;
    echo "<h1>$errorMessage</h1>";
}
else
{
    // Get deleted DM text
    $textNode = $xml->getElementsByTagName("text");
    $text = $textNode->item(0)->nodeValue;

    // Get author's profile picture
    $senderNode = $xml->getElementsByTagName("sender");
    $profilePicNode = $senderNode->item(0)->getElementsByTagName("profile_image_
            url");
    $profile_image_url = $profilePicNode->item(0)->nodeValue;

    // Print DM and user's picture
    echo "<h1>Successfully deleted the following DM:</h1>";
    echo "<img src=\"$profile_image_url\" width=\"48\" height=\"48\" />";
    echo "<p>$text</p>";
}

?>
```

Timeline Methods

The timeline is the main way all tweets are consumed by the user. It is the river of real-time incoming tweets. There are several ways to view and segment the timeline, including viewing all public tweets, the tweets of the people you follow, tweets with your name mentioned, and viewing a timeline or retweets. There are seven methods you can use to interact with the timeline, including:

- statuses/public_timeline
- statuses/friends_timeline
- statuses/user_timeline
- statuses/mentions
- statuses/retweeted_by_me
- statuses/retweeted_to_me
- statuses/retweets_of_me

Get tweets from the public timeline

The public timeline includes tweets from all public Twitter accounts with a custom profile picture. You can use the `statuses/public_timeline` to get the 20 most recent tweets from the public timeline.

This method doesn't require authentication. It does require a GET request, and is rate limited. Chapter 7 explains the concern with rate limits.

Output

This method has four output formats:

- XML
- JSON
- RSS
- Atom

On a successful call, this method returns the 20 most recent public tweets from users with a custom profile picture. This list includes the complete status object, which contains the complete user object of the tweet's author. A failed call returns an error message.

Input

This method has no input parameters.

Example

You can try the `statuses/public_timeline` method easily by typing `http://api.twitter.com/1/statuses/public_timeline.xml` into your browser's URL address bar. It returns a list of the last 20 public tweets in XML format.

In Listing 8-9, I use the `statuses/public_timeline` method to print the profile pictures of the author's of the most recent 20 public tweets.

Listing 8-9: Page Through All Your Favorites and Print Them

```
<?php

// The Twitter friendships/destroy method
$url = "http://api.twitter.com/1/statuses/public_timeline.xml";

// Get Twitter API results with cURL
$curlHandle = curl_init();
curl_setopt($curlHandle, CURLOPT_URL, "$url");
curl_setopt($curlHandle, CURLOPT_USERAGENT, "Twitter App Development For
              Dummies: Example");
curl_setopt($curlHandle, CURLOPT_RETURNTRANSFER, 1);
$apiResponse = curl_exec($curlHandle);

// Get HTTP Status Code
$info = curl_getinfo($curlHandle);
$http_code = $info['http_code'];
echo "<h1>HTTP Status Code: $http_code</h1>";

// Close cURL connection
curl_close($curlHandle);

// Get XML
$xml = new DOMDocument();
$xml->loadXML($apiResponse);

// Check for an error tag.
$errors = $xml->getElementsByTagName("error");

// If found, print the error. Else, success!
if($errors->length > 0)
{
   $errorMessage = $errors->item(0)->nodeValue;
   echo "<h1>$errorMessage</h1>";
}
else
{
   $statusNodes = $xml->getElementsByTagName("status");

   foreach($statusNodes as $status)
   {
      $profileImageNode = $status->getElementsByTagName("profile_image_url");
      $profile_image_url = $profileImageNode->item(0)->nodeValue;
      echo "<img src=\"$profile_image_url\" width=\"48\" height=\"48\" />";
   }
}

?>
```

Get your aggregated friends timeline

Your friends timeline is the aggregated stream of tweets from all the people you follow and includes your own tweets. It is the tweets you see when you go to your Twitter home page. You can retrieve this stream of tweets with the `statuses/friends_timeline` method.

This method requires authentication, a GET request, and is rate limited. Chapter 7 explains the concern with rate limits.

Output

This method has four output formats:

- XML
- JSON
- RSS
- Atom

On a successful call, this method returns an array of the 20 most recent tweets in you friends timeline. This list includes complete status objects, which contains the complete user object of each author. A failed call returns an error message.

Input

This method has four optional input parameters.

- `since_id`: The numerical id of a tweet. Use to return tweets that are more recent than the id specified.
  Example: `/statuses/friends_timeline.xml?since_id=12345`
- `max_id`: The numerical id of a tweet. Use to return tweets that are older than the id specified.
  Example: `/statuses/friends_timeline.xml?max_id=54321`
- `count`: Limits the results per page to an amount specified that is less than 200.
  Example: `/statuses/friends_timeline.xml?count=100`
- `page`: Page backwards to retrieve older tweets.
  Example: `/statuses/friends_timeline.xml?page=5`

Example

You can try the `statuses/friends_timeline` method easily by typing `http://api.twitter.com/1/statuses/friends_timeline.xml` into your browser's URL address bar. When requested by your browser, enter your Twitter user name and password. Then you receive the most recent 20 tweets in your friends timeline.

In Listing 8-10, I retrieve more than the default 20 most tweets by setting the count parameter to the maximum 200 results per page, then I incrementally increase the page parameter until the `statuses/friends_timeline` method returns no more results.

Listing 8-10: Page Through Your Friends Timeline

```
<?php
function getStatusesPage($page)
{
   // Set username and password
   $username = 'username';
   $password = 'password';

   // The Twitter statuses/friends_timeline method
   $url = "https://api.twitter.com/1/statuses/friends_timeline.
             xml?count=200&page=$page";

   // Get API results using curl
   $curlHandle = curl_init();
   curl_setopt($curlHandle, CURLOPT_URL, "$url");
   curl_setopt($curlHandle, CURLOPT_USERAGENT, "Twitter App Development For
             Dummies: Example");
   curl_setopt($curlHandle, CURLOPT_RETURNTRANSFER, 1);
   curl_setopt($curlHandle, CURLOPT_SSL_VERIFYPEER, false);
   curl_setopt($curlHandle, CURLOPT_USERPWD, "$username:$password");
   $apiResponse = curl_exec($curlHandle);

   // Get HTTP Code
   $info = curl_getinfo($curlHandle);
   $http_code = $info['http_code'];
   echo "<h1>HTTP Status Code: $http_code</h1>";

   // Close cURL connection
   curl_close($curlHandle);

   return $apiResponse;
}

$page = 1;
do
{
   echo "<h1>Page: $page</h1>";
   // Get a page of statuses
   $apiResponse = getStatusesPage($page);

   // Get XML
```

```
    $xml = new DOMDocument();
    $xml->loadXML($apiResponse);

    // Check for an error tag.
    $errors = $xml->getElementsByTagName("error");

    // If found, print the error and break. Else, keep going!
    if($errors->length > 0)
    {
        $errorMessage = $errors->item(0)->nodeValue;
        echo "<h1>$errorMessage</h1>";
        break;
    }
    else
    {
        // Get direct messages
        $statusNodes = $xml->getElementsByTagName("status");

        foreach($statusNodes as $statusNode)
        {
            // Get the tweet text
            $textNode = $statusNode->getElementsByTagName("text");
            $text = $textNode->item(0)->nodeValue;

            // Get the author's picture
            $senderNode = $statusNode->getElementsByTagName("user");
            $profilePicNode = $senderNode->item(0)->getElementsByTagName("profile_
                image_url");
            $profile_image_url = $profilePicNode->item(0)->nodeValue;

            echo "<img style=\"float:left\" src=\"$profile_image_url\" width=\"48\"
                height=\"48\" />";
            echo "<p>$text</p>";
            echo "<hr style=\"clear:both\" />";
        }
    }

    // increment page count and loop
    $page++;
}
while($statusNodes->length > 0)

?>
```

Get a user's tweets

Using the `statuses/user_timeline` method you can get a user's most recent tweets. These are the same tweet's that are viewable on a user's profile page on the Twitter Web site.

This method doesn't require authentication, but to get the tweets of a protected Twitter account, you must

- Authenticate your API call.
- Have permission to view the protected account.

This method requires a GET request and is rate limited. Chapter 7 explains the concern with rate limits.

Output

This method has four output formats:

- XML
- JSON
- RSS
- Atom

On a successful call, this method returns an array of the 20 most recent tweets in the requested user's timeline. This list includes complete status objects, which contains the complete user object of each author. A failed call returns an error message.

Input

This method has seven optional input parameters.

- `id`: The user's screen name or numerical user id.
  Example: `/notifications/leave/bob.xml`
  Example: `/notifications/leave/12345`.xml`
- `user_id`: The numerical id of the user.
  Example: `/notifications/leave.xml?user_id=12345`
- `screen_name`: The screen name of the user.
  Example: /notifications/leave.xml?screen_name=101010
- `since_id`: The numerical id of a tweet. Use to return tweets that are more recent than the id specified.
  Example: /statuses/friends_timeline.xml?since_id=12345
- `max_id`: The numerical id of a tweet. Use to return tweets that are older than the id specified.
  Example: `/statuses/friends_timeline.xml?max_id=54321`
- `count`: Limits the results per page to an amount specified that is less than 200.
  Example: `/statuses/friends_timeline.xml?count=100`
- `page`: Page backwards to retrieve older tweets.
  Example: `/statuses/friends_timeline.xml?page=5`

Avoid using the `id` parameter and use `user_id`, over `screen_name` if possible. Chapter 7 explains why.

If you want to retrieve the tweet's for the authenticated user, you don't have to specify a user id or screen name. The method retrieves the authenticated user's timeline by default.

Example

You can try the `statuses/user_timeline` method easily by typing `http://api.twitter.com/1/statuses/user_timeline.xml?screen_name=bob` into your browser's URL address bar. It returns the most recent 20 tweets in Bob's timeline.

In Listing 8-11, I retrieve more than the default 20 user tweets by setting the count parameter to the maximum 200 results per page, then I incrementally increase the page parameter until the `statuses/user_timeline` method returns no more results.

Listing 8-11: Page Through a User's Timeline

```
<?php
function getStatusesPage($page)
{
   // Set username and password
   $username = 'username';
   $password = 'password';

   // The Twitter statuses/user_timeline method
   $url = "https://api.twitter.com/1/statuses/user_timeline.
             xml?count=200&page=$page";

   // Get API results using curl
   $curlHandle = curl_init();
   curl_setopt($curlHandle, CURLOPT_URL, "$url");
   curl_setopt($curlHandle, CURLOPT_USERAGENT, "Twitter App Development For
             Dummies: Example");
   curl_setopt($curlHandle, CURLOPT_RETURNTRANSFER, 1);
   curl_setopt($curlHandle, CURLOPT_SSL_VERIFYPEER, false);
   curl_setopt($curlHandle, CURLOPT_USERPWD, "$username:$password");
   $apiResponse = curl_exec($curlHandle);

   // Get HTTP Code
   $info = curl_getinfo($curlHandle);
   $http_code = $info['http_code'];
   echo "<h1>HTTP Status Code: $http_code</h1>";

   // Close cURL connection
   curl_close($curlHandle);
```

(continued)

Listing 8-11 *(continued)*

```
    return $apiResponse;
}

$page = 1;
do
{
    echo "<h1>Page: $page</h1>";
    // Get a page of statuses
    $apiResponse = getStatusesPage($page);

    // Get XML
    $xml = new DOMDocument();
    $xml->loadXML($apiResponse);

    // Check for an error tag.
    $errors = $xml->getElementsByTagName("error");

    // If found, print the error and break. Else, keep going!
    if($errors->length > 0)
    {
        $errorMessage = $errors->item(0)->nodeValue;
        echo "<h1>$errorMessage</h1>";
        break;
    }
    else
    {
        // Get direct messages
        $statusNodes = $xml->getElementsByTagName("status");

        foreach($statusNodes as $statusNode)
        {
            // Get the tweet text
            $textNode = $statusNode->getElementsByTagName("text");
            $text = $textNode->item(0)->nodeValue;

            // Get the author's picture
            $senderNode = $statusNode->getElementsByTagName("user");
            $profilePicNode = $senderNode->item(0)->getElementsByTagName("profile_
                image_url");
            $profile_image_url = $profilePicNode->item(0)->nodeValue;

            echo "<img style=\"float:left\" src=\"$profile_image_url\" width=\"48\"
                height=\"48\" />";
            echo "<p>$text</p>";
            echo "<hr style=\"clear:both\" />";
        }
    }

    // increment page count and loop
```

```
    $page++;
}
while($statusNodes->length > 0)

?>
```

Get tweets that mention your screen name

The `statuses/mentions` method returns all the tweets that contain the authenticated user's screen name (example: @DustyReagan).

This method requires authentication, a GET request, and is rate limited. Chapter 7 explains the concern with rate limits.

Output

This method has four output formats:

- XML
- JSON
- RSS
- Atom

On a successful call, this method returns an array of the 20 most recent tweets with mentions. This list includes complete status objects, which contains the complete user object of each author. A failed call returns an error message.

Input

This method has four optional input parameters.

- `since_id`: The numerical id of a tweet. Use to return tweets that are more recent than the id specified.
  Example: /statuses/friends_timeline.xml?since_id=12345
- `max_id`: The numerical id of a tweet. Use to return tweets that are older than the id specified.
  Example: `/statuses/friends_timeline.xml?max_id=54321`
- `count`: Limits the results per page to an amount specified that is less than 200.
  Example: `/statuses/friends_timeline.xml?count=100`
- `page`: Page backwards to retrieve older tweets.
  Example: `/statuses/friends_timeline.xml?page=5`

Example

You can try the `statuses/mentions` method easily by typing `http://api.twitter.com/1/statuses/mentions.xml` into your browser's URL address bar. When requested by your browser, enter your Twitter user name and password. It returns the most recent 20 mentions in XML.

In Listing 8-12, I retrieve more than the default 20 mentions by setting the count parameter to the maximum 200 results per page, then I incrementally increase the page parameter until the `statuses/mentions` method returns no more results.

Listing 8-12: Page Through Tweets that Mention Your Screen Name

```
<?php
function getMentions($page)
{
   // Set username and password
   $username = 'username';
   $password = 'password';

   // The Twitter statuses/mentions method
   $url = "https://api.twitter.com/1/statuses/mentions.xml?count=200&page=$page";

   // Get API results using curl
   $curlHandle = curl_init();
   curl_setopt($curlHandle, CURLOPT_URL, "$url");
   curl_setopt($curlHandle, CURLOPT_USERAGENT, "Twitter App Development For
            Dummies: Example");
   curl_setopt($curlHandle, CURLOPT_RETURNTRANSFER, 1);
   curl_setopt($curlHandle, CURLOPT_SSL_VERIFYPEER, false);
   curl_setopt($curlHandle, CURLOPT_USERPWD, "$username:$password");
   $apiResponse = curl_exec($curlHandle);

   // Get HTTP Code
   $info = curl_getinfo($curlHandle);
   $http_code = $info['http_code'];
   echo "<h1>HTTP Status Code: $http_code</h1>";

   // Close cURL connection
   curl_close($curlHandle);

   return $apiResponse;
}

$page = 1;
do
```

```
{
   echo "<h1>Page: $page</h1>";
   // Get a page of mentions
   $apiResponse = getMentions($page);

   // Get XML
   $xml = new DOMDocument();
   $xml->loadXML($apiResponse);

   // Check for an error tag.
   $errors = $xml->getElementsByTagName("error");

   // If found, print the error and break. Else, keep going!
   if($errors->length > 0)
   {
      $errorMessage = $errors->item(0)->nodeValue;
      echo "<h1>$errorMessage</h1>";
      break;
   }
   else
   {
      // Get direct messages
      $statusNodes = $xml->getElementsByTagName("status");

      foreach($statusNodes as $statusNode)
      {
         // Get the tweet text
         $textNode = $statusNode->getElementsByTagName("text");
         $text = $textNode->item(0)->nodeValue;

         // Get the author's picture
         $senderNode = $statusNode->getElementsByTagName("user");
         $profilePicNode = $senderNode->item(0)->getElementsByTagName("profile_
               image_url");
         $profile_image_url = $profilePicNode->item(0)->nodeValue;

         echo "<img style=\"float:left\" src=\"$profile_image_url\" width=\"48\"
               height=\"48\" />";
         echo "<p>$text</p>";
         echo "<hr style=\"clear:both\" />";
      }
   }

   // increment page count and loop
   $page++;
}
while($statusNodes->length > 0)

?>
```

Get status updates retweeted by you

To get status updates that you have retweeted using Twitter's retweet function, use the `statuses/retweeted_by_me method`.

This method requires authentication, a GET request, and is rate limited.

Output

This method has three output formats:

- XML
- JSON
- Atom

On a successful call, this method returns an array of the authenticated user's more recent 20 retweets. This list includes complete status objects, which contains the complete user object for the original tweet's author, and the authenticated user. A failed call returns an error message.

Input

This method has four optional input parameters.

- `since_id`: The numerical id of a tweet. Use to return retweets that are more recent than the id specified.
  Example: `/statuses/retweeted_by_me?since_id=12345`
- `max_id`: The numerical id of a tweet. Use to return retweets that are older than the id specified.
  Example: `/statuses/retweeted_by_me?max_id=54321`
- `count`: Limits the results per page to an amount specified that is less than 200.
  Example: `/statuses/retweeted_by_me?count=100`
- `page`: Page backwards to retrieve older retweets.
  Example: `/statuses/retweeted_by_me?page=5`

Avoid using the `id` parameter, and use `user_id`, over `screen_name` if possible.

Example

You can try the `statuses/retweeted_by_me` method easily by typing `http://api.twitter.com/1/statuses/retweeted_by_me.xml` into your browser's URL address bar. When requested by your browser, enter your Twitter user name and password. Then you receive your last 20 retweets in XML format.

In Listing 8-13, I retrieve the authenticating user's most recent 100 retweets using `statuses/retweeted_by_me` and the count parameter.

Listing 8-13: Get User's Most Recent 100 Retweets

```
<?php

// Set username and password
$username = 'username';
$password = 'password';

// The Twitter statuses/retweeted_by_me method
$url = "https://api.twitter.com/1/statuses/retweeted_by_me.xml?count=200";

// Get API results using curl
$curlHandle = curl_init();
curl_setopt($curlHandle, CURLOPT_URL, "$url");
curl_setopt($curlHandle, CURLOPT_USERAGENT, "Twitter App Development For
               Dummies: Example");
curl_setopt($curlHandle, CURLOPT_RETURNTRANSFER, 1);
curl_setopt($curlHandle, CURLOPT_SSL_VERIFYPEER, false);
curl_setopt($curlHandle, CURLOPT_USERPWD, "$username:$password");
$apiResponse = curl_exec($curlHandle);

// Get HTTP Code
$info = curl_getinfo($curlHandle);
$http_code = $info['http_code'];
echo "<h1>HTTP Status Code: $http_code</h1>";

// Close cURL connection
curl_close($curlHandle);

// Get XML
$xml = new DOMDocument();
$xml->loadXML($apiResponse);

// Check for an error tag.
$errors = $xml->getElementsByTagName("error");

// If found, print the error and break. Else, keep going!
if($errors->length > 0)
{
  $errorMessage = $errors->item(0)->nodeValue;
  echo "<h1>$errorMessage</h1>";
  break;
}
else
{
  // Get direct messages
  $statusNodes = $xml->getElementsByTagName("status");
```

(continued)

Listing 8-12 *(continued)*

```
    foreach($statusNodes as $statusNode)
    {
        // Get the tweet text
        $textNode = $statusNode->getElementsByTagName("text");
        $text = $textNode->item(0)->nodeValue;

        // Get the author's picture
        $senderNode = $statusNode->getElementsByTagName("user");
        $profilePicNode = $senderNode->item(0)->getElementsByTagName("profile_
                image_url");
        $profile_image_url = $profilePicNode->item(0)->nodeValue;

        echo "<img style=\"float:left\" src=\"$profile_image_url\" width=\"48\"
                height=\"48\" />";
        echo "<p>$text</p>";
        echo "<hr style=\"clear:both\" />";
    }
}

?>
```

Get your friend's retweets

To get the retweets of the people you follow, use the `statuses/retweeted_to_me method`.

This method requires authentication, a GET request, and is rate limited. The sidebar "Hard Knocks" explains the concern with rate limits.

Output

This method has three output formats:

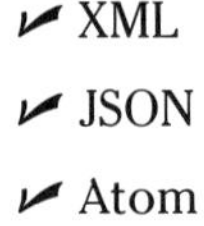

- XML
- JSON
- Atom

On a successful call, this method returns an array of the most recent 20 retweets from the people the authenticated user follows. This list includes complete status objects, which contains the complete user object for the original tweet's author, and the authenticated user. A failed call returns an error message.

Input

This method has four optional input parameters.

- since_id: The numerical id of a tweet. Use to return retweets that are more recent than the id specified.
  Example: /statuses/retweeted_to_me?since_id=12345
- max_id: The numerical id of a tweet. Use to return retweets that are older than the id specified.
  Example: /statuses/retweeted_to_me?max_id=54321
- count: Limits the results per page to an amount specified that is less than 200.
  Example: /statuses/retweeted_to_me?count=100
- page: Page backwards to retrieve older retweets.
  Example: /statuses/retweeted_to_me?page=5

Avoid using the id parameter and use user_id, over screen_name if possible.

Example

You can try the statuses/retweeted_to_me method easily by typing http://api.twitter.com/1/statuses/retweeted_to_me.xml into your browser's URL address bar. When requested by your browser, enter your Twitter user name and password. Then you receive the last 20 retweets of the people you follow retweets in XML format.

In Listing 8-14, I retrieve the retweets of the people the authenticating user follows using statuses/retweeted_by_me and the count parameter.

Listing 8-14: Get the Last 100 Retweets of the People You Follow

```
<?php

// Set username and password
$username = 'username';
$password = 'password';

// The Twitter statuses/retweeted_to_me method
$url = "https://api.twitter.com/1/statuses/retweeted_to_me.xml?count=200";

// Get API results using curl
$curlHandle = curl_init();
curl_setopt($curlHandle, CURLOPT_URL, "$url");

curl_setopt($curlHandle, CURLOPT_USERAGENT, "Twitter App Development For
            Dummies: Example");
```

(continued)

Listing 8-14 *(continued)*

```
curl_setopt($curlHandle, CURLOPT_RETURNTRANSFER, 1);
curl_setopt($curlHandle, CURLOPT_SSL_VERIFYPEER, false);
curl_setopt($curlHandle, CURLOPT_USERPWD, "$username:$password");
$apiResponse = curl_exec($curlHandle);

// Get HTTP Code
$info = curl_getinfo($curlHandle);
$http_code = $info['http_code'];
echo "<h1>HTTP Status Code: $http_code</h1>";

// Close cURL connection
curl_close($curlHandle);

// Get XML
$xml = new DOMDocument();
$xml->loadXML($apiResponse);

// Check for an error tag.
$errors = $xml->getElementsByTagName("error");

// If found, print the error and break. Else, keep going!
if($errors->length > 0)
{
  $errorMessage = $errors->item(0)->nodeValue;
  echo "<h1>$errorMessage</h1>";
  break;
}
else
{
  // Get tweets
  $statusNodes = $xml->getElementsByTagName("status");

  foreach($statusNodes as $statusNode)
  {
     // Get the tweet text
     $textNode = $statusNode->getElementsByTagName("text");
     $text = $textNode->item(0)->nodeValue;

     // Get the author's picture
     $senderNode = $statusNode->getElementsByTagName("user");
     $profilePicNode = $senderNode->item(0)->getElementsByTagName("profile_
             image_url");
     $profile_image_url = $profilePicNode->item(0)->nodeValue;

     echo "<img style=\"float:left\" src=\"$profile_image_url\" width=\"48\"
             height=\"48\" />";
     echo "<p>$text</p>";
     echo "<hr style=\"clear:both\" />";
  }
}

?>
```

Get the retweets of a specific tweet

To get the tweets of the authenticated user that others have retweeted, use the `statuses/retweets_of_me method`.

This method requires authentication, a GET request, and is rate limited. The sidebar "Hard Knocks" explains the concern with rate limits.

Output

This method has three output formats:

- XML
- JSON
- Atom

On a successful call, this method returns an array of the most recent 20 retweets of the authenticated users. This list includes complete status objects, which contains the complete user object for the original tweet's author, and the authenticated user. A failed call returns an error message.

Input

This method has four optional input parameters.

- `since_id`: The numerical id of a tweet. Use to return retweets that are more recent than the id specified.
  Example: `/statuses/retweets_of_me?since_id=12345`
- `max_id`: The numerical id of a tweet. Use to return retweets that are older than the id specified.
  Example: `/statuses/retweets_of_me?max_id=54321`
- `count`: Limits the results per page to an amount specified that is less than 200.
  Example: `/statuses/retweets_of_me?count=100`
- `page`: Page backwards to retrieve older retweets.
  Example: `/statuses/retweets_of_me?page=5`

Avoid using the `id` parameter and use `user_id`, over `screen_name` if possible.

Example

You can try the `statuses/retweets_of_me` method easily by typing `http://api.twitter.com/1/statuses/retweets_of_me.xml` into your browser's URL address bar. When requested by your browser, enter your Twitter user name and password. It returns your most recent 20 tweets that have been retweeted.

In Listing 8-15, I retrieve the authenticating user's most recent 100 tweets that have been retweeted using `statuses/retweets_of_me` and the count parameter.

Listing 8-15: Get the Retweets of a Tweet

```
<?php

// Set username and password
$username = 'username';
$password = 'password';

// The Twitter statuses/retweets_of_me method
$url = "https://api.twitter.com/1/statuses/retweets_of_me.xml?count=200";

// Get API results using curl
$curlHandle = curl_init();
curl_setopt($curlHandle, CURLOPT_URL, "$url");
curl_setopt($curlHandle, CURLOPT_USERAGENT, "Twitter App Development For
              Dummies: Example");
curl_setopt($curlHandle, CURLOPT_RETURNTRANSFER, 1);
curl_setopt($curlHandle, CURLOPT_SSL_VERIFYPEER, false);
curl_setopt($curlHandle, CURLOPT_USERPWD, "$username:$password");
$apiResponse = curl_exec($curlHandle);

// Get HTTP Code
$info = curl_getinfo($curlHandle);
$http_code = $info['http_code'];
echo "<h1>HTTP Status Code: $http_code</h1>";

// Close cURL connection
curl_close($curlHandle);

// Get XML
$xml = new DOMDocument();
$xml->loadXML($apiResponse);

// Check for an error tag.
$errors = $xml->getElementsByTagName("error");

// If found, print the error and break. Else, keep going!
if($errors->length > 0)
{
  $errorMessage = $errors->item(0)->nodeValue;
  echo "<h1>$errorMessage</h1>";
  break;
}
else
{
  // Get tweets
```

```
    $statusNodes = $xml->getElementsByTagName("status");

    foreach($statusNodes as $statusNode)
    {
        // Get the tweet text
        $textNode = $statusNode->getElementsByTagName("text");
        $text = $textNode->item(0)->nodeValue;

        // Get the author's picture
        $senderNode = $statusNode->getElementsByTagName("user");
        $profilePicNode = $senderNode->item(0)->getElementsByTagName("profile_
                image_url");
        $profile_image_url = $profilePicNode->item(0)->nodeValue;

        echo "<img style=\"float:left\" src=\"$profile_image_url\" width=\"48\"
                height=\"48\" />";
        echo "<p>$text</p>";
        echo "<hr style=\"clear:both\" />";
    }
}

?>
```

Favorite Methods

Favoriting a status update is one way to bookmark a memorable tweet. Using the API you can view a user's favorites, favorite, or un-favorite a tweet, with the following three methods:

- `favorites`
- `favorites/create`
- `favorites/destroy`

Retrieve a user's favorite tweets

You can retrieve a list of a user's favorite tweets by using the `favorites` method.

This method requires authentication, a GET request, and is rate limited. Chapter 7 explains the concern with rate limits.

To view a protected account's favorited tweet, the authenticated account must have permission to view them.

Output

This method has four output formats:

- XML
- JSON
- RSS
- Atom

On a successful call, this method returns a list of the 20 most recent favorited tweets. This list includes the complete status object, which contains the complete user object of the author. A failed call returns an error message.

Input

This method has four parameters:

- `id`: The user's screen name or numerical user id.
  Example: `/favorites/bob.xml`
- `user_id`: The numerical id of the user.
  Example: `/favorites.xml?user_id=12345`
- `screen_name`: The screen name of the user.
  Example: `/favorites.xml?screen_name=101010`
- `page`: Page to retrieve older favorites.
  Example: `/favorites.xml?page=5`

If you are authenticated, you can omit specifying the user and the method will return the favorites for the authenticated user.

Example

You can try the `favorites` method easily by typing `http://api.twitter.com/1/favorites.xml` into your browser's URL address bar. When requested by your browser, enter your Twitter user name and password. Then you receive your last 20 favorited tweets in XML format.

In Listing 8-16, I use the `favorites` method page parameter to collect all my previous tweets and display them along with the profile picture of the author.

Listing 8-16: Page Through All Your Favorites and Print Them

```
<?php
function getFavorites($screen_name, $page)
{
   // Set username and password
   $username = 'username';
   $password = 'password';

   // The Twitter statuses/friends method
   $url = "https://api.twitter.com/1/favorites.xml?page=$page";

   // Get API results using curl
   $curlHandle = curl_init();
   curl_setopt($curlHandle, CURLOPT_URL, "$url");
   curl_setopt($curlHandle, CURLOPT_USERAGENT, "Twitter App Development For
               Dummies: Example");
   curl_setopt($curlHandle, CURLOPT_RETURNTRANSFER, 1);
   curl_setopt($curlHandle, CURLOPT_SSL_VERIFYPEER, false);
   curl_setopt($curlHandle, CURLOPT_USERPWD, "$username:$password");
   $apiResponse = curl_exec($curlHandle);
   curl_close($curlHandle);

   return $apiResponse;
}

$page = 1;
do
{
   // Get a page of favorites results
   $apiResponse = getFavorites('dustyreagan', $page);

   // Get XML
   $xml = new DOMDocument();
   $xml->loadXML($apiResponse);

   // Check for an error tag.
   $errors = $xml->getElementsByTagName("error");

   // If found, print the error and break. Else, keep going!
   if($errors->length > 0)
   {
      $errorMessage = $errors->item(0)->nodeValue;
      echo "<h1>$errorMessage</h1>";
      break;
   }
   else
```

(continued)

Listing 8-16 *(continued)*

```
    {
        // Get favorited tweets
        $statusNodes = $xml->getElementsByTagName("status");

        foreach($statusNodes as $statusNode)
        {
            // Get the tweet text
            $textNode = $statusNode->getElementsByTagName("text");
            $text = $textNode->item(0)->nodeValue;

            // Get the author's picture
            $profilePicNodes = $statusNode->getElementsByTagName("profile_image_
                 url");
            $profile_image_url = $profilePicNodes->item(0)->nodeValue;

            echo "<img style=\"float:left\" src=\"$profile_image_url\" width=\"48\"
                 height=\"48\" />";
            echo "<p>$text</p>";
            echo "<hr style=\"clear:both\" />";
        }
    }

    // increment page count and loop
    $page++;
}
while($statusNodes->length > 0)
?>
```

Add a tweet to your favorites

You can add a tweet to your favorites list by authenticating and calling the `favorites/create` method.

This method requires a POST request and isn't rate limited.

Output

This method has two output formats:

- XML
- JSON

On a successful post, this method will return the details of the tweet you just added to your favorites, including the complete user details object of the author.

On a failed post, you will receive an error message explaining why you were unable to add the tweet.

Input

This method requires one parameter, the id of the tweet you want to add to your favorites.

- `id`: The numerical id of the status update.
  Example: `/favorites/destroy/1234.xml`

Example

Listing 8-17 is an example of how to programmatically add a tweet to your favorites by using PHP and cURL to post to the `favorites/create` method. If a tweet is successfully added, it displays the text of the recently added tweet and the profile picture of the author.

Listing 8-17: How to Programmatically Add a Tweet from Your Favorites

```
<?php

// Set username and password
$username = 'username';
$password = 'password';

$tweetIdToAdd = 5142491385;

// The Twitter favorites/create method
$url = "https://api.twitter.com/1/favorites/create/$tweetIdToAdd.xml";

// POST to Twitter API using curl
$curlHandle = curl_init();
curl_setopt($curlHandle, CURLOPT_URL, "$url");
curl_setopt($curlHandle, CURLOPT_USERAGENT, "Twitter App Development For
                Dummies: Example");
curl_setopt($curlHandle, CURLOPT_POST, 1);
curl_setopt($curlHandle, CURLOPT_RETURNTRANSFER, 1);
curl_setopt($curlHandle, CURLOPT_SSL_VERIFYPEER, false);
curl_setopt($curlHandle, CURLOPT_POSTFIELDS, "");
curl_setopt($curlHandle, CURLOPT_USERPWD, "$username:$password");
$apiResponse = curl_exec($curlHandle);

// Get HTTP Status Code
$info = curl_getinfo($curlHandle);
$http_code = $info['http_code'];
echo "<h1>HTTP Status Code: $http_code</h1>";
```

(continued)

Listing 8-17 *(continued)*

```
// Close cURL connection
curl_close($curlHandle);

// Get XML
$xml = new DOMDocument();
$xml->loadXML($apiResponse);

// Check for an error tag.
$errors = $xml->getElementsByTagName("error");

// If found, print the error. Else, success!
if($errors->length > 0)
{
    $errorMessage = $errors->item(0)->nodeValue;
    echo "<h1>$errorMessage</h1>";
}
else
{
    // Get favorited tweet text
    $textNode = $xml->getElementsByTagName("text");
    $text = $textNode->item(0)->nodeValue;

    // Get author's profile picture
    $profilePicNode = $xml->getElementsByTagName("profile_image_url");
    $profile_image_url = $profilePicNode->item(0)->nodeValue;

    // Print tweet and user's picture
    echo "<h1>Successfully added the following tweet to your favorites:</h1>";
    echo "<img src=\"$profile_image_url\" width=\"48\" height=\"48\" />";
    echo "<p>$text</p>";
}

?>
```

Remove a tweet from your favorites

You can remove a tweet from your favorites list by authenticating and calling the `favorites/destroy` method.

This method requires a POST or DELETE request and isn't rate limited.

Output

This method has two output formats:

- XML
- JSON

On a successful post, this method will return the details of the tweet you just removed from your favorites, including the complete user details object of the author.

On a failed post, you will receive an error message explaining why you were unable to remove the tweet.

Input

This method requires one parameter, the id of the tweet you want to remove from your favorites.

- `id`: The numerical id of the status update.
  Example: `/favorites/destroy/1234.xml`

Example

Listing 8-18 is an example of how to programmatically remove a tweet from your favorites by using PHP and cURL to post to the `favorites/destroy` method. If a tweet is successfully removed, it displays the text of the recently removed tweet and the profile picture of the author.

Listing 8-18: How to Programmatically Remove a Tweet from Your Favorites

```
<?php

// Set username and password
$username = 'username';
$password = 'password';

$tweetIdToDelete = 5142491385;

// The Twitter favorites/destroy method
$url = "https://api.twitter.com/1/favorites/destroy/$tweetIdToDelete.xml";

// POST to Twitter API using curl
$curlHandle = curl_init();
curl_setopt($curlHandle, CURLOPT_URL, "$url");
curl_setopt($curlHandle, CURLOPT_USERAGENT, "Twitter App Development For
            Dummies: Example");
curl_setopt($curlHandle, CURLOPT_POST, 1);
curl_setopt($curlHandle, CURLOPT_RETURNTRANSFER, 1);
curl_setopt($curlHandle, CURLOPT_SSL_VERIFYPEER, false);
curl_setopt($curlHandle, CURLOPT_POSTFIELDS, "");
curl_setopt($curlHandle, CURLOPT_USERPWD, "$username:$password");
$apiResponse = curl_exec($curlHandle);

// Get HTTP Status Code
$info = curl_getinfo($curlHandle);
```

(continued)

Listing 8-18 *(continued)*

```
$http_code = $info['http_code'];
echo "<h1>HTTP Status Code: $http_code</h1>";

// Close cURL connection
curl_close($curlHandle);

// Get XML
$xml = new DOMDocument();
$xml->loadXML($apiResponse);

// Check for an error tag.
$errors = $xml->getElementsByTagName("error");

// If found, print the error. Else, success!
if($errors->length > 0)
{
    $errorMessage = $errors->item(0)->nodeValue;
    echo "<h1>$errorMessage</h1>";
}
else
{
    // Get favorited tweet text
    $textNode = $xml->getElementsByTagName("text");
    $text = $textNode->item(0)->nodeValue;

    // Get author's profile picture
    $profilePicNode = $xml->getElementsByTagName("profile_image_url");
    $profile_image_url = $profilePicNode->item(0)->nodeValue;

    // Print tweet and user's picture
    echo "<h1>Successfully removed the following tweet to your favorites:</h1>";
    echo "<img src=\"$profile_image_url\" width=\"48\" height=\"48\" />";
    echo "<p>$text</p>";
}

?>
```

Saved Searches Methods

Twitter provides the Search API to allow users to search Twitter for words and phrases. If you want to regularly monitor a word or phrase on Twitter, you can save your search query as a "saved search." Twitter links to your saved searches on your Twitter home page, and 3rd party applications can interact with your saved searches using the following four methods:

- saved_searches
- saved_searches/show
- saved_searches/create
- saved_searches/destroy

Retrieve all your saved searches

You can get a list of all your saved searches by authenticating and calling the saved_searches method.

This method requires a GET request and is rate limited. Chapter 7 explains the concern with rate limits.

Output

This method has two output formats:

- XML
- JSON

On a successful method call, it returns an array of detailed saved search objects for the authenticated user's entire saved searches.

If the authenticated user has no saved searches it returns an empty array and a HTTP status of 200.

Input

This method requires no input parameters.

Example

You can try the saved_searches method easily by typing http://api.twitter.com/1/saved_searches.xml into your browser's URL address bar. When requested by your browser, enter your Twitter user name and password. Then you receive the details of all your saved searches in XML format.

In Listing 8-19, I use the saved_searches method to pull all the authenticated user's saved searches and print their queries and the date they were created.

Listing 8-19: How to Get the Details of a Saved Search

```
<?php

// Set username and password
$username = 'username';
$password = 'password';

// The Twitter saved_searches method
$url = "https://api.twitter.com/1/saved_searches.xml";

// GET Twitter API results using curl
$curlHandle = curl_init();
curl_setopt($curlHandle, CURLOPT_URL, "$url");
curl_setopt($curlHandle, CURLOPT_USERAGENT, "Twitter App Development For
               Dummies: Example");
curl_setopt($curlHandle, CURLOPT_RETURNTRANSFER, 1);
curl_setopt($curlHandle, CURLOPT_SSL_VERIFYPEER, false);
curl_setopt($curlHandle, CURLOPT_USERPWD, "$username:$password");
$apiResponse = curl_exec($curlHandle);

// Get HTTP Status Code
$info = curl_getinfo($curlHandle);
$http_code = $info['http_code'];
echo "<h1>HTTP Status Code: $http_code</h1>";

// Close cURL connection
curl_close($curlHandle);

// Get XML
$xml = new DOMDocument();
$xml->loadXML($apiResponse);

// Check for an error tag.
$errors = $xml->getElementsByTagName("error");

// If found, print the error. Else, success!
if($errors->length > 0)
{
   $errorMessage = $errors->item(0)->nodeValue;
   echo "<h1>$errorMessage</h1>";
}
else
{
   $savedSearchNodes = $xml->getElementsByTagName("saved_search");

   foreach($savedSearchNodes as $savedSearch)
   {
      // Get search query
      $queryNode = $savedSearch->getElementsByTagName("query");
      $query = $queryNode->item(0)->nodeValue;
```

```
        // Get date search was created and saved
        $createdAtNode = $savedSearch->getElementsByTagName("created_at");
        $created_at = $createdAtNode->item(0)->nodeValue;

        // Print saved search query and created date
        echo "<p>Query: $query</p>";
        echo "<p>Created On: $created_at</p>";
        echo "<hr />";
    }
}
?>
```

Get the details of a saved search

You can get the details of a specified save search for the authenticated user by calling the `saved_searches/show` method.

This method requires a GET request and is rate limited. Chapter 7 explains the concern with rate limits.

Output

This method has two output formats:

- XML
- JSON

On a successful method call, it returns the complete saved search object.

If the saved search id doesn't exist you will receive an error message and a HTTP status code of 404.

Input

This method requires one parameter, the id of the saved search.

- `id`: The numerical id of the saved search.
  Example: `/saved_searches/show/1234.xml`

Example

In Listing 8-20, I use the `saved_searches/show` method to pull the details of saved search and print the query and the date it way created.

Listing 8-20: How to Get the Details of a Saved Search

```
<?php

// Set username and password
$username = 'username';
$password = 'password';

// The Twitter saved_searches/show method
$url = "https://api.twitter.com/1/saved_searches/show/2502630.xml";

// POST to Twitter API using curl
$curlHandle = curl_init();
curl_setopt($curlHandle, CURLOPT_URL, "$url");
curl_setopt($curlHandle, CURLOPT_USERAGENT, "Twitter App Development For
            Dummies: Example");
curl_setopt($curlHandle, CURLOPT_RETURNTRANSFER, 1);
curl_setopt($curlHandle, CURLOPT_SSL_VERIFYPEER, false);
curl_setopt($curlHandle, CURLOPT_USERPWD, "$username:$password");
$apiResponse = curl_exec($curlHandle);

// Get HTTP Status Code
$info = curl_getinfo($curlHandle);
$http_code = $info['http_code'];
echo "<h1>HTTP Status Code: $http_code</h1>";

// Close cURL connection
curl_close($curlHandle);

// Get XML
$xml = new DOMDocument();
$xml->loadXML($apiResponse);

// Check for an error tag.
$errors = $xml->getElementsByTagName("error");

// If found, print the error. Else, success!
if($errors->length > 0)
{
   $errorMessage = $errors->item(0)->nodeValue;
   echo "<h1>$errorMessage</h1>";
}
else
{
   // Get search query
   $queryNode = $xml->getElementsByTagName("query");
   $query = $queryNode->item(0)->nodeValue;

   // Get date search was created and saved
   $createdAtNode = $xml->getElementsByTagName("created_at");
   $created_at = $createdAtNode->item(0)->nodeValue;
```

```
    // Print saved search query and created date
    echo "<p>Query: $query</p>";
    echo "<p>Created On: $created_at</p>";
}

?>
```

Create a saved search

To create a new saved search, authenticate as the user you want to save the search for, and call the `saved_searches/create` method.

This method requires a POST request and is rate limited. Chapter 7 explains the concern with rate limits.

Output

This method has two output formats:

- XML
- JSON

On a successful post, this method will return the details of the saved search you just created. On a failed post, you will receive an error message explaining why you were unable to create the saved search.

Input

This method requires one parameter, the query text of the search you want to save.

- `query`: The search query you want to save. Example: `/saved_searches/create.xml?query=test`

Be sure to URL encode the `query` parameter. Your query may not be saved properly otherwise. In PHP you can do this with the urlencode function, like I have in Listing 8-21.

Example

Listing 8-21 is an example of how to programmatically create a saved search using PHP and cURL to post to the `saved_searches/create` method. If a saved search is successfully create, it displays the name of the recently create search.

Listing 8-21: How to Programmatically Create a Saved Search

```
<?php

// Set username and password
$username = 'username';
$password = 'password';

$searchQuery = urlencode("#TADD");

// The Twitter saved_searches/create method
$url = "https://api.twitter.com/1/saved_searches/create.xml";

// POST to Twitter API using curl
$curlHandle = curl_init();
curl_setopt($curlHandle, CURLOPT_URL, "$url");
curl_setopt($curlHandle, CURLOPT_USERAGENT, "Twitter App Development For
               Dummies: Example");
curl_setopt($curlHandle, CURLOPT_POST, 1);
curl_setopt($curlHandle, CURLOPT_RETURNTRANSFER, 1);
curl_setopt($curlHandle, CURLOPT_SSL_VERIFYPEER, false);
curl_setopt($curlHandle, CURLOPT_POSTFIELDS, "query=$searchQuery");
curl_setopt($curlHandle, CURLOPT_USERPWD, "$username:$password");
$apiResponse = curl_exec($curlHandle);

// Get HTTP Status Code
$info = curl_getinfo($curlHandle);
$http_code = $info['http_code'];
echo "<h1>HTTP Status Code: $http_code</h1>";

// Close cURL connection
curl_close($curlHandle);

// Get XML
$xml = new DOMDocument();
$xml->loadXML($apiResponse);

// Check for an error tag.
$errors = $xml->getElementsByTagName("error");

// If found, print the error. Else, success!
if($errors->length > 0)
{
   $errorMessage = $errors->item(0)->nodeValue;
   echo "<h1>$errorMessage</h1>";
}
else
{
   // Get name of the recently created saved search
```

```
    $nameNode = $xml->getElementsByTagName("name");
    $name = $nameNode->item(0)->nodeValue;

    // Print the name of the saved search
    echo "<h1>Successfully created the saved search: $name</h1>";
}
?>
```

Remove a saved search

You can remove a saved search from your profile by authenticating and calling the `saved_searches/destroy` method.

This method requires a POST or DELETE request and is rate limited. Chapter 7 explains the concern with rate limits.

Output

This method has two output formats:

- XML
- JSON

On a successful post, this method will return the details of the saved search you just removed. On a failed post, you will receive an error message explaining why you were unable to remove the saved search.

Input

This method requires one parameter, the id of the saved search you want to remove from your profile.

- `id`: The numerical id of a saved search.
  Example: `/saved_searches/destroy/1234.xml`

Example

Listing 8-22 is an example of how to programmatically remove a saved search from your profile by using PHP and cURL to post to the `saved_searches/destroy` method. If a saved search is successfully removed, it displays the name of the recently removed saved search.

Listing 8-22: How to Programmatically Remove a Saved Search

```
<?php

// Set username and password
$username = 'username';
$password = 'password';

$savesSearchIdToRemove = 2502585;

// The Twitter saved_searches/destroy method
$url =
"https://api.twitter.com/1/saved_searches/destroy/$savesSearchIdToRemove.xml";

// POST to Twitter API using curl
$curlHandle = curl_init();
curl_setopt($curlHandle, CURLOPT_URL, "$url");
curl_setopt($curlHandle, CURLOPT_USERAGENT, "Twitter App Development For
          Dummies: Example");
curl_setopt($curlHandle, CURLOPT_POST, 1);
curl_setopt($curlHandle, CURLOPT_RETURNTRANSFER, 1);
curl_setopt($curlHandle, CURLOPT_SSL_VERIFYPEER, false);
curl_setopt($curlHandle, CURLOPT_POSTFIELDS, "");
curl_setopt($curlHandle, CURLOPT_USERPWD, "$username:$password");
$apiResponse = curl_exec($curlHandle);

// Get HTTP Status Code
$info = curl_getinfo($curlHandle);
$http_code = $info['http_code'];
echo "<h1>HTTP Status Code: $http_code</h1>";

// Close cURL connection
curl_close($curlHandle);

// Get XML
$xml = new DOMDocument();
$xml->loadXML($apiResponse);

// Check for an error tag.
$errors = $xml->getElementsByTagName("error");

// If found, print the error. Else, success!
if($errors->length > 0)
{
  $errorMessage = $errors->item(0)->nodeValue;
  echo "<h1>$errorMessage</h1>";
}
elseif($http_code == "200")
{
  // Get name of the deleted saved search
  $nameNode = $xml->getElementsByTagName("name");
  $name = $nameNode->item(0)->nodeValue;

  // Print the name of the deleted saved search
```

```
    echo "<h1>Successfully removed the saved search: $name</h1>";
}
else
    echo "<h1>Error</h1>";
?>
```

Search API Methods

The Search API allows you to find words and phrases in the Twitter public timeline. This gives you the ability to monitor what the general Twitter public is tweeting about. The Search API even provides the most popular trending topics to give you an idea of what topics are popular at the moment. You can interact with the Search API using the following methods.

- search.twitter.com/search
- search.twitter.com/trends
- search.twitter.com/trends/daily
- search.twitter.com/trends/weekly

The URL for the search API is different from the rest of the API. The search API URL is: http://search.twitter.com.

Also, remember that the Search API has a different and separate rate limit than the rest of the Twitter API that is based entirely on the requesting IP address.

How to search for tweets with the API

To search for a tweets on Twitter use the `http://search.twitter.com/search` method.

This method doesn't require authentication, it requires a GET request, and is rate limited. Chapter 7 explains the concern with rate limits.

Output

This method has two output formats:

- JSON
- Atom

On a successful post, this method will return the details of the saved search you just removed. On a failed post, you will receive an error message explaining why you were unable to remove the saved search.

Input

This method requires one parameter, the id of the saved search you want to remove from your profile. The other parameters are optional.

- `q`: The URL encoded search query to be performed.
  Example: search.twitter.com/search.atom?q=tadd
- `callback`: The callback function for JSON requests.
  Example: search.twitter.com/search.json?callback=foo&q=tadd
- `lang`: The ISO 639-1 code used to filter tweets by language.
  Example: search.twitter.com/search.atom?lang=en&q=tadd
- `locale`: Used to declare the language of the search query. "ja" is currently the only available value.
  Example: search.twitter.com/search.atom?q=東大地&locale=ja
- `rpp`: The desired amount of search results per page less than 100.
  Example: search.twitter.com/search.atom?q= tadd&rpp=15
- `page`: Page to retrieve older search results.
  Example: search.twitter.com/search.atom?q=tadd&rpp=15&page=6
- `since_id`: Returns tweets that are more recent than the id specified.
  Example: search.twitter.com/search.atom?q=tadd&since_id=12345
- `geocode`: Return results in a radius around a latitude and longitude based on the users geocode location in their profile. The string must be in the form "latitude,longitude,radius" where radius is declared as "mi" (miles) or "km" (kilometers).
  Example: search.twitter.com/search.atom?geocode=41.353129%2C-62.155203%2C60mi
- `show_user`: When set to true it adds "<user>:" to the front of retrieved tweets.
  Example: search.twitter.com/search.atom?q=twitterapi&show_user=true

Example

Listing 8-23 is an example of how to programmatically remove a saved search from your profile by using PHP and cURL to post to the `saved_searches/destroy` method. If a saved search is successfully removed, it displays the name of the recently removed saved search.

Listing 8-23: How to Search Using the API

```
<?php

// The Twitter search method
$url = "http://search.twitter.com/search.json?lang=en&q=twitter";

// Get Twitter API results with cURL
$curlHandle = curl_init();
curl_setopt($curlHandle, CURLOPT_URL, "$url");
curl_setopt($curlHandle, CURLOPT_USERAGENT, "Twitter App Development For
             Dummies: Example");
curl_setopt($curlHandle, CURLOPT_RETURNTRANSFER, 1);
$apiResponse = curl_exec($curlHandle);

// Get HTTP Status Code
$info = curl_getinfo($curlHandle);
$http_code = $info['http_code'];
echo "<h1>HTTP Status Code: $http_code</h1>";

// Close cURL connection
curl_close($curlHandle);

$json = json_decode($apiResponse);

// Print each search status
foreach($json->results as $status)
{
   $statusText = $status->text;
   $statusId = $status->id;
   $userName = $status->from_user;

   echo "<p><a href=\"http://twitter.com/$userName/statuses/$statusId\">$statusT
             ext</a></p>";
}

?>
```

Get the current trending topics

There are two methods to get the current top 10 trending topics on Twitter:

- search.twitter.com/trends
- search.twitter.com/trends/current

Both of these methods don't require authentication, require a GET request, and are rate limited. Chapter 7 explains the concern with rate limits.

Output

These methods have one output format:

- JSON

Both of these methods return the names of the top 10 trends and the time of the request. However, search.twitter.com/trends includes a URL to the search results for the current trends, while search.twitter.com/trends/current returns the search query for the trend.

A failed request will return an error message.

Input

The `search.twitter.com/trends` method has no input parameters. However, the `search.twitter.com/trends/current` method has one optional parameter:

- `exclude`: You can exclude hashtags from your results by setting this parameter value to "hashtags."
  Example: `search.twitter.com/trends/current.json?exclude=hashtags`

Example

Listing 8-24 is an example of how to retrieve the current trends on Twitter using cURL, PHP, JSON, and the `search.twitter.com/trends` method. In this example I print each of the current top 10 trends and link them to their Twitter search page.

Listing 8-24: How to Retrieve the Current Trends on Twitter

```
<?php

// The Twitter search trends method
$url = "http://search.twitter.com/trends.json";

// Get Twitter API results with cURL
$curlHandle = curl_init();
curl_setopt($curlHandle, CURLOPT_URL, "$url");
curl_setopt($curlHandle, CURLOPT_USERAGENT, "Twitter App Development For
            Dummies: Example");
curl_setopt($curlHandle, CURLOPT_RETURNTRANSFER, 1);
$apiResponse = curl_exec($curlHandle);

// Get HTTP Status Code
$info = curl_getinfo($curlHandle);
$http_code = $info['http_code'];
echo "<h1>HTTP Status Code: $http_code</h1>";
```

```
// Close cURL connection
curl_close($curlHandle);

$json = json_decode($apiResponse);

// Print each trend
foreach($json->trends as $trend)
{
   $trendName = $trend->name;
   $trendUrl = $trend->url;

   echo "<p><a href=\"$trendUrl\">$trendName</a></p>";
}

?>
```

Get the days trending topics

You can get the top 20 trends per hour for a specific day by using the `search.twitter.com/trends/daily` method.

This method doesn't require authentication, it requires a GET request, and is rate limited. Chapter 7 explains the concern with rate limits.

Output

This method has one output format:

- JSON

On a successful request this method will return an array per hour that includes the name of each trend and the search query for the trend. A failed request will return an error message.

Input

This method has two optional input parameters.

- `date`: The day you want to retrieve trends for. It should be formatted like YYYY-MM-DD.
  Example: `search.twitter.com/trends/daily.json?date=2009-03-03`
- `exclude`: You can exclude hashtags from your results by setting this parameter value to "hashtags."
  Example: `search.twitter.com/trends/daily.json?exclude=hashtags`

Example

Listing 8-25 is an example of how to retrieve today's current trends on Twitter using cURL, PHP, and JSON. The results aren't guaranteed to be in chronological order, so I make sure to sort the results in the example.

Listing 8-25: How to Retrieve the Day's Trends

```
<?php

// The Twitter search trends method
$url = "http://search.twitter.com/trends/daily.json";

// Get Twitter API results with cURL
$curlHandle = curl_init();
curl_setopt($curlHandle, CURLOPT_URL, "$url");
curl_setopt($curlHandle, CURLOPT_USERAGENT, "Twitter App Development For
                Dummies: Example");
curl_setopt($curlHandle, CURLOPT_RETURNTRANSFER, 1);
$apiResponse = curl_exec($curlHandle);

// Get HTTP Status Code
$info = curl_getinfo($curlHandle);
$http_code = $info['http_code'];
echo "<h1>HTTP Status Code: $http_code</h1>";

// Close cURL connection
curl_close($curlHandle);

$json = json_decode($apiResponse);

// The results don't come back in chronological order
// So here I add them to an array I can sort
$daysTrends = array();
foreach($json->trends as $key => $hourlyTrends){
    $daysTrends[$key] = $hourlyTrends;
}

// Sort the trends by hour
ksort($daysTrends);

// Print each hours trend
foreach($daysTrends as $key => $hourlyTrends)
{
   echo "<h1>$key</h1>";
   echo "<ul>";
   foreach($hourlyTrends as $trend)
   {
      $trendName = $trend->name;
      $trendQuery = urlencode($trend->query);
```

```
        echo "<li><a href=\"http://search.twitter.com/search?q=$trendQuery\">$tren
              dName</a></li>";
    }
    echo "</ul>";
}

?>
```

Get the weeks trending topics

You can get the top 30 trends per day for a specific week by using the `search.twitter.com/trends/weekly` method.

This method doesn't require authentication, it requires a GET request, and is rate limited. Chapter 7 explains the concern with rate limits.

Output

This method has one output format:

- JSON

On a successful request this method will return an array per day that includes the name of each trend and the search query for the trend. A failed request will return an error message.

Input

This method has two optional input parameters.

- `date`: The day you want to start your retrieved week. It should be formatted like YYYY-MM-DD.
  Example: `search.twitter.com/trends/weekly.json?date=2009-03-03`
- `exclude`: You can exclude hashtags from your results by setting this parameter value to "hashtags."
  Example: `search.twitter.com/trends/weekly.json?exclude=hashtags`

Example

Listing 8-26 is an example of how to retrieve this week's current trends on Twitter using cURL, PHP, and JSON. The results aren't guaranteed to be in chronological order, so I make sure to sort the results in the example.

Listing 8-26: How to Retrieve the Week's Trends

```
<?php

// The Twitter search trends/weekly method
$url = "http://search.twitter.com/trends/weekly.json";

// Get Twitter API results with cURL
$curlHandle = curl_init();
curl_setopt($curlHandle, CURLOPT_URL, "$url");
curl_setopt($curlHandle, CURLOPT_USERAGENT, "Twitter App Development For
            Dummies: Example");
curl_setopt($curlHandle, CURLOPT_RETURNTRANSFER, 1);
$apiResponse = curl_exec($curlHandle);

// Get HTTP Status Code
$info = curl_getinfo($curlHandle);
$http_code = $info['http_code'];
echo "<h1>HTTP Status Code: $http_code</h1>";

// Close cURL connection
curl_close($curlHandle);

$json = json_decode($apiResponse);

// The results don't come back in chronological order
// So here I add them to an array I can sort
$weeksTrends = array();
foreach($json->trends as $key => $dailyTrends){
    $weeksTrends[$key] = $dailyTrends;
}

// Sort the trends by day
ksort($weeksTrends);

// Print each hours trend
foreach($weeksTrends as $key => $dailyTrends)
{
   echo "<h1>$key</h1>";
   echo "<ul>";
   foreach($dailyTrends as $trend)
   {
      $trendName = $trend->name;
      $trendQuery = urlencode($trend->query);
      echo "<li><a href=\"http://search.twitter.com/search?q=$trendQuery\">$tren
            dName</a></li>";
   }
   echo "</ul>";
}

?>
```

Chapter 9

Selecting an Idea

In This Chapter

- How to come up with an idea for a Twitter app
- Why build a Twitter app
- A description of the demo product, Twooshes

The goal of this chapter is to cover the reasons why you might want to build a Twitter app and help you settle on an idea with wings. Whatever you decide to build, it should be something that interests you, something that users want, and something you can actually build. But the most important thing is to pick something and get started on it.

Most good ideas die before they ever have a chance of being realized. Don't spend too much time thinking up the perfect app. Pick an idea and go with it.

The discussion in this chapter is framed for Twitter applications. However, the concepts in this chapter could be applied to any consumer-based application.

If you don't need inspiration or advice on settling on a Twitter application idea, you can skip this chapter and get started on this book's project demo, Twooshes.

Imagining a Successful Twitter App

For the purpose of this chapter I define success as a popular application with many happy users that satisfies the developer's initial desires for developing the app.

To build a popular application, you can't just consider what you want. You must consider what your users want, and whether you have the skills and resources to deliver that magnificent concept in your head.

When you are thinking up your next application, consider these three points:

- What is my motivation?
- What do people want in my application?
- Do I have the available skills and resources to develop my idea?

What Is Your Motivation?

If you know you want to build a Twitter app, but you're not sure what you want to build, it's helpful to look at the reasons why you want to build an app in the first place. Identifying these reasons can help inspire you.

Understanding your motivation behind building an application is important for another reason: if you are unable to satisfy your desires for building your app, you may not develop your idea to its full potential, or abandon your app all together. Understanding your motivation and fulfilling your wants will fuel your passion for your application, and increase your work quality and output. If you are developing an application for a client, your motivation may differ from your employer, but it will still affect your work.

Your application idea is a product of your motivation to build an app. Generally, your motivation will come first, then your idea will take shape. There could be numerous reasons why you are motivated to create your application.

Enjoyment

One of the best reasons to set out on any endeavor, including Twitter app development, is the sheer enjoyment of it.

If you have an idea that someone's already done, or you don't think it will be successful, that's no reason to kill the idea. Sometimes you simply must fulfill an inner need. Usually the best products are born out of their creator's enjoyment. So stop worrying and start building!

You can always make changes to your application. Once you receive feedback from your users, you can improve it.

Make money

Making money and creating a business is a common topic in most software niches, such as iPhone and desktop application development. However, many people gloss over third-party Twitter applications making money and becoming businesses. It is possible, and you're doing yourself a disservice if you instantly discredit the idea.

Part III of this book covers money making in detail.

If you have an idea you're really excited about, but you aren't sure how to make money with it now, don't worry too much about it. Get started building your application. You can figure out how to monetize it later. Just look at Twitter. At the time of this writing, they still don't have a solid revenue model. It's important to understand, if you have a good product, you can make money with it. However, you can't make money with only an idea for a product.

Filling a need

It's cliché, but necessity is indeed the mother of invention. When I created Friend Or Follow (`http://friendorfollow.com`) I did it to help myself manage my Twitter friends and followers, and because I had a weekend to play around with the Twitter API. I had no intentions of creating a business or writing a book about Twitter application development. Luckily, I managed to fill a need not only for myself, but also for many other Twitter users.

So when you're looking for ideas on Twitter applications, ask yourself, "What do I wish Twitter could do?" If you have a good answer to that question, it's likely that at least a few other people share your need, and you have yourself a good product idea.

If your new product doesn't take off, at least you've built a cool app for yourself.

Make it better

Another common project killer is the concept that your product idea must be completely unique for it to be good. If you come up with an idea and find-out someone else, or perhaps multiple people, are also working on the same idea, you have proof that there is a market for your product. Now the key is to simply take that idea and implement it better than all your competitors. That may seem a little daunting, but you can do it.

You can differentiate yourself from your competitors by taking a different approach. If their app has tons of functionality, but is complicated to use, try making yours dead simple by including less features. You can also learn from your competitors by seeing what they've done and how their users have reacted. Find out what their users want and add that to your application.

It's like publishing a book. There are other books on Twitter application development, but you bought *this book* because it's best for *you* (I hope).

You might even want to take a piece of functionality from Twitter itself and improve upon it. Or you could reinvent the entire Twitter interface and make it your own. Brizzly (`http://brizzly.com`) is a good example of this.

Build your brand's reputation

Building a popular Twitter application can increase your reputation, or your company's. Much like how a novelist or director might gain a fan base of people who follow his or her work, if you build a useful or entertaining application that people like, they may start to watch what you are up to next. You may even become known as an expert in your domain. You can use this reputation to boost the launch of your next project or the next feature set of your current projects. This is especially true when building a popular Twitter application, because the people who are interested in your work will subscribe to your Twitter feed.

Put your Twitter username somewhere on your application!

Support a cause

You may want to build a Twitter application to promote a particular cause or charity. For example, the app TwitCause (`http://twitcause.com`) was created for Twitter users to nominate, promote, and raise donations over Twitter for a new charity every week.

Another example is Tweet Congress (`http://tweetcongress.com`). Tweet Congress advocates open and transparent government. To aid in this cause they keep track of which US senators, congressmen, and other appointed officials are on Twitter, to make it easy for their constituents to follow and interact with.

Why Do People Use a Twitter App?

People choose to use an application for a variety of reasons. It could be for anyone of, or all of, these reasons: it helps solve a problem, it's entertaining, it's easy to use, and/or because they trust it. When you are brainstorming on what you're going to build, ask yourself if your application idea can do the following:

Solves a problem

The main reason anyone uses an application is because it solves a particular problem for him or her.

A good example of an application that makes life easier for Twitter users is CoTweet (`http://cotweet.com`). CoTweet makes it easy for a team of people to manage their organization's Twitter account. It allows them to easily keep track of who on their team has corresponded to which customers, make notes about those customers for other team members, and more.

It's entertaining

If your software solves a problem, you can gain a competitive advantage if you also entertain the user as they work out their problem. However, some software aims only to entertain.

Video games are the grand daddy of entertaining applications, but users may also find entertainment in analytical sites like TweetStats (`http://tweetstats.com`). TweetStats presents a Twitter user with all kinds of stats about the tweeting behavior. A user may not have any practical use for this information, but the application can be interesting and entertaining.

It's easy to use

When given the option between an application that is confusing and one that is dead simple to use, more users usually opt for the easy to use application. However, there are exceptions to this rule.

If a user has used an application for a long time and learned all its ins and outs, they may be reluctant to switch to a competing piece of software, even if it's easier to use. This problem is common in accounting and office applications, where users have learned and used the industry standard for years. A new competing piece of software may be easier to learn and use than the established piece of software, but the learning curve may be too steep for a veteran user to switch to the competing application.

Still, as a new comer to a market, you should make your software easier to use than your competitor's to gain an advantage in the marketplace. If your application is more productive to use than your competitors, you can eventually overtake them through the word of mouth of satisfied users.

They trust it

Users want to know that their login credentials, credit card information, and user data is in trustworthy hands. If your application doesn't appear trustworthy and credible, you may not win over many users.

There are several ways to gain your user's trust:

- Avoid asking for a user's Twitter password.
- If you must authenticate the user with Twitter, use OAuth.
- Have a professional design. I cover this in detail in Chapter 13.
- Make support contact information easy to find.
- Include your name in your *application about* section.
- Use SSL (Secure Sockets Layer) when collect payment information or login credentials.
- Get user testimonials and display them.

Do You Have the Skill and Resources to Build Your App?

It takes more than a good idea and motivation to build a successful application. You need to have the skill and resources to build your idea. For example, you may really want your car to tweet when it needs an oil change. Do you have the technical knowledge to build a device that can do that? If not, do you have the money to hire someone who does? If you were to design that device, do you know how to manufacture it?

Start with a small manageable project. If you have several application concepts in your head that you are passionate about, start with the simplest idea that you believe will have audience appeal.

Enough Jibber Jabber! Start Building!

Hopefully the advice in this chapter helps you choose a viable application idea. However, it is imperative that you not get too hung up on what to build, and simply start building. Developing software and even creating a business is an iterative process. You may set out to do one thing and halfway through realize a great new opportunity. If you never start building, iterating through product versions, and getting user feedback, you will never build a successful application. If you still don't have an idea for an app, you can borrow mine, and make it better.

In the next section of the book I will walk you through the process of building a full-fledged Twitter application. The application is called Twooshes.

A twoosh is a tweet that is exactly 140 characters long.

Twooshes is a Twitter game. It will monitor the Twitter streams of the users that follow the @Twooshes account and look for tweets that are exactly 140 characters. If it finds a twoosh, it will give that user 1 point. To make the game a little more interesting, if Twooshes finds a tweet that contains a current trending topic, it will subtract a point from the user. There is no real practical use for the Twooshes application. It's all just good fun. To monetize Twooshes, I intend to use the Featured Users (`http://featuredusers.com`) ad network, and a liberal use of Magpie (`http://be-a-magpie.com`) sponsored tweets.

I use the domain name and Twitter account "Twooshes" for the example application in this book. You will need to create your own application name to follow along. It can be anything you like, but avoid including the word Twitter in your name. That's trademark infringement. Use your imagination, but don't spend too much time thinking about it. It's time to start coding!

Part III

Creation — Developing Your Application

"This program's really helped me learn a new language. It's so buggy I'm constantly talking with overseas service reps."

In this part . . .

The chapters in this part show you how to take control of your application and detail it. When you look behind the curtain, this is the stuff you see the great Wizard reading while he twists knobs and throws switches.

Chapter 10

Selecting Libraries, Design Patterns, and Frameworks

In This Chapter

- Leveraging existing tools and patterns
- Picking out a library and framework for Twooshes
- Understanding the MVC design pattern

When you sit down to start coding your Web application, you shouldn't start from scratch. Much like how you don't have to start coding from 0's and 1's, you don't have to start from a blank PHP file. You can build on top of the previous generation's breakthroughs by using free, high-quality libraries, frameworks, and design patterns. Leveraging these tools saves you time, increases your code quality, and lets you get straight to the core of your project.

Twitter API Libraries Can Speed Up Development

Earlier in this book, I showed you how to interact with the Twitter API. You may have noticed it is pretty straightforward but the code is a little redundant. Every time you connect to Twitter using cURL, and parse data using DOMDocument, the code looks the same as the last time you called the API. This is a great opportunity to create libraries, functions, or classes to reduce the amount of redundant code, and make interacting with the Twitter API easy.

By centralizing your code and removing redundancies, you make it easier to read, maintain, and consequently decrease the potential for bugs. However, you don't need to build your own library from scratch. Other developers have already created open-source libraries, in numerous programming languages, that you can use for free. Thanks to their efforts, you can skip all this legwork, and get to the part of development you're interested in.

If building libraries is what you're interested in, then by all means create your own. Or you can contribute to a pre-existing library and improve it for yourself and the rest of the Twitter community.

You can view a fairly comprehensive list of open source Twitter libraries, maintained by Twitter, on the Twitter API Wiki at `http://apiwiki.twitter.com/Libraries`.

For the Twooshes project, I use the Twitter library found in the PHP Zend Framework. It isn't the most comprehensive Twitter PHP library available, but it's built into the rest of the Zend Framework.

Web Application Frameworks

Web application frameworks are code projects that encapsulate common Web development tasks. They serve as a Web application's foundation, which the developer then builds upon. The framework's purposes are to

- Decrease development time, by relieving the developer from coding common Web application tasks
- Increase the quality of the project, by abstracting common tasks using tested code.

Use software frameworks whenever possible:

- They prevent you from reinventing the wheel.
- They usually encourage good design patterns.

  Having good design patterns and leveraging a popular framework also makes it easier for other developers to work on your product, due to recognizable methods and patterns.

For us PHP developers, there are several PHP frameworks. These are popular:

- Agavi: `http://agavi.org`
- CakePHP: `http://cakephp.org`
- CodeIgniter: `http://codeigniter.com`
- Symfony: `http://symfony-project.org`
- Zend Framework: `http://framework.zend.com`

  I use the Zend Framework (ZF) for the Twooshes project in this book because it is one of the most popular PHP frameworks. Finding books, reference material, and support groups for ZF is fairly easy. ZF also has a corporate sponsor, Zend Technologies, which is co-founded by two PHP core developers, Andi Gutmans and Zeev Suraski. There have also been technical contributions from corporations like IBM, Google, Microsoft, and Adobe Systems. With heavyweights like this working on ZF, you know it has to meet a high level of quality.

Another big selling point for ZF is it has a Twitter API library built in. In addition, ZF supports and encourages the model-view-controller design pattern.

Model View Control

This chapter is about avoiding reinventing things: design patterns are no exception. Design patterns are conceptual ideas on how to structure software that has been observed, reused, and tested in numerous applications.

Model-view-control (MVC) is a popular software design pattern. I use it on the Twooshes project in this book. It is named after its three conceptual parts:

- Model: This is where data comes from.
- View: This is where the HTML is.
- Controller: This is where the business logic is, and where the view gets its data.

The strength of the MVC design pattern comes from the isolation of its three parts. By separating the HTML, data access code, and business logic, you divide your problem into smaller, more manageable pieces. This makes your application easier to build, scale, test, and maintain.

The MVC design pattern also requires isolation of its parts. The model and view aren't on speaking terms, and they always use the controller to talk to one another. The basic workflow for the MVC pattern is illustrated in Figure 10-1.

Walking through the MVC workflow goes something like the following:

1. A user requests a Web page.
2. The controller notices the requested Web page requires data from the database, so the controller asks for the data from the model.
3. The model gathers the data and gives it to the controller.

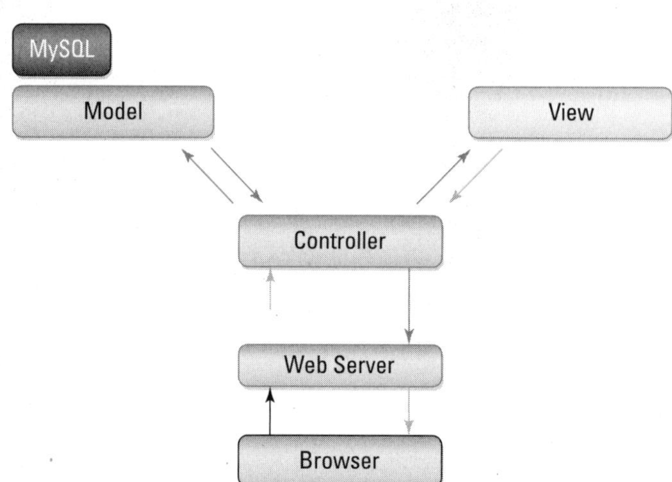

Figure 10-1: MVC pattern workflow.

4. The controller hands the data over to the view to integrate it into the HTML.
5. The controller gives the completed HTML to the Web user.

Here are a few tips to help you conform to the MVC pattern:

- You should never have SQL code in your view.
- Your view should never reference anything in the model.
- The controller should be lightweight, with as little code as possible.
- The model can be fat with code, but it should only deal in gathering and interfacing with data.

Now that you have a grasp on the libraries, frameworks, and design patterns, and you know which ones are used to build Twooshes, it's time to set up our server.

Chapter 11

Hosting In the Clouds

In This Chapter

- Hosting solution options
- Setting up your servers for the Twooshes project
- Uploading project files to your Web server

Before you jump in with the Twooshes project, you need to set up your servers. This chapter includes a brief overview of the Web hosting solutions available to you. I also select a Web hosting solution for the Twooshes project and walk you through the setup process. You also learn how to transfer files to your server and how to setup your domain name.

Types of Web Hosting Solutions

There are numerous Web hosting solutions to choose from. Here are the three most popular solutions for your consideration.

Shared web hosting

Shared Web hosting is usually the most inexpensive way to have your Web content hosted. In a shared Web hosting environment, everyone shares the same computing resources. Each user is limited to the amount of resources they can use.

This can be a major drawback if your application requires a lot of processing power, memory, bandwidth, or disk space.

However, shared Web hosting is an excellent solution for many users who host small Web sites that haven't yet gained a large audience.

Dedicated web hosting

To get the most Web hosting power possible, you can run your Web site on a server completely dedicated to your app. This is dedicated Web hosting. It comes in a few different flavors.

- Leased: You can lease a physical server from an Internet service provider (ISP) and then manage the server yourself.
- Managed: You can lease a physical server and signup for a support contract from your ISP, where someone manages and keeps an eye on your server 24/7.

  This tends to be the most expensive hosting option.
- Co-location: If you own your own servers, you can host it at an ISP's data center by paying a co-location lease. In this lease, you're paying for the physical space your server takes up, the electricity, the bandwidth, and the facility features like air conditioning and backup electricity generators.

Dedicated Web hosting is the most expensive hosting option, but if your site's audience grows to enormous sizes, you may need this kind of capacity.

Cloud computing

Cloud computing is a fluffy term, but the concept of "cloud computing" or "cloud hosting" refers to computing resources that are available on demand, over the Internet, for use by a consumer. Examples of computing resources vary from Google's Gmail, to on-demand disk storage space such as Amazon's S3 (`http://aws.amazon.com/s3`).

In the loosest sense of the term, Twitter could be considered a cloud computing resource. For example, you send the Twitter API a request over the Internet and it performs an action and sends you the results.

With cloud computing, the consumer needs no knowledge of the infrastructure required to run the computing resources. The consumer simply requests what resources they need from the "cloud" and the cloud returns the results.

Hosting in the cloud refers to outsourcing your Web server needs to cloud computing services. This way, you don't need to consider server infrastructure. Further, you can increase or decrease your server's resources on demand.

This is great for a small Web application that needs the ability to scale quickly.

It's more expensive than shared Web hosting, but it offers more flexibility, and is usually much cheaper than starting with a dedicated server.

Choosing a Hosting Provider

You should always start with the smallest Web hosting solution and grow into the next largest solution. There is no reason to spend money on resources you don't need. I usually recommend individuals start with shared Web hosting. If you have less than a few hundred visitors per day, shared Web hosting works fine and is much less expensive than other hosting solutions. If your application starts to peak above approximately 300 visitors per day, you need to start preparing to migrate to a larger Web host.

If possible, get a Web host with a static IP address. Shared Web hosts usually assign a dynamic IP address. In the past, Twitter has banned large blocks of IP addresses belonging to shared Web hosts, due to Twitter API abuse originating from an IP address owned by the Web host. The consequence to this is Twitter creates collateral damage banning well behaving Twitter apps running on the same shared Web host. For this reason if your application begins to gather an audience you need to get a static IP address.

For Twooshes, I go against my own advice of starting on a shared Web host, and opt for a cloud hosting solution. This is because I predict Twooshes will receive more traffic than a shared host can handle, but not enough to warrant a dedicated Web server. The service I use is Rackspace Cloud Servers (`http://rackspacecloud.com`). With Rackspace Cloud Servers, I can set up a virtual server with dedicated resources and increase or decrease those resources on demand. This is great for a modestly popular Web site that may need to grow quickly.

There is really no reason to start a project with a dedicated Web server. Dedicated servers are something you grow into, not start with.

For Twooshes, I use two Rackspace Cloud virtual servers to create

- Web server
- Database server

Splitting the application's workload horizontally, across more servers, scales to handle more traffic, for less money, than using fewer more powerful servers. However, you don't need to split these two servers right away. To save money, you could run your Web server and database server on the same virtual machine until you need more capacity. At that point, you could split the workload across two machines. However, because Rackspace Cloud allows me to increase my server's resources on demand, it's easy to grow in capacity vertically (giving the servers more power). However, you can't split your database and Web server on demand. It requires a bit of work and server downtime. I prefer to start my projects with the database and Web server on different machines, and use the smallest possible virtual machine for both servers. This is the most obvious horizontal scaling trick you can make for your Web application.

Setting Up Your Servers

To get started, create a Rackspace Cloud Server account at `http://rackspacecloud.com`. After you have set up your billing information and created your account, log in to Rackspace Cloud at `http://manage.rackspacecloud.com`. Once logged in, you are greeted with your Rackspace dashboard.

Setting up Apache and PHP

It's time to create your Apache Web server. Follow these steps:

1. **Click the "Hosting" tab on the left-hand navigation menu.**
2. **Click "Cloud Servers" in the drop-down menu.**

   This is your Cloud Servers dashboard. Figure 11-1 is a screenshot of my Cloud Servers dashboard. Yours should look similar, but without any existing servers listed.
3. **Click the "Add New Server" button at the top of your dashboard.**

   At the top of the new page, you are presented with a menu of server sizes.
4. **Select the smallest server size (currently 256 MB).**

   Below the server sizes menu is a field to enter the name of your server and a menu of "Default Cloud Server Images."

5. **Name your server anything you like.**

   I prefer to use the name of my project with the server type prefixed to it. So since this is the Web server I've named mine "TwooshesWeb."
6. **For the "Default Cloud Server Images," select Ubuntu Hardy (currently listed as: Ubuntu 8.04.2 LTS (hardy)).**

Figure 11-1: My Cloud Servers dashboard.

7. **Click "Add Cloud Server."**

   After clicking "Add Cloud Server," you are taken to your new server's dashboard, as seen in Figure 11-2. Your server takes a few moments to build.

8. **Jot down the root password displayed at the top of the screen and go grab a cup of coffee.**

   Once your server is done building the status on the dashboard says "Active" and you receive an email from Rackspace with your server's IP address and root password.

When your server is built, it's time to install the Apache Web server on it.

Before you can install Apache, you must open your server's command prompt. Follow these steps:

1. **Still logged in and looking at your server's dashboard, click the "Console" button on the "Overview" tab under "Actions For This Server," at the top of the screen.**

   A dialog box opens to remind you to make sure Javascript is enabled on your browser.

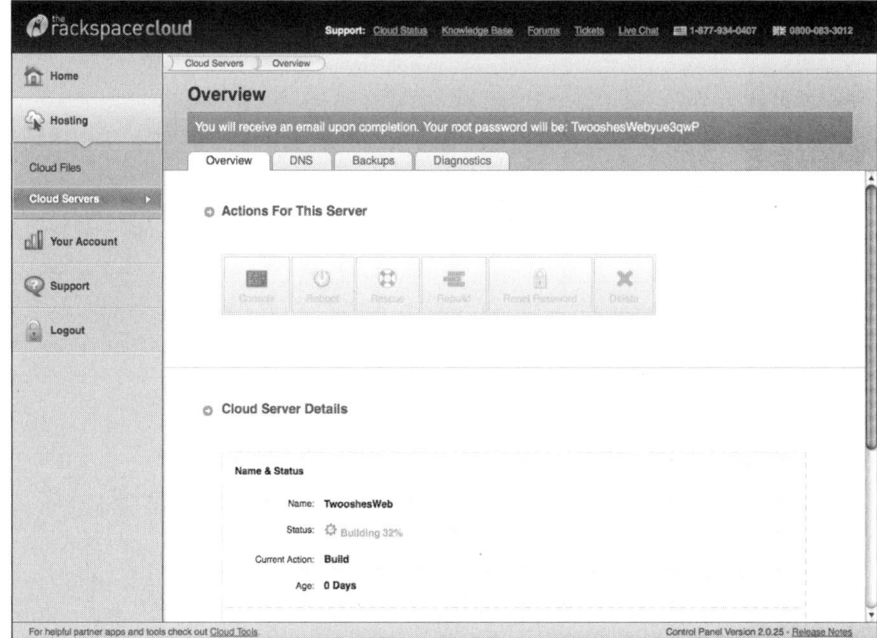

Figure 11-2: The Twooshes Web server dashboard.

2. **Click the "Open Console" button to dismiss this dialog box and continue.**

   A new browser window opens, with content similar to Figure 11-3, showing your server's command line.

   Sometimes, the console window opens too small. Maximize the window to be sure you can see everything.

   From here, you can log in to your Web server for the first time.

3. **Type in `root` as the login name, then enter the root password you jotted down when you created your server.**

   You didn't write down the root password? You can look it up in the e-mail Rackspace sent you after the server finished building.

   Once logged in, you are presented with a blank command prompt that looks something like this, except "TwooshesWeb" is replaced with whatever you named your server when you created it:

```
root@TwooshesWeb:~#
```

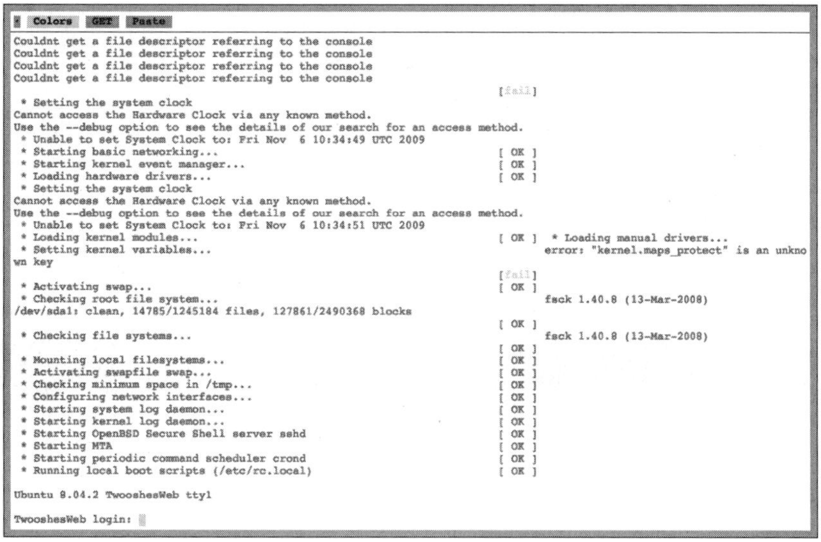

```
* Colors GET Paste
Couldnt get a file descriptor referring to the console
Couldnt get a file descriptor referring to the console
Couldnt get a file descriptor referring to the console
Couldnt get a file descriptor referring to the console
                                                              [fail]
 * Setting the system clock
Cannot access the Hardware Clock via any known method.
Use the --debug option to see the details of our search for an access method.
 * Unable to set System Clock to: Fri Nov  6 10:34:49 UTC 2009
 * Starting basic networking...                               [ OK ]
 * Starting kernel event manager...                           [ OK ]
 * Loading hardware drivers...                                [ OK ]
 * Setting the system clock
Cannot access the Hardware Clock via any known method.
Use the --debug option to see the details of our search for an access method.
 * Unable to set System Clock to: Fri Nov  6 10:34:51 UTC 2009
 * Loading kernel modules...                                  [ OK ]  * Loading manual drivers...
 * Setting kernel variables...                                       error: "kernel.maps_protect" is an unkno
wn key
                                                              [fail]
 * Activating swap...                                         [ OK ]
 * Checking root file system...                                      fsck 1.40.8 (13-Mar-2008)
/dev/sda1: clean, 14785/1245184 files, 127861/2490368 blocks
                                                              [ OK ]
 * Checking file systems...                                          fsck 1.40.8 (13-Mar-2008)
                                                              [ OK ]
 * Mounting local filesystems...                              [ OK ]
 * Activating swapfile swap...                                [ OK ]
 * Checking minimum space in /tmp...                          [ OK ]
 * Configuring network interfaces...                          [ OK ]
 * Starting system log daemon...                              [ OK ]
 * Starting kernel log daemon...                              [ OK ]
 * Starting OpenBSD Secure Shell server sshd                  [ OK ]
 * Starting MTA                                               [ OK ]
 * Starting periodic command scheduler crond                  [ OK ]
 * Running local boot scripts (/etc/rc.local)                 [ OK ]

Ubuntu 8.04.2 TwooshesWeb tty1

TwooshesWeb login:
```

Figure 11-3: Your server console inside your Web browser.

Install Apache and PHP

After your command prompt is open, you can install Apache and PHP on your new server. Follow these steps:

1. **Type the command `apt-get update` in the command prompt and press enter to update Ubuntu's install package libraries.**
2. **Type the command `apt-get install apache2` and press enter to install the Apache Web server.**

   The installer stops to ask you if you want to use disk space. Type Y and press Enter.
3. **Type the command `apt-get install php5` and press enter to install PHP.**

   The installer stops to ask you if you want to use disk space. Type Y and press Enter.
4. **Type the command `apt-get install libapache2-mod-php5` and press enter to integrate Apache and PHP.**

   The installer stops to ask you if you want to use disk space. Type Y and press Enter.

5. **Type the command `apt-get install php5-mysql` and press enter to install MySQL module for PHP.**

   The installer stops to ask you if you want to use disk space. Type Y and press Enter.

6. **Type the command `apt-get install curl php5-curl` and press Enter to install cURL for PHP.**

7. **Restart Apache by typing the command `/etc/init.d/apache2 restart` and pressing Enter.**

Once you've completed the installation of apache, you can test it by typing your server's IP address in your browser's address bar. You should see a blank Web page with the words "It works!" in the top left.

Your server's IP address can be found on your server's Rackspace Cloud dashboard and in the e-mail you received after your server finished building.

Install mod_rewrite

Next, you need to setup support for .htaccess files by installing and enabling mod_rewrite. This is a requirement for the Zend Framework I use for the Twooses project. Follow these steps:

1. **With the command prompt still open, install mod_rewrite by typing the command `a2enmod rewrite` and pressing Enter.**

2. **Type the command `/etc/init.d/apache2 force-reload` and press Enter to enable the module.**

3. **Navigate to the Apache install directory by typing `cd /etc/apache2/sites-available`.**

4. **Type `nano default` and press Enter to open the configuration file.**

5. **In the configuration file, replace the first two occurrences of `AllowOverride None` with `AllowOverride All`.**

   Your file should look like Figure 11-4.

6. **Save the configuration file by pressing Ctrl+X.**

   When asked to "Save modified buffer?" press Y, then press Enter when presented with the filename.

7. **Restart Apache by typing the command `/etc/init.d/apache2 restart` and pressing Enter.**

Now that your Web server is up, it's time to get your database server going.

Figure 11-4: The apache2/sites-available configuration file.

Setting up your MySQL server

Return to your "Cloud Servers" dashboard by clicking the "Hosting" tab on the left-hand navigation menu. Then click "Cloud Servers" in the drop-down menu. You should see your Cloud Servers dashboard with your newly created Web server listed.

If you want to run MySQL on a separate server, follow these steps. If you want to run Apache and MySQL on one server you can skip this process:

1. **Click the "Add New Server" button at the top of your dashboard.**

   At the top of the new page you are presented with a menu of server sizes. Select the smallest server size (currently 256 MB).

   Below the server sizes menu is a field to enter the name of your server and a menu of "Default Cloud Server Images." You can name your server anything you like. I prefer to use the name of my project with the server type prefixed to it. This is the database server, so I've named mine "TwooshesDB."

2. **For the "Default Cloud Server Images," select Ubuntu Hardy (currently listed as: Ubuntu 8.04.2 LTS (hardy)).**

3. **Click "Add Cloud Server."**

   After clicking "Add Cloud Server," you are taken to your new server's dashboard, it looks similar to Figure 11-2.

Your server takes a few moments to build, so jot down the root password displayed at the top, and take a moment to refill your coffee.

Once your server is done building, the status on the dashboard says "Active" and you receive an email from Rackspace with your server's IP address, and root password.

Once your server is built, you can install MySQL by first opening up your server's command prompt using the following steps:

1. **Still logged in and looking at your server's dashboard, click the "Console" button on the "Overview" tab under "Actions For This Server," at the top of the screen.**

   A dialog box opens to remind you to make sure Javascript is enabled on your browser. Click the "Open Console" button to dismiss this dialog box and continue.

   A new browser window opens, with content similar to Figure 11-3, showing your server's command line.

   Sometimes the console window opens too small, maximize the window to be sure you can see everything. From here you can log in to your Web server for the first time.

2. **Type `root` as the login name, then enter the root password you wrote down earlier when you created your server.**

   Once logged in, you are presented with a blank command prompt.

Install MySQL on your new server:

1. **Type the command `apt-get update` in the command prompt and press Enter to update Ubuntu's install package libraries.**
2. **Type the command `apt-get install mysql-server` and press enter to install MySQL server.**

   The installer stops to ask you if you want to use disk space. Type Y and press enter. Next you are prompted to enter a MySQL root password.

   This password is case sensitive.

3. **Type a password you will remember and press Enter. Repeat the password when prompted.**

   Remember this password. You need it later.

Now you need to create your project database and a new database user that your application can use to connect to the database.

Don't use the root username and password to connect your application to your database. That is a security vulnerability. By using a different login dedicated to your Web app you can limit that accounts permissions to only what it requires. That way if the username and password is compromised, the intruder's access is limited.

1. **Type the command `mysqladmin -p create twooshes` in the command prompt (where twooshes is the name of your database).**

   When requested, type the password you assigned to the root database user when you installed MySQL.

2. **Type the command `mysql -p` and press Enter.**

   This logs you in to MySQL monitor and gives you a new command prompt: `mysql>`

3. **Type the command `use twooshes` and press Enter (where twooshes is the name of your database).**

   This focuses your next commands on your project database.

4. **Create the new database user by typing `GRANT ALL ON twooshes.* TO 'twooshesUser'@'%' IDENTIFIED BY 'password';` and then press Enter.**

   Be sure to replace password with an actual password for the User.

5. **Type `exit` and press Enter to return to the server's normal command prompt.**

To allow connections from other computers, you must update the `my.cnf` file. Here, I set up MySQL to allow access from all IP addresses. This allows your application to access the database from the Web server. It also allows you to access the database from your desktop.

This MySQL server setup isn't the most secure setup, but it is the easiest to get started with. To secure your MySQL server, you need to restrict access to only allow IP addresses from computers you know:

1. **Type `cd /etc/mysql` in the command prompt and press Enter.**

   The cd command changes your current directory to `/etc/mysql`.

2. **Type `nano my.cnf` to edit the MySQL configuration file.**

   This opens the MySQL configuration file with nano, a Linux-based command line text editor.

3. **With the MySQL configuration file open, find the line with the contents: `bind-address = 127.0.0.1`. Comment the line out by adding a # to the front of the line.**

   Figure 11-5 shows a screenshot of the command line with the my.cnf file open to this line.

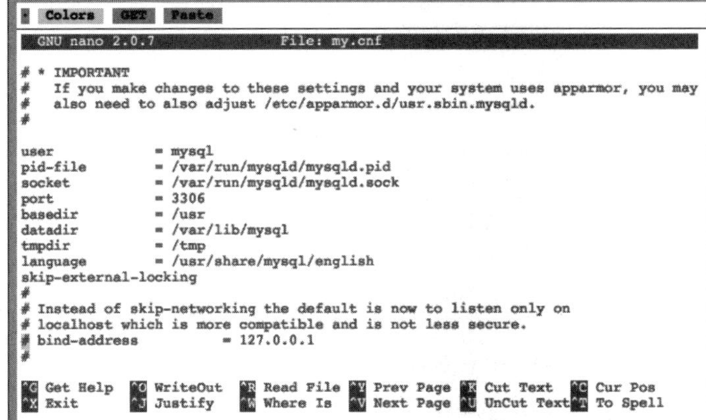

Figure 11-5: MySQL my.cnf file open with nano.

4. **Save the configuration file by pressing Ctrl+X.**

   When asked to "Save modified buffer?" press Y and then press enter when presented with the filename.

5. **To make the new configuration file take effect, restart your MySQL server.**

   Type **`/etc/init.d/mysql restart`** in the command line and press Enter.

Uploading Files to Your Web Server

To upload files to your Rackspace Cloud Web server you can use any secure file transfer protocol (SFTP) client you like. I prefer to user FileZilla (`http://filezilla-project.org`).

1. **To log in to your Web server via SFTP:**

   - Use your Web server's IP address as the host address.
   - Use your server's root username and password as the login credentials.

2. **After you've logged in, navigate to the `/var` directory.**

   Your public files are to be uploaded to the `/var/www` directory.

   By default Apache places a single `index.html` file in the `www` directory. Delete that file so it doesn't compete with the `index.php` file you create in Chapter 12.

The first time you log in, you need to create two new folders in the `/var` directory:

- `application`: Holds the core of your application files.
- `library`: Holds the Zend Framework library files.

These folders will hold nonpublic files that you create in Chapter 12.

Setting Up Your Domain Name

At this point, you can access your Web server using its IP address. That's fine, but you need an easy-to-remember domain name. Here's how:

1. **Identify a domain name that is available, and buy it.**

   I prefer to buy my domain names from Nearly Free Speech (`http://nearlyfreespeech.net`). Many people prefer the GoDaddy service (`http://godaddy.com`).

2. **Update your domain's nameserver records so they point to Rackspace Cloud's nameservers.**

   Rackspace Cloud's nameservers are

   - dns1.stabletransit.com
   - dns2.stabletransit.com

   Refer to your domain name host for instructions on how to update your domain's name servers. Every host is a little different.

3. **Configure your domain name server (DNS) records at RackSpace Cloud:**

   a. Go to your Web server dashboard and click the "DNS" tab at the top of the page. Once there, click Add Domain. A popup appears asking for your domain name, as seen in Figure 11-6.

   b. Type your domain name in the box (excluding the "http://" protocol) and click OK.

      Now your new domain is listed in the "Domain Management" box.

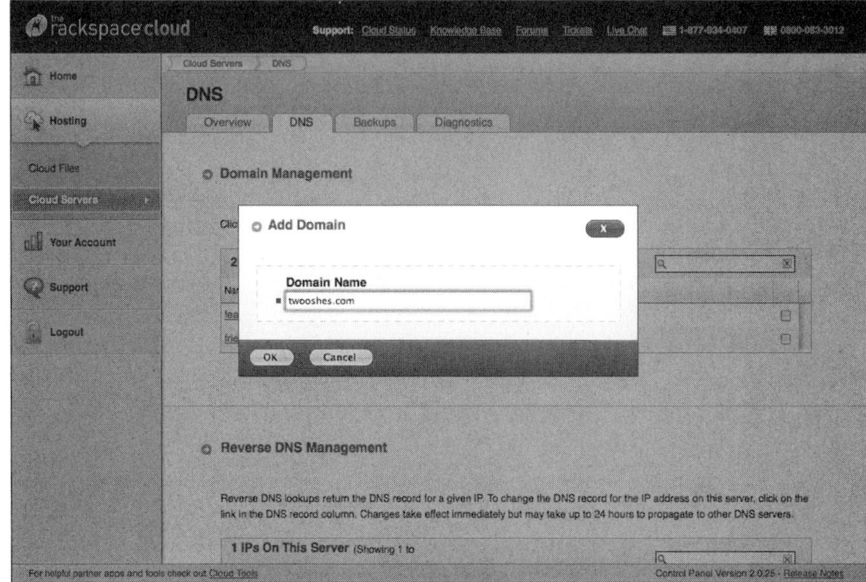

Figure 11-6: Adding a new domain name to my DNS records.

c. Click your domain name to modify the DNS records. Once on the DNS page, click the “Add” button on the top of the page.

   A popup appears.

d. In the “Name” field, type your domain name (without the “http://” protocol and without any trailing slashes).

e. In the “Content” field, type the IP address to your Web server.

f. In the TTL field, type **`60`**.

   Leave the “Type” dropdown set to “A.”

g. Click “Ok.”

It may take up to 24 hours before your domain starts working, which makes it a great time to start programming your application. Read on!

Chapter 12

Coding Your Application

In This Chapter

- Setting up the Zend Framework
- Building your Data Models
- Automating tasks with cron jobs
- Creating your game's scoreboard

Finally! It's time to start coding.

If you skipped to this chapter to get to the fun stuff, I recommend taking a look at Chapter 9 to get an idea of the application you're building here. Also, I use the Zend Framework and its included Twitter API library heavily in this chapter. If you aren't familiar with Web development frameworks like Zend, please check out Chapter 10. Finally, this Web application is based on a LAMP (Linux, Apache, MySQL, & PHP) stack. If you don't have your servers set up yet, please review Chapter 11.

Still here? Okay, time to get to work.

Setting Up the Zend Framework

In Chapter 10, I discussed how Twitter API libraries could speed up development by saving you from reinventing basic functionality, and it can make your code more robust by encouraging a solid design pattern. I've chosen the Zend Framework and its included Twitter API library for the Twooshes project. To get started with the Zend Framework, the first thing you need to do is set up your directory structure.

Create your project's initial directories

Stake a place on your hard drive and copy the folder structure illustrated in Figure 12-1.

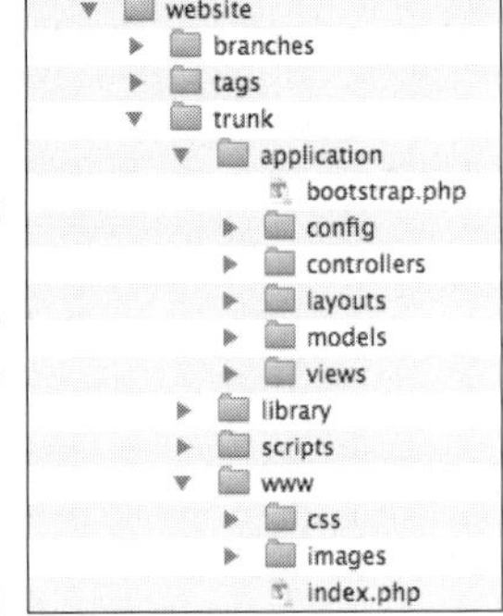

Figure 12-1: Your directory structure looks like this.

Underneath your project folder, titled `Twooshes` for this example application, is a directory called `website`. Underneath the `website` folder are three folders titled `branches`, `tags`, and `trunks`. This is a common Subversion folder structure:

- The `trunk` folder holds the main working code for your project.
- The `branches` folder is used for instances when you need to make a copy of the trunk. For example, if you want to try some experimental code but you don't want to break anything in the trunk, you make a copy of the trunk in the `branches` directory and try your experimental code there.
- The `tags` directory is used for storing version snapshots, or copies, of the trunk that you don't intend to modify. Copies stored in `tags` are used for instances where you want to roll your project back to a specific point in time.

These common subversion folders prove useful as your project matures, the code base grows, and more developers begin working together on your code. It is helpful to be familiar with this pattern because you are likely to run into it again if you work on anyone else's Web project.

Underneath the `trunk` folder is where your main project code is stored. It contains four folders: `application`, `library`, `scripts`, and www.

- The `application` folder is where the majority of your custom written PHP code resides.
- The `library` folder is where you store the Zend Framework code.

- The `scripts` folder is used to store SQL script files.
- The www folder is the only folder that you'll make public when you upload your project to your Web server. It contains the publicly accessible files, such as images, CSS, Javascript, and Zend Framework loader files.

Install the Zend Framework

By "install the Zend Framework" I really mean go to the Zend Framework Web site, download the framework, and copy it to your `library` folder.

To do that, first go to the Zend Framework Web site (`http://framework.zend.com/download/latest`) and download the latest version of the framework (version 1.9.6 as of this writing). Choose the "Minimal Package." You will most likely be asked to login or register a Zend account before you can download the free framework.

Using a site like BugMeNot (`http://bugmenot.com`) can help you skip compulsory registration.

Uncompress your freshly downloaded file. In its contents is a folder labeled `Zend`. It can be found as a subdirectory to the `library` folder. Copy the `Zend` folder and its contents to your project's `library` directory. Glimpsing at your library folder, it should look similar to Figure 12-2.

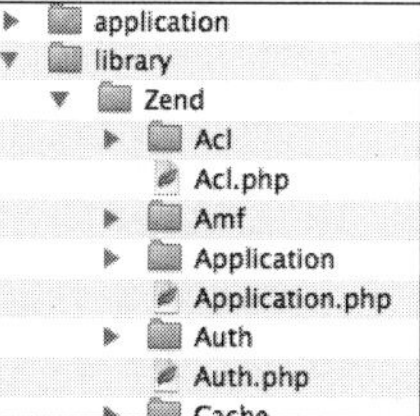

Figure 12-2: A view of the top few folders of the `library` directory.

Once your directories are set up and your Zend Framework files are in place, you need to set up and understand the Zend Framework bootstrap process.

Bootstrapping your application

The Zend Framework uses a design pattern called the Front Controller Pattern. This design pattern routes all application requests through one central script. That script then handles all the common housekeeping tasks and runs the appropriate request specific scripts. In the case of the Zend Framework, the central entry script is `index.php`.

To ensure that your application's environment variables are set up correctly, and that all requests are routed through `index.php`, you will use a process known as bootstrapping. An `.htaccess` file in your public root folder will direct all `HTTP` traffic to your `index.php` file, also in your public root folder. The `index.php` file will then call the `bootstrap.php` file that resides in your publicly inaccessible application folder. Then the `bootstrap.php` file sets up all of your environment variables stored in the `app.ini` file in your `config` folder, and it will call the correct request specific controller based on the user's requested URL. See Figure 12-3 for an illustration of this workflow.

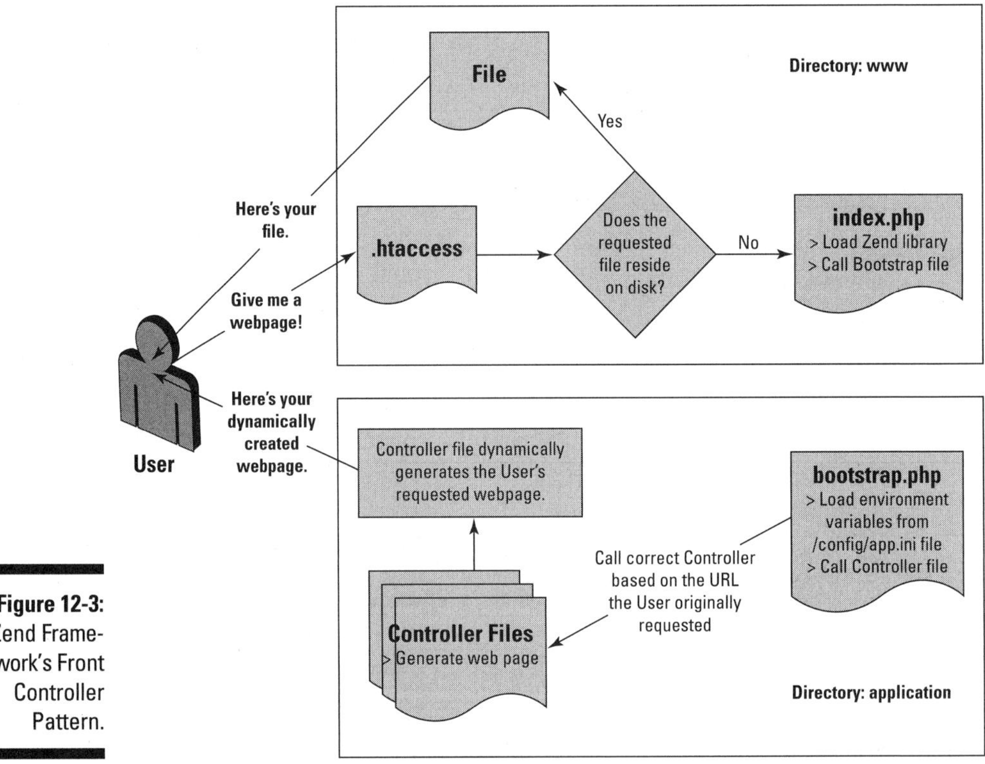

Figure 12-3: Zend Framework's Front Controller Pattern.

Create your .htaccess file

Create a new file in your www directory titled `.htaccess` and add the code shown in Listing 12-1.

In Chapter 11, you set up your Web server to support .htaccess files. If you skipped Chapter 11, make sure your Apache install is configured to support `.htaccess` files. You can do this by verifying that the setting `AllowOverride All` is in your `httpd.conf` file and by making certain you have enabled the `mod_rewrite` extension. See Chapter 11 for detailed instructions on this process.

Listing 12-1: www/.htaccess

```
RewriteEngine On
RewriteOptions MaxRedirects=250
RewriteCond %{REQUEST_FILENAME} -s [OR]
RewriteCond %{REQUEST_FILENAME} -l [OR]
RewriteCond %{REQUEST_FILENAME} -d
RewriteRule ^.*$ - [NC,L]
RewriteRule ^.*$ /index.php [NC,L]
```

The code in Listing 12-1 simply says "if a requested file exists, serve that file; else go to `index.php`."

Create your index.php file

Now create a file named `index.php` in your www directory. This file loads the Zend library and runs your bootstrap file.

Step 1: Create a constant for your application directory path

The first thing you need to do in your `index.php` file is open the PHP script tag and define a named constant to store the folder path of your `application` directory. You can see how this is done if Listing 12-2.

Listing 12-2: The Beginning of Your index.php File

```
<?php
defined('APPLICATION_PATH')
    || define('APPLICATION_PATH', realpath(dirname(__
        FILE__) . '/../application'));
```

You can use the APPLICATION_PATH constant anywhere in your application when you need to reference the path to your application folder.

Step 2: Define your environment

Next, you need to create another named constant defining your application's environment. In most cases, this refers to either:

- development: Used when you're working locally.
- testing: Used on servers that are dedicated to testing and not customer use.
- production: Used for servers your customers use.

But you can invent as many or as few environments as you want. I define the environment as "development" in Listing 12-3. When this code is placed on a live customer facing Web server, the environment should be defined as "production."

Listing 12-3: Defining the Application Environment in Your index.php File

```
defined('APPLICATION_ENV')
    || define('APPLICATION_ENV', (getenv('APPLICATION_ENV') ?
            getenv('APPLICATION_ENV') : 'development'));
```

Defining your application's environment allows you to store different settings for each environment in your configuration (config) file. For example, you may store connection settings in your config file for a database used for test data and a database used for live customer data. Defining the environment tells your application which database connection settings to use.

Step 3: Include the Zend Framework library files

Now, use the APPLICATION_PATH constant to point PHP's include_path to the Zend Framework stored in your library directory, as seen in Listing 12-4. This tells PHP where to look for Zend Framework files and classes.

Listing 12-4: Set Include Path to the Zend Framework Library

```
set_include_path(APPLICATION_PATH . '/../library' . PATH_SEPARATOR . get_
            include_path());
```

Step 4: Load the bootstrap file

Finally, create the Zend_Application object by passing it the application environment, and configuration file path as parameter, and run the bootstrap file. This is done in Listing 12-5.

Listing 12-5: Create Zend_Application and Run Bootstrap

```
require_once 'Zend/Application.php';

// Create application, bootstrap, and run
$application = new Zend_Application(
    APPLICATION_ENV,
    APPLICATION_PATH . '/config/app.ini'
);
$application->bootstrap()->run();
```

Your complete `index.php` file should look like Listing 12-6.

Listing 12-6: The Complete `index.php` File

```
<?php

// Define path to application directory
defined('APPLICATION_PATH')
    || define('APPLICATION_PATH', realpath(dirname(__FILE__) . '/../
              application'));

// Define application environment
defined('APPLICATION_ENV')
    || define('APPLICATION_ENV', (getenv('APPLICATION_ENV') ?
              getenv('APPLICATION_ENV') : 'testing'));

// Ensure library/ is on include_path
set_include_path(APPLICATION_PATH . '/../library' . PATH_SEPARATOR . get_
              include_path());

// Create application, bootstrap, and run
require_once 'Zend/Application.php';

$application = new Zend_Application(
    APPLICATION_ENV,
    APPLICATION_PATH . '/config/app.ini'
);
$application->bootstrap()->run();
```

Create your bootstrap file

Your bootstrap file is used to run common generic startup code. In your `application` folder, create a new file called `bootstrap.php` and add the code in Listing 12-7 into the file.

Listing 12-7: application/bootstrap.php

```
<?php

class Bootstrap extends Zend_Application_Bootstrap_Bootstrap
{
    protected function _initAutoload()
    {
        $moduleLoader = new Zend_Application_Module_Autoloader(array(
            'namespace' => '',
            'basePath'  => APPLICATION_PATH));
        return $moduleLoader;
    }

    function _initViewHelpers()
    {
        $this->bootstrap('layout');
        $layout = $this->getResource('layout');
        $view = $layout->getView();

        $view->doctype('XHTML1_STRICT');
        $view->headMeta()->appendHttpEquiv('Content-Type', 'text/
                html;charset=utf-8');
        $view->headTitle()->setSeparator(' - ');
        $view->headTitle('Twooshes');
    }
}
```

The `_initAutoload` function automatically loads required Zend Framework classes. This saves you from needing to constantly write 'require' or 'include' statements when referencing a Zend Framework class.

The `_initViewHelpers` function specifies the file used for the default HTML page layout. It looks for a file named `layout.phtml` in the `application/layouts` directory. You create this file later in this chapter. It also sets the global doctype, content type, and generic page title across all pages in your application.

Create your config file

Create a file named `app.ini` in your `config` folder. This is your config file and holds your environment specific variables. Add the contents of the example config file, seen in Listing 12-8, to your app.ini.

Listing 12-8: application/config/app.ini

```
[production]
phpSettings.display_startup_errors = 0
phpSettings.display_errors = 0
phpSettings.date.timezone = "UTC"
includePaths.library = APPLICATION_PATH "/../library"
bootstrap.path = APPLICATION_PATH "/bootstrap.php"
bootstrap.class = "Bootstrap"
resources.frontController.controllerDirectory = APPLICATION_PATH "/controllers"
resources.db.adapter = PDO_MYSQL
resources.db.params.host = 192.168.1.1
resources.db.params.username = twooshesUser
resources.db.params.password = password
resources.db.params.dbname = twooshes
resources.layout.layoutpath = APPLICATION_PATH "/layouts"

[staging : production]

[testing : production]
phpSettings.display_startup_errors = 1
phpSettings.display_errors = 1

[development : production]
phpSettings.display_startup_errors = 1
phpSettings.display_errors = 1
```

In Chapter 11, you created a MySQL database server and a new MySQL user for this project. You need to modify Listing 12-8's database connection settings to match your database's connection settings. The settings your need to update are

- `resources.db.params.host`: The IP address of your database server.
- `resources.db.params.username`: The username of your database user. (This shouldn't be the `root` user.)
- `resources.db.params.password`: The password for the database user.
- `resources.db.params.dbname`: The name of your project's database.

Create your layout template

The layout template allows you to build a common site-wide HTML framework that you plug dynamic page specific content into. This is useful for things like headers and footers, and saves you from having to make edits in numerous places due to redundant code.

To make your layout template, create a file called `layout.phtml` in your `application/layouts` directory and insert the code in Listing 12-9.

Listing 12-9: application/layouts/layout.phtml

```
<?php echo $this->doctype(); ?>
<html xmlns="http://www.w3.org/1999/xhtml" xml:lang="en" lang="en">
<head>
    <?php echo $this->HeadMeta(); ?>
    <?php echo $this->headTitle(); ?>
    <?php echo $this->headLink()->prependStylesheet($this->baseUrl().'/css/site.
            css'); ?>
</head>
<body>
<div id="content">
    <?php echo $this->layout()->content; ?>
</div>
</body>
</html>
```

In Listing 12-9, the doctype, meta tags, and page title are being populated by variables set in your `bootstrap.php` file. This line of code between the div tags in Listing 12-9 is where your page specific controllers insert their output:

```
<?php echo $this->layout()->content; ?>
```

The next step is to create a skeleton view and controller.

Create your first view and controller

The Zend Framework uses the Model-View-Controller (MVC) design pattern. For our purposes, consider the model as the data, the view as the HTML, and the controller as the code you write to generate dynamic content.

Review Chapter 9 for additional details on the MVC pattern.

The first view and controller you need is for the home index page. That is the page you get when you visit `http://twooshes.com`.

View

To make your first view, create a new directory called `scripts` under your `application/views` directory. Under your new `scripts` directory, create a subdirectory titled `index`. In the `index` directory, create a new file titled `index.phtml`.

This file is the HTML template for the controller. In Listing 12-10, I create a variable called `foobar` between the <h1> tags. This variable's value is set from the controller. Add the code in Listing 12-10 to your `index.phtml` file.

Listing 12-10: application/views/scripts/index.phtml

```
<h1><?=$this->foobar?></h1>
```

Controller

Create a new file called `IndexContoller.php` under your `application/controllers` directory

The capitalization of the filename matters.

In Listing 12-11, the value of the view variable `foobar` is set to "Hello World." Insert the code in Listing 12-11 into your IndexController.php file.

Listing 12-11: application/controllers/IndexController.php

```
<?php

class IndexController extends Zend_Controller_Action
{
   public function indexAction()
   {
      $this->view->foobar = "Hello World";
   }
}
```

Give it a test

Test your Zend Framework install and your new view and controller by uploading the following folders and their contents to your Web server's `var` directory:

- `www`
- `application`
- `library`

If you need a refresher, Chapter 11 contains details on how to upload files to your Web server.

Once your files have been uploaded, visit your Web site with your browser of choice. You should see a white page with "Hello World" written in the top-left corner.

Setting Up Your Data Structure

For the Twooshes game, you give the Twitter user a point when they tweet something that is exactly 140 characters long, and you deduct a point when they post a tweet with any Trending Topics.

To keep up with this, you need two database tables:

- user
- tweet

The first table keeps up with the player's data and their total score. I title this table `user`. The second table keeps a historical record of the tweets that make up the user's score. I title this table `tweet`.

For this tutorial, you use the MySQL database you set up in Chapter 11.

Build the User table

When I access the Twitter API to get data, I prefer to store the majority of the data that the API returns whether I'm going to use it immediately or not. I do this because calling the Twitter API is expensive, in that the API calls are slow, and I can only perform so many API calls per hour due to Twitter's API rate limiting. So, I try to maximize the value I receive from each call. The alternative to this approach is to store only the data you know you will need for your app. This is an equally acceptable approach, and it's beneficial because it will keep your data structures lean. For the purposes of keeping this tutorial from being inundated with long lists of variable names, I only store the most necessary data fields.

Name your data fields exactly the same way they are named in the Twitter API results. This keeps confusion to a minimum and makes mapping the API data to the database straightforward. I make one exception in this example with the `twitter_id` field. This is the ID that Twitter has attached to a user. Twitter calls this field `id`. To avoid confusing it with my table's primary key `userId`, I store Twitter's `id` field as `twitter_id`.

Listing 12-12: 'User' Table Creation SQL

```
CREATE TABLE  `twooshes`.`user` (
  `userId` int(10) unsigned NOT NULL auto_increment,
  `created` timestamp NOT NULL default '0000-00-00 00:00:00',
  `updated` timestamp NOT NULL default CURRENT_TIMESTAMP on update CURRENT_
              TIMESTAMP,
  `score` int(10) NOT NULL,
```

```
  `trendingTopics` int(10) NOT NULL,
  `twooshes` int(10) NOT NULL,
  `enabled` tinyint(1) unsigned default '1',
  `twitter_id` int(10) unsigned NOT NULL,
  `screen_name` varchar(30) NOT NULL,
  `profile_image_url` varchar(400) NOT NULL,
  `url` varchar(400) default NULL,
`created_at` timestamp NOT NULL default '0000-00-00 00:00:00',
PRIMARY KEY  (`userId`),
  UNIQUE KEY `userId` (`userId`),
  UNIQUE KEY `twitter_id` (`twitter_id`),
  UNIQUE KEY `screen_name` (`screen_name`),
  KEY `score` (`score`),
  KEY `trendingTopics` (`trendingTopics`),
  KEY `twooshes` (`twooshes`)
) ENGINE=InnoDB DEFAULT CHARSET=utf8;
```

Have a look at the SQL in Listing 12-12. All the fields in this table will be populated using the Twitter API, except for the first seven fields listed:

- `userId` is the primary key of the table and is an auto incremented integer. This is your own proprietary user ID and isn't the same as the ID that Twitter returns for the user. You store the ID that Twitter returns as `twitter_id`.
- `created` is the date and time that the user record was created. It must be manually set when you insert a new row into the user table.
- `updated` is the date and time of the last time any field on that row was updated. That field updates itself automatically so you don't need to manage it.
- `score` is that users total up-to-date game score.
- `trendingTopics` is the number of tweets for that user that contain a trending topic.
- `twooshes` is the number of tweets for that user that contain exactly 140 characters.
- `enabled` is by default set to true, but if a user stops following your game's Twitter account, this field is be set to false.

You'll eventually need to sort the users by score to display a leader board. So, the `score`, `trendingTopics`, and `twooshes` fields are set as keys, so they'll be indexed. This will speed up the sorting.

Build the Tweet table

You'll use the `tweet` table to keep a record of how a user's score was calculated. You may also eventually use this table to show the user the tweets that make up their score.

Listing 12-13: 'Tweet' Table Creation SQL

```
CREATE TABLE  `twooshes`.`tweet` (
  `tweetId` int(10) unsigned NOT NULL auto_increment,
  `userId` int(10) unsigned NOT NULL,
  `created` timestamp NOT NULL default CURRENT_TIMESTAMP,
  `status_id` bigint(20) unsigned NOT NULL,
  `status` varchar(140) NOT NULL,
  `created_at` timestamp NOT NULL default '0000-00-00 00:00:00',
  `twoosh` tinyint(1) unsigned default '0',
  `trendingTopic` varchar(60) default NULL,
  PRIMARY KEY  (`tweetId`),
  UNIQUE KEY `tweetId` (`tweetId`),
  UNIQUE KEY `status_id` (`status_id`),
  KEY `user_ibfk_1` (`userId`),
  CONSTRAINT `user_ibfk_1` FOREIGN KEY (`userId`) REFERENCES `user` (`userId`)
            ON DELETE CASCADE
) ENGINE=InnoDB DEFAULT CHARSET=utf8;
```

In Listing 12-13, I have written the SQL to create the tweet table. Notice the `twoosh` field and `trendingTopic` field. If a tweet is exactly 140 characters long, you will place a 1, signifying a truth Boolean, in the `twoosh` column. If a tweet contains a trending topic, you will put the trending phrase in the `trendingTopic` field. It is possible that a tweet contains more than one trending topic. In that case, you'll simply store the first trending topic you find in the tweet.

Also notice in Listing 12-13 that the `created` column is auto populated, so you don't need to worry about populating that field when you insert data. There is also a foreign key constraint on the `userId`. This prevents the accidental deletion of a user record that still has tweets associated with it.

Finally, run the create table statements in Listings 12-12 and 12-13 on your Twooshes database. You can use any MySQL client, such as phpMyAdmin, the standard MySQL command-line, or MySQL Query Browser.

Create Your Data Models

Once you have created your MySQL tables, you need to create a Table Data Gateway. This is a design pattern the Zend Framework uses to manage the creation of most of your SQL code. You interact with the database tables via objects. This is the *model* part of the model-view-controller design pattern.

When you abstract your data in a data model, you can retrieve data from your controller by making simple calls like this:

```
$user = new user("dustyreagan");
$user->location = "Austin";
```

That code creates a new user named "dustyreagan" and sets that user's `location` to "Austin."

See how readable that code is? Data models help keep the code complexity in your controllers to a minimum.

Define your tables

First, create a new folder under your `models` folder called `DbTable`. Under `DbTable` create two new files: `User.php` and `Tweet.php`. These files represent your two database tables.

In Listing 12-14, I have the code for the `User.php` file. It defines the name of the table and the dependent tweet table. Add the code in Listing 12-14 to your `User.php` file.

Listing 12-14: application/models/DbTable/User.php

```
<?php
class Model_DbTable_User extends Zend_Db_Table_Abstract
{
   protected $_name = 'user';
   protected $_dependentTables = array('Model_DbTable_Tweet');
}
```

For the `Tweet.php` file, you define the name of the table and create a reference map to the parent `user` table. The code for this is in Listing 12-15.

Listing 12-15: application/models/DbTable/Tweet.php

```
<?php
class Model_DbTable_Tweet extends Zend_Db_Table_Abstract
{
   protected $_name    = 'tweet';
   protected $_referenceMap    = array(
      'User' => array(
         'columns'          => 'userId',
         'refTableClass'    => 'Model_DbTable_User',
         'refColumns'       => 'userId',
         'onDelete'         => self::CASCADE,
         'onUpdate'         => self::CASCADE
      )
   );
}
```

Once you define your tables for the Zend Framework, you need to further abstract the data model into usable objects.

TIP

Keep SQL statements delegated to models. Don't add SQL statements to your controllers.

Create the Tweet model

The tweet model is very simple. It performs two functions for your game:

- Map status update data to an object.
- Provide a function that returns the `status_id` of the latest tweet in your `tweet` table.

First, create a file called `Tweet.php` in your `application/models` directory.

To map tweet data to your `Tweet` object, define the tweet fields as public variables, then take the data in as parameters in your constructor and map the parameters to your public variables. Listing 12-16 shows how to achieve this.

Listing 12-16: application/models/Tweet.php

```
<?php

class Tweet
{
   public $status_id;
   public $status;
   public $created_at;
   public $twoosh;
```

```
    public $trendingTopic;

    public function __construct($status_id, $status, $created_at, $twoosh,
            $trendingTopic)
    {
        $this->status_id = $status_id;
        $this->status = $status;
        $this->created_at = $created_at;
        $this->twoosh = $twoosh;
        $this->trendingTopic = $trendingTopic;
    }
}
```

For Twooshes, you need to poll the Twitter stream of the game's Twitter account on a consistent basis, looking for tweets that earn the player a point. After you have observed and processed a set of tweets for points, you don't need to observe them again. To avoid reviewing old tweets, you need the `status_id` of the latest tweet you have stored in your `tweet` table. To do that, add a static function to your Tweet model that runs a SQL query to return the max `status_id`. This function is seen in Listing 12-17.

Listing 12-17: application/models/Tweet.php : getLastStatusId()

```
public static function getLastStatusId()
{
    $db = Zend_Db_Table::getDefaultAdapter();

    $select = 'select max(status_id) as status_id from tweet';
    $lastStatusId = $db->fetchOne($select);

    if(empty($lastStatusId))
        $lastStatusId = 1;

    return $lastStatusId;
}
```

In Listing 12-17, I load the `Zend_Db_Table` object using the default connection found in the `config/app.ini` file. Then I run a SQL statement that returns the max `status_id`. If you haven't stored any status updates yet, your max `status_id` will come back NULL. If you use the Twitter API to request the latest tweets, giving it a variable `since_id` equal to NULL, the API returns no results. This isn't what you want. So if the max `status_id` comes back NULL, I set `status_id` equal to 1.

Your final `Tweet.php` file looks like Listing 12-18.

Listing 12-18: Final Tweet.php file

```
<?php

class Tweet
{
   public $status_id;
   public $status;
   public $created_at;
   public $twoosh;
   public $trendingTopic;

   public function __construct($status_id, $status, $created_at, $twoosh,
            $trendingTopic)
   {
      $this->status_id = $status_id;
      $this->status = $status;
      $this->created_at = $created_at;
      $this->twoosh = $twoosh;
      $this->trendingTopic = $trendingTopic;
   }

   public static function getLastStatusId()
   {
      $db = Zend_Db_Table::getDefaultAdapter();

      $select = 'select max(status_id) as status_id from tweet';
      $lastStatusId = $db->fetchOne($select);

      if(empty($lastStatusId))
         $lastStatusId = 1;

      return $lastStatusId;
   }
}
```

Create the User model

The `User` model in Twooshes is more complicated than the `Tweet` model. But never fear. I tackle it a section at a time.

Your `User` model needs to provide a variety of functions for your Twitter game:

- Access the fields associated with a user.
- Load a user from the database by their screen name or Twitter Id.
- Load a User object using the data retrieved from the Twitter API.
- Save the current user object to the database.

- Store a Tweet associated to the user.
- Add a point to the user's score.
- Subtract a point from the user's score.

The first thing you need to do is create a file called `User.php` in your `application/models` directory. Then, in that file define the following publicly accessible variables:

- `twitter_id`: The ID Twitter assigned to the user.
- `screen_name`: The user's Twitter screen name.
- `profile_image_url`: The URL to the user's profile image.
- `created_at`: The date the user created their Twitter account.
- `enabled`: Set to 0 if the user is no longer playing Twooshes, set to 1 by default for active players.

You also need a private field for the `userId`. This is the value of the primary key field for the user in your user database table. You need this value to save a tweet to the user. You don't need the `userId` value outside of the User model, so keep that value private.

Listing 12-19 shows how to start the `User` class and define all the fields.

Listing 12-19: application/models/User.php

```
<?php

class User
{
   public $twitter_id;
   public $screen_name;
   public $profile_image_url;
   public $created_at;
   public $enabled = 1;

   private $userId;
}
```

Next, add a class constructor so you can load the user from the database based on their `screen_name` or `twitter_id`. This gives you the ability to load a user and the user's properties from a controller like this:

```
$user = new user("dustyreagan");
$location = $user->location;
```

To do this, your constructor needs to load the user data table object, determine whether you are searching on screen_name or twitter_id, and then map the row results to the class' variables. Listing 12-20 illustrates how this is done.

Listing 12-20: application/models/User.php : constructor

```
public function __construct($identifier = null)
{
    if(!empty($identifier))
    {
        $userTable = $this->getUserTable();

        if(is_numeric($identifier))
            $select = $userTable->select()->where('twitter_id = ?', $identifier);
        else
            $select = $userTable->select()->where('screen_name = ?', $identifier);

        $row = $userTable->fetchRow($select);
        $this->mapResponse($row);
    }
}

private $_userTable;
private function getUserTable()
{
    if (null === $this->_userTable)
    {
        require_once APPLICATION_PATH . '/models/DbTable/User.php';
        $this->_userTable = new Model_DbTable_User;
    }
    return $this->_userTable;
}
```

In Listing 12-20, the constructor tests whether a parameter called $identifier is included when the User object is created. If $identifier isn't null, the constructor then loads the user table by calling a private function named getUserTable, also seen in Listing 12-20.

The getUserTable function checks whether the user table has already been loaded; if not, it loads the table and stores it in a private variable $_userTable. If the getUserTable function is called more than once, instead of reloading the table, it simply returns the set private variable $_userTable for efficiency.

After the user table is loaded, the constructor then tests whether the $identifier is a number. If so, it assumes it's the twitter_id, else it assumes it's the screen_name. The SQL select statement is created depending on whether the $identifier is the twitter_id or the screen_name. Then the user row is fetched from the user table and passed to the public function mapResponse.

The code for the mapResponse function is shown in Listing 12-21.

Listing 12-21: application/models/User.php : mapResponse()

```
public function mapResponse($response)
{
    // basic check that $response is actually user data
    if(!empty($response->screen_name))
    {
        // if $reponse contains twitter_id you're mapping row data
        if(!empty($response->twitter_id))
        {
            $this->twitter_id = $response->twitter_id;
            $this->enabled = $response->enabled;
            $this->userId = $response->userId;
        }
        // else you're mapping API data
        else
            $this->twitter_id = $response->id;

        // these mappings are the same in the API & your database
        $this->screen_name = $response->screen_name;
        $this->profile_image_url = $response->profile_image_url;
        $this->created_at = $this->formatCreatedAt($response->created_at);
    }
}

private function formatCreatedAt($created_at)
{
  return date('Y-m-d H:i:s', strtotime($created_at));
}
```

The mapResponse function seen in Listing 12-21 loads either Twitter data returned from the API, or from your user table, to the User class variables.

The private function formatCreatedAt, also seen in Listing 12-21, formats the date and time returned by the Twitter API to conform to MySQL standards.

You need the ability to save your User object to the database using a command like this from the controller:

```
$user->save();
```

To do that, you need to create a public function in your User model named save. The save function needs to be smart enough to insert new data if it doesn't already exist in your database, and update old data if it does. You can do this by running a SQL statement to check whether the row already exists, then by running another SQL statement to do the insert or update as appropriate. However, since you are using MySQL you can use ON DUPLICATE KEY UPDATE to do all this in one command. Listing 12-22 shows how this is done.

Listing 12-22: application/models/User.php : save()

```
public function save()
{
   $db = Zend_Db_Table::getDefaultAdapter();

   $sql = 'INSERT INTO user (
            created,
            twitter_id,
            screen_name,
            profile_image_url,
            created_at,
            enabled) VALUES (now(), ?, ?, ?, ?, ?)
      ON DUPLICATE KEY UPDATE
            updated = now(),
            twitter_id = ?,
            screen_name = ?,
            profile_image_url = ?,
            created_at = ?,
            enabled = ?';

     $data = array(
      'twitter_id'=>$this->twitter_id,
      'screen_name'=>$this->screen_name,
      'profile_image_url'=>$this->profile_image_url,
      'created_at'=>$this->created_at,
      'enabled'=>$this->enabled
     );

     $db->query($sql, array_merge(array_values($data), array_values($data)));
}
```

You need to be able to save a user's tweets, and add the appropriate points, from the constructor like this:

```
$user->addTweet($tweet);
```

I do this using a function called `addTweet`, seen in Listing 12-23.

Listing 12-23: application/models/User.php : addTweet()

```
public function addTweet($tweetObj)
{
  $data = array(
     'userId' => $this->userId,
      'created_at' => $this->formatCreatedAt($tweetObj->created_at),
      'status_id' => $tweetObj->status_id,
      'status' => $tweetObj->status,
      'twoosh' => $tweetObj->twoosh,
      'trendingTopic' => $tweetObj->trendingTopic
```

```
    );

    $this->getTweetTable()->insert($data);

    if($tweetObj->twoosh == 1)
        $this->addPoint();

    if(!empty($tweetObj->trendingTopic))
        $this->subPoint();
}

private $_tweetTable;
private function getTweetTable()
{
    if (null === $this->_tweetTable)
    {
        require_once APPLICATION_PATH . '/models/DbTable/Tweet.php';
        $this->_tweetTable = new Model_DbTable_Tweet;
    }
    return $this->_tweetTable;
}
```

Missing from Listing 12-23 are the `addPoint` and `subPoint` functions. These two functions run an update statement on the score of the user's record. These function and their update statements are seen in Listing 12-24.

Listing 12-24: application/models/User.php : addPoint() and subPoint()

```
private function addPoint()
{
    $db = Zend_Db_Table::getDefaultAdapter();

    $sql = 'update user set score = score + 1, twooshes = twooshes + 1
        where userId = ' . $this->userId;

    $db->query($sql);
}

private function subPoint()
{
    $db = Zend_Db_Table::getDefaultAdapter();

    $sql = 'update user set score = score - 1, trendingTopics = trendingTopics + 1
        where userId = ' . $this->userId;

    $db->query($sql);
}
```

Listing 12-25 is the complete `User.php` file.

Listing 12-25: The Complete User.php File

```
<?php

class User
{
   public $twitter_id;
   public $screen_name;
   public $profile_image_url;
   public $created_at;
   public $enabled = 1;

   private $userId;

   public function __construct($identifier = null)
   {
      if(!empty($identifier))
      {
         $userTable = $this->getUserTable();

         if(is_numeric($identifier))
            $select = $userTable->select()->where('twitter_id = ?', $identifier);
         else
            $select = $userTable->select()->where('screen_name = ?',
               $identifier);

         $row = $userTable->fetchRow($select);
         $this->mapResponse($row);
      }
   }

   private $_userTable;
   private function getUserTable()
   {
      if (null === $this->_userTable)
      {
         require_once APPLICATION_PATH . '/models/DbTable/User.php';
         $this->_userTable = new Model_DbTable_User;
      }
      return $this->_userTable;
   }

   public function mapResponse($response)
   {
      // basic check that $response is actually user data
      if(!empty($response->screen_name))
      {
         // if $reponse contains twitter_id you're mapping row data
         if(!empty($response->twitter_id))
         {
```

```
            $this->twitter_id = $response->twitter_id;
            $this->enabled = $response->enabled;
            $this->userId = $response->userId;
        }
        // else you're mapping API data
        else
            $this->twitter_id = $response->id;

        // these mappings are the same in the API & your database
        $this->screen_name = $response->screen_name;
        $this->profile_image_url = $response->profile_image_url;
        $this->created_at = $this->formatCreatedAt($response->created_at);
    }
}

private function formatCreatedAt($created_at)
{
  return date('Y-m-d H:i:s', strtotime($created_at));
}

public function save()
{
   $db = Zend_Db_Table::getDefaultAdapter();

   $sql = 'INSERT INTO user (
            created,
            twitter_id,
            screen_name,
            profile_image_url,
            created_at,
            enabled) VALUES (now(), ?, ?, ?, ?, ?)
      ON DUPLICATE KEY UPDATE
            updated = now(),
            twitter_id = ?,
            screen_name = ?,
            profile_image_url = ?,
            created_at = ?,
            enabled = ?';

     $data = array(
      'twitter_id'=>$this->twitter_id,
      'screen_name'=>$this->screen_name,
      'profile_image_url'=>$this->profile_image_url,
      'created_at'=>$this->created_at,
      'enabled'=>$this->enabled
     );

     $db->query($sql, array_merge(array_values($data), array_values($data)));
}
```

(continued)

Listing 12-25 ***(continued)***

```
public function addTweet($tweetObj)
{
  $data = array(
     'userId' => $this->userId,
      'created_at' => $this->formatCreatedAt($tweetObj->created_at),
      'status_id' => $tweetObj->status_id,
      'status' => $tweetObj->status,
      'twoosh' => $tweetObj->twoosh,
      'trendingTopic' => $tweetObj->trendingTopic
  );

  $this->getTweetTable()->insert($data);

  if($tweetObj->twoosh == 1)
     $this->addPoint();

  if(!empty($tweetObj->trendingTopic))
     $this->subPoint();
}

private $_tweetTable;
private function getTweetTable()
{
   if (null === $this->_tweetTable)
   {
      require_once APPLICATION_PATH . '/models/DbTable/Tweet.php';
      $this->_tweetTable = new Model_DbTable_Tweet;
   }
   return $this->_tweetTable;
}

private function addPoint()
{
  $db = Zend_Db_Table::getDefaultAdapter();

  $sql = 'update user set score = score + 1, twooshes = twooshes + 1
        where userId = ' . $this->userId;

  $db->query($sql);
}

private function subPoint()
{
  $db = Zend_Db_Table::getDefaultAdapter();

  $sql = 'update user set score = score - 1, trendingTopics = trendingTopics
            + 1
        where userId = ' . $this->userId;

  $db->query($sql);
}
```

The Cron Jobs

In order for people to play Twooshes, they must follow your application's Twitter account. After they follow the account, you need to follow them back so you can monitor their Twitter stream for Twooshes and trending topics. To do that there are two tasks that need to be automated here:

- You need to automatically follow users back who start following your apps Twitter account.
- You need to continuously monitor your applications Twitter stream to identify tweets that are 140 characters long or contain a trending topic.

You can solve these problems by writing a script that performs these tasks and then schedule it to run every few minutes using a cron job.

Cron is a job scheduler found in Unix and Linux based operating systems. You give the cron a basic command line and tell it when to run.

To tackle this problem start by writing the script that will auto-follow users back.

1. Creating your auto-follow script

First, you need to create a new controller and view for your auto-follow script. To create your controller, make a new file titled `FollowcronController.php` in your `application/controllers` directory and insert the code in Listing 12-26.

Listing 12-26: application/controllers/FollowcronController.php

```
<?php

class FollowcronController extends Zend_Controller_Action
{
   public function indexAction()
   {
      // Disable layout
      $layout = Zend_Layout::getMvcInstance();
      $layout->disableLayout();

      // your auto follow script code goes here
   }
}
```

The cron script doesn't need to render HTML so I've disabled the rendering of the Web site layout in Listing 12-19.

To create your view, make a new directory under your `application/views/scripts` directory titled `followcron`. In this directory, create a new file called `index.phtml`. Leave this file empty. You have to create this file to adhere to Zend Frameworks MVC pattern, but you don't need to use it.

For your Twitter application account, you want to keep a strict one-to-one ratio of following to follower. If someone stops following your account, they are opting out of the game and you want to stop calculating their score. Conversely, if someone starts following your account, you must follow them back in order to calculate their score.

You can figure out who you need to follow and unfollow by using the two Twitter API social graph methods:

- `friends/ids`: returns the IDs of everyone the user is following.
- `followers/ids`: returns the IDs of everyone who is following the user.

These methods return a list of Twitter user IDs and nothing more. There is one gotcha, however. As of Zend Framework 1.9, these methods aren't included in Zend's Twitter methods library. Indeed this is a bummer, but you can correct this by simply adding the missing methods to your copy of Zend's Twitter library.

Adding the missing methods

You'll find Zend's Twitter service methods in the `Twitter.php` file located in your `library/Zend/Service` directory. Open this file up and add the two new methods listed in Listing 12-27 to the bottom of the `Twitter.php` file before the last closing bracket.

Listing 12-27: library/Zend/Service/Twitter.php : Add Social Graph Methods

```
public function userFriendsIds($screen_name = null)
{
    $_params = "screen_name=$screen_name";

    $path = '/friends/ids.xml';

    $username = $this->_username;
    $password = $this->_password;
    $credentials = sprintf("%s:%s", $username, $password);

    $ch = curl_init('http://twitter.com'. $path . '?' . $_params);

    curl_setopt($ch, CURLOPT_USERPWD, $credentials);
    curl_setopt($ch, CURLOPT_RETURNTRANSFER, true);
```

```
    $data = curl_exec($ch);

    curl_close($ch);

    return new Zend_Rest_Client_Result($data);
}

public function userFollowersIds($screen_name = null)
{
    $_params = "screen_name=$screen_name";

    $path = '/followers/ids.xml';

    $username = $this->_username;
    $password = $this->_password;
    $credentials = sprintf("%s:%s", $username, $password);

    $ch = curl_init('http://twitter.com'. $path . '?' . $_params);

    curl_setopt($ch, CURLOPT_USERPWD, $credentials);
    curl_setopt($ch, CURLOPT_RETURNTRANSFER, true);

    $data = curl_exec($ch);

    curl_close($ch);

    return new Zend_Rest_Client_Result($data);
}
```

The two methods in Listing 12-27 take an optional Twitter screen name as input. Then, they grab the authentication credentials provided when the Twitter service object is created. Finally, they call the Twitter API using cURL and the authentication credentials provided which returns the IDs for the screen name provide, or if no screen name is provided, it returns the IDs for the authenticated user.

Back to the mission at hand

Now that you have the Twitter API library methods you need, you can get back to writing your auto follow script.

Go back to your `FollowcronController.php` file. The first thing you need to do is create a new `Zend_Service_Twitter` object. Listing 12-28 shows how this is done with the new code lines in bold.

Listing 12-28: application/controllers/FollowcronController.php

```
<?php
class FollowcronController extends Zend_Controller_Action
{
   private $_twitter = null;

   public function indexAction()
   {
      // Disable layout
      $layout = Zend_Layout::getMvcInstance();
      $layout->disableLayout();

      $this->_twitter = new Zend_Service_Twitter('Twooshes', 'password123');
   }
}
```

Next, you need to create a function that collects the IDs of the users that are following your game's Twitter account. To do that, add the function in Listing 12-29 to your `FollowcronController` class.

Listing 12-29: application/controllers/FollowcronController.php

```
private $_followerIds = null;
private function getFollowerIds()
{
   if($this->_followerIds == null)
   {
      $response = $this->_twitter->user->followersIds();
      if(!empty($response->id))
      {
         foreach($response->id as $twitter_id)
            $this->_followerIds[] = (string) $twitter_id;
      }
      else
         $this->_followerIds = array();
   }
   return $this->_followerIds;
}
```

The function in Listing 12-29 has an associated private variable called `$_followerIds`. When the function is called for the first time, it checks whether `$_followerIds` has a null value. If so, it calls the `userFollower-sIds` method you recently added to Zend's Twitter library. Then, it takes the IDs returned from the method call and adds them to an array that you can easily work with. Once this is done, the function assigns that array to `$_fol-lowerIds`. If the function is called again in this HTTP request, it will simply return the results it has already stored in the `$_followerIds` variable. This saves you from unnecessary additional API calls.

You also need a function for collecting the IDs of people our game's Twitter account is following. Add the function in Listing 12-23 to your `FollowcronController` class.

The function in Listing 12-30 works just like the function in Listing 12-29, except it returns the IDs of the users you are following.

Listing 12-30: application/controllers/FollowcronController.php

```
private $_followingIds = null;
private function getFollowingIds()
{
   if($this->_followingIds == null)
   {
      $response = $this->_twitter->user->friendsIds();
      if(!empty($response->id))
      {
         foreach($response->id as $twitter_id)
            $this->_followingIds[] = (string) $twitter_id;
      }
      else
         $this->_followingIds = array();
   }
   return $this->_followingIds;
}
```

Now you have a list of the people who are following your account and a list of the people you're following. Next, you need to figure out who you aren't following and who isn't following you. You can do this by evaluating the differences in your two lists. To find out who you aren't following, look to see who is in your followers list but not in your following list, and vice versa to find out who isn't following you.

Fortunately, PHP provides an array function that does this work for you called `array_diff`. `array_diff` returns an array containing all the entries from the first array parameter that aren't present in the second array parameter. Thus, the parameter order is important. To keep things straight, add the two functions listed in Listing 12-31 to your FollowcronController class.

Listing 12-31: application/controllers/FollowcronController.php

```
private function getNonFollowersIds()
{
   $following = $this->getFollowingIds();
   $followers = $this->getFollowerIds();

   return array_diff($following, $followers);
}

private function getNewFollowersIds()
{
   $following = $this->getFollowingIds();
   $followers = $this->getFollowerIds();

   return array_diff($followers, $following);
}
```

In Listing 12-31, the functions are nearly identical except for the order of the parameters in `array_diff` function.

Next, take the arrays of people you need to unfollow and follow and loop through both of them, calling the Zend Twitter library's destroy and create friendship methods, respectively, inside the loop. You also need to disable User accounts you unfollow and create User accounts you follow. You can do that using the User data model. You may also want to print the amount of people your script has followed and unfollowed so you can easily see what it's doing. Finally, you need to close your Twitter session using Zend's `endSession` method. After you've done all this your `indexAction` function should look similar to Listing 12-32.

At this point, you need to be very careful with which Twitter account you're authenticating with. Use a Twitter account dedicated to this application you're building, not your personal Twitter account. If you don't do this, you may unintentionally drop and follow people by running this script.

Listing 12-32: application/controllers/FollowcronController.php : indexAction()

```
public function indexAction()
{
   // Disable layout
   $layout = Zend_Layout::getMvcInstance();
   $layout->disableLayout();

   $this->_twitter = new Zend_Service_Twitter('Twooshes',
          'password123');

   $nonFollowersIds = $this->getNonFollowersIds();
   $newFollowersIds = $this->getNewFollowersIds();

   print_r($nonFollowersIds);
   echo "<hr/>";
   print_r($newFollowersIds);
   echo "<hr/>";

   require_once APPLICATION_PATH . '/models/User.php';

   foreach ($nonFollowersIds as $value)
   {
      $this->_twitter->friendship->destroy($value);

      $user = new User($value);
      $user->enabled = 0;
      $user->save();
   }
```

```
    foreach ($newFollowersIds as $value)
    {
       $response = $this->_twitter->friendship-
           >create($value);

       $user = new User();
       $user->mapResponse($response);
       $user->save();
    }

    echo "Followed " . count($newFollowersIds) . "<br />";
    echo "UnFollowed " . count($nonFollowersIds);

    $this->_twitter->account->endSession();
}
```

2. Creating your Tweet monitor script

The tweet monitor script uses the Twitter API to get your friends timeline. Then, it loops through each tweet looking for tweets that are exactly 140 characters long or that contain a trending topic. Finally, it saves any twooshes or tweets with trending topics to that user's record.

First, you need to create a new controller and view for your tweet monitor script. To create your view, make a new directory under your `application/views/scripts` directory titled `tweetcron` and add a new file titled `index.phtml`. Leave this file empty, just like you did for `followcron`.

To create your controller, make a new file titled `TweetcronController.php` in your `application\controllers` directory and insert the code in Listing 12-33.

Listing 12-33: application/controllers/TweetcronController.php

```
<?php
class TweetcronController extends Zend_Controller_Action
{
   public function indexAction()
   {
      // Disable layout
      $layout = Zend_Layout::getMvcInstance();
      $layout->disableLayout();

      $twitter = new Zend_Service_Twitter('Twooshes', 'password123');

      require_once APPLICATION_PATH . '/models/User.php';
      require_once APPLICATION_PATH . '/models/Tweet.php';
```

(continued)

Listing 12-33 ***(continued)***

```
      // call public static method to get max since_id
      $lastStatusId = Tweet::getLastStatusId();

      $data = array(
         'count'=>200,
         'since_id'=>$lastStatusId
      );

      // Get current tweets
      $response = $twitter->status->friendsTimeline($data);

      $twitter_search = new Zend_Service_Twitter_Search();
      $twitter_trends = $twitter_search->trends();

      // loop through each tweet
      foreach($response as $value)
      {
         // if length is 140 mark it a Twoosh
         $twoosh = 0;
         if(strlen($value->text) == 140)
            $twoosh = 1;

         // loop through each trending topic
         $trendingTopic = null;
         foreach($twitter_trends['trends'] as $trend)
         {
            // if the tweet contains a trending topic mark it
            if(strlen(stristr($value->text, $trend['name'])) > 0)
            {
               echo $trend['name'];
               $trendingTopic = $trend['name'];
               break;
            }
         }

         // if the tweet is a twoosh or contained a trending topic, process it
         if($twoosh == 1 || !empty($trendingTopic))
         {
            // create a new tweet object
            $tweet = new tweet($value->id, $value->text, $value->created_at,
               $twoosh, $trendingTopic);

            // associate the tweet to a user
            $user = new user((int) $value->user->id);
            $user->addTweet($tweet);

            // update the user DB record while you have fresh API data
            $user->mapResponse($value->user);
            $user->save;
         }
      }
   }
}
```

Schedule your Cron jobs

To automate the running of your auto-follow and tweet monitor scripts, you need to modify your Web server's crontab file. This file can usually be found in `/etc/crontab`. Use a command line terminal to SSH into your Web server. Once in, enter the command:

```
sudo nano /etc/crontab
```

Enter your password when prompted. Then, in the command line text editor add the bold lines in Listing 12-34. Make sure to replace the domain name with your own domain name.

Listing 12-34: /etc/crontab

```
# m h dom mon dow user  command
*/1 *    * * * root     /usr/bin/curl http://yourdomain.com/tweetcron
*/5 *    * * * root     /usr/bin/curl http://yourdomain.com/followcron
```

These two lines will have the cron job call the tweecron script every minute and call the followcron script every five minutes.

Exit and save the crontab file. Finally, restart the cron with the following command:

```
sudo /etc/init.d/cron restart
```

Creating the Scoreboard

Now that your game's Twitter account is following players and keeping score, it's high time to create a scoreboard that players can page through to see their score. To do this, you need to revisit the very first view and controller you created when you set up the Zend Framework. Look at your `IndexController.php` file first.

Update your IndexController

Your original `IndexController` file simply set an example value in the View. Now, you need it to display a pageable table of players ordered by score. Sounds complicated, but it isn't that bad if you enlist the help of the `Zend_Paginator` class. This class takes a `Zend_DbTable` object and a page number as input. It is clever enough to figure out the most optimal way to retrieve data from your database, freeing you up to deal with the appearance of the table. Have a look at how your new `IndexController.php` file looks in Listing 12-35.

Listing 12-35: application/controllers/IndexController.php

```
<?php

class IndexController extends Zend_Controller_Action
{
   public function indexAction()
   {
      $pageNumber = $this->_getParam('page');

      if(empty($pageNumber))
         $pageNumber = 1;

      $userTable = $this->getUserTable();

      $select = $userTable->select()
         ->where('enabled = ?', 1)
         ->order("score desc, screen_name");

      Zend_Paginator::setDefaultScrollingStyle('Sliding');
      Zend_View_Helper_PaginationControl::setDefaultViewPartial(
         'pagination_control.phtml');

      $paginator = new Zend_Paginator(new Zend_Paginator_Adapter_
            DbTableSelect($select));
      $paginator->setItemCountPerPage(5);
      $paginator->setCurrentPageNumber($pageNumber);

      $this->view->paginator = $paginator;
   }

   private $_userTable;
   private function getUserTable()
   {
      if (null === $this->_userTable) {
         require_once APPLICATION_PATH . '/models/DbTable/User.php';
         $this->_userTable = new Model_DbTable_User;
      }
      return $this->_userTable;
   }
}
```

In Listing 12-35, I look for a page number value in the query-string using the `_getParam` method. If a value isn't found I set `$pageNumber = 1`. Next, I set up the `Zend_DbTable` select statement. Finally, I set up the `Zend_Paginator` class and assign it to the view.

Take a look at this line during the `Zend_Paginator` setup:

```
Zend_View_Helper_PaginationControl::setDefaultViewPartial(
   'pagination_control.phtml');
```

That line of code points to a new file you need to create in your `application/views/scripts` directory called `pagination_control.phtml`. This file contains the HTML template for page buttons used to go to a new page.

Add your pagination template

Create the file pagination_control.phtml in your application/views/scripts directory and add the code in Listing 12-36 to the file.

Listing 12-36 application/views/scripts/pagination_control.phtml

```
<?php if ($this->pageCount): ?>
<div class="paginationControl">

<!-- First page link -->
<?php if ($this->current != $this->first): ?>
  <a href="<?php echo $this->url() . '?page=' . $this->first; ?>">
    &lt;&lt;</a> |
<?php else: ?>
  <span class="disabled">&lt;&lt; |</span>
<?php endif; ?>

<!-- Previous page link -->
<?php if (isset($this->previous)): ?>
  <a href="<?php echo $this->url() . '?page=' . $this->previous; ?>">
    &lt;</a> |
<?php else: ?>
  <span class="disabled">&lt; |</span>
<?php endif; ?>

<!-- Numbered page links -->
<?php foreach ($this->pagesInRange as $page): ?>
  <?php if ($page != $this->current): ?>
    <a href="<?php echo $this->url() . '?page=' . $page; ?>">
        <?php echo $page; ?></a> |
  <?php else: ?>
    <?php echo $page; ?> |
  <?php endif; ?>
<?php endforeach; ?>

<!-- Next page link -->
<?php if (isset($this->next)): ?>
  <a href="<?php echo $this->url() . '?page=' . $this->next; ?>">
    &gt;</a> |
<?php else: ?>
  <span class="disabled">&gt; |</span>
<?php endif; ?>
```

continued

Listing 12-36 *(continued)*

```
<!-- First page link -->
<?php if ($this->current != $this->last): ?>
  <a href="<?php echo $this->url() . '?page=' . $this->last; ?>">
    &gt;&gt;</a>
<?php else: ?>
  <span class="disabled">&gt;&gt;</span>
<?php endif; ?>

</div>
<?php endif; ?>
```

You can use pagination_control.phtml to modify the appearance of the pagination buttons.

Update your Index view

Finally, update the IndexController view, otherwise known as the index.phtml file found in application/views/scripts/index, with the code found in Listing 12-37.

Listing 12-37: application/views/scripts/index/index.phtml

```
<h1>Twooshes</h1>

<p>Twooshes Leader Board</p>

<div class="leader-board">
   <?php if (count($this->paginator)): ?>
      <table class="niceTableInverse">
      <tr>
         <th></th>
         <th>screen_name</th>
         <th>twooshes</th>
         <th>trends</th>
         <th>score</th>
      </tr>
      <?php foreach ($this->paginator as $item): ?>
         <tr>
            <td><img src="<?php echo $item->profile_image_url; ?>" /></td>
            <td><?php echo $item->screen_name; ?></td>
            <td><?php echo $item->twooshes; ?></td>
            <td><?php echo $item->trendingTopics; ?></td>
            <td><?php echo $item->score; ?></td>
         </tr>
      <?php endforeach; ?>
      </table>
   <?php endif; ?>
   <?php echo $this->paginator; ?>
</div>
```

Notice that the View checks whether any paginator items exist. If they exist, it loops through the paginator items and adds them as table rows. Finally, it prints the paginator buttons under the scoreboard results table and before the final closing div tag.

For more details on the Zend_Paginator class, check Chapter 39 of the Zend Framework Programmer's Reference Guide (`http://framework.zend.com/manual/en/zend.paginator.html`).

With all this done after you've uploaded all these files to your production server, the index of your Web site should look something like Figure 12-4. (Provided you've got a few followers and some scores.)

Twooshes

Twooshes Leader Board

	screen_name	twooshes	trends	score
	frank_souders	3	0	3
	jdeeringdavis	1	0	1
	dacort	0	0	0
	c9	0	0	0
	katiefeltman	0	0	0

<< | < | 1 | 2 | 3 | 4 | > | >>

Figure 12-4: A scoreboard with pagination, where players can see how they rank.

Release Early and Often

Okay! You're done! Well, kind of. The basics of your Twitter app are done, but there are still a lot of enhancements that could be made. Think about all the cool features you could add. Also, the site is still pretty ugly. You could definitely spend some time making it more aesthetically pleasing. You are now at a crossroads. You have two options: show your friends your site now, or wait until you make some more enhancements.

If you are working solo, with no external pressure from your boss, investors, or teammates, my advice to you is release your software right now! As soon as it is somewhat stable and functional, it's time to show it to your friends. In fact I've already shown the Twooshes Twitter app to my Twitter followers and I haven't even finished writing this chapter.

I recommend releasing early for two reasons:

- You need user feedback to learn what the next steps are in improving your application.
- If you wait to release your app until it's perfect, you may never release it. Or when you release it, you may find it isn't what your users needed or wanted.

After your initial release, you need to frequently make improvements to your application.

Keep your project's feature roadmap to yourself, or between you and your teammates. Telling your users about your feature roadmap is as good as promising them the features. They may begin to make plans based on your feature roadmap, and if you later decide not to implement a feature, your users may become upset or consider you flakey. If you keep your roadmap to yourself you will delight users with new unexpected features, and you'll retain your creative freedom.

Chapter 13

Making It Pretty Makes It Credible

In This Chapter

- Considering good design
- Making your app pretty
- Integrating design into your Web app

Once you have built a Twitter application, the next step is convincing people to use it. An app with compelling functionality that fills a need goes a long way in attracting and retaining users, but there is another issue besides functionality that you must consider: form. Just how people form first impressions of others based on looks, people will form a first impression of your application based on its looks. All things being equal, if two sites perform the same functionality, a more attractive design may be the deciding factor for users. To stay competitive, you need your app to look good.

Even more important than first impressions and building a more competitive product, a beautifully designed application gives your app credibility. It gives the user the impression that your app is here to stay and that you're serious about supporting your application. A cobbled together design gives the user the impression that you may have built the app on your lunch break and aren't serious about maintaining the application for the long haul. If your application requires the user's trust, such as asking for payment, login credentials, or OAuth authorization, you need your application to appear credible. This chapter explains how to do that.

Although this chapter's slant on design is primarily toward Web applications, the general principles in this chapter are applicable to desktop and mobile applications as well.

Hire a Designer

If you're a stud Web designer, you can skip this section. However, if you don't make your living doing Web design, I strongly recommend hiring a professional designer to design your application. It may seem like a decadent expenditure for an application with little to no upfront capital, but the gain in credibility is worth the expense. Remember, you aren't Coca-Cola, so it isn't necessary to spend a fortune on a design agency, but hiring a modestly priced freelance designer will go a long way for the aesthetics of your application.

How much to spend on design is up to you. To get an idea of what it costs to have your app professionally designed, try comparing several project bids. You can post your gig to Craigslist (`http://craigslist.org`), Elance (`http://elance.com`), or even to your Twitter stream. You should take time to review each candidate's portfolio and select a designer whose aesthetics you like.

If hiring a designer is financially not feasible, do your best to make your application pretty and user-friendly on your own, and release it to the public anyway. You can revisit the app design later.

If you're creating your own site design, keep it simple and try to focus on making the functionality the centerpiece:

- For low-form, high-functionality design
  - Strive for minimalism.
  - Mimic successful sites like Craigslist and Google.

- Consider modifying an open source design.

  Sites like Open Source Web Design (`http://oswd.org`) have a library of free designs you can tweak to fit your application.

PSD to XHTML

Design is usually done in Adobe Photoshop or a similar creative application. The files Photoshop creates are PSD files and need to be converted into HTML to be useable on the Web. There is no good way to do this automatically. You must mark up the design in HTML yourself.

When marking up the HTML of your design, strive to adhere to W3C standards; code in XHTML 1.0 Strict, using table-less CSS markup; and arrange your page as semantically as possible.

Having this type of clean markup will make it easy to integrate the HTML into your app. It will also help with search engine optimization (SEO), as I cover in detail in Chapter 18.

If you're looking to contract out your PSD to HTML markup work, there is an excellent service that I use often called "PSD to HTML" (`http://psd2html.com`). It isn't an automated file conversion system. Human developers painstakingly mark up your HTML by hand. They have a fast turnaround time, produce quality HTML, and are very affordable.

Integrating Your Design

To integrate your design's HTML into your application, you need to break it up into multiple files of smaller functional pieces, such as header, navigation, and footer. Then you include those files in your site's layout.

In Chapter 12 you created a file named `layout.phtml` (found in your `/application/layouts/` directory). This file, shown in Listing 13-1, is the basic HTML layout for the Twooshes Web site.

Listing 13-1: Twooshes layout.phtml

```
<?php echo $this->doctype(); ?>
<html xmlns="http://www.w3.org/1999/xhtml" xml:lang="en" lang="en">
<head>
   <?php echo $this->HeadMeta(); ?>
   <?php echo $this->headTitle(); ?>
   <?php echo
      $this->headLink()->prependStylesheet($this->baseUrl().'/css/site.css'); ?>
</head>
<body>
<div id="content">
   <?php echo $this->layout()->content; ?>
</div>
</body>
</html>
```

The layout contains all the common elements found across all your Web site pages. This prevents you from having to include the same HTML markup on every single page in your app, and is a step in reducing markup redundancy. However, you aren't limited to one layout. Your application may have numerous layouts. For example, Friend Or Follow (`http://friendorfollow.com`) uses two different layouts: a front page and an interior page. Figure 13-1 shows Friend Or Follow's front page on the left and interior page on the right.

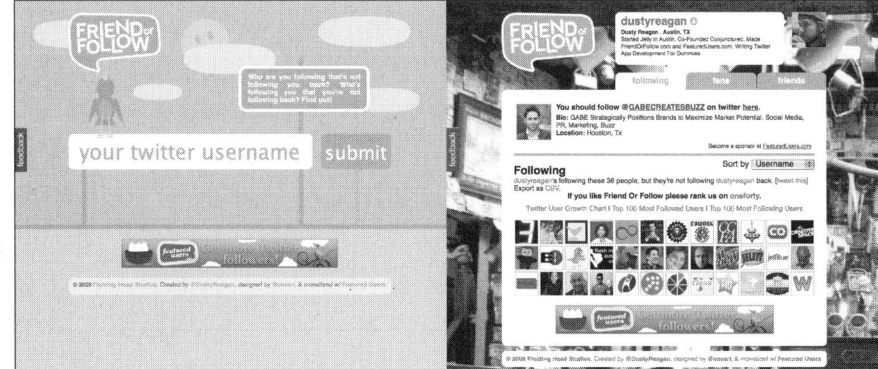

Figure 13-1: Friend Or Follow layouts.

Even though there are two separate layouts for Friend Or Follow, both layouts still share common HTML markup elements, such as

- Nonvisible Meta data in the HTML header
- Logo
- Footer
- Nonvisible JavaScript code used for analytics tracking at the bottom of the HTML

To avoid duplicating similar markup in your projects, you can break up your HTML into many external files and reference those files in each layout file. Listing 13-2 adds four external file references to the original Twooshes `layout.phtml` file:

- `htmlHead.phtml`
- `header.phtml`
- `footer.phtml`
- `tracking.phtml`

However, you can create as many external file references as you need.

Listing 13-2: Twooshes layout.phtml with References to Other Files

```
<?php echo $this->doctype(); ?>
<html xmlns="http://www.w3.org/1999/xhtml" xml:lang="en" lang="en">
<head>
   <?php echo $this->HeadMeta(); ?>
   <?php echo $this->headTitle(); ?>
   <?php echo
```

```
        $this->headLink()->prependStylesheet($this->baseUrl().'/css/site.css'); ?>
    <?= $this->render('htmlHead.phtml') ?>
</head>
<body>
<?= $this->render(header.phtml') ?>
<div id="content">
    <?php echo $this->layout()->content; ?>
</div>
<?= $this->render('footer.phtml') ?>
<?= $this->render('tracking.phtml') ?>
</body>
</html>
```

Now that your HTML is designed into functional sections, you can reuse the same markup across multiple layouts.

The example in this section shows how to split up and reuse HTML markup using the Zend Framework. However, this method of breaking up HTML markup into multiple files and referencing those files is prevalent across Web development frameworks. Even if you aren't using a framework, you can achieve the same effect from inside standard HTML files with

- Server Side Includes (SSI), like this:

  ```
  <!--#include virtual="filename.html" -->
  ```

  Your Web server must have SSI enabled for Server Side Includes to work.
- PHP includes, like this:

  ```
  <?php include("filename.html"); ?>
  ```

Chapter 14

What You Need to Know to Grow

In This Chapter

- Battling code complexity
- Managing multiple developers
- Dealing with performance issues

As your application grows in features, it become more complicated. Complexity is the kiss of death in software development. It breeds bugs and makes your code harder to maintain and enhance. To combat this, developers

- Use abstraction to hide sub-routines and keep functional code as simple as possible.
- Use automated testing to make sure new code doesn't break old features.

In addition to your application's growing complexity, your application will suffer from scaling pains as you gain more users. As your user base increases, so does your server load, disk space requirements, database hits, and Twitter API calls. You must address these scaling issues first, or your application is at risk of crashing.

This chapter is here to warn you of potential growing pains and point you in the direction of potential solutions.

Automating Acceptance Testing

Acceptance testing is done from the user interface side of your application. For example, if your app has a login mechanism, to do acceptance testing on that mechanism means you type a username and password, press the login button and verify the login page loaded. This is the most common and simple type of software testing. Acceptance testing can be done manually by a tester or the developer, but it's difficult and time consuming to test every feature of an application, and do it the same way each time. Fortunately, acceptance testing can be automated.

There are open source acceptance testing automation frameworks for nearly every popular platform, including desktop, mobile, and Web development. Some test frameworks require you to write your testing scripts in their in own language, while other test frameworks allow you to write tests in any language the framework supports. Once the tests are written you can play them back as frequently as you need.

This beats manually remembering to test the 100 different features in your application every time you make a major change in your code.

To get started with acceptance testing for Web applications, give Selenium (`http://seleniumhq.org`) a try. Selenium has an optional Firefox extension called Selenium IDE that gives you a visual user interface, seen in Figure 14-1, that you can use to record tests for Web application. Using the visual test recorder and player will help introduce you to automated acceptance testing.

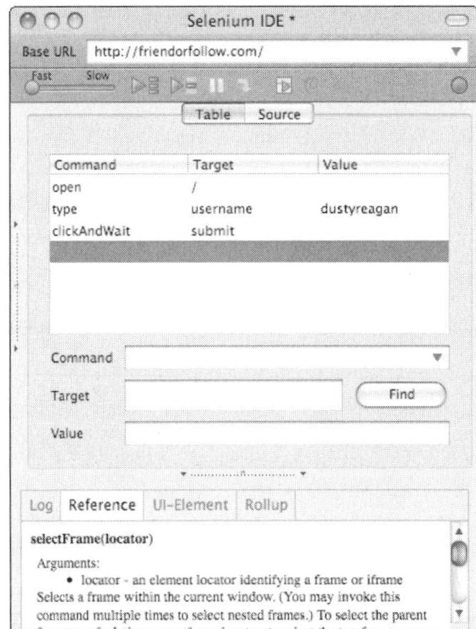

Figure 14-1: Selenium IDE user interface.

Having acceptance tests for you application will stave off new bugs and allow your application to grow larger.

The problem with acceptance tests is they can't tell you exactly where in your code the bug is. They can alert you that there is a problem, but you're left with only vague guesses as to what that problem might be.

Unit Testing

Unit tests are small tests that cover a functional piece of code. For example, if you have a method that takes two numbers as input and returns their sum, you can test that method by writing a unit test. The unit test passes two parameters to the method and tests whether the method output matches the correct summation of the number. The amount of methods you test is called *code coverage.* If every piece of code in your application is covered with a unit test, you have 100 percent code coverage.

The beauty of unit testing is the tests run extremely quickly, and if you write granular tests, when a test fails, you know exactly where the problem is.

Much like automated acceptance testing frameworks, there are open source unit testing frameworks for nearly every popular language. For PHP the popular unit-testing framework is PHPUnit. There is even a wrapper class around PHPUnit in the Zend Framework. You can get more information on writing unit tests in the Zend Framework at `http://framework.zend.com/manual/en/zend.test.html`

Continuous Integration

The larger your project team grows, the more helpful continuous integration becomes. If you're still a one- or two-person operation, setting up a continuous integration server is probably overkill, but it could be helpful later in your project's lifespan.

When you introduce new developers in to your team, you increase the chance of bug introductions, and of having developers step on each others' toes. Using version control software is a good way to keep programmers from unwittingly overwriting each others code, but that doesn't stop the introduction of new bugs. To do that, you need to use continuous integration. Continuous integration runs your entire automated unit and acceptance test cases every time a developer checks in code to version control. If a test case fails, the entire team is alerted and the bug is identified, along with the programmer who introduced the bug. Continuous integration is not intended to shame the guilty developer. It's intended to indentify bugs before they slip into production and catch them while the code is still fresh on the introducer's mind.

To set up continuous integration, your team needs to be using version control software, such as Subversion (`http://subversion.tigris.org`) or Git (`http://git-scm.com`). Then you need a server running continuous integration software, such as CruiseControl (http://cruisecontrol.sourceforge.net). The continuous integration software will poll your version control system looking for changes or check ins. If it notices a new check-in, it will kick off all your automated test scripts. If a test fails, the version control software will alert your team.

Performance Concerns

Aside from a growingly complex code base, you must also concern yourself with your application's performance and ability to scale as you gain more users. Scalability is a major problem with Web applications, because all your users are sharing the same server resources. Desktop applications have to share computing resources with the operating system, but in general don't need to worry about scaling with an increase of users, because new users come with their own processor, disk space, and RAM. However, due to Twitter's API rate limits, even desktop and mobile applications have to watch the frequency that they access the API.

One way to desktop and mobile applications manage API limits is by authenticating the user and having them use their own rate limit allowance. The desktop application TweetDeck (http://tweetdeck.com) shows the users their current rate limit in the top right of the application, as seen in Figure 14-2. Web applications can use this same trick for Twitter API rate limits.

Figure 14-2: Remaining API displayed in TweetDeck

Along with making the end user aware and responsible for their own API access, you can cache API data. For example, to show a user's Twitter profile you must request it from the Twitter API. Once you have that data, it's safe to assume it will not change significantly in the next few hours. You can save that data to a database and reuse it, instead of requesting it from Twitter again.

A big bottleneck in scaling Web applications is data storage. Relational database systems, such as MySQL, are commonly run on one server. The problem with this is that eventually you will not be able to upgrade a single server's performance any further. Your only option at that point is to add additional servers and split the work. It can be tricky to divide a relational database across multiple servers. For example, if you're doing most of your data writing to one table, you can't split that table across more than one server without running into data integrity issues. To handle a situation like this, you can fracture your data stores. Fracturing your data means breaking it up into smaller, but logical, pieces. So if your application is constantly writing to a users table, you could split that table up across multiple servers by placing users A-M on one server and N-Z on the other. Another option is using a non-relational data storage system such as CouchDB (`http://couchdb.apache.org`) or Amazon SimpleDB (`http://aws.amazon.com/simpledb`). These non-relational systems have the ability to scale and sync data horizontally across servers natively.

Your Web server is also susceptible to performance degradation due to increased traffic. To increase the performance of your Web server you can

- Add additional Web servers to your project and use a load-balancing server to direct traffic between your Web servers.
- Move your static content, such as images, to Web servers that specialize in serving static content.

Part IV
Monetization — Making Money with Your Application

"This is getting downright annoying. He tweets me every time he's about to go down a chimney."

In this part . . .

Hey, there's more to life than money. That's why we keep the money stuff safely tucked away here.

Chapter 15

How Twitter Makes Money

In This Chapter

- Understanding how Twitter runs without making money
- Speculating how Twitter might make money
- Funding the development of your Twitter app

After you build your Twitter app, you may want to start recouping your server costs or even start making a profit from your app. If you'd like to try your hand in business, you'll like the next four chapters, which cover moneymaking and promotion strategies for your application.

Since you are building a product on the back of another business, Twitter, you should take the time to learn the financial position of your business partner. Are you making a wise decision partnering with Twitter? I think you are, but Twitter doesn't yet generate any significant revenue. In fact, instead of earning money, they spend it. How is this possible? They have investors, and lots of them. These investors are gambling that Twitter will eventually start turning a sizable profit. In this chapter, I cover some of the common speculations on how Twitter will make money.

Once you understand Twitter's financial position, it is time to look at your own predicament. How will you fund the development of your application? You may already know the answer to this question, but I recommend reading on. You may learn about new funding options that you can leverage to build and grow your app.

Understanding Venture Capital

Venture capital (VC) is money that groups of private investors put into small, immature businesses. These businesses are often young and unproven, thus making them a risky investment, too risky for a bank loan or line of credit. Venture capital firms employ experts in the fields they invest in and fund managers to manage the firms' investments. VC firms invest in risky fledgling companies with the hope that these companies will become publicly traded or be purchased by a larger company. At that point, the VC investors will earn the return on their investments.

Spreading Rumors

No one knows for sure how Twitter will start making money. Well, maybe the founders Evan Williams (@ev), and Biz Stone (@biz) know, but they aren't telling anyone. The fact that Twitter has earned so much investment money without a clear path to revenue or profitability has raised a lot of eyebrows, and caused many speculations on how Twitter will actually start generating revenue. Here are some of the most common Twitter revenue model speculations:

- One idea is that Twitter could establish a pro version of its popular Web site. The current version of Twitter would continue to be free, but the pro version would offer additional features for a monthly fee. The feature set would most likely cater to businesses and power users who want to manage their brand effectively on Twitter.

  In Chapter 4, I mention two Twitter CRM Web sites: CoTweet, and HootSuite. Both of the Web sites are an excellent example of what a Twitter pro version could be like. Maybe Twitter will acquire one of these companies and monetize it.

- One of the most obvious ways for Twitter to start making money is by adding advertising to their Web site. They could build their own proprietary ad auction marketplace that would place clearly defined, sponsored ads on the side of your Twitter stream, or they could integrate a third-party ad network such as Google AdSense. The ads could be removed for any pro versions of Twitter while advertising would subsidize the free version of Twitter.

  Twitter has been reluctant to integrate ads into their site, but they have added a small Twitter application definition box on the side bar. This box randomly displays the name and a brief description of third-party Twitter applications. There have been spottings of paid ads in this box for third-party Twitter applications. But the amount of revenue these ads have generated is speculated to be insignificant compared to Twitter's size and expenses.

- A more controversial advertising possibility is for Twitter to occasionally include an ad in the user's Twitter stream. The ad would be matched to users based on the topics they Tweet about and whom they follow.

  A few companies have tried building a system like this independently of Twitter by leveraging the Twitter API. In Chapter 4, I profile a company called Magpie, which is trying this type of advertising. It has had harsh user push back, so it's unlikely that Twitter will adopt a similar model.

- An attractive revenue model for Twitter is SMS (Short Message Service) revenue sharing from mobile providers. SMS is commonly known as text messaging. As you know, Twitter allows you to update your status via SMS. They also broadcast your tweets to any of your followers who follow your updates via SMS. Currently, Twitter pays mobile providers to send and receive text messages. However, mobile providers make money from the sender and the receiver of a text message. If Twitter increases SMS messages, the company may be able to reverse the deal and negotiate for a share of the mobile provider's SMS revenue. Twitter's ultimatum might be that they would take their business to another provider if they aren't provided with some sort of revenue sharing.

Along with investing money in a business, VC firms will often take an active role in the business' decision-making processes and in advising its managers.

Twitter started as a side project in the podcasting company, Odeo, in 2006. After the project was well received at South By South West Interactive 2007, a technology conference in Austin, Twitter was spun off as its own company. Due to its success, in July 2007 Twitter was able to raise $5 million in venture capital funding. It raised $15 million more in VC funding in May 2008, an additional $35 million in funding in February 2009, and a whopping $100 million in funding in September 2009. These investors see great potential in Twitter, and are betting that Twitter will eventually become a publicly traded company or sell to a larger company like Google. However, Twitter will eventually have to start earning revenue to be a sustainable venture.

How to Fund Your Application

When you build a Web application you're essentially building a product. Whether you choose to turn that product into a business is up to you. However, if you're interested in creating a business with your Twitter application, like Twitter, you will need to eventually make money. And, like Twitter, you will need money to fund your endeavor to get it started. There are several ways to fund the building of your Twitter application.

Self-funding

Bootstrapping is the easiest way to go about funding your Twitter application. Bootstrapping means using your own money to fund your business and when your business starts making money, reinvesting that money back into the business until it is profitable.

You can bootstrap by not quitting your day job. Build your application on the side, after work. If you're a freelancer, work on your application in between gigs.

It's feasible to successfully build a supplemental, passive income outside your full-time job. If you find that your new business is requiring more of your time, you may want to consider focusing on it full time. To do this, you will need money to live on and money to continue funding your business. You can continue to fund your business by bootstrapping, relying on savings, and growing revenue.

Outside investors

If your business requires a large amount of money up front before it can start generating revenue, you may want to seek investors:

- Friends and family are the first sources you may want to consider when seeking investors.
  - Friends and family will usually loan money with few strings.
  - There are fewer legal consequences if your business fails.
- Angel investors are individuals who invest their own money in your startup in exchange for equity or some other monetary return.

  Angel investors generally seek a return of 20 to 30 times their investment within five to seven years. There are organizations of angel investors, called angel networks, who pool their resources when making investments.

  If you don't know any angel investors, seek an angel network in your area by using Google or Twitter.
- To raise more money than friends, family, and angel investors can provide, you will need to seek venture capital.
  - It can be difficult to raise venture capital. Though VC firms make risky investments, they turn down far more businesses than they fund.
  - Raising money from a VC firm will decrease the amount of control you have over your business. The firms take a significant role in securing the success of their investment.

  To get VC funding, you need to find a VC group in your area and pitch them your business concept. These groups usually have procedures in place that instruct you how and when to present your idea. You can seek out VC firms using Google and Twitter and start a conversation with people in the firm.

The best way to fund your business is to start generating revenue as soon as possible, then bootstrap your growth. If you later choose to seek investors and your business is already making revenue, investors will give your pitch more consideration.

Now that you have a good understanding of how to fund your business, you are ready to explore revenue-generating options. These options are covered in the rest of Part IV.

Chapter 16

Advertising

In This Chapter

- Joining an Ad Network
- Twitter as a vertical ad network
- Selling your own ads

One of the most obvious ways of monetizing any Web site or application is through advertising. However, just because advertising is obvious doesn't mean it can't earn you excellent revenue.

Many Web site and application owners have built their businesses through advertising, including the mighty Google. I can't promise you Google-sized revenue, but I can show you how to make money through advertising.

Selecting a Traditional Ad Network

Online advertising has been around since the early days of the World Wide Web. The industry has had time to mature and produce numerous advertising networks. Ad networks are companies that bring advertisers and Web site owners together, streamlining the transaction of buying and selling ad space on the Web.

As a Twitter application owner, you can partner with an ad network as a publisher. Your partnered ad network will sell ad space on your site, give you a percentage of the earnings, and keep the rest. This is beneficial because integrating an ad network into your site is usually incredibly easy and instantly starts generating revenue for you.

However, you need to consider the best ad network for your site. Not all ad networks are created equal, and many perform well on one type of site but not another.

If your Twitter app is a desktop or mobile client, make sure that the ad network you choose allows non–Web-based applications in the term of service. If you own a mobile app, note that there are ad networks like AdMob (`http://admob.com`) that cater specifically to mobile advertising. You can see an example AdMob ad in Figure 16-1.

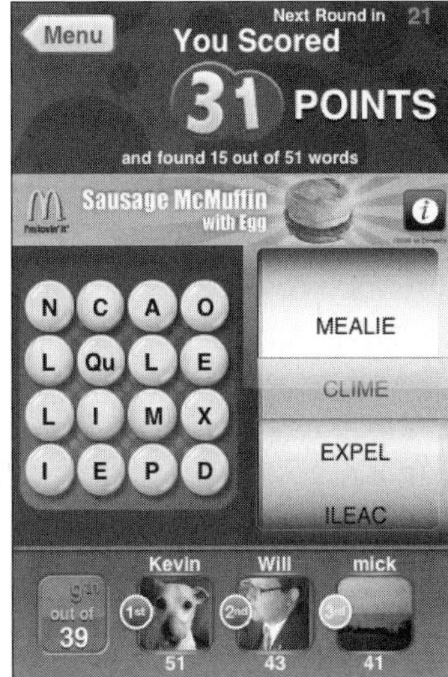

Figure 16-1: An AdMob ad on the iPhone for a Sausage McMuffin.

Ad networks also pay on different criteria. There are four basic flavors of ad networks: pay per click (PPC), cost per thousand (CPM), pay per action (CPA), and cost per time (CPT).

Pay Per Click (PPC)

PPC networks pay publishers only when a user clicks on an ad. The amount an advertiser pays for each click is called the *cost per click* or CPC.

PPC networks are popular with advertisers because they pay only for traffic that is sent to their Web site. It also ensures that the publishers' and advertisers' interests are aligned in driving ad clicks.

However, this model is open to abuse in the form of illegitimate clicks from unethical publishers trying to increase their earnings and from the advertiser's competitors trying to waste the advertiser's marketing budget. This type of fraud benefits the ad network but is harmful to their reputation. Because of this, many PPC ad networks try to defend against click fraud.

You're probably familiar with the biggest PPC ad network, Google. Google has made billions through online PPC in its search results and in the form of a network called Google AdSense. (Figure 16-2 shows a sample AdSense ad.) It's incredibly easy to sign up for Google AdSense and integrate it into your Web site. Due to its low barrier to entry, I suggest trying AdSense first in your attempt to monetize your site. However, Google's PPC network has some disadvantages. When you sign up for AdSense, Google will start crawling your Web site to determine what type of content is on your site so it can serve related ads. It may be that your Twitter application is low on textual content and high on functionality. In this case, Google may not be able to match appropriate ads to your content, which will cause your site to have a low click through rate (CTR) and consequently decrease your earnings. If this happens, you should investigate alternative ad networks.

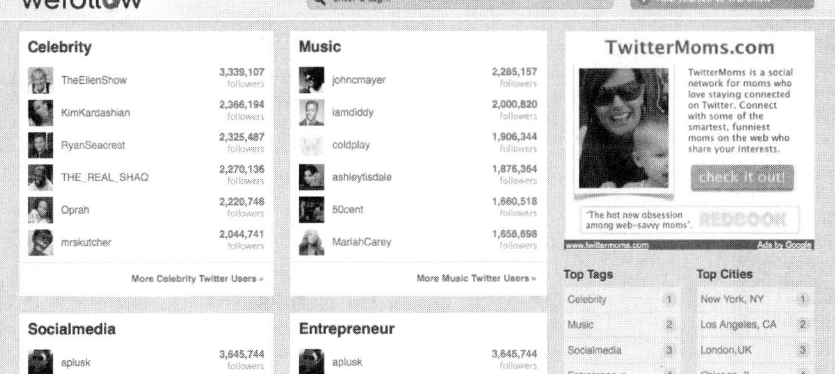

Figure 16-2: Google AdSense ad in the upper-right corner of WeFollow.

Cost Per Thousand (CPM)

In CPM networks, advertisers pay simply to have their ad displayed on a Web site. Each time an ad is displayed is called an impression.

CPM networks generally deal in units of 1,000 impressions, hence the Roman numeral M for 1,000 in the abbreviation CPM. Publishers are paid for each ad impression their site generates.

Popular CPM ad networks usually have high qualification for publishers. Tribal Fusion (`http://tribalfusion.com`), for example, requires your site to have a minimum of 5,000 unique visitors per day. However, if your site meets such qualifications, you can earn excellent payouts for your Web traffic.

Some other examples of CPM networks are

- Casale Media (`http://casalemedia.com`)
- ValueClick (`http://valueclick.com`)
- Gorilla Nation (`http://gorillanation.com`)

Pay Per Action (PPA)

PPA networks pay publishers only when a user performs an action desired by the advertiser, such as follows:

- Purchasing a product
- Signing up for an e-mail newsletter

The amount the advertiser pays per action is called the cost per action or CPA.

Some PPA networks include the following:

- Commission Junction (`http://cj.com`)
- LinkShare (`http://linkshare.com`)

PPA is a perfect fit for an application in some scenarios. For example, say you develop a Twitter application that allows users to share the books they are reading with other users. You could integrate an Amazon affiliate code in every recommended book link. Then you will be paid each time a user purchases a book based on your affiliate links. As I mention in Chapter 4, the music-sharing site Blip.fm makes a portion of its revenue doing iTunes and Amazon affiliate music sales, as shown in Figure 16-3.

Figure 16-3: Blip.fm links to Amazon and iTunes with affiliate links.

maczter Black Moth Super Rainbow + The Octopus Project – "All The Friends You Can Eat"
Black Moth Super Rainbow + The Octopus Project – All The Friends You Can Eat | play
POSTED ON SEP 12 AT 4:17 AM | AMAZON | ITUNES

Cost Per Time (CPT)

Advertisers may pay to have their ad displayed for a set amount of time (like a billboard) regardless of the amount of impressions, clicks, or actions.

The amount the advertiser pays is called the cost per time.

The advertising agreement could span days, weeks, or months. When purchasing CPT ads, advertisers look at the traffic history of a site to estimate what the cost per thousand impressions might be. This is called the eCPM. Advertisers can then use the eCPM to compare offers and get the best deal.

Selling ads in blocks of time is a great way to start selling your own ads. It requires little to no infrastructure to place an ad for a set amount of time on your site. You can also cut out the ad network position as the middleman and pocket 100 percent of the ad revenue.

However, selling ad space still requires quite a bit of effort. If you aren't interested in booking your own ad space, you can use a service like BuySellAds.com (`http://buysellads.com`) to automate the process and help sell your inventory of ad space. Figure 16-4 shows a screenshot of BuySellAds.com.

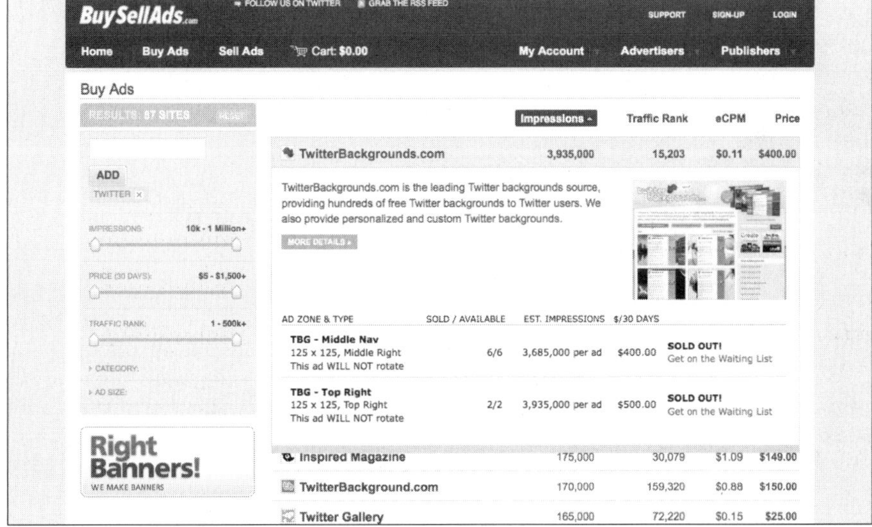

Figure 16-4: BuySellAds.com sells ads by CPT.

Going Vertical

Vertical ad networks are networks that contain sites that target a specific topic. An example might be an ad network that contains only high-quality Web sites about cooking. Businesses selling cookware will then have an excellent place to run an advertising campaign.

The opposite of this is a horizontal ad network that contains sites about all sorts of topics.

One vertical ad segment that may be obvious to you, given the topic of this book, is Twitter. There are several companies trying to leverage Twitter for advertising.

The Magpie Network

The Magpie network (`http://be-a-magpie.com`) marries advertisers and Twitterers. Through the help of the Magpie network, advertisers draft a tweet for their products, then pay Twitter users to post that tweet to their profile.

If you have an application that requires users to follow a particular Twitter account (like the Twooshes game example that's built in this book), you can post occasional ads from the Magpie network to that account.

Don't post too many ads. You don't want to annoy and run off your application's users. However, users usually accept a small amount of relevant ads.

The Featured Users Network

Featured Users (`http://featuredusers.com`) is my own creation. It's a network of Twitter applications that advertises Twitter profiles. Twitter users purchase impressions on Featured Users to gain new followers and increase brand exposure. Ad revenue is split between Featured Users and its publishers. It is much like a typical CPM ad network except that it focuses on a tight vertical niche, promoting a Twitter account.

Integrating Featured Users into your Twitter application is about as easy as integrating Google AdSense:

1. Apply for a publisher account.
2. Once approved, simply add the javascript code to your Web site.

The ads are the benefit that Featured Users has over other ad networks, since the profiles of Twitter users are relevant to a Twitter app, and the payout is very competitive. A Featured Users profile ad is shown in Figure 16-5.

Figure 16-5: A Featured Users ad promoting a Twitter account.

Do It Yourself

It's possible to sell your own ads. By selling your own ad inventory, you don't have to share your revenue with an ad network. You keep 100 percent of the revenue.

Here are the basic steps for selling your own ads.

1. **Determine where you will place your ads.**

   What are you offering a potential advertiser? A high-profile, large banner ad above the fold of your Web site, or perhaps a text ad in the sidebar? You can request more money for high-profile ad locations.

2. **Price your ads competitively.**

   Check the rates on an ad network that sells ads by CPT (`http://BuySellAds.com`, for example). Look up sites like yours and see how much advertisers are paying to be on those sites.

3. **Attract advertisers**:

   - Add placeholder "advertise here" banners where your paid ads will go.
   - Promote your ad spots via your Web site, blog, and Twitter account.

4. **Once you sell some ads, show your advertisers that you appreciate them.**

   You may consider offering discounts if they purchase several months in advance.

If keeping track of ads that you have booked is getting out of hand, consider using ad management software, such as Google Ad Manager or OpenX. These software tools will help you manage ad bookings, placement, and performance tracking.

If you're truly adventurous, you might consider building your own proprietary ad management system. This is how I created Featured Users.

Chapter 17

Monetizing with Other Models

In This Chapter

- Making money with your app
- Relying on the generosity of strangers
- Making recurring revenue with subscriptions
- Merchandising
- Earning money indirectly through your app
- Selling your business

In this chapter, I cover seven common revenue models, including ways that customers can pay you for your application's service, how you can sell physical and virtual goods, and long range revenue strategies. This certainly isn't an exhaustive list, but it should give you some ideas to help you start making money with your app.

Some software lends itself to certain monetization models better than others. To find the optimal revenue generator you should experiment with multiple models and exploit the ones that work the best for you.

Requesting Payment for Service

It is customary to pay someone for the services they provide. If you've ever worked a day job you are probably familiar with this concept. Your application provides a service for your users, so it isn't much of a stretch to consider asking for payment in exchange for the services your application renders. There are numerous ways you can go about asking for payment. Here I cover three of the most common ways:

- Asking for donations
- Charging a fee in exchange for a copy of your application
- Charging a subscription for access to your application

Ask for donations

Asking for donations may be the easiest way to start making money with your Web site. Possibly even easier than partnering with an ad network.

Donations aren't the most effective means of generating revenue. They are unpredictable and rely on the generosity of your users. With a donation-based system, you will do well to cover your operational costs. Don't rely on donations to turn your Web site into a profitable business.

Still, if your goal is to simply keep the servers running, a donation-based model can work. Wikipedia raised $6 million in donations to cover their operational cost for the 2009 fiscal year. You can see Wikipedia's donation page in Figure 17-1.

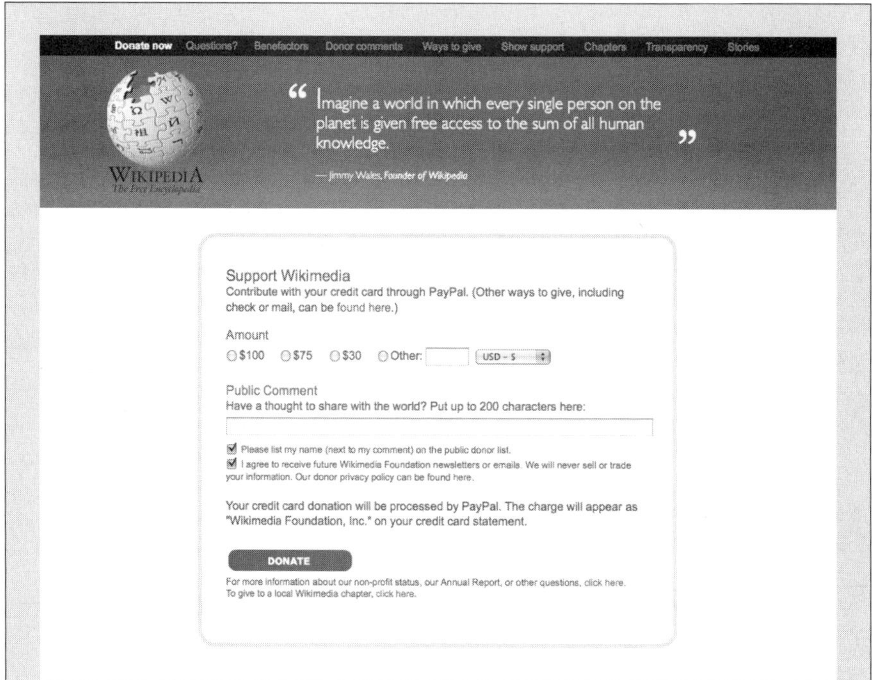

Figure 17-1: Donating to Wikipedia.

For a donation model to really work, your application needs to strike an emotional chord with your users. Wikipedia, for example, provides millions of users with a vast amount of free up-to-date information on a variety of topics. Before Wikipedia, encyclopedias were sold in book sets and cost hundreds of dollars. Not only were printed encyclopedias expensive, the printed information quickly went out of date. This meant that if readers wanted the most up-to-date information, they had to annually replace their encyclopedias.

Wikipedia solves this problem and benefits humanity by making knowledge free, not a luxury to those who can afford it. This is a compelling reason for people to donate money. Your application doesn't have to solve humanities problems on the same level as Wikipedia to garner donations. If you can help one person in a way that they truly appreciate it, such as saving them time, you can earn their appreciation and, consequently, donations.

Make it as easy as possible for your users to give you money. To take donations, you need to accept online payments. You could have your users mail you a check, but I suspect you would receive very few checks. The easiest way to start taking online payments is to sign up for PayPal, Google Checkout, or Amazon Payments. Each one of these services has a donation button you can set up and easily integrate into your app. Make sure your donation button is in an easy-to-find, high profile location on your application. Just like PBS, NPR, and Wikipedia, you may even want to run a fund drive, where for a period of time, you actively promote that you're taking donations.

Sell your software

One tried-and-true method to make money is to license your application and sell it to each user. This is how Microsoft made its fortune, and it's how a lot of software is still sold.

A good example of this in the Twitter ecosystem is the iPhone app, Tweetie. Tweetie is sold for $2.99 in the Apple iPhone App Store (see Figure 17-2). You pay for the app once, and then you have access to that software pretty much for life. Or more realistically, until that software is out of date.

Figure 17-2: Tweetie is for sale in the iPhone App Store.

As a software merchant, after you've sold to your entire marketplace, you can reinvent your software and sell it all over again. Consider all the versions of Microsoft Windows through the years.

Apple has made this sort of online software distribution easy with the iPhone App Store. But what do you do if you're selling desktop software? For small teams of developers on a budget, your best option is to sell it online and let users download your software.

A common way to get started selling your desktop software online is to use the shareware model. Shareware allows users to download a trial of your software and then pay for it if they like it. The trial may

- Expire after a certain amount of time.
- Disable some features.
- Display an annoying pop-up to remind the user to pay for their copy.

When users pay, they receive a key to unlock their shareware copy to the full version.

Twitterrific for Mac is an example of a shareware Twitter app. You can download an ad-supported version of Twitterrific for free. If you upgrade to the paid version of Twitterrific, you are given a code to remove the ads.

Sell subscriptions

What if your Twitter app is a Web application? You could sell access to your Web site once and give the user access for life, but there are other options. You could sell a subscription to your Web app.

With Web applications, users run the software online, on a remote Web server. They don't need to download, install, run, or store data locally on their computer. They can even store their documents, photos, and other files online with the Web application. Positioned this way, it's easy to think of a Web application as a service.

The term "software as a service," or SaaS, represents this view.

Because Web applications manage so much for the user and have the ability to restrict access, it's natural to charge a subscription fee. In fact, this model has become very common.

Typically, subscriptions to Web applications are sold in a tiered hierarchy where each tier contains more features than the one below it.

Often, the bottom tier is given away for free to gain market share and give users a sample of the application's features. This is called the *freemium* model. The popular online photo-sharing site Flickr (`http://flickr.com`) is an excellent example of the freemium model. Flickr has two product tiers:

- A free version that displays ads and limits uploads.
- A pro version that removes upload restrictions and adds features the user would appreciate, like the removal of ads. The first page of Fickr's pro version sign up form is shown in Figure 17-3.

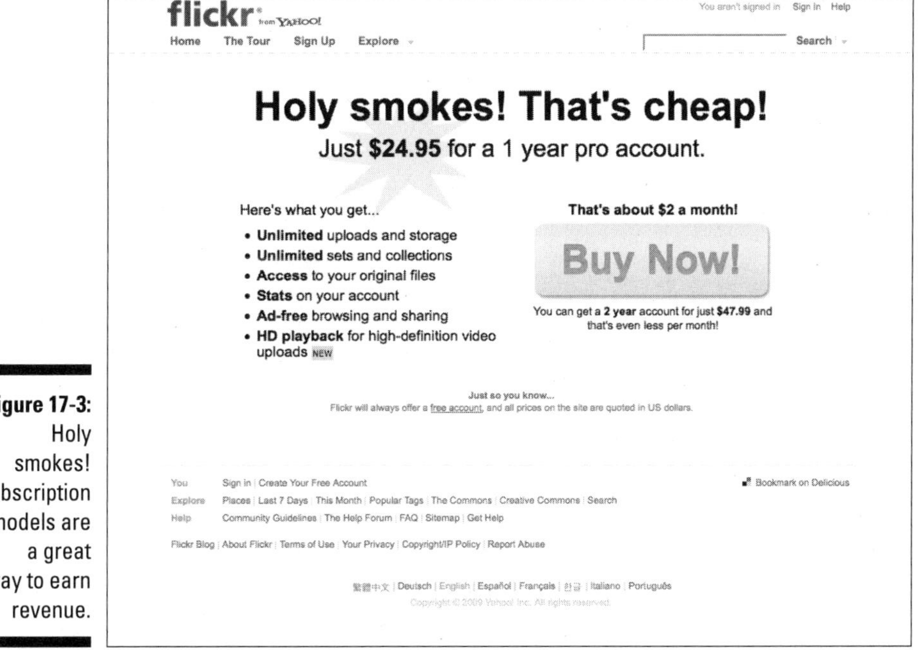

Figure 17-3: Holy smokes! Subscription models are a great way to earn revenue.

Selling Goods

In contrast to requesting money for the services your application provides, you can sell physical or virtual goods that compliment your application. Selling physical goods is a common practice online as ecommerce and offline in the traditional marketplace. Selling intangible virtual goods for use in your application is a relatively new and developing revenue generating practice. You should consider both options.

Physical goods

If you're manufacturing a Twitter hardware device, selling the physical hardware is the obvious way to revenue. However, selling physical goods is a less obvious approach to revenue if you're building software. But that doesn't mean it is impossible.

You can monetize your Twitter application by using it to sell physical goods by either

- Joining affiliate programs (as in Chapter 16).
- Selling your own complimentary products.
  - Twitterrific sells T-shirts with their logo on it at `http://twitterrific.com/gear`.
  - 140tees (`http://140tees.com`) uses the Twitter API to tie into your account and help you select your favorite tweets that you can then order on a T-shirt. Their homepage is seen in Figure 17-4.

An easy way to get started selling products via your Twitter app is to use a site like CafePress (`http://cafepress.com`). CafePress allows you to create a virtual storefront with a variety of products you can slap your logo on. They also provide an API that you can use to create custom-made products for each of your users.

Figure 17-4: Put your friend's updates on a T-shirt with 140tees.

Virtual goods

Virtual goods are goods that exist only online and may be purchased, but have no intrinsic value. The term virtual good is usually applied to concepts such as digital gifts, items in video games, and avatar accessories. The term is usually not applied to

- Digital media (such as videos and music files)
- Digital content (such as written news and entertainment)

Games

Virtual goods are found primarily in online video games. A common scenario in games involves players paying for in-game items that they would otherwise have to spend time earning. For example, these types of virtual items might include weapons that help a player's performance, or they might be purely aesthetic items such as character clothing, player avatars, or props. Players can also purchase in-game currency with real-world money. They then use the virtual currency to purchase in-game items. Sometimes, the creators of the games participate in the virtual goods marketplace, selling items to players. Other times, the terms of the game ban the purchase of all in-game items using real-world money. This usually leads to a black market where players try to hide their transactions from game administrators.

Social networking

On social networking sites, virtual items are often gifted between members. The gifts usually take the form of a badge or icon that the recipients can display on their profile.

Facebook (`http://facebook.com`) is a popular social networking site with a virtual gift marketplace (see Figure 17-5). Some gifts are free, while other gifts must be purchased from Facebook.

Because the price of virtual gifts is public information, a user may opt to purchase an expensive gift in an effort to impress the recipient. This behavior was observed on the popular dating site HOT or NOT (`http://hotornot.com`), where users could gift a virtual rose priced between $2 and $10. Because suitors wanted to impress their love interest, they often chose the $10 rose to signal the seriousness of their admiration.

How can you apply virtual gifts to your Twitter app? It will take some creativity to be sure. Perhaps you could use the Twitter API to publicly announce bestowing of a gift and host the gift on your site. Or if you create a game on Twitter, maybe you could sell special items that will help a player's performance.

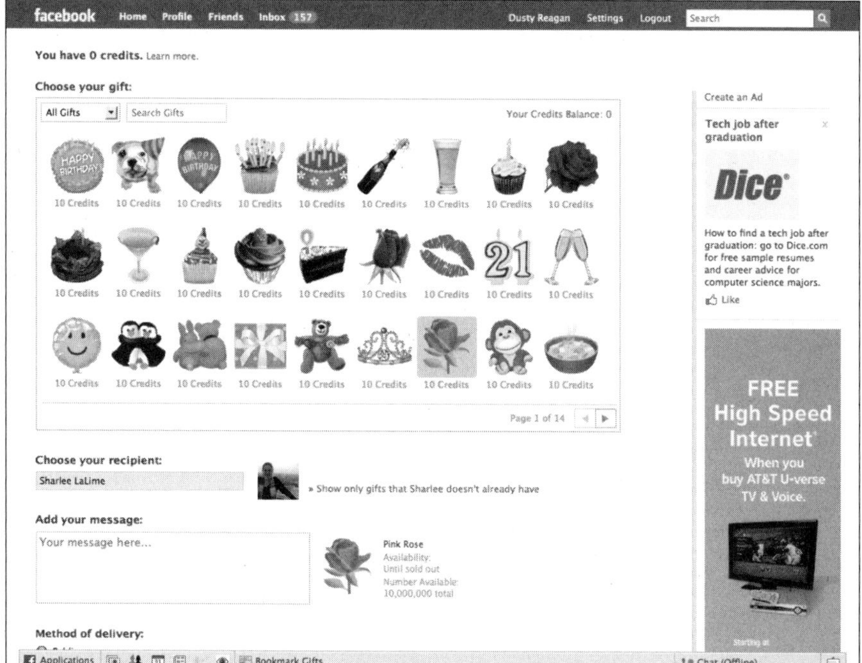

Figure 17-5: Buying my wife a virtual rose.

Building Your Business

Instead of creating a direct stream of revenue immediately, your application may generate revenue indirectly by creating opportunities through increased brand exposure. It is also possible that your application doesn't generate revenue until another company finally acquires it. Either of these cases means that your application is building a business.

Brand awareness

Brand building refers to creating name recognition. This can be either

- A company's brand name
- Your own name

By building name recognition, you can gain renown and social capital that you can later cash in on. One effective way to leverage brand building is to become known as an expert in a particular topic or field. Your renown as an expert can then lead to gigs, speaking engagements, and book deals, which, in turn, further your brand.

There are more ways to leverage brand building than becoming an expert and landing project gigs. Say you build a popular Twitter app that entertains thousands of users. Some of those users will recognize the joy you bring them and in return start following you on Twitter. You are building social capital with these individuals. The next project you launch now has a built-in audience of fans from your last project. Success leads to more success.

If you want to leverage brand building, it's important that your audience knows who you are. You can't build an awesome product and expect people to know innately that you built it. You have to tell them.

You can do this subtly by creating an "about us" page or by putting your name in the footer of your app. If you'd like to put your name in bold at the top of your app, that's fine, too.

The next step is to go beyond listing your name and actually give your users a call to action. Of course, in your case, you want them to follow you on Twitter, so ask them. Somewhere on your Twitter app, put "If you like my app, please follow me on Twitter." You may be surprised by the results.

Be acquired

An acquisition is when a large company purchases a smaller company. Acquisitions happen for many reasons. Your business might be seen as a threat or as an opportunity. Perhaps you have technology that complements the acquiring company. Or it might be due to all these reasons and more.

Being acquired is a jackpot exit strategy if you're a company founder. It means a huge payday, your creation gets to live on, and you get to move on to your next project.

Some companies are built from the start with the goal of eventually being acquired. Founders and investors attempt to make their company attractive for acquisition. In these cases, gathering market share may be more important than generating revenue. Take the poster child of Web acquisitions, YouTube (`http://youtube.com`), for example. In 2006, after YouTube had not made a dime in revenue, Google acquired the company for $1.65 billion in cash and stock option. Google saw the advertising potential in YouTube and decided to purchase the company and crack the revenue-generation nut themselves.

The most famous acquisition in the Twitter ecosystem is Twitter's acquisition of Summize in 2008. Summize is the company behind Twitter's search engine (shown in Figure 17-6), but it was once an independent third-party Twitter application (see Figure 17-7). It is estimated that Summize was purchased for around $15 million in cash and stock options. After the acquisition, five of the six Summize employees were hired by Twitter, and the founder of Summize moved on to a new project.

Maybe Twitter will be interested in purchasing your Twitter app.

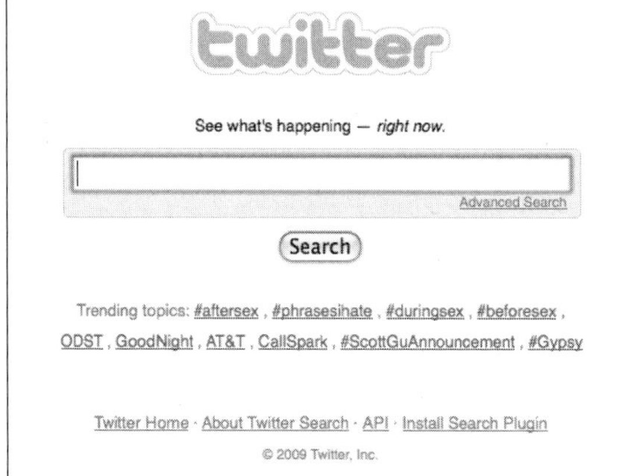

Figure 17-6: After Summize acquisition.

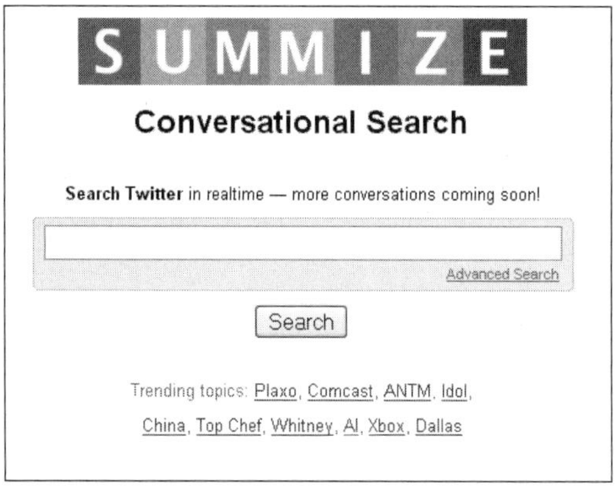

SUMMIZE

Conversational Search

Search Twitter in realtime — more conversations coming soon!

Advanced Search

Search

Trending topics: Plaxo, Comcast, ANTM, Idol,
China, Top Chef, Whitney, AI, Xbox, Dallas

Figure 17-7: Before Summize acquisition.

Chapter 18

Promoting Your Application

In This Chapter

- Leveraging online social networks
- Using viral marketing to promote your app
- How to manage your own PR
- Advertise your app
- Make your app easy to find via search engines

As a developer, I know how exciting it is to invent and bring to life a new product. I also know how disheartening it can be to launch your product to the sound of crickets chirping. This scenario happens all the time to entrepreneurial software developers. It's a common pitfall to expect a barrage of users excited about your product right after you launch. In your heart, you know you've built something wonderfully useful and entertaining, but if nobody knows your application exists, they can't fall in love with it like you have.

If you don't love your project, how can you expect your users to love it? You can't. Consider moving on to another project you're excited about.

When your application has launched, your work has just begun. It's time to spread the word about your app. I cover several promotion strategies you can use in this chapter, but they all focus on driving traffic to your Web site. If you have a desktop or mobile application, you absolutely must have a central Web presence. From there you can direct visitors to download or purchase your application.

There are some common promotional strategies you can leverage to build your user base. The strategies I cover in this chapter include social media, viral marketing, public relations, advertising, and search engine optimization (SEO).

Social Networking

If you're promoting anything, take advantage of online social networks.

The idea behind social networking for marketing is gathering an audience. You need to create lists of people who are interested in what you have to say, and you need to communicate with those people regularly on their preferred platform. This may include gaining followers on Twitter, friends and fans in Facebook, subscribers to your blog RSS feed, or subscribers to your e-mail newsletter. Building an audience of active listeners allows you to establish relationships with your customers and potential customers. It's a bit like rounding up all your warm leads and keeping in constant contact with them. When you have an audience you don't have to market to uninterested people. Instead you can market to your audience, who has invited you to keep them informed about your product.

How should you get involved in social networking? At a minimum, your brand should have a Twitter account and Facebook fan page. With a little extra effort, you would do well to have a blog and an email list.

Twitter strategy

When your product is complete, announce it on your personal Twitter account. If possible, ask your good friends to retweet your announcement. Make sure somewhere on your application you link to your personal Twitter account and ask your users to follow you. This will help promote your personal brand, so the next time you launch a project, fans of your last project will hear about it. It is acceptable to tweet about your application when you work on it or make updates. However, you may annoy your friends if you deal with a lot of product support requests from your personal Twitter account. So, if you don't have one already, you need to create a Twitter account for your product or company brand.

From your product's Twitter account, you can tweet about deals, updates, and handle support requests. Just like your personal account, you need to list your product's Twitter account on your application and ask your users to follow it. You can push your Twitter strategy further by posting to your brand's account regularly. If you don't have enough product news, you can tweet about topics your market segment might find valuable. For example, if you have a Twitter application that helps users share pictures, try tweeting links to some of your favorite photos or photography tutorials.

Make sure your tweets are relevant to your audience and provide value. The goal is to make the tweets from your brand's Twitter account a welcome addition to your follower's Twitter stream. When you accomplish this, you have built trust with your users and each of your tweets will help keep your brand on top of your customer's mind.

You can also do more than just post updates to your Twitter account. One strategy we use with Featured Users (`http://featuredusers.com`) is to automatically send our customers a direct message via Twitter when they run out of banner impressions. This gives us an opportunity to ask them to purchase more impressions. We also use Twitter's favorite feature to star any tweets that would make a good product testimonial. We then display our favorite tweets on our Web site, as seen in Figure 18-1.

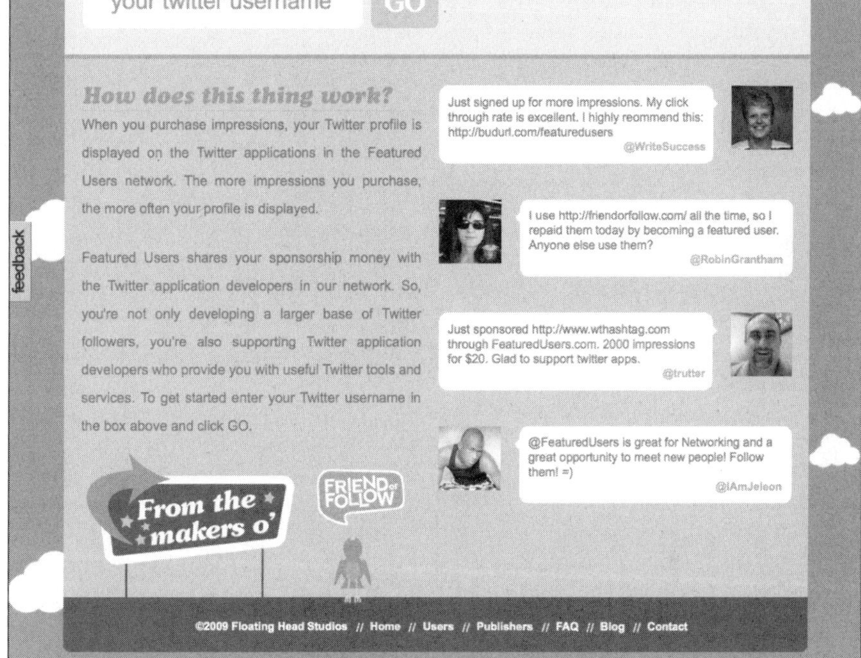

Figure 18-1: On the bottom of every page of Featured Users.com is a tweeted testimonial.

Facebook strategy

Facebook is the largest social networking site online. You would be doing your brand a disservice not to have some sort of presence on the site. You want to be sure your brand is marketed where your customers are. It's a good bet that when your users aren't on Twitter, or using your Twitter app, they're probably spending time on Facebook.

First, you need a personal Facebook profile page for yourself. In addition, you can recruit your friends and colleagues to help you promote your project via Facebook.

If you're passionate about your project, your friends won't mind trying to help you out by spreading the word about your app.

Next, create a Facebook fan page for your application. Fan pages allow people to confess their satisfaction with your brand. You can use the page to share links, photos, news, and event dates with your fans. If you plan on doing most of your product updates from Twitter, it is possible to pipe your Twitter updates to your Facebook fan page. However, this is unsupported and tricky to set up. You can also have your blog update your fan page status.

Once you have a fan page created, ask your friends to become a fan. Once they fan your page, their friends will be alerted to your page, giving you an extra bit of exposure. It's also a good idea to have a link to your fan page somewhere on your application. Facebook even provides a fan page widget you can add to your site. Having a lot of fans on Facebook is an additional display of your product's legitimacy.

Web site blog

A product blog is a great way to post updates to your users. It gives you a public place to communicate with your customers on your own terms. That means no 140-character limits. Take all the characters you need! Further, your customers can communicate back in the form of public comments.

An often-overlooked benefit to keeping a well-groomed blog is their SEO (search engine optimization) value. Today's search engines feed on content, and a frequently updated blog is a content generation machine. This means a user may find content on your blog through a search and consequently be introduced to your Web site.

Further, posting good content to your blog will hopefully cause people to link to your blog posts. These incoming links will drive traffic and signify to search engines like Google that your Web site has link-worthy content. The more incoming links you have, the more important your Web site is perceived, which increases how high your Web site appears in search rankings.

There are several platforms you can use to run your blog. Some popular blog platforms include Wordpress, Blogger, and Movable Type. You want your blog to share your brand's URL. In addition, you want your domain to get credit for all incoming links. To accomplish this, I recommend installing and running your own copy of Wordpress in a subfolder on your official domain, so that the URL looks like this: `http://yourbrand.com/blog`.

If managing your own installation of Wordpress seems too bothersome, use the hosted version of Wordpress or Blogger, but use their respective domain masking features to point to a sub domain of your branded URL. You URL should look something like: `http://blog.yourbrand.com`.

Don't use a third-party URL for your blog. Doing so wastes a lot of branding and SEO opportunity.

Opt-in e-mail list

Managing an e-mail list may seem a little old fashioned in today's online marketing environment. However, it's still an effective means to distribute your message.

It's very important your e-mail list is an opt-in list. An opt-in list means that users willingly and knowingly join your list because they're interested in what you have to say.

Don't send e-mails to people who didn't opt-in to your mailing list. Spam damages your brand's reputation.

To manage an effective e-mail newsletter, you need an e-mail list manager and a means to recruit subscribers. An e-mail list manager is a Web service that helps you maintain your list, create your e-mails, deliver them, and provides click and opening statistics. These services usually charge based on the amount of e-mails you send. Two services I recommend are MailChimp (`http://mailchimp.com`) and Emma (`http://myemma.com`).

To start building your e-mail list, first ask your Twitter followers and Facebook friends to join. Then you should consider putting a newsletter signup form on your Web site. Both MailChimp and Emma provide code to easily integrate a form on your site. Beyond these steps, consider asking your customers to subscribe when you send them a receipt, or when they sign up for your service. Once you have a system in place to build your list, use it to make product announcements.

Try not to wear out your welcome. Two or three e-mails per month are plenty.

Go Viral

One of the most effective ways to spread the word about your application is to use viral marketing. Viral marketing is the term used for the strategy of building a marketing campaign that spreads organically as one person tells another person about your offer. Social media sites like Twitter, Facebook, and MySpace are the perfect vehicles for this type of marketing.

The key to viral marketing is to make something people will want to share with their friends. Then you need to make it easy to share. Tweetmeme's (`http://tweetmeme.com`) "tweet this" button that makes it easy for blog readers to tweet about a post is a good example. You can see the Tweetmeme button in Figure 18-2.

Viral marketing needs to link with your product, somehow. A viral video of your cat is funny, but to gain any value from it your brand needs to be associated with video.

Figure 18-2: Tweetmeme makes it easy to tweet about a blog post.

One way to jump start a viral marketing effort is to provide an incentive for your users to tell their friends. An excellent example of viral marketing in a Twitter app is WeFollow (`http://wefollow.com`). WeFollow is a Twitter user directory where every user gets to pick five categories to describe themselves. People want to be listed in the directory so other users with similar interests can find them. However, to get listed in WeFollow you must first publicly tweet your chosen categories and include a link back to WeFollow, as seen in Figure 18-3. When a user joins, their friends are alerted. Now those users have a social incentive to join. When they join the cycle repeats, and you have a wonderful example of viral marketing.

It takes some creativity to come up with a good viral marketing campaign, but it is well worth the effort.

Added self to http://wefollow.com twitter directory #austin_tx #digitalmedia #businessdevelopment #socialmedia #musicindustry #filmindustry

2 minutes ago from web

frank_souders

Figure 18-3: A tweet to join the WeFollow user directory.

Public Relations Strategies

Public relations, or PR, is the art of dealing with the public and the press. Many large companies employ the services of a PR firm to manage the company's brand image. They do this by pitching news stories to media outlets, hosting events, and crafting marketing campaigns that portray the company's brand in a positive light.

PR firms can be very expensive. If you aim to turn your Twitter app into a business, hiring a PR firm early may not be the best use of your funds. However, you can try do-it-yourself PR. You may consider writing press releases and pitching them to individuals that cover news in your industry, such as writers at TechCrunch (`http://techcrunch.com`) and Mashable (`http://mashable.com`).

As a new developer, your time is better spent focusing on the following three areas: network in your industry, toot your own horn, and be authentic.

Network in your industry

Networking in your industry is really networking in your customer's industry. Wherever your customers are, you need to be there. This means attending tradeshows, conferences, happy hours, and meetups. You should spend time mingling with your customers, making connections, building trust, and building friendships.

Don't try to make hard sells at these types of events. Become a member of your customer's community. You need to earn your seat at the table. People prefer to do business with people they know and trust. You may also make connections that will help you sell or market your product. The important thing is to get out there and make sure your customers know you exist.

Toot your own horn

When it comes to promoting your own product, don't be modest.

For example, if a Twitter celebrity sends you a note that they like your app, seize the opportunity and ask them for a testimonial that you can publish on your Web site. If your app is mentioned on a popular technology blog, tell everyone you know and proudly link to the article from your Web site. All these little victories add credibility to your work. It's similar to the saying if a tree falls in the forest and no one hears it, did it actually fall? The same goes for PR. If McHammer tells you he likes your Twitter app (see Figure 18-4), but nobody knows he endorses it, then it didn't really benefit your brand at all.

check out friendorfollow.com ... it's real cool...

12:53 AM Nov 8th, 2008 from web

MCHammer

Hammer

Figure 18-4: @ MCHammer digs Friend Or Follow.

Be authentic

When you hire a PR firm, they spend time coaching you on how to talk to the media. If you can't afford a PR firm, my advice to you is to just act like yourself. Don't try to be someone you aren't. You aren't the CEO of ExxonMobil, so don't act like it. People find authenticity refreshing, and it's a lot easier to pull off being yourself, than to sling out stunted corporate marketing talk.

Be passionate, be respectful, be yourself.

Advertise

There are many outlets for paid advertising: billboards, Web banners, radio spots, TV commercials, and printed ads just to name a few.

If you're early in your brand's life, start with Web banners and text ads. These types of ads cost little to nothing to produce and are an ideal way to drive Web traffic. Other forms of advertising like billboards or TV commercials require a lot of upfront production cost, such as printing the billboard screen, or hiring a film crew. You have to pay these production costs before you can even begin to pay for the advertising spot. You can also directly measure your return on investment (ROI) with Web advertising by tracking the click through rate (CTR) and conversions. Most online ad networks have tools to help you track this.

The first place you should start your online ad campaign is Google AdWords. AdWords is the grand daddy of online text ads. Google provides plenty of metrics and tools, and you don't need any banner images. AdWords allows you to target keywords you think are relative to your Twitter app and it allows you to set a daily budget. You can even track sales conversions and measure your ROI.

When you decide to branch out from text ads to graphical banner ads, your first hurtle will be obtaining the banner images. If you or a friend is a designer, problem solved. Otherwise, you might be interested in Right Banners (`http://rightbanners.com`). Right Banners is a Web service that specializes in making banner ads. Now that you have a resource for creating your banner images you can use ad networks like BuySellAds.com (`http://buysellads.com`) and Project Wonderful (`http://projectwonderful.com`) to find relative sites to advertise on.

SEO

SEO stands for search engine optimization. It is the craft of optimizing your Web site's content so that users can easily find it via search engines. If you host a desktop or mobile application, SEO doesn't apply directly to your application. However, it does apply to the Web site you use to promote your application.

You'll score big by following two rules:

- Use semantically correct HTML markup
- Provide unique content that people will want to link to

Using semantically correct HTML markup means using each HTML element as it is intended to be used. For example, the <p> tag stands for paragraph, so you should only use it to denote a paragraph. The <h1> tag means "header 1," so you should only use it for a section header. Search engines try to use the semantic meanings of HTML tags to determine what is most important on your page. They also use the position of the text on the page as an indicator. For example, the text in an <h1> tag at the top of the page will be considered more important than a <p> tag at the bottom of the page.

Keep all style elements separate from your content by using external CSS files. Ultimately, you should be able to remove the reference to your CSS file and still have a site that is clearly readable. If you can't read your site without the CSS, search engines like Google probably can't read your site. Removing style elements and complex code also makes your Web site easier to index and load faster for users.

To help enforce semantically correct HTML, validate your Web site as XHTML 1.0 Strict. XHTML 1.0 Strict is a set of rules that ensures your markup meets a minimum level of quality. You can use the W3C Markup Validation Service found at `http://validator.w3.org` to validate your code. Figure 18-5 shows the W3C Validation Web site.

Figure 18-5: Validate your code using the W3C Markup Validation Service.

The next thing you need to do for SEO is have a lot of quality incoming links. Search engines see links that point to your Web site as an indicator that your site is important. Google uses a 10-point scale called *page rank* to measure your site's perceived importance. However, search engines don't just look at the quantity of incoming links. They also look at the quality of the links. This means if a well-established blog with a page rank of eight links to your site, that is much more influential to Google than a link from a site with a page rank of two.

The best way to get incoming Web links is to have good unique content that people will want to link to. Hosting your own blog with thoughtful posts will often do the trick. Of course, if you have an awesome Web app that people want to tell their friends about, that will also create quality incoming links.

There are many Twitter application lists and review sites that you to your application for free. Some examples are oneforty (`http://oneforty.com`), Twtbase (`http://twtbase.com`), and Twitdom (`http://twitdom.com`).

Part V
The Part of Tens

In this part . . .

Two great chapters. Two great lists. Too much!

Chapter 19

Ten Traits of a Respectable Twitter Developer

In This Chapter

- Gaining the respect of your peers
- Gaining the respect of your users

Twitter's API is open, which means anybody can start developing a Twitter app. This has led to a multitude of applications and a flourishing community of Twitter developers. Just like any other community, there are highly respected members, and there are those who are considered a burden on the rest of the community. You should strive to be a respected, contributing Twitter developer.

In this chapter, I list ten traits of a respectable Twitter developer. Follow these traits and your peers and customers will hold you in high regard.

Ask Permission

Don't perform any action on users' behalf without first getting their consent.

- Don't send a tweet on users' behalf without first getting their permission. Just because they authenticated with your application doesn't mean they gave gratis to post whatever you want to their Twitter stream.
- Don't make users follow your application's Twitter account without first asking for their permission.

Read the Documentation First

Before you ask a question in the Twitter API Google Group (`http://groups.google.com/group/twitter-development-talk`), make sure you first

- Look for an answer in the Twitter API wiki.
- Search previous posts in the Google Group.

The developer community is a great resource, but they frown upon unnecessary queries. Nothing is more agitating to community contributors than answering the same questions over and over again. Be a good community member and do your homework before you recruit help.

Stay within Your Rate Limit

Twitter limits the amount of API requests an authenticated user and an IP address can make per hour. This limit is in place to help with Twitter's server load and prevent rogue applications from degrading API access for everyone. You need to monitor your API use using the `account/rate_limit_status` method, and avoid going over your limit.

If you need more API requests per hour, you can apply for whitelisting at `http://twitter.com/help/request_whitelisting`.

Don't Promote Mass Following

The Twitter community at large frowns on the practice of mass following to gain reciprocal followers. There are several tactics for accomplishing this, but they all involve following a large number of people and dropping those who don't follow back.

You're better than this. Don't do it.

Even shadier is dropping all but a few people to give the appearance of false popularity. Using the API to automate this practice is highly frowned upon and may be against Twitter's terms of service. If you create an app of this nature, you will not receive much love from either the developer community or the support staff at Twitter.

Be Cautious of Trademarks

Twitter legally must protect its trademarks. This includes the word "twitter."

Avoid using the word "twitter" anywhere in your product or domain name.

To be extra safe, strive to deviate from Twitter's branding as much as possible. Numerous apps have adopted prefixing "tw" to their brand. *Break out of the pack.* Avoid "twitter," "tweet," "twit," for sure, and I'll give you bonus points for avoiding "tw" altogether.

Give Back

The Twitter developer community is strong, and it's a great resource when you're seeking API help. Whenever possible, you should try to give back to the community with such contributions as these:

- Answering questions on the developer Google Group
- Contributing to open source Twitter libraries that make it easy for other developers to get involved in Twitter development

Doing these sorts of things will garner goodwill in the community, and the next time you need assistance, people will go the extra mile to help you.

Cache Your Data

You should strive to access the API as little as possible. One key to doing this is to cache the data you retrieve from the API. Reuse the data you've already retrieved as much as possible. This takes load off of Twitter's servers and speeds up your application. It also saves your rate limit.

Use OAuth

If you must authenticate a user with Twitter, you should use OAuth instead of basic authentication. Basic authentication requires that you, the developer, manage users' passwords. This is a risk for the user and a liability for the developer. Further, users have become skeptical of applications that ask for their passwords, for fear that their account might be compromised.

With OAuth, you never have to deal with users' passwords. Users give your application permission to access their private data from Twitter's side of the fence.

Don't Be Evil

Take a tip from Google's company motto and don't be evil. This includes honoring the wishes of private account holders. Private users may give your application permission to access their tweets. Keep these users' data confidential.

When users give you their trust, you should work hard not to break that trust.

Communicate with Your Users

Users will want to give you feedback, report bugs, and ask you questions about your application. You should make yourself available by either

- Providing contact information
- Integrating a reporting tool into your application, such as
  - UserVoice (`http://uservoice.com`)
  - GetSatisfaction (`http://getsatisfaction.com`)

Identifying yourself to your users gives your application credibility and shows you aren't a fly-by-night operation.

Chapter 20

Ten Twitter API Tips

In This Chapter

- Gleaning advice from other Twitter developers

One of the best ways to learn is to do. However, the next best way to learn is to glean advice from other people's experience. You've heard a lot from me in this book about my experience with the Twitter API, now here are some tips from other Twitter developers.

Develop Defensively

"Develop defensively. For instance, when passing in scoping parameters like `since_id`, assume that the Twitter API will break one day and disregard `since_id` when building the result set."

–Barry Hess (@bjhess), co-creator of Follow Cost (`http://followcost.com`)

Degrade Gracefully

"The Twitter API can and will go down. Applications should have some sort of monitoring, graceful degradation, and informative error messages for users in the event that this happens. Because if you don't, your app gets blamed, not Twitter."

–Damon Cortesi (@dacort), creator of TweetStats (`http://tweetstats.com`) and TweepSearch (`http://tweepsearch.com`)

Don't Rely on screen_name

"Always use `user_id` to reference accounts instead of `screen_name`. `screen_name` could change at anytime."

–Abraham Williams (@abraham)

Use 64-Bit Integers

"Be sure to use long integers (Int64 in the .NET world) for storing ID values. 32-bit integers aren't large enough for the ID values that Twitter is producing."

–Duane Roelands (@DWRoelands), creator of Quitter (`http://getquitter.com`)

Subscribe to the Google Group

"Expect things to change. Twitter is a rapidly developing service, and what is true now may not be true in 12 months. Subscribe to the developer announcement list (`http://groups.google.com/group/twitter-development-talk`) and read it religiously."

–David Fisher (@tibbon), Web Ecology Project (`http://webecologyproject.org`)

Access the API in the Background

"If you're building a Web app, do as much of your Twitter communication outside the request-response cycle as you can. API calls to Twitter will often have errors or take unpredictable amounts of time. When possible, move API calls to background processes or cron jobs, batch them and cache the results. This gives users a more consistent experience, allows you to more easily handle errors and helps with staying under rate limits since your API calls are less of a function of the number of requests your app gets."

–Hayes Davis (@hayesdavis), creator of CheapTweet (`http://cheaptweet.com`) and TweetReach (`http://tweetreach.com`)

Use JSON

"Get to know JSON. Even if you aren't writing javascript, there are JSON parsers in most every language. JSON is leaner and meaner than XML and super easy to understand once you take 5 minutes to learn it. Every Twitter API method can return JSON data, so use it!"

–Chad Etzel (@JazzyChad), creator of TweetGrid (`http://tweetgrid.com`) and TweetHook (`http://tweethook.com`)

Optimize Caching

"Learn everything you can about efficient caching and database queries. If your app gets popular, these two things will make or break your success."

–Noah Coffey (@noahwesley), creator of TweetFX (`http://tweetfx.com`)

Support International Characters

"Make sure your app supports more than just English characters, especially when updating a user's status. For OAuth, this can mean extra legwork, since the content of the status update is part of what is used to authenticate the request — so it's crucial it gets encoded properly. It seems some developers don't test international characters — but Twitter is part of an international community, and this detail shouldn't be overlooked."

–Andrew Perrin (@mageuzi), creator of Trowl (`http://mageuzi.com/trowl/`)

Do It Client Side

"Twibes uses the powerful (and under-hyped) JASONP support in the Twitter API to get around usage quotas. By using Javascript to perform searches, a Web page can become more like a desktop app — connecting directly to Twitter and only sending the relevant new results up to a Web server. Distributing your application logic to many clients takes load off your server and distributes the Twitter API calls (thus using none of your app's API quota)."

–Adam Loving (@adamloving), creator of Twibes (`http://twibes.com`)

Appendix A

Twitter API Reference

This appendix includes a break down of all the Twitter API methods available as of this writing. It is to serve as a quick reference guide. The methods are in alphabetical order by their path name.

All methods referenced in this appendix refer to version 1 of the API. As such, the root of all method paths is

```
http://api.twitter.com/1/
```

Account Methods

- account/verify_credentials
- account/rate_limit_status
- account/end_session
- account/update_delivery_device
- account/update_profile_colors
- account/update_profile_image
- account/update_profile_background_image
- account/update_profile

account/verify_credentials

Use to verify that the supplied credentials are valid.

Path	*Output Formats*	*HTTP Methods*	*Authentication*	*Rate Limited*
/account/verify_credentials	XML, JSON	GET	TRUE	FALSE

account/rate_limit_status

Returns the amount of remaining API requests available for the hour for the authenticated user. If you aren't authenticated, the rate limit for the current IP address is returned.

Path	Output Formats	HTTP Methods	Authentication	Rate Limited
/account/rate_limit_status	XML, JSON	GET	FALSE	FALSE

account/end_session

Ends the session for the current logged in user.

Path	Output Formats	HTTP Methods	Authentication	Rate Limited
/account/end_session	XML, JSON	GET	TRUE	FALSE

account/update_delivery_device

Updates the device that Twitter forwards tweets to.

As of this writing, IM is not supported.

Path	Output Formats	HTTP Methods	Authentication	Rate Limited
/account/update_delivery_device	XML, JSON	POST	TRUE	FALSE

Parameter	Description	Examples
device	Values include: sms, none	device=sms

account/update_profile_colors

Sets user defined colors for the elements on the user's Twitter page for the authenticated user.

Path	Output Formats	HTTP Methods	Authentication	Rate Limited
/account/update_profile_colors	XML, JSON	POST	TRUE	FALSE

Parameter	Description	Examples
profile_background_color	Hexadecimal color code for the background, if no background image is present.	profile_background_color=333
profile_text_color	Hexadecimal color code for text.	profile_text_color=000000
profile_link_color	Hexadecimal color code for links.	profile_link_color=00C2FC
profile_sidebar_fill_color	Hexadecimal color code for the background of the sidebar.	profile_sidebar_fill_color=fff
profile_sidebar_border_color	Hexadecimal color code for the border around the sidebar.	profile_sidebar_border_color=000

account/update_profile_image

Sets the profile image for the authenticated user.

Path	Output Formats	HTTP Methods	Authentication	Rate Limited
/account/update_profile_image	XML, JSON	POST	TRUE	FALSE

Parameter	Description	Examples
image	A GIF, JPG, or PNG image less than 700 kilobytes. Widths greater than 500 pixels are scaled down.	image=@'mypic.png;type=image/png'

account/update_profile_background_image

Sets the profile background image for the authenticated user.

Path	Output Formats	HTTP Methods	Authentication	Rate Limited
/account/update_profile_background_image	XML, JSON	POST	TRUE	FALSE

Parameter	Description	Examples
image	A GIF, JPG, or PNG image less than 800 kilobytes. Widths greater than 2048 pixels are scaled down.	image=@'mypic.png;type=image/png'
tile	Tile the background image by setting a value of true.	title=true

account/update_profile

Sets the authenticated user's profile text fields.

Path	Output Formats	HTTP Methods	Authentication	Rate Limited
/account/update_profile	XML, JSON	POST	TRUE	FALSE

Parameter	Description	Examples
name	A string under 20 characters intended for the full name of the user.	name=Dusty Reagan
url	A string under 100 characters intended for the personal URL of the user. "http://" is added if not already included.	url=http://google.com
location	A string under 30 characters intended for the geographical location of the user.	location=Texas
description	A string under 160 characters intended to describe the user.	description=awesome dude

Block Methods

- blocks/blocking
- blocks/blocking/ids

- blocks/create
- blocks/destroy
- blocks/exists

blocks/blocking

Returns the user details object for the 20 most recently blocked users by the authenticating user.

Path	*Output Formats*	*HTTP Methods*	*Authentication*	*Rate Limited*
/blocks/blocking	XML, JSON	GET	TRUE	TRUE

Parameter	*Description*	*Examples*
page	Page to retrieve older blocked users.	/blocks/blocking.xml?page=5

blocks/blocking/ids

Get the numeric user ids of users the authenticating user has blocked.

Path	*Output Formats*	*HTTP Methods*	*Authentication*	*Rate Limited*
/blocks/blocking/id	XML, JSON	GET	TRUE	TRUE

blocks/create

Block the specified user for the authenticated user.

Path	*Output Formats*	*HTTP Methods*	*Authentication*	*Rate Limited*
/blocks/create	XML, JSON	POST	TRUE	FALSE

Parameter	*Description*	*Examples*
id	The numeric user ID or screen name of the desired user.	/blocks/create/12345.xml /blocks/create/bob.xml

Parameter	*Description*	*Example*
user_id	The numeric ID of the user.	/blocks/create.xml?user_id=12345
screen_name	The screen name of the user.	/blocks/create.xml?screen_name=101010

blocks/destroy

Removes the block of a specified user for the authenticated user.

Path	*Output Formats*	*HTTP Methods*	*Authentication*	*Rate Limited*
/blocks/destroy	XML, JSON	POST, DELETE	TRUE	FALSE

Parameter	*Description*	*Examples*
id	The numeric user ID or screen name of the desired user.	/blocks/destroy/12345.xml/blocks/destroy/bob.xml
user_id	The numeric ID of the user.	/blocks/destroy.xml?user_id=12345
screen_name	The screen name of the user.	/blocks/destory.xml?screen_name=101010

blocks/exists

Check if the authenticating user has blocked a specified user.

Path	*Output Formats*	*HTTP Methods*	*Authentication*	*Rate Limited*
/blocks/exists	XML, JSON	GET	TRUE	FALSE

Parameter	*Description*	*Examples*
id	The numeric user ID or screen name of the desired user.	/blocks/exists/12345.xml /blocks/exists/bob.xml
user_id	The numeric ID of the user.	/blocks/exists.xml?user_id=12345

Parameter	Description	Example
screen_ name	The screen name of the user.	/blocks/exists. xml?screen_ name=101010

Direct Message Methods

- direct_messages
- direct_messages/destroy
- direct_messages/new
- direct_messages/sent

direct_messages

Get the authenticated user's 20 most recently received direct messages.

Path	Output Formats	HTTP Methods	Authentication	Rate Limited
/direct_messages	XML, JSON, RSS, ATOM	GET	TRUE	TRUE

Parameter	Description	Examples
since_id	The numerical id of a direct message. Use to return direct messages that are more recent than the id specified.	/direct_messages.xml? since_id=12345
max_id	The numerical id of a direct message. Use to return direct messages that are older than the id specified.	/direct_messages.xml? max_id=54321
count	Limits the results per page to an amount specified that is less than 200.	/direct_messages.xml? count=100
page	Page backwards to retrieve older direct messages.	/direct_messages.xml? page=5

direct_messages/sent

Get the authenticated user's 20 most recently sent direct messages.

Path	*Output Formats*	*HTTP Methods*	*Authentication*	*Rate Limited*
/direct_messages/ sent	XML, JSON, RSS, ATOM	GET	TRUE	TRUE

Parameter	*Description*	*Examples*
since_id	Returns direct messages that are more recent than the id specified.	/direct_messages/sent.xml? since_id=12345
max_id	Returns direct messages that older than the id specified.	/direct_messages/sent.xml? max_id=54321
count	Limits the results to an amount specified that is less than 200.	/direct_messages/sent.xml? count=100
page	Page backwards to retrieve older direct messages.	/direct_messages/sent.xml? page=5

direct_messages/new

Send a new direct message to a user.

While the `id` parameter can take either a screen name or numeric user id as a parameter, there are cases when a screen name and numeric user id may conflict. For example, a user's screen name might be 101010. There might also be a numeric user id 101010. For this reason you should use either the `user_id` or `screen_name` parameter.

Path	*Output Formats*	*HTTP Methods*	*Authentication*	*Rate Limited*
/direct_ messages/new	XML, JSON	POST	TRUE	FALSE

Parameter	*Description*	*Examples*
user	The numeric user ID or screen name of the desired user.	/direct_messages/new/12345. xml/direct_messages/new/ bob.xml

Parameter	Description	Example
user_id	The numeric ID of the user.	/direct_messages/new.xml?user_id=12345
screen_name	The screen name of the user.	/direct_messages/new.xml?screen_name=101010
text	The content of the direct message. Must be URL encoded and less than 140 characters.	/direct_messages/new.xml?user_id=123&text=hi

direct_messages/destroy

Deletes a specified received direct message of the authenticating user.

Path	Output Formats	HTTP Methods	Authentication	Rate Limited
/direct_messages/destroy/	XML, JSON	POST, DELETE	TRUE	FALSE

Parameter	Description	Examples
id	The numeric id of the direct message you want to delete.	/direct_messages/destroy/12345.xml /direct_messages/destroy/12345.json

Favorite Methods

- favorites
- favorites/create
- favorites/destroy

favorites

Returns the 20 most recently favorited tweets for the authenticated user or the user you request.

Path	Output Formats	HTTP Methods	Authentication	Rate Limited
/favorites	XML, JSON	GET	FALSE	TRUE

Parameter	*Description*	*Examples*
id	The numeric user ID or screen name of the desired user.	/favorites/12345.xml /favorites/bob.xml
user_id	The numeric ID of the user.	/favorites.xml?user_id=12345
screen_name	The screen name of the user.	/favorites.xml?screen_name=101010
page	Page backwards to retrieve older favorited tweets.	/favorites.xml?page=5

favorites/create

Mark a tweet as a favorite for the authenticated user.

Path	*Output Formats*	*HTTP Methods*	*Authentication*	*Rate Limited*
/favorites/create/	XML, JSON	POST	TRUE	FALSE

Parameter	*Description*	*Examples*
id	The numeric id of the tweet you want to favorite.	/favorites/create/12345.xml /favorites/create/12345.json

favorites/destroy

Remove a marked favorite tweet for the authenticated user.

Path	*Output Formats*	*HTTP Methods*	*Authentication*	*Rate Limited*
/favorites/destroy/	XML, JSON	POST, DELETE	TRUE	FALSE

Parameter	*Description*	*Examples*
id	The numeric id of the tweet you want to un-favorite.	/favorites/destroy/12345.xml /favorites/destroy/12345.json

Social Graph Methods

- followers/ids
- friends/ids

followers/ids

Get to numeric user ids of the entire user's following a target user.

Path	*Output Formats*	*HTTP Methods*	*Authentication*	*Rate Limited*
/followers/ids	XML, JSON	GET	FALSE	TRUE

Parameter	*Description*	*Examples*
id	The numeric user ID or screen name of a user.	/followers/ids/12345.xml /followers/ids/bob.xml
user_id	The numeric ID of a user.	/followers/ids.xml?user_id=12345
screen_name	The screen name of a user.	/followers/ids.xml?screen_name=101010
cursor	Splits results into pages of a maximum of 5000 ids. Pass a value of -1 to begin paging.	/followers/ids/bob.xml?cursor=-1/followers/ids/bob.xml?cursor=-1300794057949944903

friends/ids

Get to numeric user ids of all the users a person is following.

Path	*Output Formats*	*HTTP Methods*	*Authentication*	*Rate Limited*
/friends/ids	XML, JSON	GET	FALSE	TRUE

Parameter	*Description*	*Examples*
id	The numeric user ID or screen name of a user.	/friends/ids/12345.xml /friends/ids/bob.xml
user_id	The numeric ID of a user.	/friends/ids.xml?user_id=12345
screen_name	The screen name of a user.	/friends/ids.xml?screen_name=101010
cursor	Splits results into pages of a maximum of 5000 ids. Pass a value of -1 to begin paging.	/friends/ids/bob.xml?cursor=-1 /friends/ids/bob.xml?cursor=-1300794057949944903

Friendship Methods

- friendships/create
- friendships/destory
- friendships/exists
- friendships/show

friendships/create

Have the authenticated user follow the specified Twitter user.

Path	*Output Formats*	*HTTP Methods*	*Authentication*	*Rate Limited*
/friendships/ create	XML, JSON	POST	TRUE	FALSE

Parameter	*Description*	*Examples*
id	The numeric user ID or screen name of the desired user.	/friendships/create/ 12345.xml/friendships/ create/bob.xml
user_id	The numeric ID of the user.	/friendships/create. xml?user_id=12345
screen_name	The screen name of the user.	/friendships/create. xml?screen_ name=101010
follow	Enabled following via SMS in addition to become a Twitter follower.	/friendships/create/bob. xml?follow=true

friendships/destroy

Have the authenticated user unfollow a specified user.

Path	*Output Formats*	*HTTP Methods*	*Authentication*	*Rate Limited*
/friendships/ destroy/	XML, JSON	POST, DELETE	TRUE	FALSE

Parameter	Description	Examples
id	The numeric user ID or screen name of the desired user.	/friendships/destroy/12345.xml /friendships/destroy / bob.xml
user_id	The numeric ID of the user.	/friendships/destroy.xml?user_id=12345
screen_name	The screen name of the user.	/friendships/destroy.xml?screen_name=101010

friendships/exists

Discover if one user follows another user. Returns true or false. If either of the users is protected, you must be authenticated as a user with permission to view that user's tweets.

Path	Output Formats	HTTP Methods	Authentication	Rate Limited
/friendships/exists	XML, JSON	GET	FALSE	TRUE

Parameter	Description	Examples
user_a	The id or screen_name of a user.	/friendships/exists.xml?user_a=dougw&user_b=al3x
user_b	The id or screen_name of a user whom you want to know if user_a is following.	/friendships/exists.xml?user_a=dougw&user_b=al3x

friendships/show

Returns the bi-directional following status of two users.

Path	Output Formats	HTTP Methods	Authentication	Rate Limited
/friendships/show	XML, JSON	GET	FALSE	TRUE

If you want to compare the following status between the authenticated user and another user, you are only required to supply either the target_id or target_screen_name parameters. Otherwise, you must supply both a source user and a target user.

Parameter	Description	Examples
source_id	The numeric id of a user.	/friendships/show.xml?source_id=123&target_id=456
source_screen_name	The screen_name of a user.	/friendships/show.xml?source_screen_name=bob &target_id=456
target_id	The numeric id of another user.	/friendships/show.xml?target_id=456
target_screen_name	The screen_name of another user.	/friendships/show.xml?target_screen_name=bob

Help Methods

- help/test

help/test

Used to test your connection to Twitter's API.

Path	Output Formats	HTTP Methods	Authentication	Rate Limited
/help/test	XML, JSON	GET	FALSE	FALSE

Notification Methods

- notifications/follow
- notifications/leave

notifications/follow

Have Twitter send the tweets of a specified user the authenticated user's device.

Path	Output Formats	HTTP Methods	Authentication	Rate Limited
/notifications/follow	XML, JSON	POST	TRUE	FALSE

Parameter	Description	Examples
id	The numeric user ID or screen name of the desired user.	/notifications/follow/12345.xml /notifications/follow/bob.xml
user_id	The numeric ID of the user.	/notifications/follow.xml?user_id=12345
screen_name	The screen name of the user.	/notifications/follow.xml?screen_name=101010

notifications/leave

Have Twitter stop sending the tweets of a specified user to the authenticated user's device.

Path	Output Formats	HTTP Methods	Authentication	Rate Limited
/notifications/leave	XML, JSON	POST	TRUE	FALSE

Parameter	Description	Examples
id	The numeric user ID or screen name of the desired user.	/notifications/leave/12345.xml /notifications/leave/bob.xml
user_id	The numeric ID of the user.	/notifications/leave.xml?user_id=12345
screen_name	The screen name of the user.	/notifications/leave.xml?screen_name=101010

OAuth Methods

- oauth/access_token
- oauth/authenticate
- oauth/authorize
- oauth/request_token

oauth/access_token

Path	Output Formats	HTTP Methods	Authentication	Rate Limited
/oauth/access_token	TEXT	POST	FALSE	FALSE

oath/authenticate

Path	Output Formats	HTTP Methods	Authentication	Rate Limited
/oauth/authenticate	NONE	GET	FALSE	FALSE

oauth/authorize

Path	Output Formats	HTTP Methods	Authentication	Rate Limited
/oauth/authorize	NONE	GET	FALSE	FALSE

oauth/request_token

Path	Output Formats	HTTP Methods	Authentication	Rate Limited
/oauth/request_token	TEXT	GET	FALSE	FALSE

Saved Searches Methods

- saved_searches
- saved_searches/create
- saved_searches/destroy
- saved_searches/show

saved_searches

Get the authenticated user's saved searches.

Path	*Output Formats*	*HTTP Methods*	*Authentication*	*Rate Limited*
/saved_searches	XML, JSON	GET	TRUE	TRUE

saved_searches/create

Add a search query to the authenticated user's saved searches

Path	*Output Formats*	*HTTP Methods*	*Authentication*	*Rate Limited*
/saved_searches/create	XML, JSON	POST	TRUE	TRUE

Parameter	*Description*	*Examples*
query	The search query you want to save.	query=test

saved_searches/destroy

Remove a search query from the authenticated user's saved searches.

Path	*Output Formats*	*HTTP Methods*	*Authentication*	*Rate Limited*
/savedsearches/destroy	XML, JSON	POST, DELETE	TRUE	TRUE

Parameter	*Description*	*Examples*
id	The numeric id of the search to be removed.	/saved_searches/destroy/12345.xml

saved_searches/show

Remove a search query from the authenticated user's saved searches.

Path	*Output Formats*	*HTTP Methods*	*Authentication*	*Rate Limited*
/saved_searches/show	XML, JSON	GET	TRUE	TRUE

Parameter	Description	Examples
id	The numeric id of a saved search.	/saved_searches/ show/12345.xml

Search Methods

As of this writing search methods have a different domain than the rest of the Twitter API. Twitter plans to eventually merge the search API with the rest of the API system.

- search
- trends
- trends/daily
- trends/current
- trends/weekly

search

Path	Output Formats	HTTP Methods	Authentication	Rate Limited
search.twitter. com/search	JSON, ATOM	GET	FALSE	TRUE

Parameter	Description	Examples
q	The URL encoded search query to be performed.	search.twitter.com/search. atom?q=test
callback	The callback function for JSON requests.	search.twitter.com/search. json?callback=foo&q=tadd
lang	The ISO 639-1 code used to filter tweets by language.	search.twitter.com/search. atom?lang=en&q=tadd
locale	Used to declare the language of the search query. "ja" is currently the only available value.	search.twitter.com/search. atom?q=&locale=ja
rpp	The desired amount of search results per page less than 100.	search.twitter.com/search. atom?q= tadd&rpp=15

Parameter	*Description*	*Examples*
page	Page to retrieve older search results.	search.twitter.com/search.atom?q=tadd&rpp=15&page=6
since_id	Returns tweets that are more recent than the id specified.	search.twitter.com/search.atom?q=tadd&since_id=12345
geocode	Return results in a radius around a latitude and longitude based on the user's geocode location in their profile. The string must be in the form "latitude,longitude,radius" where radius is declared as "mi" (miles) or "km" (kilometers).	search.twitter.com/search.atom?geocode=41.353129%2C-62.155203%2C60mi
show_user		search.twitter.com/search.atom?q=twitterapi&show_user=true

trends

Get the top ten currently trending search topics.

Path	*Output Formats*	*HTTP Methods*	*Authentication*	*Rate Limited*
search.twitter.com/trends	JSON	GET	FALSE	TRUE

trends/daily

Get the top 20 hourly trending search topics for a given day.

Path	*Output Formats*	*HTTP Methods*	*Authentication*	*Rate Limited*
search.twitter.com/trends/daily	JSON	GET	FALSE	TRUE

Parameter	*Description*	*Examples*
date	Start date in YYYY-MM-DD format.	search.twitter.com/trends/daily.json?date=2009-01-10
exclude	Exclude hashtags from the results by setting the value to "hashtags."	search.twitter.com/trends/daily.json?exclude=hashtags

trends/current

Get the top ten current trending search topics.

Path	*Output Formats*	*HTTP Methods*	*Authentication*	*Rate Limited*
search.twitter.com/trends/current	JSON	GET	FALSE	TRUE

Parameter	*Description*	*Examples*
exclude	Exclude hashtags from the results by setting the value to "hashtags."	search.twitter.com/trends/current.json?exclude=hashtags

trends/weekly

Get the top 30 daily trending search topics for a given week.

Path	*Output Formats*	*HTTP Methods*	*Authentication*	*Rate Limited*
search.twitter.com/trends/weekly	JSON	GET	FALSE	TRUE

Parameter	*Description*	*Examples*
date	Start date in YYYY-MM-DD format.	search.twitter.com/trends/weekly.json?date=2009-01-10
exclude	Exclude hashtags from the results by setting the value to "hashtags."	search.twitter.com/trends/weekly.json?exclude=hashtags

Spam Reporting Methods

- report_spam

report_spam

Block the specified user for the authenticated user and reports them as spam.

Path	Output Formats	HTTP Methods	Authentication	Rate Limited
/report_spam	XML, JSON	POST	TRUE	FALSE

Parameter	Description	Examples
id	The numeric user ID or screen name of the desired user.	/report_spam/12345.xml /report_spam/bob.xml
user_id	The numeric ID of the user.	/report_spam.xml?user_id=12345
screen_name	The screen name of the user.	/report_spam.xml?screen_name=101010

Status Methods

- statuses/destroy
- statuses/followers
- statuses/friends
- statuses/friends_timeline
- statuses/home_timeline
- statuses/mentions
- statuses/public_timeline
- statuses/retweet
- statuses/retweeted_by_me
- statuses/retweeted_of_me
- statuses/retweeted_to_me
- statuses/retweets
- statuses/show
- statuses/update
- statuses/user_timeline

statuses/destroy

Deletes a specific status update.

You can only delete a status update that belongs to the user you're authenticating with.

Path	Output Formats	HTTP Methods	Authentication	Rate Limited
/statuses/destroy/	XML, JSON	POST, DELETE	TRUE	FALSE

Parameter	Description	Examples
id	The numeric id of the tweet you want to delete.	/statuses/destroy/12345.xml /statuses/destroy/12345.json

statuses/followers

Retrieves a list of a user's followers and includes their profile details and last tweet. Only retrieves 100 users at a time.

If you request follower data for a protected user, you must authenticate and be allowed to view the protected user.

If you provide no parameters the method will return the follower details for the user you have authenticated with. If you have not authenticated, you must provide a parameter to identify the user whose follower details you want to retrieve.

Path	Output Formats	HTTP Methods	Authentication	Rate Limited
/statuses/followers	XML, JSON	GET	FALSE	FALSE

Parameter	Description	Examples
id	The numeric user ID or screen name of the desired user.	/statuses/followers/12345.xml/statuses/followers/bob.xml
user_id	The numeric ID of the user.	/statuses/followers.xml?user_id=12345
screen_name	The screen name of the user.	/statuses/followers.xml?screen_name=101010

Parameter	Description	Examples
cursor	Splits results into pages of a maximum of 100 users. Pass a value of -1 to begin paging.	/statuses/followers/bob.xml?cursor=-1/statuses/followers/bob.ml?cursor=-1300794057949944903

statuses/friends

Retrieves a list of who the user is following and includes their profile details and last tweet. Only retrieves 100 users at a time.

If you request following data for a protected user, you must authenticate and be allowed to view the protected user.

If you provide no parameters, the method will return the following details for the user you have authenticated with. If you have not authenticated, you must provide a parameter to identify the user whose following details you want to retrieve.

Path	Output Formats	HTTP Methods	Authentication	Rate Limited
/statuses/friends	XML, JSON	GET	FALSE	FALSE

Parameter	Description	Examples
id	The numeric user ID or screen name of the desired user.	/statuses/friends/12345.xml /statuses/friends/bob.xml
Parameter	***Description***	***Examples***
user_id	The numeric ID of the user.	/statuses/friends.xml?user_id=12345
screen_name	The screen name of the user.	/statuses/friends.xml?screen_name=101010
cursor	Splits results into pages of a maximum of 100 users. Pass a value of -1 to begin paging.	/statuses/friends/bob.xml?cursor=-1 /statuses/friends/bob.xml?cursor=1300794057949944903

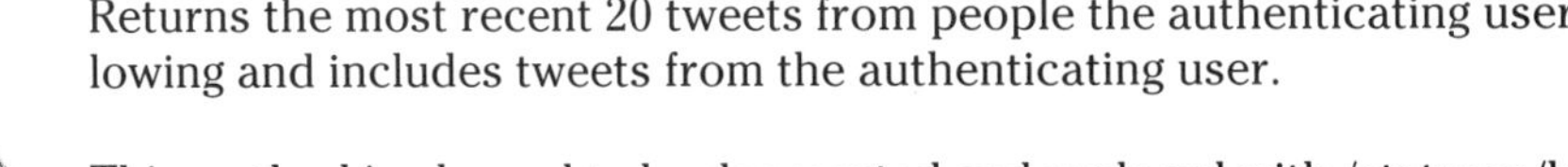

statuses/friends_timeline

Returns the most recent 20 tweets from people the authenticating user is following and includes tweets from the authenticating user.

This method is planned to be deprecated and replaced with /statuses/home_timeline.

Path	*Output Formats*	*HTTP Methods*	*Authentication*	*Rate Limited*
/statuses/friends_timeline	XML, JSON, RSS, ATOM	GET	TRUE	TRUE

Parameter	*Description*	*Examples*
since_id	Returns tweets that are more recent than the id specified.	/statuses/friends_timeline.xml?since_id=12345
max_id	Returns tweets that are older than the id specified.	/statuses/friends_timeline.xml?max_id=54321
count	Limits the results to an amount specified that is less than 200.	/statuses/friends_timeline.xml?count=100
page	Page backwards to retrieve older tweets.	/statuses/friends_timeline?page=5

statuses/home_timeline

Returns the most recent 20 tweets from people the authenticating user is following, including retweets, and tweets from the authenticating user.

This method is the same as /statuses/friends_timeline, except that it includes retweets.

Path	*Output Formats*	*HTTP Methods*	*Authentication*	*Rate Limited*
/statuses/home_timeline	XML, JSON, ATOM	GET	TRUE	TRUE

Parameter	*Description*	*Examples*
since_id	Returns tweets that are more recent than the id specified.	/statuses/home_timeline.xml?since_id=12345

Parameters	*Description*	*Examples*
max_id	Returns tweets that are older than the id specified.	/statuses/home_timeline.xml?max_id=54321
count	Limits the results to an amount specified that is less than 200.	/statuses/home_timeline.xml?count=100
page	Page backwards to retrieve older tweets.	/statuses/home_timeline?page=5

statuses/mentions

Returns the most recent 20 tweets that contain the username of the authenticated user.

Path	*Output Formats*	*HTTP Methods*	*Authentication*	*Rate Limited*
/statuses/mentions	XML, JSON, RSS, ATOM	GET	TRUE	TRUE

Parameter	*Description*	*Examples*
since_id	Returns tweets that are more recent than the id specified.	/statuses/mentions.xml?since_id=12345
max_id	Returns tweets that are older than the id specified.	/statuses/mentions.xml?max_id=54321
count	Limits the results to an amount specified that is less than 200.	/statuses/mentions.xml?count=100
page	Page backwards to retrieve older tweets.	/statuses/mentions?page=5

statuses/public_timeline

Returns the most recent 20 public tweets of users who have a custom profile image. The public timeline is cached and only returns new results every 60 seconds.

Path	*Output Formats*	*HTTP Methods*	*Authentication*	*Rate Limited*
/statuses/public_timeline	XML, JSON, RSS, ATOM	GET	FALSE	TRUE

statuses/retweet

Retweets a tweet. You must be authenticated as the user who wants to retweet.

Path	***Output Formats***	***HTTP Methods***	***Authentication***	***Rate Limited***
/statuses/retweet	XML, JSON	POST, PUT	TRUE	FALSE

Parameter	***Description***	***Examples***
id	The numerical id of a tweet you want to retweet.	/statuses/retweet/1234.xml

statuses/retweeted_by_me

Get the authenticated user's most recent 20 retweets.

Path	***Output Formats***	***HTTP Methods***	***Authentication***	***Rate Limited***
/statuses /retweeted_by_me	XML, JSON, ATOM	GET	TRUE	TRUE

Parameter	***Description***	***Examples***
since_id	Returns tweets that are more recent than the id specified.	/statuses/retweeted_by_me.xml?since_id=12345
max_id	Returns tweets that are older than the id specified.	/statuses/retweeted_by_me.xml?max_id=54321
count	Limits the results to an amount specified that is less than 200.	/statuses/retweeted_by_me.xml?count=100
page	Page backwards to retrieve older tweets.	/statuses/retweeted_by_me?page=5

statuses/retweeted_of_me

Get the authenticated user's most recent 20 retweets that have been retweeted.

Path	Output Formats	HTTP Methods	Authentication	Rate Limited
/statuses/retweeted_of_me	XML, JSON, ATOM	GET	TRUE	TRUE

Parameter	Description	Examples
since_id	Returns tweets that are more recent than the id specified.	/statuses/retweeted_of_me.xml?since_id=12345
max_id	Returns tweets that are older than the id specified.	/statuses/retweeted_of_me.xml?max_id=54321
count	Limits the results to an amount specified that is less than 200.	/statuses/retweeted_of_me.xml?count=100
page	Page backwards to retrieve older tweets.	/statuses/retweeted_of_me?page=5

statuses/retweeted_to_me

Get the authenticated user's friends most recent 20 retweets.

Path	Output Formats	HTTP Methods	Authentication	Rate Limited
/statuses/retweeted_to_me	XML, JSON, ATOM	GET	TRUE	TRUE

Parameter	Description	Examples
since_id	Returns tweets that are more recent than the id specified.	/statuses/retweeted_to_me.xml?since_id=12345
max_id	Returns tweets that are older than the id specified.	/statuses/retweeted_to_me.xml?max_id=54321
Parameter	**Description**	**Examples**
count	Limits the results to an amount specified that is less than 200.	/statuses/retweeted_to_me.xml?count=100
page	Page backwards to retrieve older tweets.	/statuses/retweeted_to_me?page=5

statuses/retweets

Get a tweet's most recent 100 retweets.

Path	Output Formats	HTTP Methods	Authentication	Rate Limited
/statuses/retweets	XML, JSON	GET	TRUE	TRUE

Parameter	Description	Examples
id	The numerical id of a tweet you want to retweet.	/statuses/retweets/1234.xml
count	Limits the results to an amount specified that is less than 100.	/statuses/retweets/1234.xml?count=4

statuses/show

Get the details of a tweet and its author. If an author is protected, the authenticated user must have permission to view that user's tweets.

Path	Output Formats	HTTP Methods	Authentication	Rate Limited
/statuses/show	XML, JSON	GET	TRUE	TRUE

Parameter	Description	Examples
id	The numerical id of a tweet you want details on.	/statuses/show/1234.xml

statuses/update

Create a new tweet of 140 characters or less for the authenticated user. Duplicate tweets are not allowed. There is an unspecified limit to the amount of status updates a user may tweet per day. If the limit is reached, a 403 HTTP error is returned.

Path	Output Formats	HTTP Methods	Authentication	Rate Limited
/statuses/update	XML, JSON	POST	TRUE	FALSE

Parameter	Description	Examples
status	The contents of the tweet. Anything over 140 characters is truncated.	status=Hello

Parameter	Description	Examples
in_reply_to_status_id	The id of a tweet that is being replied to. The new tweet reply must contain the username of the author of the original tweet, or this parameter is ignored.	in_reply_to_status_id=1234
lat	The geographical latitude of the tweet. Must be a valid latitude value between -90.0 and +90.0, the long parameter must be valid, and the user must not have geo_enabled disabled, otherwise this parameter is ignored.	lat=30.4
long	The geographical longitude of the tweet. Must be a valid longitude value between -180.0 and +180.0, the lat parameter must be valid, and the user must not have geo_enabled disabled, otherwise this parameter is ignored.	long=35.6

statuses/user_timeline

Returns the authenticated user's most recent 20 tweets, unless you include an id or screen_name for another user. If you request data for a protected user, the authenticated user must be allowed to view the protected user.

While the `id` parameter can take either a screen name or numeric user id as a parameter, there are cases when a screen name and numeric user id may conflict. For example, a user's screen name might be 101010. There might also be a numeric user id 101010. For this reason you should use either the `user_id` or `screen_name` parameter.

Path	Output Formats	HTTP Methods	Authentication	Rate Limited
/statuses/user_timeline	XML, JSON, RSS, ATOM	GET	FALSE	TRUE

Parameter	Description	Examples
id	The numeric user ID or screen name of the desired user.	/statuses/user_timeline/12345.xml/statuses/user_timeline/bob.xml
user_id	The numeric ID of the user.	/statuses/user_timeline.xml?user_id=12345

Parameter	*Description*	*Examples*
screen_name	The screen name of the user.	/statuses/user_timeline.xml?screen_name=101010
since_id	Returns tweets that are more recent than the id specified.	/statuses/user_timeline.xml?since_id=12345
max_id	Returns tweets that are older than the id specified.	/statuses/user_timeline.xml?max_id=54321
count	Limits the results to an amount specified that is less than 200.	/statuses/user_timeline.xml?count=100
page	Page backwards to retrieve older tweets.	/statuses/user_timeline?page=5

User Methods

- Get User's Profile Information: /users/show

users/show

Returns the profile information for a requested user.

While the `id` parameter can take either a screen name or numeric user id as a parameter, there are cases when a screen name and numeric user id may conflict. For example, a user's screen name might be 101010. There might also be a numeric user id 101010. For this reason you should use either the `user_id` or `screen_name` parameter.

If you request data for a protected user, you must authenticate and be allowed to view the protected user.

Path	*Output Formats*	*HTTP Methods*	*Authentication*	*Rate Limited*
/users/show	XML, JSON	GET	FALSE	TRUE

Parameter	*Description*	*Examples*
id	The numeric user ID or screen name of the desired user.	/users/show/12345.xml /users/show/bob.xml
user_id	The numeric ID of the user.	/users/show.xml?user_id=12345
screen_name	The screen name of the user.	/users/show.xml?screen_name=101010

Appendix B

Gallery of Twitter Applications

In This Appendix

- Pictures for inspiration

Twitter applications and products can take shapes wild or practical. I've selected some of my favorite examples of fun or functional products for you. These pages show the unique looks that you can create for a Twitter product.

Many of these products are described in detail in Chapter 4.

TWEET THIS!
BakerTweet
TWEET WHAT'S FRESH
Baker Sign in
Pain Au Chocolat
01:27
vimeo
The weather at Hansel and Gretel's looks like citrus showers. Lemon Drizzle Cake, a tart and sweet warm front, cooling fast.
1 month, 1 week ago from Albion's oven
What is it?
BakerTweet is a way for busy bakers to tell the world that something hot and fresh has just come out of the oven. It's as simple as turning the dial and hitting the button. All of the baker's followers get a Twitter alert to tell them that it's bun-time. Or bread time. Or whatever.
The first BakerTweet device has been installed at the Albion Cafe on Boundary Street in Shoreditch, London. To find out what's cooking follow @albionsoven on Twitter.

Figure B-1: BakerTweet announces fresh products to customers.

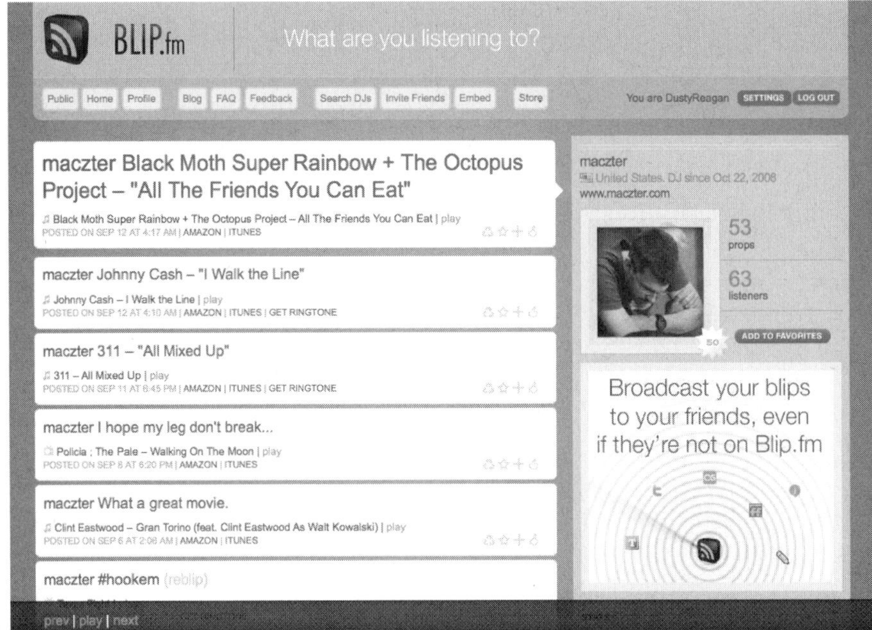

Figure B-2: Blip.fm shares your favorite music with your friends.

Figure B-3: Botanicalls plant monitoring kit.

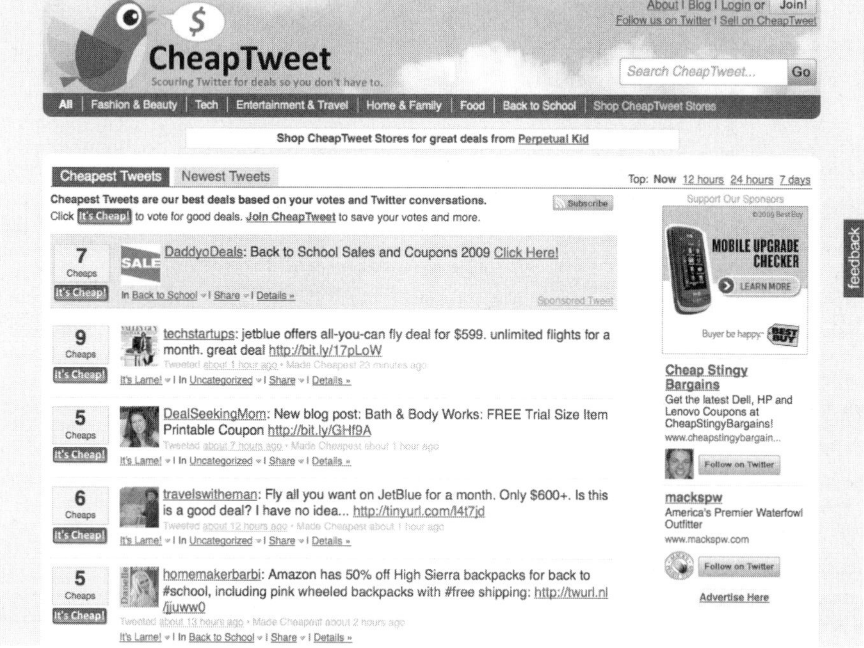

Figure B-4: CheapTweet finds great deals and discounts.

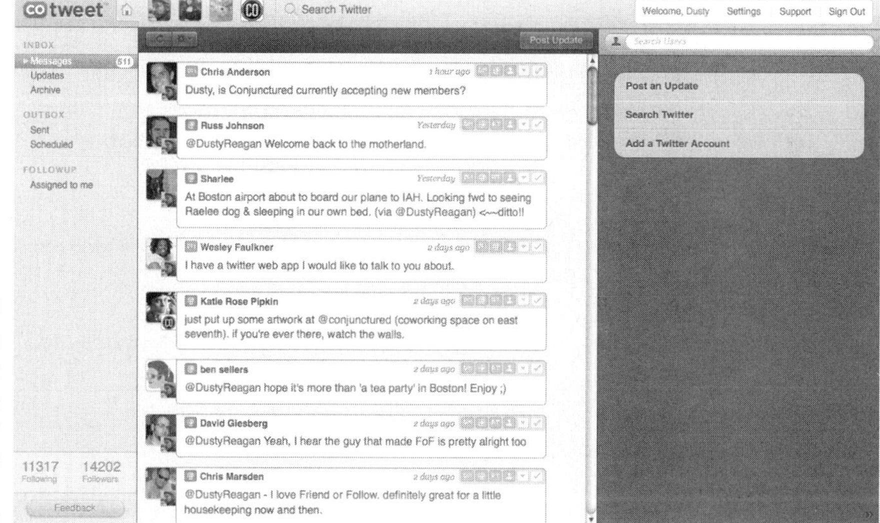

Figure B-5: CoTweet manages contacts for business tweeting.

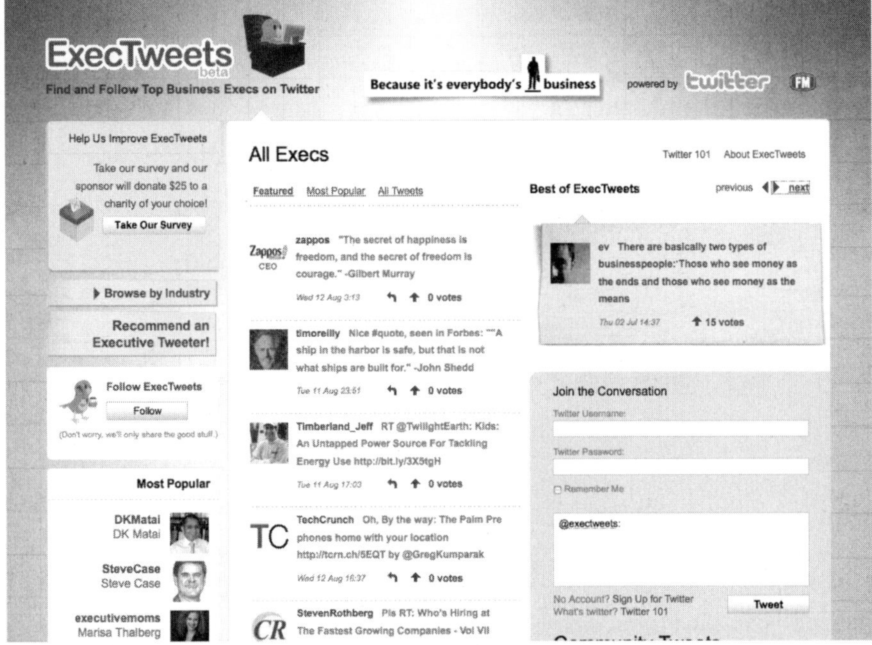

Figure B-6: ExecTweets aggregates messages fromprominent executives.

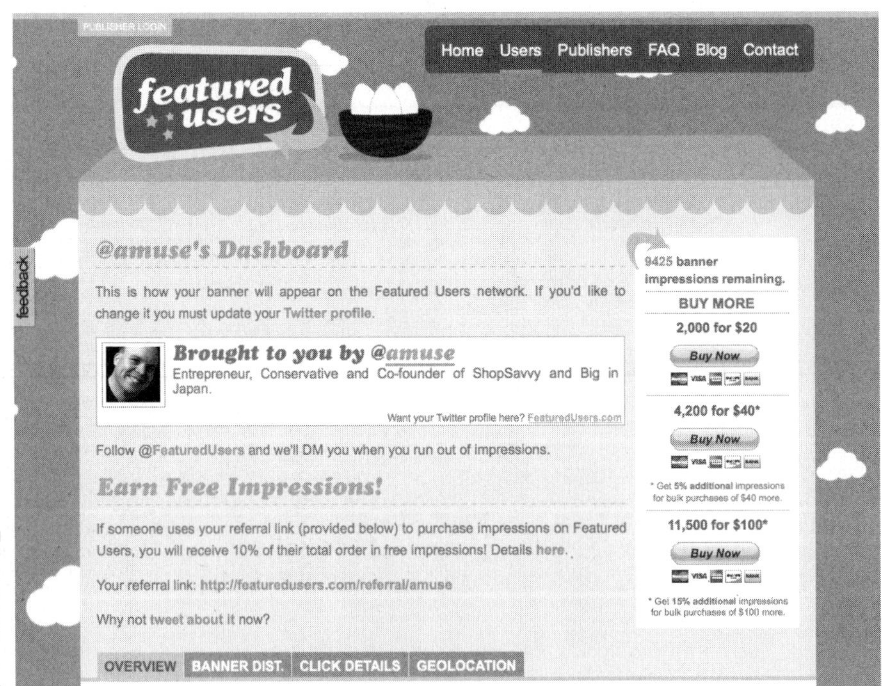

Figure B-7: Featured Users ad network.

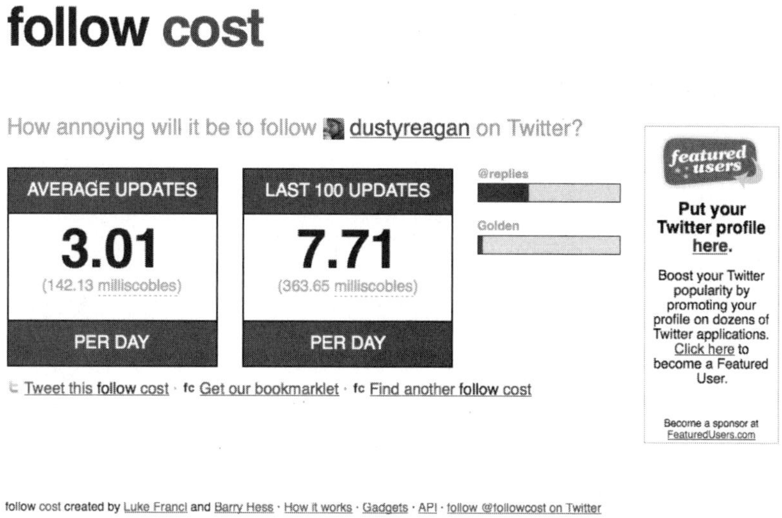

follow cost

How annoying will it be to follow dustyreagan on Twitter?

AVERAGE UPDATES
3.01
(142.13 milliscobles)
PER DAY

LAST 100 UPDATES
7.71
(363.65 milliscobles)
PER DAY

@replies
Golden

Tweet this follow cost · fc Get our bookmarklet · fc Find another follow cost

featured users
Put your Twitter profile here.
Boost your Twitter popularity by promoting your profile on dozens of Twitter applications. Click here to become a Featured User.
Become a sponsor at FeaturedUsers.com

follow cost created by Luke Francl and Barry Hess · How it works · Gadgets · API · follow @followcost on Twitter

Figure B-8: Follow Cost finds how frequently other users tweet.

Figure B-9: Friend Or Follow shows users who aren't following their friends.

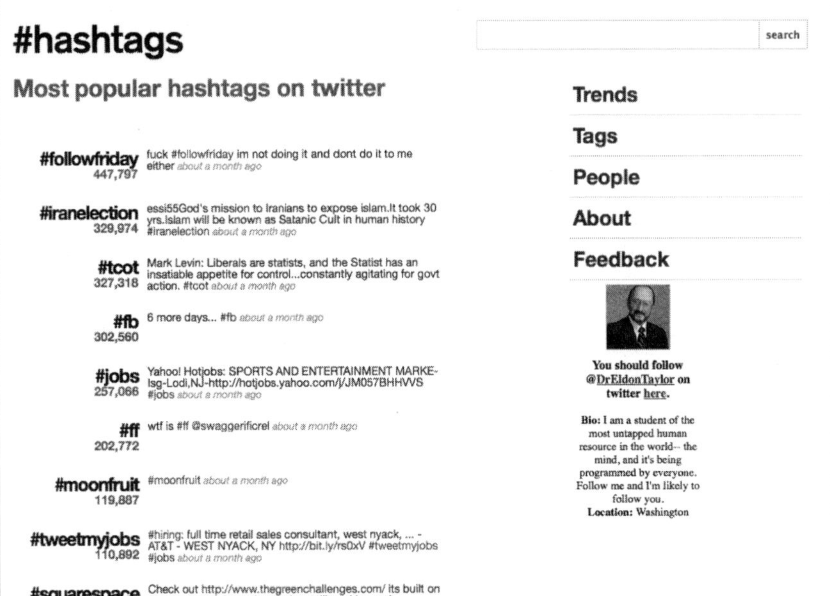

Figure B-10: Hashtags.org tracks and searches Twitter hashtags.

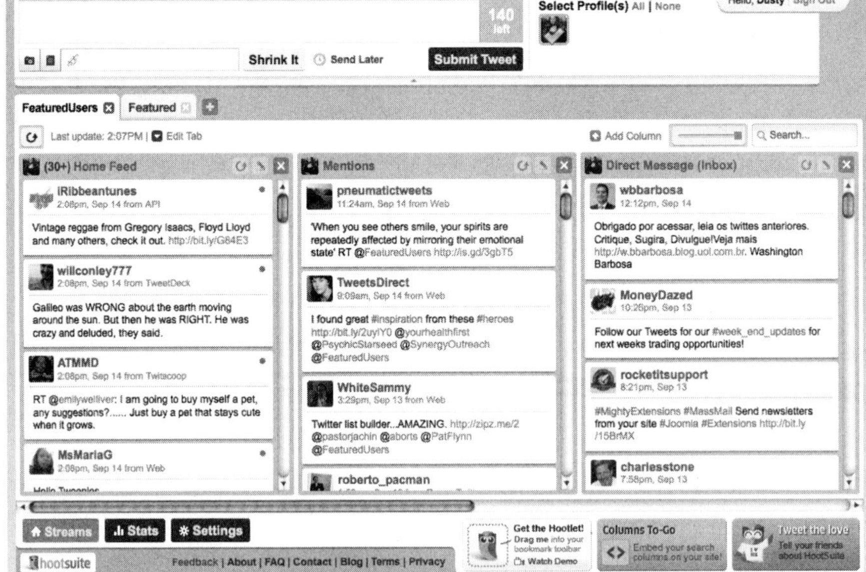

Figure B-11: HootSuite manages multiple Twitter accounts for multiple users.

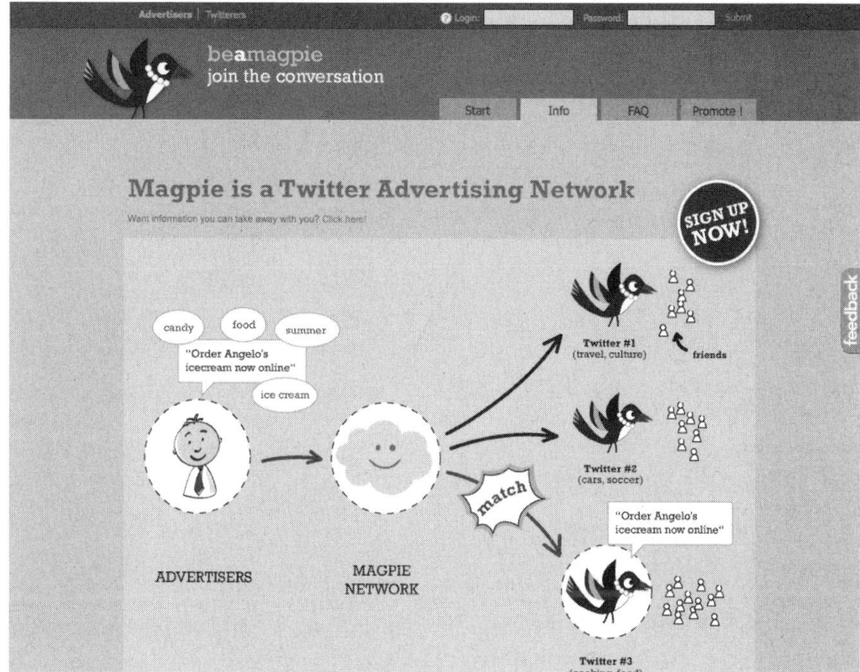

Figure B-12: Magpie ad network.

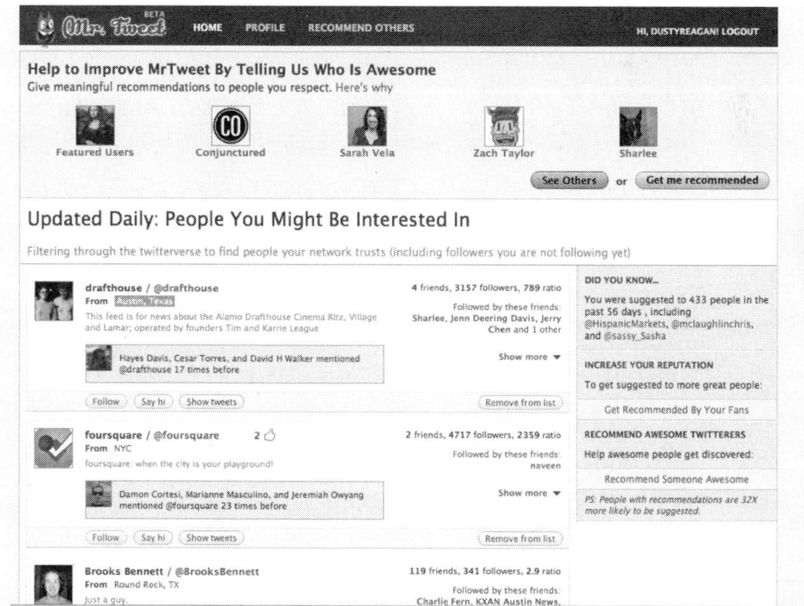

Figure B-13: Mr. Tweet recommends users for you to follow.

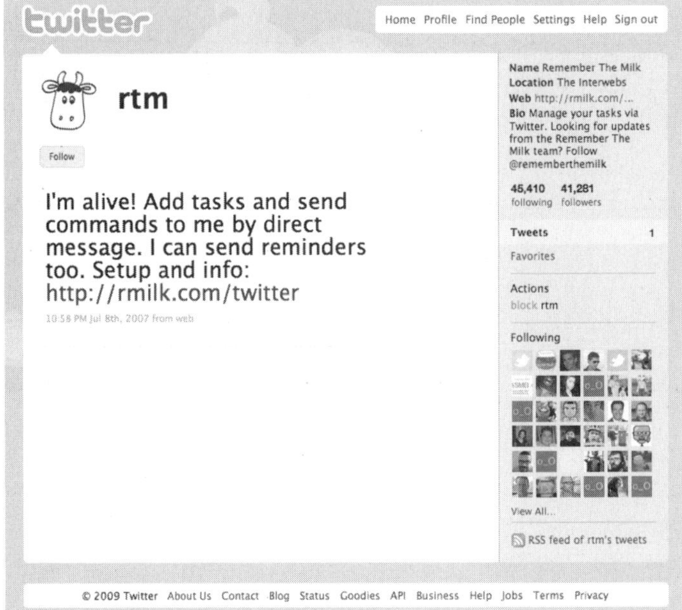

Figure B-14: Remember The Milk® to-do list.

Figure B-15: Secret Tweet posts your secrets, but anonymously. Spill your guts safely!

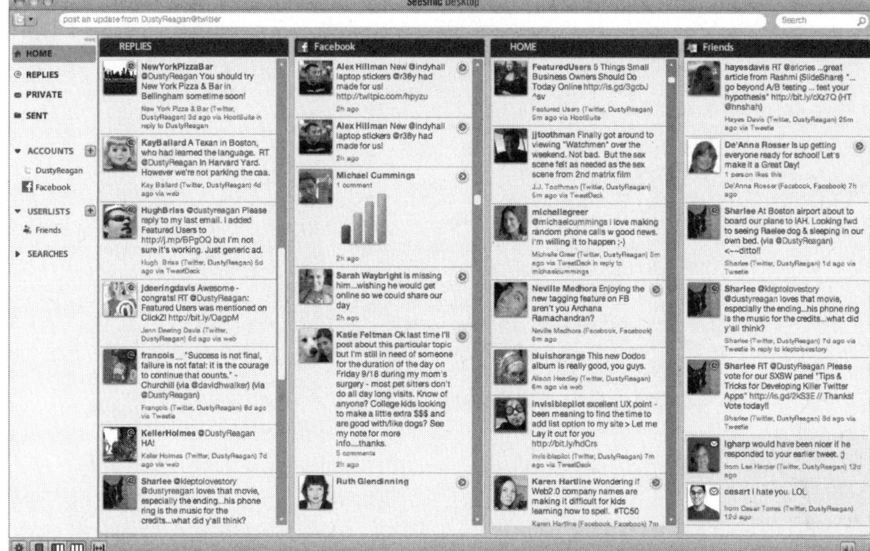

Figure B-16: Seesmic Desktop is a Twitter Web client.

Easily Share Flickr Pictures on Twitter

All messages sent via SnapTweet are **publicly viewable.** SnapTweet is not affiliated with Twitter or Flickr.
© Kismet Ventures, LLC. SnapTweet and DoesFollow are brought to you by damon. Email us with questions.

Say what? Login

Signup

Send your Flickr photos to Twitter with SnapTweet

1. Your account information for *SnapTweet* is the same as Twitter.

   Twitter User **Password** why?

2. Enter your Flickr URL so we can look up your latest photo.

   Flickr URL
   http://flickr.com/photos/iamcal

3. You can tweet your latest photo by sending a **DIRECT MESSAGE** to SnapTweet on Twitter with your message. If you send a blank message, we'll use the photo's title.

   Fully automated and tag-based posting are also available.

Join

Figure B-17: SnapTweet links your photos from Flickr to Twitter.

Figure B-18: Tiny Twitter is a Twitter client for any Java-enabled phone.

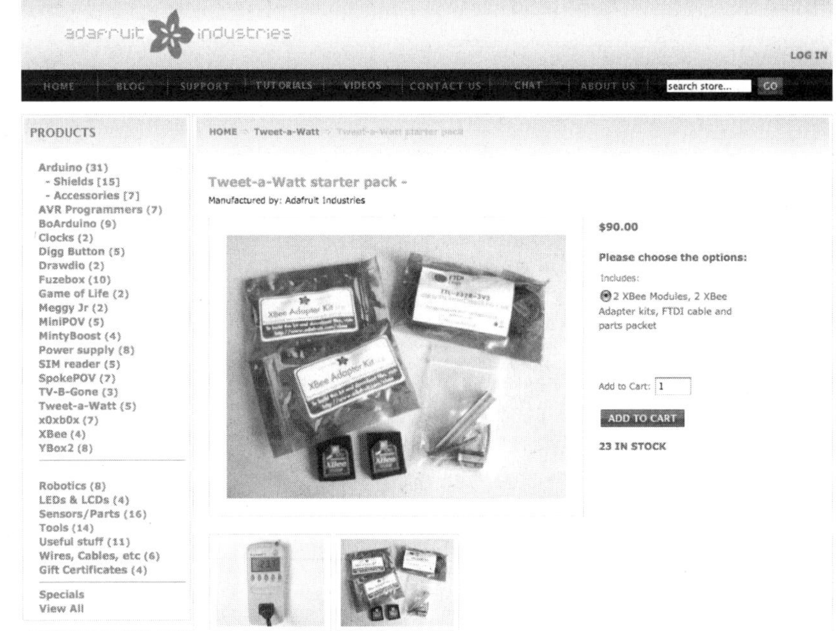

Figure B-19: Tweet-a-Watt power consumption meter.

Figure B-20: TweetDeck manages Twitter, Facebook, LinkedIn, and MySpace.

Figure B-21: Tweeting Too Hard finds blow-hards, so you don't have to.

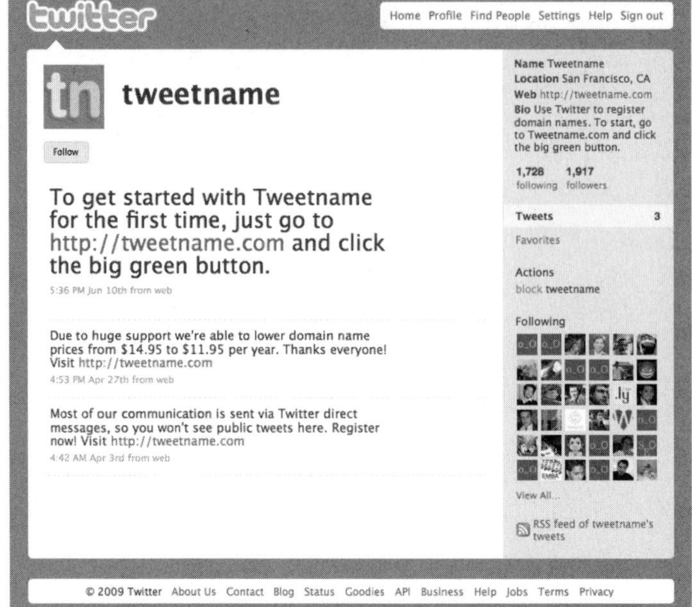

Figure B-22: Tweetname looks for available domain names.

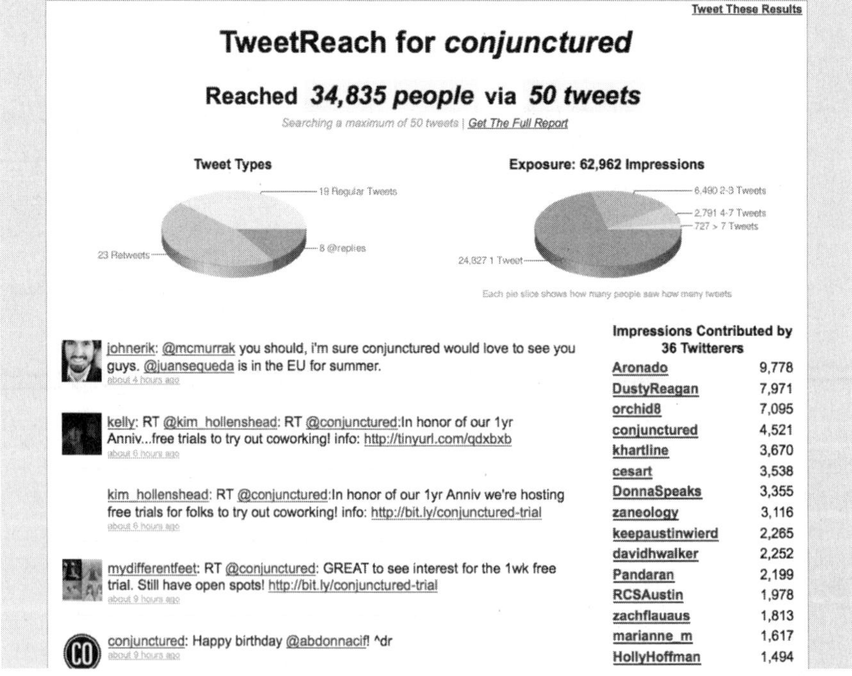

Figure B-23: TweetReach reports how frequently a phrase or URL is tweeted.

Figure B-24: TweetStats reports your own tweets.

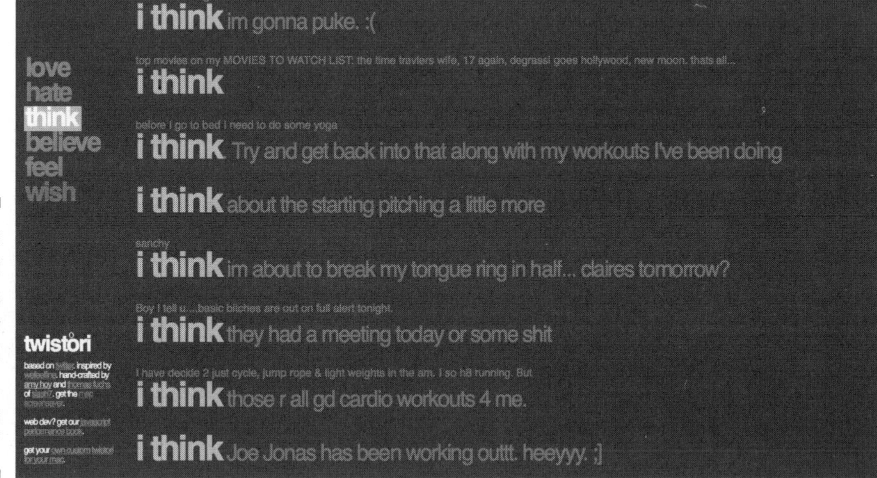

Figure B-25: Twistori finds tweets by emotional phrases, such as "I think."

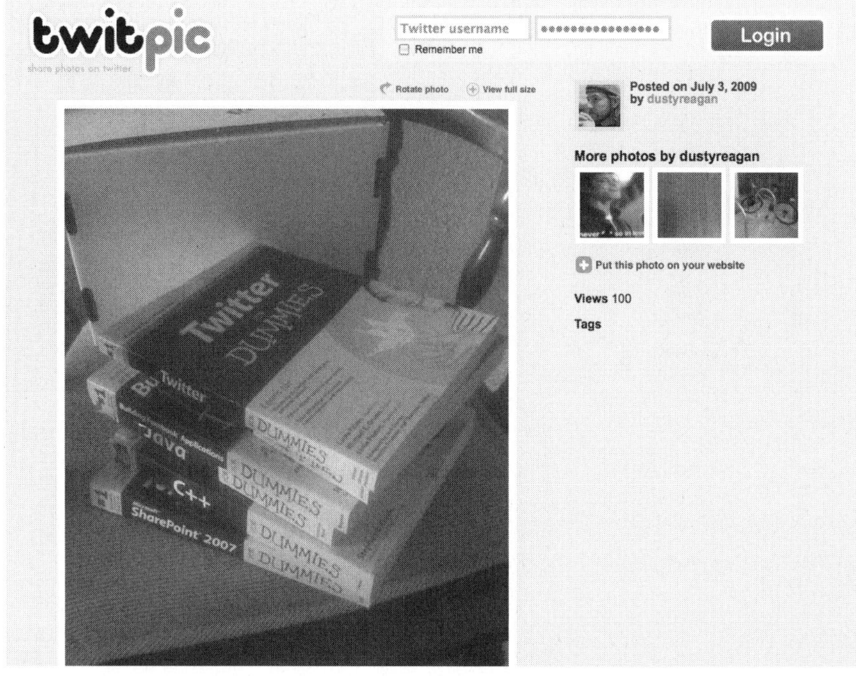

Figure B-26: TwitPic is the most popular photo-sharing site on Twitter.

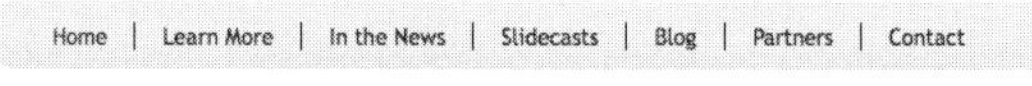

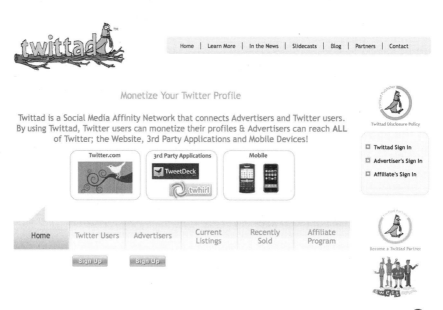

Figure B-27: Twittad background advertising.

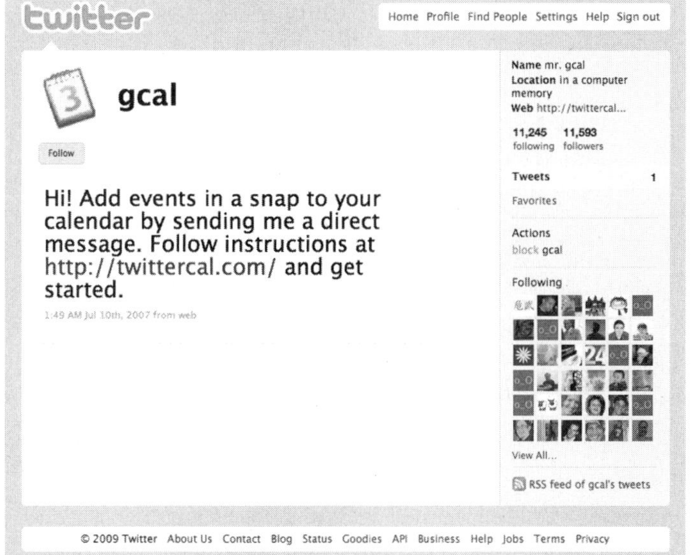

Figure B-28: Twittercal bot for Google Calendars.

Figure B-29: Twitter Counter tells the world how many followers you have.

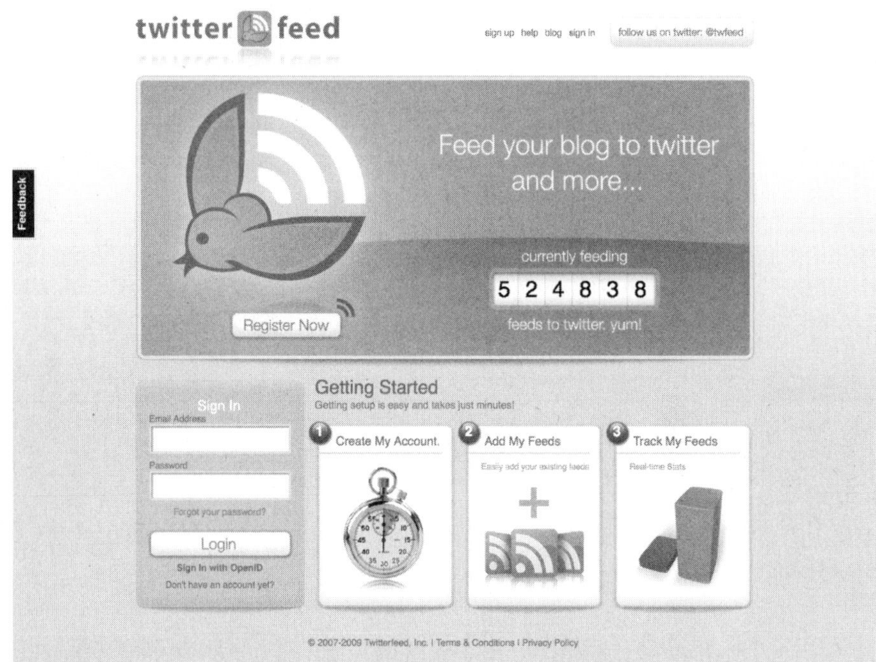

Figure B-30: Twitterfeed pushes RSS feeds.

Figure B-31: Twitterrific is a Twitter client for Mac OS X and iPhone.

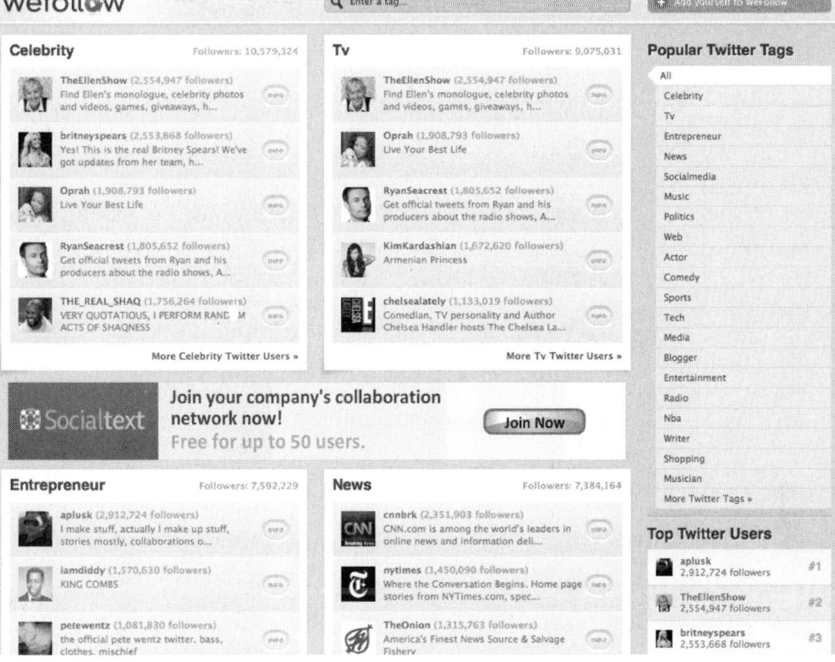

Figure B-32: WeFollow helps Twitter uses link to each other based on your tags.

Index

Symbols & Numerics

@ replies, 8, 9
@AusTraffic, 8
@big_ben_clock, 8
64-bit integers, using, 362
140tees Web site, 340

• A •

acceptance testing, automating, 315–316
access tokens, getting, 99–103
accessing API in background, 362
account management
  checking rate limits, 81–83, 358
  description of, 79–80
  ending user sessions, 83–84
  overview of, 365–368
  updating user notification devices, 85–86
  updating user profile background images, 93–95
  updating user profile colors, 89–91
  updating user profile pictures, 91–93
  updating user profiles, 86–89
  verifying user credentials, 80–81
account methods
  account/end_session, 83–84, 366
  account/rate_limit_status, 68, 81–83, 358, 366
  account/update_delivery_device, 85–86, 366
  account/update_profile, 86–89, 368
  account/update_profile_background_image, 93–95, 367–368
  account/update_profile_colors, 89–91, 366–367
  account/update_profile_image, 91–92, 367
  account/verify_credentials, 80–81, 365
account/end_session method, 83–84, 366
account/rate_limit_status method
  description of, 81–83, 366
  to retrieve current rate limit status, 68, 358
accounts. *See also* personal accounts; protected accounts; public accounts
  developer, creating, 39–40
  granting permission to applications to access, 74
  private, keeping data in confidential, 360
  for products, 346
  reporting as spam, 176–178
  Twooshes game app and, 300
  user, and @ sign, 8
account/update_delivery_device method, 85–86, 366
account/update_profile method, 86–89, 368
account/update_profile_background_image method, 93–95, 367–368
account/update_profile_colors method, 89–91, 366–367
account/update_profile_image method, 91–92, 367
account/verify_credentials method, 80–81, 365
acquisition of businesses, 343–344
ad management software, 334
ad networks
  cost per thousand, 329–330
  cost per time, 331
  description of, 327–328
  pay per action, 330
  pay per click, 328–329
  vertical, 332–333
addPoint function, 291
addTweet function, 290–291
AdMob ads, 328
advertising. *See also* promotion strategies
  adding to Twitter, 324

advertising *(continued)*
apps for, 58–59
paid, to promote applications, 352–353
selling, 333–334
traditional ad networks, 327–331
vertical ad networks, 332–333
Agavi framework, 252
alt attribute, 18
Amazon
Payments service, 337
SimpleDB data storage system, 319
S3 on-demand disk storage space, 256
anchor tags, 17
angel investors, 326
Apache servers, setting up, 258–263
API (Application Programming Interface). *See also* methods; rate limits; Search API; Search API methods
accessing in background, 362
authentication, 73–78
components of, 65–66
defining payload, 71–73
description of, 63
Google Group for, 358, 362
HTTP response status codes and errors, 69–70
libraries, 251–252
REST, 66, 67–68
Streaming, 66
terms of service, 63–65
tips for, 361–363
versioning, 66–67
`app.ini` file, creating, 276–277
application definition box, 324
application design
converting into HTML, 310–311
first impressions and, 309
hiring professional for, 309–310
integrating, 311–313
application ecosystem
categories in, 47
desktop clients, 47–49
hardware integration, 60–61
mobile clients, 49–50
Twitter bots, 59–60
Web applications, 50–59
`application` folder, 270
Application Programming Interface. *See* API
`APPLICATION_PATH` constant, 274
applications. *See also* application design; application ecosystem; developing applications; growing pains for applications
feature roadmap, 308
growth in complexity of, 315
licensing and selling, 337–338
reasons to develop, 11–12, 242–244
reasons to use, 244–246
registering with Twitter, 76–77
releasing, 308
writing first, 41–43
`array_diff` function, 31, 299
`array_intersect` function, 31
`array_merge` function, 31
arrays, 30–31
`array_values` function, 31
asymmetrical relationship model, 9
@ replies, 8, 9
Austin American Statesmen (newspaper), 8
@AusTraffic, 8
authentication, 73–78
authenticity in public relations activities, 352
auto-follow script, creating, 295–301
automating acceptance testing, 315–316
avoiding timeouts, 113

• B •

background, accessing API in, 362
background color, getting from user data, 107–108
background style, 23
Bailey, Cody Marx (developer), 57
BakerTweet wireless device, 61, 395
banner ads, 352, 353
basic HTTP authentication, 74
Beanstalk Web site, 40
bids, getting for designers, 310
@big_ben_clock, 8
blacklisting, 69
Blip.fm app, 55, 330, 396
block methods
`blocks/blocking`, 172–174, 369
`blocks/blocking/ids`, 174–176, 369

blocks/create, 166–167, 369–370
blocks/destroy, 168–169, 370
blocks/exists, 170–172, 370–371
overview of, 165–166, 368–369
blocking
checking for, 170–172
getting user details list of blocked users, 172–174
retrieving lists of blocked user IDs, 174–176
unblocking users, 168–169
users, 166–167
block-level elements, 16–17
blocks/blocking method, 172–174, 369
blocks/blocking/ids method, 174–176, 369
blocks/create method, 166–167, 369–370
blocks/destroy method, 168–169, 370
blocks/exists method, 170–172, 370–371
Blogger blog platform, 348
blogs for product, 348–349
body of HTML documents, 16–18
bootstrap.php file, creating, 275–276
bootstrapping process
for applications, 272
for self-funding, 325
borders, specifying for boxes, 22
Botanicalls Kit plant monitoring kit, 61, 396
box model, 21
branches folder, 270
brand name. *See also* product
building awareness of, 342–343
building reputation of, 244
monitoring mentions of, 11
promoting, 12
break tags, closed, 15
breaking design HTML into smaller files, 311–313
Britcher, Loren (developer), 49
Brizzly, 244
browsers
opening apps in, 42
server console inside, 261
Brunel, Fred (developer), 59
BugMeNot Web site, 271
building applications. *See* developing applications
Burkert, Ben (developer), 57
business issues
acquisitions, 343–344
building on top of Twitter, 11, 342–344
partnering with Twitter, 323
venture capital, 323, 325
BuySellAds Web site, 331, 353

• C •

caching, optimizing, 359, 363
CafePress Web site, 340
CakePHP framework, 252
Casale Media ad network, 330
Cascading Style Sheets (CSS)
basic styles, 21–23
description of, 13–14
selectors, 20–21
SEO and, 353
styling HTML with, 18–21
case sensitivity of XHTML tags, 15
causes, supporting, 12, 244
Cawley, Kevin (developer), 50
CheapTweet app, 55–56, 397
checking. *See* testing
class selectors, 20
clauses (MySQL), 36
click fraud, 328
click through rate (CTR), 329
Clinkscales, Damon (developer), 54
closed break tags, 15
cloud computing, 256–257
code coverage, 317
CodeIgniter framework, 252
Coffey, Noah (developer), 363
co-location of servers, 256
colons in method paths, 116
commands (MySQL), 36
comments syntax, 25–26
Commission Junction ad network, 330
communication with users, 360
comparing differences between files, 40
comparison operators, 27
competition, differentiation from, 243–244
complexity of software, 315

conditional statements, 26–28
configuration file
  creating, 276–277
  defining application environment and, 274
constant for directory path, creating, 273–274
constants (cURL), 32–33
contact management apps, 52–53
content, separating from style, 14
content tags, 16
continuous integration, 317–318
controller
  for auto-follow script, 295–296
  creating, 279
  in model-view-control design pattern, 253–254
  for tweet monitor script, 301–302
converting files from PSD to HTML, 310–311
Cortesi, Damon (developer), 54, 361
cost per thousand (CPM) networks, 329–330
cost per time (CPT) networks, 331
CoTweet app
  description of 51
  as pro version example, 324
  screenshot, 397
  as solving problem, 245
CouchDB data storage system, 319
count function, 31
CPM (cost per thousand) networks, 329–330
CPT (cost per time) networks, 331
Craigslist for design bids, 310
create statement, 37
`created` field, 281
`created_at` variable, 287
credibility and application design, 309
CRM (customer relationship management) apps, 51, 324
cron jobs
  auto-follow script, 295–301
  description of, 295
  scheduling, 303
  tweet monitor script, 301–302
CruiseControl continuous integration software, 317–318
CSS (Cascading Style Sheets)
  basic styles, 21–23
  description of, 13–14
  selectors, 20–21
  SEO and, 353
  styling HTML with, 18–21
CTR (click through rate), 329
Cummings, Michael (developer), 56
cURL
  description of, 31–33
  reading HTTP status codes with, 69–70
`cursor` parameter
  paging through user ids using, 113
  printing profile pictures using, 109–111
customer relationship management (CRM) apps, 51, 324

• D •

daily trending topics, retrieving, 237–239
data fields, naming, 280
data models, creating
  defining tables, 283–284
  `Tweet` model, 284–286
  `User` model, 286–294
data storage, 319
data structure, setting up, 280–282
Davis, Hayes (developer), 53, 54, 362
Davis, Jenn Deering (developer), 54
dedicated Web hosting, 256, 257
defining application environment, 274
degrade gracefully tip, 361
delete statement, 38
deleting
  direct messages, 196–198
  lists, 124–126
  members from lists, 138–140
  saved searches, 231–233
  tweets, 184–186
  tweets from favorites, 222–224
descendant selectors, 20
design of application
  converting into HTML, 310–311
  first impressions and, 309

hiring professional for, 309–310
integrating, 311–313
desktop client applications
ad networks and, 328
examples of, 47–49
selling online, 338
details, getting
on protected accounts, 109–111
on public users, 106–108
on specific lists, 122–124
develop defensively tip, 361
developer accounts, creating, 39–40
developer announcement list, 358, 362
developer etiquette, 65, 357–360
developing applications
feature roadmap for, 308
ideas for, 241
as iterative process, 247
libraries and, 251–252
model-view-control design pattern and, 253–254
motivations for, 11–12, 242–244
releasing applications, 308
skills for, 246
success, defining, 241–242
Web application frameworks and, 252–253
differentiating product from competition, 243–244
direct message methods
`direct_messages`, 191–194, 371
`direct_messages/destroy`, 196–198, 373
`direct_messages/new`, 194–196, 372–373
`direct_messages/sent`, 191–194, 372
overview of, 190, 371
direct messages (DMs)
deleting, 196–198
description of, 9
retrieving, 191–194
sending, 194–196
`direct_messages` method, 191–194, 371
`direct_messages/destroy` method, 196–198, 373
`direct_messages/new` method, 194–196, 372–373
`direct_messages/sent` method, 191–194, 372
directory path, creating constant for, 273–274
directory structure, creating, 270–271
display style, 23
displaying
blocked users, 173–174
maximum amount of tweets in lists, 127–129
rate limits, 318
div tags, 17
DMs. *See* direct messages
doctypes (HTML), 14–15
documentation, reading, 358
Dodsworth, Iain (developer), 48, 50
domain names, setting up, 267–268
DOMDocument class, 33–35
DOMNodeList object, 34–35
donations, asking for, 336–337
do-while loops, 20
download size, decreasing with external CSS files, 19
downloading Zend Framework, 271

• E •

ease-of-use of applications, 245
echo command, 25
Elance for design bids, 310
Eliason, James (developer), 59
elseif parts, 27–28
e-mail lists for promoting applications, 349
embedding CSS, 19
Emma e-mail list manager, 349
`enabled` field, 281
`enabled` variable, 287
encoding and OAuth, 78, 97
ending user sessions, 83–84
enjoyment in building applications, 242
entertaining with applications, 245
environment, defining, 274
`/etc/crontab` file, 303
Etzel, Chad (developer), 363
Everett, Noah (developer), 54
evil, avoiding, tip about, 360

ExecTweets app, 56, 398
Extensible Hypertext Markup Language (XHTML)
  document example, 15
  1.0 Strict, 310, 353
Extensible Markup Language (XML)
  formatting in, 24
  PHP DOMDocument class and, 33
  Web browsers and, 42
external CSS files, creating, 19

• F •

Facebook
  promoting applications on, 347–348
  virtual goods sold on, 341, 342
FailWhale image, 9
family members, as investors, 326
Farnham, Aaron (developer), 57
favorite methods
  `favorites`, 217–220, 373–374
  `favorites/create`, 220–222, 374
  `favorites/destroy`, 222–224, 374
  overview of, 217, 373
`favorites` method, 217–220, 373–374
`favorites/create` method, 220–222, 374
`favorites/destroy` method, 222–224, 374
feature roadmap, 308
Featured Users app
  description of, 58
  integrating into applications, 332–333
  screenshot, 398
  tweeted testimonials for, 347
  Twooshes app and, 247
files
  breaking design HTML into smaller, 311–313
  converting from PSD to HTML, 310–311
  external CSS, creating, 19
  rolling back to previous versions, 40
  uploading to Web servers, 266–267
filling needs as reason to build applications, 243
Firefox browser and XML, 42
Firehose method, 66
Fisher, David (developer), 362
Flickr
  product tiers, 339
  SnapTweet and, 403
floating style, 23
Follow Cost app, 54, 399
`FollowcronController.php` file, 295
`$_followerIds` variable, 298
followers. *See also* following
  churning, 64
  description of, 7
  getting lists of, 143–145
  getting user details on, 109–111
  getting user IDs of, 112–115
`followers/ids` method
  adding to Zend Framework library, 296–297
  description of, 112–115, 375
following. *See also* followers
  mass, promotion of, 358
  users, stopping, 154–155
  users programmatically, 152–153
  users to phones, 161–163
following lists
  starting, 145–147
  stopping, 147–149
  testing users for, 149–151
font styles, specifying, 22–23
foreach loops, 28–29
form tags, 17
`formatCreatedAt` function, 289
fracturing data stores, 319
frameset doctype of HTML, 15
Francl, Luke (developer), 54
freemium model, 339
frequency of interaction with system, limits on, 67
Friend Or Follow app
  description of, 11, 52
  layouts of, 311–312
  screenshot, 399
friends
  getting user details on, 109–111
  getting user IDs of, 112–115
  as investors, 326
  retweets of, getting, 212–214
friends timeline, getting, 201–203
friendship methods
  `friendship/create`, 152–153, 376
  `friendship/destroy`, 154–155, 376–377

friendships/exists, 156–158, 377
friendships/show, 158–161, 377–378
overview of, 151, 376
friendship/create method, 152–153, 376
friendship/destroy method, 154–155, 376–377
friendships/exists method, 156–158, 377
friendships/show method, 158–161, 377–378
friends/ids method
adding to Zend Framework library, 296–297
description of, 112–115, 375
Front Controller design pattern, 272
Fuchs, Thomas (developer), 56
functions
addPoint, 291
addTweet, 290–291
array_diff, 31, 299
array_intersect, 31
array_merge, 31
array_values, 31
count, 31
cURL, 32
formatCreatedAt, 289
getFollowerIds, 298
getFollowingIds, 298–299
getUserTable, 288
indexAction, 300–301
_initAutoload, 276
_initViewHelpers, 276
json_decode, 35
ksort, 31
mapResponse, 288–289
PHP, 29–30, 31
rawurlencode, 97
save, 289
subPoint, 291
fund drives, 337
funding applications
with investors, 326
self-funding, 325
Fung, Yu-Shan (developer), 52

• G •

games, selling, 341
geolocation, parameters to facilitate, 182
GET requests and REST API rate limit, 67–68
getElementsByTagName method, 34, 35
getFollowerIds function, 298
getFollowingIds function, 298–299
getting
access tokens, 99–103
background colors from user data, 107–108
current top 10 trending topics, 235–237
details on protected accounts, 109–111
details on public users, 106–108
details on specific lists, 122–124
details on tweets, 180–181
direct messages, 191–194
favorite tweets of users, 217–220
friends timeline, 201–203
information about relationships between users, 158–161
lists of followers, 143–145
members of lists, 134–136
protected account details, 109–111
public account details, 106–108
request tokens, 96–99
retweeted status updates, 210–212
retweets of friends, 212–214
retweets of specific tweets, 188–190, 215–217
subscribers to lists, 143–145
timelines for lists, 126–129
top 20 trending topics per hour, 237–239
top 30 trending topics per week, 239–240
tweets from public timeline, 199–200
tweets that mention screen names, 207–209
user details list of blocked users, 172–174
user details on followers, 109–111
user details on friends, 109–111
user IDs of followers, 112–115
user IDs of friends, 112–115
user timeline, 203–207
getUserTable function, 288
GitHub Web site, 40

giving back to developer community, 359
GoDaddy service, 267
Google
  Ad Manager, 334
  AdSense, 329
  AdWords, 352
  Calendar, updating, 8
  Checkout service, 337
  Chrome browser and XML, 42
  developer announcement list, 358, 362
  Gmail, 256
  Group for Twitter API, 358, 362
  page rank, 354
  YouTube acquisition, 343
Gorilla Nation ad network, 330
graphical banner ads, 352, 353
growing pains for applications
  automating acceptance testing and, 315–316
  continuous integration and, 317–318
  performance concerns and, 318–319
  unit testing and, 317

• H •

Hanson, Keith (developer), 56
hardware devices, 60–61
hashtags, 8, 9
Hashtags.org Web site, 57, 400
head of HTML documents, 16
heading tags, 16
height attribute, 18
height of element, specifying, 22
help methods, 378
`help/test` method, 378
Hess, Barry (developer), 54, 361
hiring designers, 310
HootSuite app, 51, 324, 400
horizontal ad networks, 332
horizontal scaling, 257–258
hosted version control repositories, 40
HOT or NOT dating site, 341
Hoy, Amy (developer), 56
`.htaccess` file, creating, 273
HTML (Hypertext Markup Language)
  breaking design file into smaller files, 311–313
  converting files from PSD to, 310–311
  CSS and, 13–14, 18–21
  description of, 13
  elements of, 16–18
  making valid XHTML, 15
  SEO and, 353
  specification documents, 14–15
HTTP response status codes and errors, 69–70
Hypertext Markup Language. *See* HTML

• I •

`id` parameter, 106, 107
ID selectors, 20
ideas
  going with, 241, 247
  monetizing, 243
  motivation and, 242
if-then-else statements, 26
image tags, 18
improving applications, 308
`include_path` (PHP), 274
`indexAction` function, 300–301
`IndexController.php` file
  creating, 279
  updating, 303–305
`index.php` file, creating, 273–275
`index.php` script, 272
`index.phtml` file
  creating, 279
  updating, 306–307
industry, networking in, 351
information aggregation apps, 55–57
information publishing apps, 57–58
`_initAutoload` function, 276
`_initViewHelpers` function, 276
inline elements, 17–18
insert statement, 38
installing
  Apache and PHP on servers, 261–263
  MySQL on servers, 264–266
  Zend Framework, 271

integrating
  design HTML into applications, 311–313
  Featured Users into applications, 332–333
international characters, supporting, 363
Internet Explorer browser and XML, 42
investors
  seeking, 326
  venture capital and, 323, 325
IP addresses
  static, 257
  white listing and, 68
iPhone App Store, 337, 338
iterative process, development as, 247

• J •

JASONP support, 363
JSON (JavaScript Object Notation), 24, 363
json_decode function, 35

• K •

Kaplan, Philip (developer), 59
ksort function, 31

• L •

LAMP (Linux, Apache, MySQL, and PHP) stack as development platform, 13
layout template, creating, 277–278
`layout.phtml` file
  creating, 278
  HTML layout for, 311
  with references to other files, 312–313
Le Meur, Loic (developer), 48
leased servers, 256
libcurl, 32
libraries
  OAuth authentication methods, 78
  Twitter API, 251–252
`library` folder, 270, 271
licensing and selling applications, 337–338
limits. *See* rate limits
line break tags, 18
link tags, 16
links and SEO, 354
LinkShare ad network, 330
list members methods
  overview of, 134
  `:user/:list_id/members`, 134–140
  `:user/:list_id/members/:id`, 140–142
list methods
  behavior of, 115
  colons and, 116
  `:user/lists`, 116–118, 120–122
  `:user/lists/:id`, 118–120, 122–126
  `:user/lists/:list_id/statuses`, 126–129
  `:user/lists/memberships`, 129–131
  `:user/lists/subscriptions`, 132–134
list subscribers methods
  overview of, 142–143
  `:user/:list_id/subscribers`, 143–149
  `:user/:list_id/subscribers/:id`, 149–151
listings
  `application/bootstrap.php` File, 276
  `application/config/app.ini` File, 277
  `application/controllers/FollowcronController.php` File, 295
  `application/controllers/IndexController.php` File, 279
  `application/controllers/IndexController.php` File, Updated, 304
  `application/controllers/TweetcronController.php` File, 301–302
  `application/layouts/layout.phtml` File, 278
  `application/models/DbTable/Tweet.php` File, 284
  `application/models/DbTable/User.php` File, 283
  `application/models/Tweet.php` File, 284–285
  `application/models/Tweet.php:getLastStatusId()` File, 285
  `application/models/User.php` File, 287
  `application/models/User.php:addPoint() and subPoint()` File, 291

listings *(continued)*
application/models/User.php:addTweet() File, 290–291
application/models/User.php:constructor File, 288
application/models/User.php:mapResponse() File, 289
application/models/User.php:save() File, 290
applications/views/scripts/index/index.phtml File, 306
application/views/scripts/index.phtml File, 279
application/views/scripts/pagination_control.phtml File, 305–306
array_dif Function, 299
Authentication Login URL, 96
Background Styles, 23
Blocking Users, 167
Border Styles, 22
Check if Two Users Follow Each Other, 160–161
Check if User Is Blocked, 171–172
Check Length of DOMNodeList, 35
Concatenated oauth_signature String Before Encrypting and Parameter Encoding, 97, 101
Count and List of Blocked User IDs, Getting, 175–176
Create Statement, 37
Creating Array, 30
Creating DOMDocument Object, 34
Current Trends, Retrieving, 236–237
Cursor, Using to Print Profile Pictures, 110–111
Daily Trending Topics, Retrieving, 238–239
Delete Statement, 38
Deleting Direct Message, 197–198
Deleting Tweet, 185–186
Display Style, 23
Displaying Blocked Users, 173–174
do-while Loop that Counts to 10, 20
ElseIf Part, 27–28
Ending Persistent Basic HTTP Auth Session, 84
Error Message in XML, 70
/etc/crontab File, 303
Favorites, Adding Tweet to, 221–222
Favorites, Removing Tweet from, 223–224
Floating Style, 23
Following New Users, 153
Font Decorations, 23
foreach Loop, 28, 29
Function example, 30
Generating Access Token, 101–103
Generating Request Token, 98–99
getElementsByTagName, 34, 35
getFollowerIds Function, 298
getFollowingIds Function, 299
Go Straight to First Node in DOMNodeList Object, 34
Height and Width, 22
HelloTwitter.html, 41
If-Then-Else, 26
indexAction Function, 300–301
index.php File, Beginning of, 273
index.php File, Complete, 275
index.php File, Defining Application Environment in, 274
Insert Statement, 38
JSON Object example, 24
Last 100 Retweets of Friends, Getting, 213–214
library/Zend/Service/Twitter.php Directory, Adding Social Graph Methods, 296–297
List, Creating, 117–118
List, Deleting, 125–126
List, Updating, 119–120
List Details, Getting, 123–124
List Followers, Getting, 144–145
List Members, Adding, 137–138
List Members, Removing, 139–140
List Membership, Checking, 141–142
List Subscribers, Adding, 146–147
List Tweets, Getting, 128–129
Lists User Belongs To, Getting, 130–131
Lists User Subscribes To, Getting, 132–134
Loop through DOMNodeList Object, 34
Margin and Padding, 21
Margin and Padding Shorthand, 22
Marking Users as Spam, 177–178
Most Recent 100 Retweets, Getting, 211–212

Most Recent 100 Retweets of Tweets, Getting, 216–217
oauth/access_token Response Body, 100
oauth/request_token Response Body, 96
Paging Through Friends Timeline, 202–203
Paging Through Tweets that Mention Screen Name, 208–209
Paging Through User Timeline, 205–207
PHP Comments Syntax, 26
Post Tweet (curl command line client), 32
Post Tweet (libcurl), 33
Post Tweet (statuses/update method), 183–184
Previous Tweets, Retrieving and Displaying, 219–220
Print String to Screen, 25
Profile Colors, Updating, 90–91
Profile Pictures of Most Recent 20 Public Tweets, Printing, 200
Pull Up Public Timeline, 32
Rate Limit Status, Looking Up, 82–83
Reading HTTP Status Code with PHP and cURL, 69
Received Direct Messages, Getting Using Paging, 192–194
Receiving Notifications from Users, 162–163
Retweeting Tweets, 187–188
Retweets of Specific Tweets, Retrieving, 189–190
Saved Search Details, Getting, 228–229
Saved Searches, Creating, 230–231
Saved Searches, Removing, 232–233
Saved Searches, Retrieving All, 226–227
Searching For Tweets Using API, 235
Select Query Using Group By and Having Clause, 37
Select Query Using Where, Order By, and Limit Clause, 37
Sending Direct Message, 195–196
SQL Select Query, 36
SQL Select Query Using Join, 37
status Object in XML, 72–73
Subscription Status, Checking, 150–151
Testing if One User Follows Another, 157–158
Turning Off SMS Notifications, 164–165
Tweet Details, Getting, 180–181
Tweet Table, Creating, 282
Tweet.php File, 286
Twitter Status Update XML Response, 42–43
Twooshes layout.phtml File, 311
Twooshes layout.phtml File With References to Other Files, 312–313
Unblocking Users, 168–169
Unfollowing Lists, 148–149
Unfollowing Users, 154–155
Update Statement, 38
Updating Device Settings, 85–86
Updating Twitter Background, 93–95
Updating Twitter Picture, 92–93
Updating Twitter Profile, 87–89
User Agent String to Increase Search API Rate Limit, 68
User Data, Getting with users/show Method, 107–108
User IDs of Mutual Followers, Getting, 114–115
User Is Not Blocked Message, 170
user Object in XML example, 71–72
User Table, Creating, 280–281
Username and Password, Checking, 81
User.php File, 292–294
Users List Follows, Getting, 135–136
Users List of Lists, Getting, 121–122
Weekly Trending Topics, Retrieving, 240
www/.htaccess File, Creating, 273
XML Object, 24
XML Response from friendships/show Method, 158–159
Zend_Application Object, Creating and Running Bootstrap, 275
Zend_Service_Twitter Object, Creating, 298

lists
- adding members to, 136–138
- of blocked user IDs, getting, 174–176
- of blocked users, getting, 172–174
- creating new, 116–118
- deleting, 124–126
- deleting members from, 138–140
- description of, 115
- details on specific lists, getting, 122–124
- following, 145–147

lists *(continued)*
members of, getting, 134–136
stop following, 147–149
subscribers to, getting, 143–145
testing if users are members of, 140–142
timelines for, getting, 126–129
updating existing, 118–120
user belongs to, getting, 129–131
user follows, getting, 132–134
user list of lists, getting, 120–122
local cache of detailed user data, 114
logging in
authentication, 73–78
users with OAuth, 95–96
logical operators, 27
loops, 28–29
Loving, Adam (developer), 363

• M •

Magpie ad network
description of, 58, 324, 332
screenshot, 401
Twooshes app and, 247
MailChump e-mail list manager, 349
managed servers, 256
`mapResponse` function, 288–289
margins, specifying for boxes, 21–22
Mashable Web site, 351
mass following, promotion of, 358
`max_id` parameter, 192
media sharing apps, 54–55
members
adding to lists, 136–138
deleting from lists, 138–140
of lists, getting, 134–136
testing if users are list members, 140–142
Menti, Mario (developer), 58
mentions
of brand name, monitoring, 11
description of, 9
of screen name, getting, 207–209
meta tags, 16
methods
account management, 79–91, 365–368
block, 165–176, 368–371
colons in method paths, 116
direct messages, 190–198, 371–373
favorite, 217–224, 373–374
friendship, 151–161, 376–378
help, 378
list, 115–134
list members, 134–142
list subscribers, 142–151
notification, 161–165, 378–379
OAuth authentication, 78, 95–103, 379–380
saved searches, 224–233, 380–382
Search API, 233–240, 382–384
social graph, 112–115, 296–297, 374–375
spam reporting, 176–178, 384–385
status, 179–190, 385–394
timeline, 198–217
user, 105–111, 394
version numbers of, 67
for working with OAuth, 75
mobile client applications
ad networks and, 328
examples of, 49–50
mobile providers, SMS revenue sharing from, 324
model-view-control design pattern, 253–254. *See also* controller; view
mod_rewrite, installing, 262–263
money, making. *See also* advertising
asking for donations, 336–337
building businesses, 342–344
developing apps, 12
as reason to build applications, 242–243
requesting payment for service, 335–339
revenue model speculations regarding Twitter, 324
revenue models, 337–338
selling goods, 339–342
selling subscriptions, 338–339
monitoring
bakeries for fresh items, 61, 395
mentions of brand name or product, 11
plants for water needs, 61, 396
trending words, 10, 236–240
Morse, Jacob (developer), 56
motivations for building applications, 11–12, 242–244
Movable Type blog platform, 348
Mr. Tweet app, 52, 401

MVC (model-view-control) design pattern, 253–254. *See also* controller; view
My Cloud Servers dashboard, 259
my.cnf file (MySQL), 265, 266
MySQL
  description of, 35
  my.cnf file, 265, 266
  servers, setting up, 263–266

• N •

name recognition, building, 342–343. *See also* brand name
name squatting, 64
naming data fields, 280
Nearly Free Speech Web hosting company, 267
networking in industry, 351
news organizations, updates from, 10
next_cursor node, 109–110
non-relational data storage systems, 319
notification methods
  notifications/follow, 161–163, 378–379
  notifications/leave, 163–165, 379
  overview of, 161, 378
notifications/follow method, 161–163, 378–379
notifications/leave method, 163–165, 379
numeric userIDs, 107

• O •

OAuth
  access tokens, getting, 99–103
  description of, 74–78
  methods, 379
  parameter encoding with, 78, 97
  request tokens, getting, 96–99
  using, 359–360
oauth/access_token method, 99–103, 380
oauth/authenticate method, 75, 95–96, 380
oauth/authorize method, 75, 95–96, 380
oauth/request_token method, 96–99, 380
Odeo podcasting company, 325
ON DUPLICATE KEY UPDATE command, 289–290
oneforty Web site, 354
140tees Web site, 340
online payments, accepting, 337
open API, 11
Open Source Web Design Web site, 310
OpenX ad management software, 334
opt-in e-mail lists, 349
output, 71–73

• P •

padding, specifying for boxes, 21–22
pagination_control.phtml file, 305–306
paragraph tags, 16
parameter encoding with OAuth, 78, 97
parameters to facilitate geolocation, 182
parsing standard DOM markup, 33
partnering with Twitter, 323
passwords
  root, using to connect applications to databases, 265
  of users, checking, 80–81
  of users, handling, 74
pay per action (PPA) networks, 330
pay per click (PPC) networks, 328–329
payload, defining, 71–73
payment for services, requesting, 335–339
PayPal service, 337
performance concerns, 318–319
permission
  asking before acting on user's behalf, 357
  granting to applications to access accounts, 74
Perrin, Andrew (developer), 363
personal accounts
  allowing access to, 41
  for development, creating, 39–40
  experience with, 39
Philips, Trey (developer), 56
phones, following users to, 161–163
photo-sharing sites, 408

PHP
- arrays, 30–31
- comments syntax, 25–26
- conditional statements, 26–28
- cURL, 31–33
- description of, 25
- DOMDocument class, 33–35
- echo command, 25
- frameworks, 252
- functions, 29–30
- includes, 313
- json_decode function, 35
- loops, 28–29
- online manual, 31
- `rawurlencode` function, 97
- reading HTTP status codes with, 69–70
- servers, setting up, 258–263

PHP Zend Framework
- adding methods to library, 296–297
- bootstrap process, 272
- `bootstrap.php` file, creating, 275–276
- configuration file, creating, 276–277
- description of, 252–253
- directory structure, creating, 270–271
- `include_path`, setting to library, 274
- installing, 271
- layout template, creating, 277–278
- mod_rewrite, installing, 262–263
- scoreboard, creating, 303–307
- setting up, 269–279
- Table Data Gateway design pattern, 283
- testing, 279
- unit tests and, 317
- view and controller, creating, 278–279

PHPUnit unit-testing framework, 317
physical goods, selling, 339–340
plant monitoring kits, 61, 396
platforms for blogs, 348
popular applications, imagining and building, 241–242
power consumption, tracking, 61, 404
PPA (pay per action) networks, 330
PPC (pay per click) networks, 328–329
`previous_cursor` node, 109–110
printing profile pictures
- of most recent 20 public tweets, 200
- of people followed, 110–111

private accounts, keeping data in confidential, 360
problem solving with applications, 245
product. *See also* brand name
- blogs for, 348–349
- differentiating from competition, 243–244
- Facebook fan pages for, 348
- monitoring mentions of, 11
- Twitter accounts for, 346

`profile_image_url` variable, 287
profiles
- background images, updating, 93–95
- colors, updating, 89–91
- data in, 79
- pictures, updating, 91–93
- updating, 86–89

Project Wonderful Web site, 353
promotion strategies. *See also* advertising
- blogs, 348–349
- on Facebook, 347–348
- opt-in e-mail lists, 349
- overview of, 345
- public relations, 351–352
- search engine optimization, 353–354
- social networking, 346–349
- on Twitter, 346–347
- viral marketing, 349–350

protected accounts
- following, 152–153
- getting details of, 109–111

PSD to HTML file conversion service, 311
public accounts
- asymmetrical relationship model and, 9
- getting details of, 106–108

public relations strategies, 351–352
public timeline
- getting tweets from, 199–200
- Search API and, 233

quotation marks and XHTML tag attributes, 15

• R •

Rackspace Cloud Servers
  Apache and PHP, setting up, 258–263
  description of, 257
  domain names, setting up, 267–268
  MySQL, setting up, 263–266
  uploading files to, 266–267
rate limits
  blacklisting and, 69
  checking, 81–83
  displaying, 318
  getting around, 363
  REST API, 67–68
  Search API, 68–69, 233
  staying within, 358
  storing API results locally and, 107
`rawurlencode` function, 97
reading documentation, 358
Reagan, Dusty (developer), 52, 58
receiving notifications from users, 162–163
registering applications, 76–77
registration page, 76, 77
relational databases, 36, 319
relationship between users, getting information about, 158–161
relationship structure, 9
releasing applications, 308
Remember The Milk app, 60, 402
removing
  direct messages, 196–198
  lists, 124–126
  members from lists, 138–140
  saved searches, 231–233
  tweets, 184–186
  tweets from favorites, 222–224
reporting tools, 360
`report_spam` method, 176–178, 384–385
Representational State Transfer (REST), 63
reputation, building by developing applications, 12, 244
request tokens, getting, 96–99
resources
  for building applications, 246
  online, 65
REST (Representational State Transfer), 63
REST API
  description of, 66
  rate limit, 67–68
result set, 71–73
retrieving
  access tokens, 99–103
  background colors from user data, 107–108
  current top 10 trending topics, 235–237
  details on protected accounts, 109–111
  details on public users, 106–108
  details on specific lists, 122–124
  details on tweets, 180–181
  direct messages, 191–194
  favorite tweets of users, 217–220
  friends timeline, 201–203
  information about relationships between users, 158–161
  lists of followers, 143–145
  members of lists, 134–136
  protected account details, 109–111
  public account details, 106–108
  request tokens, 96–99
  retweeted status updates, 210–212
  retweets of friends, 212–214
  retweets of specific tweets, 188–190, 215–217
  subscribers to lists, 143–145
  timelines for lists, 126–129
  top 20 trending topics per hour, 237–239
  top 30 trending topics per week, 239–240
  tweets from public timeline, 199–200
  tweets that mention screen names, 207–209
  user details list of blocked users, 172–174
  user details on followers, 109–111
  user details on friends, 109–111
  user IDs of followers, 112–115
  user IDs of friends, 112–115
  user timeline, 203–207
retweeting tweets, 186–188
retweets (RTs)
  description of, 8, 9
  of specific tweets, retrieving, 188–190, 215–217
reusing markup across multiple layouts, 313

revenue model speculations about Twitter, 324
revenue models
 asking for donations, 336–337
 building businesses, 342–344
 licensing and selling software, 337–338
 requesting payment for services, 335–339
 selling goods, 339–342
 selling subscriptions, 338–339
Right Banners service, 353
Roelands, Duane (developer), 362
rolling back files to previous versions, 40
root usernames and passwords, using to connect applications to databases, 265
Rose, Kevin (developer), 52
RTs. *See* retweets
rules
 for developers, 65
 general, 64

• S •

SaaS (software as a service) view, 338
Safari browser and XML, 42
`save` function, 289
saved searches
 creating, 229–231
 details, getting, 227–229
 removing, 231–233
 retrieving all, 225–227
saved searches methods
 overview of, 224–225, 380
 `saved_searches`, 225–227, 381
 `saved_searches/create`, 229–231, 381
 `saved_searches/destroy`, 231–233, 381
 `saved_searches/show`, 227–229, 381–382
`saved_searches` method, 225–227, 381
`saved_searches/create` method, 229–231, 381
`saved_searches/destroy` method, 231–233, 381
`saved_searches/show` method, 227–229, 381–382
saving `User` object to database, 289
scalability of Web applications, 318–319
scheduling cron jobs, 303
`score` field, 281
scoreboard for Twooshes game, creating, 303–307
screen names
 @ replies and, 8
 tweets that mention, getting, 207–209
`screen_name` parameter, 107, 362
`screen_name` variable, 287
script tags, 16
`scripts` folder, 271
Search API
 description of, 66
 rate limit, 68–69
Search API methods
 overview of, 233, 382
 `search.tweet.com/search`, 233–235, 382–383
 `search.twitter.com/trends`, 235–237, 383
 `search.twitter.com/trends/current`, 235–237, 384
 `search.twitter.com/trends/daily`, 237–239, 383–384
 `search.twitter.com/trends/weekly`, 239–240, 384
search engine optimization (SEO), 348, 353–354
search functionality, 11
searching for tweets, 233–235
`search.twitter.com/search` method, 233–235, 382–383
`search.twitter.com/trends` method, 235–237, 383
`search.twitter.com/trends/current` method, 235–237, 384
`search.twitter.com/trends/daily` method, 237–239, 383–384
`search.twitter.com/trends/weekly` method, 239–240, 384
SecretTweet app, 57, 402
Secure Sockets Layer (SSL), 246
securing MySQL server, 265–266
Seesmic Desktop app, 48, 403
select query, 36
selectors (CSS), 20
Selenium, acceptance testing with, 316
self-funding applications, 325

selling
advertising, 333–334
applications, 337–338
goods, 339–342
subscriptions, 338–339
sending
direct messages, 194–196
status updates, 183–184
SEO (search engine optimization), 348, 353–354
server console inside Web browsers, 261
Server Side Includes (SSI), 313
servers
Apache and PHP, setting up, 258–263
domain names, setting up, 267–268
hosting providers, selecting, 257–258
increasing performance of, 319
MySQL, setting up, 263–266
splitting workload across, 257–258
uploading files to, 266–267
Web hosting solutions, 255–257
shared Web hosting, 255, 257
shareware model, 338
Short Message Service (SMS) revenue sharing from mobile providers, 324
64-bit integers, using, 362
Smith, Brian (developer), 57
Smith, Kevin (developer), 57
SMS (Short Message Service) revenue sharing from mobile providers, 324
SMS updates
turning off, 164–165
usefulness of, 10
SnapTweet app, 55, 403
social capital, building, 342–343
social graph methods
adding to Zend Framework library, 296–297
overview of, 374–375
user IDs of friends and followers, getting, 112–115
social networking sites
promotion strategies using, 346–349
virtual goods sold on, 341–342
software. *See* applications
software as a service (SaaS) view, 338
software frameworks, 252–253
solving problems with applications, 245
source code, viewing, 42
spam reporting method, 176–178, 384–385
splitting workload across servers, 257–258
SSI (Server Side Includes), 313
SSL (Secure Sockets Layer), 246
static IP addresses, 257
statistical analysis apps, 53
status methods
overview of, 179, 385
`statuses/destroy`, 184–186, 386
`statuses/retweet`, 186–188, 390
`statuses/retweets`, 188–190, 392
`statuses/show`, 180–181, 392
`statuses/update`, 182–184, 392–393
`status` objects, 71, 72–73
status updates, retweeted, getting, 210–212
`statuses/destroy` method, 184–186, 386
`statuses/followers` method, 109–111, 386–387
`statuses/friends` method, 109–111, 387
`statuses/friends_timeline` method, 201–203, 388
`statuses/home_timeline` method, 388–389
`statuses/mentions` method, 207–209, 389
`statuses/public_timeline` method, 199–200, 389
`statuses/retweet` method, 186–188, 390
`statuses/retweeted_by_me` method, 210–212, 390
`statuses/retweeted_to_me` method, 212–214, 391
`statuses/retweets` method, 188–190, 392
`statuses/retweets_of_me` method, 215–217, 390–391
`statuses/show` method, 180–181, 392
`statuses/update` method, 182–184, 392–393
`statuses/user_timeline` method, 203–207, 393–394

Stone, Biz (founder), 324
stop following
 lists, 147–149
 users, 154–155
stop receiving notifications from users, 163–165
storing API results locally, 107, 280
Streaming API, 66
"strict" doctype of HTML, 15, 310, 353
strong tags, 18
style, separating from content, 14
style attribute, 18
style tags, 16, 19
subPoint function, 291
subscribers to lists
 adding, 146–147
 getting, 143–145
 testing for, 149–151
subscribing to Google developer announcement list, 358, 362
subscriptions, selling, 338–339
Subversion version control system, 40, 317
success, definition of, 241
Summize acquisition, 343–344
Symfony framework, 252

• T •

Table Data Gateway design pattern, 283
table tags, 17
tables, creating in MySQL, 37
tags directory, 270
TechCrunch Web site, 351
terminology, 9
terms of service
 developer etiquette, 65
 general, 64
testing
 automating acceptance testing, 315–316
 if users are list members, 140–142
 if users follow lists, 149–151
 if users follow users, 156–158
 unit, 317
 users for blocking, 170–172
 Zend Framework, 279
text ads, 352
text parameter, 195
textual data formatting, 24
timeline methods
 overview of, 198–199
 statuses/friends_timeline, 201–203, 388
 statuses/mentions, 207–209, 389
 statuses/public_timeline, 199–200, 389
 statuses/retweeted_by_me, 210–212, 390
 statuses/retweeted_to_me, 212–214, 392
 statuses/retweets_of_me, 215–217, 390–391
 statuses/user_timeline, 203–207, 393–394
timelines
 for lists, getting, 126–129
 public, 199–200, 233
timeouts, avoiding, 113
Tiny Twitter app, 50, 404
title attribute, 18
title tags, 16
tooting own horn, 351
Torrone, Phil (developer), 61
tracking
 ads sold, 334
 file changes over time, 40
 power consumption, 61, 404
trademarks, 359
traffic reports, accessing, 8
traits of respectable developers, 357–360
transitional doctype of HTML, 15
trending topics
 current top 10, getting, 235–237
 monitoring, 10
 top 20 per hour, getting, 237–239
 top 30 per week, retrieving, 239–240
trendingTopics field, 281
Tribal Fusion ad network, 329
trunk folder, 270
trust, building with users, 246, 346
turning off SMS updates, 164–165
Tweet Congress application, 244

tweet database table, building, 282
Tweet model, creating, 284–286
Tweet-a-Watt device, 61, 404
TweetcronController.php file, 301–302
TweetDeck app
for desktops, 48
managing API limits with, 318
for mobile phones, 50
screenshot, 405
Tweetie app, 49–50, 337
Tweeting Too Hard app, 56, 405
Tweetmeme app, 349–350
Tweetname bot, 60, 406
Tweet.php file, 284–286
TweetReach app, 53, 406
tweets. *See also* timeline methods
adding to favorites, 220–222
creating, 182–184
deleting, 184–186
description of, 7, 9
details of, getting, 180–181
favorite, retrieving, 217–220
in lists, displaying maximum amount of, 127–129
mentioning screen name, getting, 207–209
from public timeline, getting, 199–200
purposes of, 7–8
removing from favorites, 222–224
retrieving retweets of, 188–190, 215–217
retweeting, 186–188
searching for, 233–235
TweetStats app, 54, 245, 407
Twibes, 363
Twistori app, 56–57, 407
TwitCause application, 244
Twitdom Web site, 354
TwitPic app, 54–55, 408
Twittad app, 59, 408
Twitter
application definition box, 324
bots, 59–60
building businesses on top of, 11, 342–344
description of, 7
features of, 8, 9–11
open API, 11
partnering with, 323
promoting applications on, 346–347
relationship structure of, 9
revenue model speculations, 324
SMS updates, 10
Summize acquisition, 343–344
terminology of, 9
trends and searches, 10–11
wiki, 78, 252
Twitter-async library, 78
Twittercal bot, 59, 409
TwitterCounter app, 53, 409
Twitterfeed app, 57–58, 410
twitter_id field, 280
twitter_id variable, 287
Twitterrific for Mac app
description of, 49, 338
logo T-shirts, 340
screenshot, 410
twooshes field, 281
Twooshes game app
auto-follow script, creating, 295–301
bootstrap.php file, creating, 275–276
bootstrapping, 272
cloud hosting solution for, 257
configuration file, creating, 276–277
cron jobs, creating, 295–303
data models, creating, 283–294
data structure, setting up, 280–282
description of, 9, 247
directory structure, creating, 270–271
.htaccess file, creating, 273
index.php file, creating, 273–275
layout template, creating, 277–278
scoreboard, creating, 303–307
view and controller, creating, 278–279
Web server dashboard, 260
Zend Framework, installing, 271
Twtbase Web site, 354
type selectors, 20

• U •

unblocking users, 168–169
unfollowing
lists, 147–149
users, 154–155

Unfuddle Web site, 40
unit testing, 317
unordered list tags, 16
update statement, 38
updated field, 281
updates, following and posting, 10
updating
  existing lists, 118–120
  Google Calendar, 8
  user notification devices, 85–86
  user profile background images, 93–95
  user profile colors, 89–91
  user profile pictures, 91–93
  user profiles, 86–89
uploading files to Web servers, 266–267
usage quotas, getting around, 363
user accounts and @ sign, 8
User Agent string to increase Search API rate limit, 68–69
user credentials, verifying, 80–81
user database table, building, 280–281
user details list
  of blocked users, getting, 172–174
  of friends and followers, getting, 109–111
user IDs
  of friends and followers, getting, 112–115
  list of blocked, getting, 174–176
user methods
  details of friends and followers, getting, 109–111
  details of users, getting, 106–108
  overview of, 105, 394
User model, creating, 286–294
user notification devices, updating, 85–86
user objects, 71–72
user passwords, handling, 74
user profiles
  background images, updating, 93–95
  colors, updating, 89–91
  data in, 79
  pictures, updating, 91–93
  updating, 86–89
user sessions, ending, 83–84
user timeline, getting, 203–207
userId field, 281
user_id parameter, 107, 362
:user/:list_id/members method
  adding members to lists, 136–138
  getting lists of members, 134–136
  removing members from lists, 138–140
:user/:list_id/members/:id method, 140–142
:user/:list_id/subscribers method
  following lists, 145–147
  getting list of followers, 143–145
  stop following lists, 147–149
:user/:list_id/subscribers/:id method, 149–151
:user/lists method, 116–118, 120–122
:user/lists/:id method, 118–120, 122–126
:user/lists/:list_id/statuses method, 126–129
:user/lists/memberships method, 129–131
:user/lists/subscriptions method, 132–134
usernames
  checking, 80–81
  root, using to connect applications to databases, 265
User.php file
  complete syntax, 292–294
  creating, 283
  starting class and defining fields, 287
users
  blocking, 166–167
  building trust with, 246, 346
  checking for blocking, 170–172
  communication with, 360
  favorite tweets of, retrieving, 217–220
  following, 152–153
  getting information about relationship between, 158–161
  list of lists, getting, 120–122
  receiving notifications from, 161–163
  stop following, 154–155
  stopping notifications from, 163–165
  unblocking, 168–169
users/show method, 106–108, 394

• V •

validating Web sites as XHTML 1.0 Strict, 353–354
ValueClick ad network, 330
van Zanten, Boris Veldhuijzen (developer), 53
Venneman, Brian (developer), 54
venture capital
  description of, 323, 325
  seeking, 326
verifying user credentials, 80–81
version control, 40, 317
versioning of API, 66–67
vertical ad networks, 332–333
view
  for auto-follow script, 296
  creating, 278–279
  in model-view-control design pattern, 253–254
viewing source code, 42
viral marketing, 349–350
virtual goods, selling, 339, 341–342

• W •

Web application frameworks
  breaking up HTML markup and, 313
  description of, 252–253
Web applications
  advertising, 58–59
  contact management, 52–53
  customer relationship management, 51
  description of, 50–51
  information aggregation, 55–57
  information publishing, 57–58
  media sharing, 54–55
  selling subscriptions for, 338–339
  statistical analysis, 53
Web banners, 352, 353
Web browsers
  opening apps in, 42
  server console inside, 261
Web development. *See also* CSS; HTML; MySQL; PHP
  LAMP (Linux, Apache, MySQL, and PHP) stack and, 13
  separating content from style in, 14
  standards for, 14
Web hosting companies, 257–258
Web hosting solutions
  cloud computing, 256–257
  dedicated, 256
  shared, 255
Web servers
  Apache and PHP, setting up, 258–263
  domain names, setting up, 267–268
  hosting providers, selecting, 257–258
  increasing performance of, 319
  MySQL, setting up, 263–266
  splitting workload across, 257–258
  uploading files to, 266–267
  Web hosting solutions, 255–257
Web sites
  ad networks, 329–330, 331, 332, 353
  AdMob, 328
  advertising apps, 58–59
  Brizzly, 244
  BugMeNot, 271
  BuySellAds, 331
  CafePress, 340
  cloud computing examples, 256
  contact management apps, 52–53
  CoTweet, 245
  CRM apps, 51
  CruiseControl, 318
  for design bids, 310
  desktop clients, 48–49
  developer announcement list, 362
  for domain names, 267
  e-mail list managers, 349
  Facebook, 341, 342
  Featured Users, 247, 332–333
  hardware devices, 61
  hosted version control repositories, 40
  HOT or NOT, 341
  information aggregation apps, 55–57
  information publishing apps, 57–58
  lists and reviews, 354
  Magpie ad network, 247, 332
  media sharing applications, 54–55
  mobile clients, 50

Web sites *(continued)*
- non-relational data storage systems, 319
- 140tees, 340
- Open Source Web Design, 310
- PHP frameworks, 252
- PHP manual, 31
- PSD to HTML file conversion service, 311
- Rackspace Cloud Servers, 257
- reporting tools, 360
- resources, 65
- Right Banners, 353
- statistical analysis apps, 53
- Streaming API, 66
- Subversion, 317
- tech writers, 351
- Tribal Fusion ad network, 329
- Tweet Congress, 244
- TweetDeck, 318
- TweetStats, 245
- TwitCause, 244
- Twitter bots, 59–60
- Twitter wiki, 78, 252
- validating as XHTML 1.0 Strict, 353–354
- white listing application, 68, 107
- `Zend_Paginator` class, 307

WebFollow app, 52–53
`website` directory, 270
weekly trending topics, retrieving, 239–240
WeFollow app, 350, 411
weight attribute, 18
white listing, 68, 107
width of element, specifying, 22
Wikipedia donation page, 336–337
Williams, Abraham (developer), 362
Williams, Evan (founder), 324
Wilson, Mike (@2drinksbehind), 10
Wordpress blog platform, 348
workflow of model-view-control design pattern, 253–254
workload, splitting across servers, 257–258
World Wide Web Consortium (W3C), 14
writing first app, 41–43
W3C (World Wide Web Consortium), 14
W3C Markup Validation Service, 353–354
`www` folder, 271

XHTML (Extensible Hypertext Markup Language)
- document example, 15
- 1.0 Strict, 310, 353

XML (Extensible Markup Language)
- formatting in, 24
- PHP DOMDocument class and, 33
- Web browsers and, 42

xmlns attribute, 15

• Y •

Yasuda, Jeff (developer), 54
YouTube, acquisition of, 343

• Z •

Zend Framework
- adding methods to library, 296–297
- bootstrap process, 272
- `bootstrap.php` file, creating, 275–276
- configuration file, creating, 276–277
- description of, 252–253
- directory structure, creating, 270–271
- `include_path`, setting to library, 274
- installing, 271
- layout template, creating, 277–278
- mod_rewrite, installing, 262–263
- scoreboard, creating, 303–307
- setting up, 269–279
- Table Data Gateway design pattern, 283
- testing, 279
- unit tests and, 317
- view and controller, creating, 278–279

`Zend_Application` object, creating, 274–275
`Zend_Paginator` class, 303, 304, 307
`Zend_Service_Twitter object, creating`, 297–298